RETHINKING CRIMINAL LAW THEORY

In the last two decades, the philosophy of criminal law has undergone a vibrant revival in Canada. The adoption of the Charter of Rights and Freedoms has given the Supreme Court of Canada unprecedented latitude to engage with principles of legal, moral, and political philosophy when elaborating its criminal law jurisprudence. Canadian scholars have followed suit by paying increased attention to the philosophical foundations of domestic criminal law. Because of Canada's leadership in international criminal law, both at the level of the International Criminal Court and of specific war crimes tribunals, they have also begun to turn their attention to international criminal law per se. This collection seeks to bring all these Canadian voices together for the first time, and evidence the fact that criminal law theory is no longer to be associated exclusively with the older British, German and American traditions. The topics covered include the legitimate scope of domestic and international criminalization, rationales for criminal law defences in both domestic and international law, the philosophical underpinnings of specific crimes and forms of joint responsibility, as well as the theorization of criminal procedure and evidence law.

Rethinking Criminal Law Theory

New Canadian Perspectives in the Philosophy of Domestic, Transnational, and International Criminal Law

Edited by
François Tanguay-Renaud
and
James Stribopoulos

·HART·
PUBLISHING

OXFORD AND PORTLAND, OREGON
2012

Published in the United Kingdom by Hart Publishing Ltd
16C Worcester Place, Oxford, OX1 2JW
Telephone: +44 (0)1865 517530
Fax: +44 (0)1865 510710
E-mail: mail@hartpub.co.uk
Website: http://www.hartpub.co.uk

Published in North America (US and Canada) by
Hart Publishing
c/o International Specialized Book Services
920 NE 58th Avenue, Suite 300
Portland, OR 97213-3786
USA
Tel: +1 503 287 3093 or toll-free: (1) 800 944 6190
Fax: +1 503 280 8832
E-mail: orders@isbs.com
Website: http://www.isbs.com

British Library Cataloguing in Publication Data
Data Available

ISBN: 978-1-84946-010-1

Typeset by Hope Services, Abingdon
Printed and bound in Great Britain by
TJ International Ltd, Padstow, Cornwall

MIX
Paper from responsible sources
FSC® C013056
FSC
www.fsc.org

PREFACE

The philosophy of criminal law is at a turning point in Canada. The adoption of the Charter of Rights and Freedoms in 1982 has given the Supreme Court of Canada unprecedented latitude to engage with principles of moral, political, and legal philosophy when elaborating its criminal law jurisprudence. Be it in the context of discussions about the constitutionalization of various aspects of moral innocence, the proper contours of criminal law defences, the legitimate scope of criminalization, the rule of law, the availability of legal rights to corporate entities, the justification of state punishment, or the nature of crimes with international dimensions, the works of philosophers like John Stuart Mill, Immanuel Kant, Jeremy Bentham, Hans Kelsen, HLA Hart, Joel Feinberg, Joseph Raz, and George P Fletcher are already given significant judicial attention. Given all of this, an appraisal of such works and the puzzles they address in light of Canada's distinctive problems and opportunities is overdue.

Canadian law schools and philosophy departments have sought to keep up with this development by hiring, in recent years, a number of criminal law theorists able to participate in philosophical debate and contribute to its healthy development. The number of Canadian legal and moral theorists interested in criminal law who have been hired by foreign institutions has also witnessed a marked increase. The result has been a significant deepening of Canadian scholarship in the philosophy of criminal law, both in relation to Charter-related questions and broader *problématiques*, since the time that the now defunct Law Reform Commission of Canada (1971–1993) and Law Commission of Canada (1997–2006) last looked at these fundamental issues. Criminal law theory is now alive and well in Canada and, thus, no longer to be associated exclusively with the older British, German, and American traditions.

This Canadian momentum is not only being felt in respect of the study of domestic criminal law. Because of Canada's leadership in international criminal law, both at the level of the International Criminal Court and of specific war crimes tribunals, Canadian legal theorists have also begun to turn their attention to international criminal law per se, building on their domestic expertise.

The present collection seeks to capitalize on this rapidly developing expertise and bring together for the first time the work of leading Canadian theorists of domestic and international criminal law – both newer voices as well as older voices addressing new questions or old questions from new perspectives. The topics covered are wide-ranging and ambitious. They address questions of philosophical methodology, the legitimate scope of domestic and international criminalization, the nature of criminal responsibility and blame, as well as various rationales for justificatory and excusatory defences. Theoretical questions related to the criminal process, evidence, and the form of punishment are also given focal importance. To be sure, authors and topics were selected to reflect the broad diversity of philosophical work currently being done by Canadians on all aspects of domestic and international criminal law, in a way that balances consideration of more local issues with the general and timeless puzzles that they engage. Thus, it is our hope that this collection will become an enduring contribution to theorizing about criminal law, not only in Canada, but also internationally.

The essays compiled in this book were first presented at a conference sharing its title, held at Osgoode Hall Law School, York University, in Toronto on 10–12 September, 2010. Financial support for the conference was primarily provided by Osgoode Hall's Jack and Mae Nathanson Centre on Transnational Human Rights, Crime and Security. We owe sincere thanks to the Centre's Director, Professor Craig Scott, for showing so much enthusiasm for this project from the very start and for his willingness to integrate criminal law theory into the Centre's mandate. We also wish to thank Osgoode Hall Law School and its Dean, Professor Lorne Sossin, as well as the following law firms, for their generous support: Cooper & Sandler LLP, Di Luca Copeland Davies LLP Barristers, Fenton Smith Barristers, Henein and Associates, Kapoor Barristers, and Lacy Wilkinson LLP. The conference also benefited from the tireless administrative support of Ms Lielle Gonsalves, Administrative Assistant of the Nathanson Centre, as well as that of Mohamad Al-Hakim (PhD candidate in philosophy, York University) and Joshua Tong (JD student, Osgoode Hall Law School). Joshua Tong is also to be thanked for his invaluable editorial assistance in preparing the manuscript for publication.

A special expression of gratitude is also owed to our British colleagues Antony Duff (Stirling/Minnesota), Sandra Marshall (Stirling), and Victor Tadros (Warwick) who so generously offered to use some of the funding tied to their multi-year Criminalization research project (funded by the Arts and Humanities Research Council of the United Kingdom) to attend the conference and offer thoughtful commentaries on some of the chapters. Their advice in the organization of the conference and their input during the event were invaluable, as well as a fine illustration of what the future of a more transnationalized pooling of resources for the study of criminal law theory holds in store. Significant thanks are also owed to our American colleagues Stuart P Green (Rutgers-Newark) and Ekow Yankah (Cardozo), to our Indian colleague Neha Jain (Georgetown), as well as to our very own Susan Dimock (York) for their helpful and challenging responses to some of the chapters. Finally, we want to express our appreciation to Osgoode, York, and McMaster University colleagues who kindly agreed to act as panel chairs – namely, Louis-Philippe Hodgson, Dan Priel, Craig Scott, Wil Waluchow, and Alan Young. The future of Canadian criminal law theory is all the brighter for their contributions.

François Tanguay-Renaud
James Stribopoulos
Osgoode Hall Law School
Toronto, 4 March 2011

TABLE OF CONTENTS

NOTES ON CONTRIBUTORS

Annalise Acorn is Lawlor Professor of Law and Ethics at the Faculty of Law of the University of Alberta. She holds a BA and LLB from the University of Alberta, and a BCL from the University of Oxford. Her main area of research is the theory of emotions in the context of conflict and justice. She is the author of *Compulsory Compassion: A Critique of Restorative Justice* (Vancouver, UBC Press, 2004) and has published numerous articles in journals such as the *Oxford Journal of Legal Studies*, the *Osgoode Hall Law Journal*, the *Valparaiso Law Review*, and the *UCLA Women's Law Journal*.

Benjamin L Berger is Associate Professor of Law at Osgoode Hall Law School. He holds a BA (Hons) (Alberta), LLB (UVic), LLM (Yale), and JSD (Yale). His research addresses questions related to constitutional and criminal law and theory, the law of evidence, and law and religion. He has published broadly in these areas and his work has appeared in multiple edited collections and in legal and interdisciplinary journals such as the *Canadian Journal of Law and Jurisprudence*, *Law, Culture and the Humanities*, the *McGill Law Journal*, the *Osgoode Hall Law Journal*, and the *Journal of Comparative Law*. He is on the editorial board of the *Canadian Journal of Law and Society* and *Studies in Religion/ Sciences Religieuses*, is the book review editor for the *Review of Constitutional Studies*, and is an Associate Editor for the Hart Publishing series *Constitutional Systems of the World*.

Andrew Botterell is Assistant Professor at the University of Western Ontario, where he is jointly appointed to the Department of Philosophy and the Faculty of Law. He received his BA from McGill University, his PhD from MIT, and his JD from the University of Toronto. He has published in leading journals such as *Legal Theory* and *Law and Philosophy*. He currently serves as the Associate Editor of the *Canadian Journal of Law & Jurisprudence*.

Kimberley Brownlee is Senior Lecturer in Political Philosophy at the University of Manchester. She holds a BA (McGill), MPhil (Cambridge) and DPhil (Oxford) in philosophy, and is the Honorary Secretary of the Society for Applied Philosophy. She works on topics in moral, political, and legal philosophy. She is the editor (with Adam Cureton) of *Disability and Disadvantage* (Oxford, OUP, 2009) and has published in numerous leading philosophy journals.

Alan Brudner is Albert Abel Professor of Law at the Faculty of Law, and Professor at the Department of Political Science, at the University of Toronto. He is the author of *Punishment and Freedom: A Liberal Theory of Penal Justice* (Oxford, OUP, 2009),

Constitutional Goods (Oxford, OUP, 2004), and *The Unity of the Common Law: Studies in Hegelian Jurisprudence* (Berkeley, UC Press, 1995), as well as numerous journal articles on a variety of topics in legal and political theory. He was the editor of the University of Toronto Law Journal from 2000 to 2007.

Michael Giudice is Associate Professor of Philosophy at York University and Adjunct Professor of Law at Osgoode Hall Law School. He holds a BA from the University of New Brunswick, as well as an MA and PhD from McMaster University. He is also a Research Associate of the Jack and Mae Nathanson Centre on Transnational Human Rights, Crime and Security, and a member of the editorial committee of *Transnational Legal Theory*. He is the author (with Keith Culver) of *Legality's Borders: An Essay in General Jurisprudence* (New York, OUP, 2010).

Leslie Green is Professor of the Philosophy of Law and Pauline and Max Gordon Fellow of Balliol College at the University of Oxford. He also holds a part-time appointment as Professor of Law and Distinguished University Fellow at Queen's University. He is the author of *The Authority of the State* (Oxford, Clarendon Press, 1990), as well as numerous articles on a variety of topics in legal and political philosophy. He serves on the editorial board of many law journals, and is co-editor of *Oxford Studies in the Philosophy of Law*.

Dennis Klimchuk is Associate Professor of Philosophy at the University of Western Ontario, and is cross-appointed to the Faculty of Law. He holds a PhD in philosophy from the University of Toronto. His main research interests are in philosophy of law and the history of political philosophy, and he has published work in many leading philosophy journals and law reviews.

Margaret Martin is Assistant Professor of Law at the University of Western Ontario. She holds a BA (Hons) and MA from McMaster University, MSL from the University of Toronto, and PhD from the University of Cambridge. Her main research interests are legal philosophy, constitutional law and international criminal law. Her publications include *Judging Positivism* (Oxford, Hart Publishing, forthcoming 2011).

Dwight Newman is Professor at the University of Saskatchewan College of Law. He holds a JD from the University of Saskatchewan, as well as his BCL, MPhil and DPhil from the University of Oxford. He researches in areas of constitutional law, international law, Aboriginal law, and legal/political theory. His publications include *The Duty to Consult: New Relationships with Aboriginal Peoples* (Saskatoon, Purich Publishing, 2009) and *Community and Collective Rights: A Theoretical Framework for Rights Held by Groups* (Oxford, Hart Publishing, forthcoming 2011).

Jens David Ohlin is Associate Professor of Law at Cornell University. He holds a PhD in philosophy from Columbia University, and a JD from Columbia Law

School, where he also served as an associate-in-law for two years. His research interests are focused on criminal law theory, public international law, and international criminal law. He is the author (with George Fletcher) of *Defending Humanity: When Force is Justified and Why* (Oxford, OUP, 2008). His work has also appeared in the *Columbia Law Review*, the *Harvard International Law Journal*, the *American Journal of International Law*, the *Journal of Criminal Law & Criminology*, and the *Journal of International Criminal Justice*. He is also a member of an international working group developing general rules and principles of international criminal procedure.

Matthew Schaeffer is a doctoral candidate in the Department of Philosophy at York University. He also holds a BA and MA from York University.

Hamish Stewart is an Associate Professor of Law at the University of Toronto. In addition to an LLB (Toronto), he holds a BA (Toronto) and a PhD (Harvard) in Economics. His research focuses on criminal law, the law of evidence, and legal theory. He recently contributed the Evidence title to *Halsbury's Laws of Canada* (LexisNexis, 2010). He is also principal author of *Sexual Offences in Canadian Law* (Canada Law Boook, 2004), general editor of *Evidence: A Canadian Casebook*, 2d edn (Emond Montgomery, 2006), an associate editor of the *Canadian Criminal Cases*, and book review editor of the *University of Toronto Law Journal*.

James Stribopoulos is Associate Professor of Law at Osgoode Hall Law School. He holds a BA (York), JD (Osgoode), LLM and JSD (Columbia). At Osgoode, he is Director of Mooting and Co-Director of the Part-Time LLM Program Specializing in Criminal Law. In the past, he has also served as Director of the Criminal Intensive Program, Director of Clinical Education and Editor-in-Chief of the faculty's blog (TheCourt.ca). His research focuses on topics related to criminal law, criminal procedure, evidence, comparative criminal procedure, constitutional law, advocacy, legal ethics, the legal profession and the legal process. He is an associate editor of *Criminal Law and Procedure: Cases and Materials*, 10th edn (Toronto, Emond Montgomery, 2010) and *Evidence: A Canadian Casebook*, 2d edn (Toronto, Emond Montgomery, 2006). He is also the editor (with Jamie Cameron) of *The Charter and Criminal Justice: Twenty-Five Years Later* (Toronto, LexisNexis, 2008).

François Tanguay-Renaud is Assistant Professor of Law at Osgoode Hall Law School, and a member of the Graduate Faculty of the Department of Philosophy at York University in Toronto. He is currently Associate Director (Acting Director, 2009-2011) of the Jack and Mae Nathanson Centre on Transnational Human Rights, Crime and Security, as well as HLA Hart Visiting Fellow at the Oxford Centre for Ethics and Philosophy of Law. He holds law degrees in both civil and common law from McGill University, as well as BCL, MPhil, and DPhil degrees from the University of Oxford. His research focuses on issues in criminal law theory, constitutional theory, general jurisprudence, as well as moral and political philosophy. He has published articles in leading journals such as *Ethics*, *Legal Theory*, and *Res Publica*, as well as in several edited collections, and he is a member of the editorial committee of *Transnational Legal Theory*.

Malcolm Thorburn is Associate Professor of Law and Canada Research Chair in Crime, Security and Constitutionalism at the Faculty of Law of Queen's University. He holds a BA (Toronto) and MA (Penn) in Philosophy, and a JD (Toronto), LLM and JSD (Columbia). His research focuses on theoretical issues in criminal law, criminal procedure and sentencing. His work has appeared in such publications as the *Yale Law Journal*, the *Boston University Law Review*, the *University of Toronto Law Journal*, the *Queen's Law Journal* and several books at Oxford University Press and Hart Publishing. He is a member of the Surveillance Studies Centre at Queen's University, an associate editor of the *New Criminal Law Review* and a member of the editorial board of *Law and Philosophy*.

PART I

Rethinking the Philosophical Foundations of Substantive Domestic Criminal Law

A

The Legitimate Scope of Criminal Law and the Methodology of Criminal Law Theory

1

Two Conceptions of Equality before the (Criminal) Law

MALCOLM THORBURN*

I INTRODUCTION

Equality before the law is one of the central ideals in modern legal thinking, but its precise meaning is the object of considerable dispute. It is important for criminal law theorists to get a clear sense of the meaning of this ideal, however, for it plays an important part in our understanding of the law of justification defences. This is because criminal law justification defences seem to undermine our equality before the law by permitting some people to do the very things that others are criminally prohibited from doing. For example, the prison official who punishes a duly convicted offender is entitled to a justification for his conduct, but a private citizen who takes it upon himself to punish a wrongdoer in the same way is treated as a criminal vigilante. Any attempt to explain the legitimacy of justification defences will have to find some way to square the ideal of equality before the law with the way in which justifications privilege some to act in ways that are foreclosed to others.

In this chapter, I contrast two different conceptions of the ideal of equality before the law and their implications for criminal law justifications doctrine. In section II, I set out the two ideals, which, for the sake of simplicity, I call 'Diceyan' and 'Kantian' and I articulate some of their implications for criminal law justifications doctrine. In section III, I show how contemporary criminal law doctrine – as well as doctrines in Canadian and American constitutional law and elsewhere in our legal systems – seems to fit more neatly with the Kantian account of equality before the law. That said, I point out that the fit is far from perfect – there are still a number of older doctrines that seem to fit better with the Diceyan picture. In this section, I argue that the root of my disagreement with John Gardner (and

* Thanks to Larissa Katz, Dennis Klimchuk, Sandra Marshall, Hamish Stewart, François Tanguay-Renaud, Mark Walters and to all the participants in the conference that led to this volume for valuable comments and discussion. Thanks also to the Social Sciences and Humanities Research Council of Canada for its financial support.

others)[1] on the structure and rationale of justification defences in contemporary criminal law is at least in part the result of a deeper disagreement on the nature of the ideal of equality before the law. In section IV, I conclude by pointing out that there is much more at work in justification defences than the issues that dominate contemporary criminal law theory debates in this area. Rather than arguing about whose intuitions about justification are best, we should look to the prior question of what role justifications are supposed to play within a legitimate legal order. It is this issue, which animates the dispute over the ideal of equality before the law that should be at the heart of the criminal law theory debate.

II THE TWO CONCEPTIONS CONTRASTED

A The Diceyan Ideal

The first account of equality before the law is what I shall (somewhat loosely) call 'the Diceyan ideal'.[2] Although this ideal of equality before the law is almost never made explicit in criminal law theory debates – probably because it is thought to be too obvious to be worthy of mention – it is the one that has dominated Anglo-American criminal law theory for at least a generation. According to this way of thinking, the key to equality before the law is the absence of any special legal status for the conduct of state officials – or anyone else, for that matter. One of the deep problems with late nineteenth-century French *droit administratif*, in Dicey's opinion, was the fact that 'affairs or disputes in which the government or its servants are concerned are beyond the sphere of the civil courts and must be dealt with by special and more or less official bodies (*tribunaux administratifs*)'.[3] That is, it had one set of rules designed only for private citizens (administered by the ordinary courts) and another set of rules designed only for public officials (administered by a parallel set of courts that concerned themselves only with public law matters). By contrast, the great virtue of the common law, in Dicey's opinion, was

[1] My disagreement with John Gardner is on a point where he is in agreement with most of the current orthodoxy in Anglo-American criminal law theory. So, although I focus my comments on his position, I believe that most of my comments also apply, mutatis mutandis, to most other English-speaking criminal law theorists, as well.

[2] I use this expression as a sort of shorthand. I do not pretend to be faithful to the writings of AV Dicey in every aspect of this ideal. I should also add that I am using Dicey to stand in for a stronger set of claims than the ones I made in his name in an earlier article: M Thorburn, 'Justifications, Powers, and Authority' (2008) 117 *Yale Law Journal* 1070. In that article, I invoked Dicey in support of the ideal that everyone may be held criminally liable unless he can provide an adequate justification defence for his prima facie wrongful conduct. But I did not invoke the stronger claim, which is part of the larger Diceyan ideal that justification defences apply to us in virtue of our factual position rather than in virtue of our legal standing. There as here, I rejected that stronger Diceyan claim.

[3] This, at least, is Dicey's characterization of the situation in the early editions of his great book, *An Introduction to the Study of the Law of the Constitution* (eg, at 215–16 of the 1885 edition). There is reason to believe that this was not, strictly speaking, the case even at the time when Dicey was writing. But the accuracy of Dicey's description of the French legal system is not relevant for present purposes.

the fact that it subjected everyone – public officials and private citizens alike – to the same set of rules administered by the same court system. As Dicey puts it:

> Every official, from the Prime Minister down to a constable or a collector of taxes, is under the same responsibility for every act done without legal justification as any other citizen. The Reports abound with cases in which officials have been brought before the Courts, and made, in their personal capacity, liable to punishment, or to the payment of damages, for acts done in their official character but in excess of their lawful authority.[4]

But, of course, in the common law world, public officials are often able to claim justifications that are not open to the rest of us. Police officers, to take only one example, are entitled to make arrests on the basis of reasonable suspicion of the commission of an indictable offence but private citizens are not.[5] So what is the real substance of the Diceyan ideal of equality before the law? In order for it to escape the charge of empty formalism – merely demanding that public officials be tried in the same courts but allowing them to be tried according to an altogether different set of rules – something more must be added. That 'something more' is the claim that any differences between the justification defences available to public officials and those open to private citizens is merely a reflection of their different factual circumstances.

According to the old common law adage, a police officer is only 'a person paid to perform as a matter of duty acts which if he were so minded he might have done voluntarily'.[6] That is, the justifications available to police officers are for the most part the same as the ones open to the rest of us; and where they are different this is not in virtue of any difference in legal status for officials. Instead, it is merely because the law recognizes that police officers (and other public officials) find themselves in a different set of circumstances from the rest us. As Dicey puts it, 'officers, magistrates, soldiers, policemen, ordinary citizens, all occupy in the eye of the law *the same position*' (emphasis added).[7] Those circumstances are different in such a way that, applying the *same* basic normative standards, we should permit public officials to do things that others are prohibited from doing. Gardner has recently endorsed this position in the following terms:

[4] AV Dicey, *An Introduction to the Study of the Law of the Constitution* 8th edn (Indianapolis, Liberty Fund, 1982) 124.

[5] In Canadian criminal law, the difference is set out in the Criminal Code RSC 1985 ch C-46, ss 494 (concerning ordinary citizens) and 495 (concerning police officers).

[6] The Royal Commission on the Police, cited in G Marshall, *Police and Government: The Status and Accountability of the English Constable* (London, Methuen, 1965) 17.

[7] Dicey, *An Introduction* (n 4) 185. Dicey elaborates on this point as follows:

> [T]hey are, each and all of them, bound to withstand and put down breaches of the peace, such as riots and other disturbances; they are, each and all of them, authorised to employ so much force, even to the taking of life, as may be necessary for that purpose, and they are none of them entitled to use more; they are, each and all of them, liable to be called to account before a jury for the use of excessive, that is, of unnecessary force; they are each, it must be added – for this is often forgotten – liable, in theory at least, to be called to account before the Courts for non-performance of their duty as citizens in putting down riots, though of course the degree and kind of energy which each is reasonably bound to exert in the maintenance of order may depend upon and differ with his position as officer, magistrate, soldier, or ordinary citizen.

> [T]he legal power of ordinary members of the public to effect an arrest is the basic power, and the extra arrest powers of police officers, including the power to arrest on reasonable suspicion of the commission of an offence, are special extensions of that. This reflects the general common law doctrine, of which Dicey made so much, that public officials are regulated first by the ordinary law of the land applicable to private persons, to which ordinary law of the land all specifically public powers, duties and permissions must be read as either extensions or exceptions.[8]

But if public officials are no different in their legal standing from ordinary citizens, why should the law ever grant them permission to do things that the rest of us are forbidden from doing? One reason concerns their expertise: for example, if they are trained in the use of firearms and other coercive tools in a way that the rest of us are not, then there might be good prudential reasons for the law to grant them the exclusive right to use coercive force. Another reason for doing so is the need to coordinate the activities of a plurality of actors: for example, it is best to give the right to use coercive force exclusively to *someone* in order to avoid violent chaos. But these reasons merely track factual circumstances that are not necessarily related the officer's status as a public official. In other cases, it might be some private citizen who has the relevant expertise (say, a doctor, who may perform surgeries that the rest of us may not) or who is the one we pick out of the crowd for reasons of social coordination (as we might privilege the person closest to the scene of an accident as the person to take charge of the situation). Gardner makes clear his commitment to this point in the following terms:

> [O]ccasionally people have additional legal powers by virtue of being public officials, such as police officers. But although these additional powers are the powers of public officials, nothing turns, for the criminal law, on the fact that they are the powers of public officials . . . In the criminal court . . . their public character is neither here nor there.[9]

According to the Diceyan ideal, then, understanding the structure of justification defences is a fairly straightforward affair. There is a single phenomenon of justification that is the same both inside and outside the criminal law. The justification defences made available in a legitimate criminal justice system should track as closely as possible the sorts of reasons that an individual might present to justify his conduct morally outside the legal system. So the criminal law theorist's main task when making sense of justification defences, it seems, is to read the current literature in moral philosophy and to take careful notes. If we believe that all individuals are morally justified in killing in self-defence, then we should advocate in favour of a justification defence of self-defence open to all. If we believe that police officers are morally justified (given the institutional arrangements in which they find themselves) in using force to apprehend criminal suspects in ways that the rest of us are not, then we should advocate in favour of a special justification defence of

[8] J Gardner, 'Justification under Authority' (2010) 23 *Canadian Journal of Law and Jurisprudence* 71, 95–96.

[9] ibid 97.

lawful arrest available to police officers. And if we think that individuals are justified in damaging others' property as part of an effort to resist immoral laws, then we should advocate in favour of a justification defence of civil disobedience. And this is precisely how contemporary criminal law has treated the question of justification defences. The debate is little more than a repeat of the same discussions from the moral philosophy literature about moral justification. The details of precisely how to adjust such justifications to suit the criminal law context might be grounds for some dispute,[10] but these are largely afterthoughts that need not trouble us as we make sense of the basic moral 'gist'[11] of these claims of justification.

B The Kantian Ideal

There is a second ideal of equality under the law, however, that is worthy of consideration and that can give rise to a rather different understanding of justification defences in criminal law. It is what I shall (again, somewhat loosely) call 'the Kantian ideal'.[12] According to the Kantian ideal, we preserve equality before the law by introducing the very feature that was considered problematic under the Diceyan ideal: a difference in legal status between private actors and public officials. Now, there might be an air of paradox to the suggestion that we may guarantee equality under the law by recognizing two different types of legal actors, especially where one class of actors is permitted to do a number of things that members of the other class are prohibited from doing. That air of paradox, however, dissipates on closer inspection. To see how, we need to take a step back to discover the sort of equality that matters under this ideal and why.

The best way to set out the Kantian conception of equality before the law is to contrast it with its Diceyan counterpart. Under most versions of the Diceyan story,[13] the idea of equality before the law is a purely negative one: the law should

[10] One notable dispute is the importance of mistakes. One sort of mistake – where a person reasonably but mistakenly believes that the justifying grounds for his conduct are present – has been the subject of intense dispute; another sort of mistake – where a person mistakenly believes that there are no justifying grounds for his conduct – has also been subject of intense dispute. And, of course, there is a deep disagreement as to moral theory. Utilitarians such as Paul Robinson take one view of what conduct is morally justified; non-consequentialist writers such as George Fletcher and John Gardner take a quite different view.

[11] I take this expression from Gardner's article 'The Gist of Excuses' (1997) 2 *Buffalo Criminal Law Review* 575. It is clear from his treatment of both justification and excuse that he takes these legal doctrines as institutionalized versions of the same basic concepts as understood in moral theory.

[12] It might just as easily be called the 'Roman law ideal' since it is based on the centrality of a distinction between public and private that arises first in Roman law, but I will stick with the 'Kantian' terminology in order to stress a connection to a particular conception of equality before the law.

[13] Not all, of course. Writers such as Gardner actually rely on a well-developed account of the law's authority, taken from the work of Joseph Raz. According to his account, the law has authority over us just in case it guides us to conform better to the reasons that already apply to us than if we tried to do so without its help. See, eg, J Gardner, 'Justifications and Reasons' in *Offences and Defences: Selected Essays in the Philosophy of Criminal Law* (New York, Oxford University Press, 2007) citing J Raz, *Practical Reason and Norms* (London, Hutchinson, 1975). Nevertheless, Gardner's views on authority are just additional support for these negative claims; they are not at odds with them.

not draw distinctions among people based on status. But under the Kantian ideal, the law ought not only to avoid creating new inequalities, it must also play a crucial role in *securing* the equality of all in the first place. The basic idea is this: in the absence of legal rules and institutions, not only are the clever and the powerful *in fact* free to run the lives of the not-so-clever and the not-so-powerful (simply because they are clever and powerful enough to get away with it), there also appear to be good reasons why they *should* be allowed to run the lives of the not-so-clever and not-so-powerful as well. It seems that the clever should be allowed to make decisions for the not-so-clever simply because they are more likely to come to the morally right answer; and it seems that the powerful should make broad organizational decisions for everyone simply because they are more likely actually to get the mass of people to abide by their decisions. But this situation – where clever and powerful people are entitled to call all the shots – strikes most of us as deeply wrong. When pressed, we might say that the reason why it is so objectionable is that it seems to confuse two distinct issues. Although it is important to do what we can to come to the morally right outcome when exercising jurisdiction that is our own, this does not mean that we should allocate jurisdiction in whatever way is likely to generate the right outcomes in most cases. The allocation of jurisdiction should operate on a different principle: viz, the principle that everyone should be equally entitled to make decisions about his or her own affairs, free from interference by others.

The Kantian ideal provides a mechanism through which we may simultaneously recognize the value in both of these two claims: viz, that it is important to make morally right decisions *and* that it is also important that *we* make the decisions about our own affairs. Taking each person's claim to personal sovereignty seriously, we recognize that none of us has the standing to force others to come to the morally right conclusions about how to run her own life. But, once again taking each person's claim to personal sovereignty seriously, we also recognize that the legal system must articulate each person's sphere of personal sovereignty and vindicate it when it is under threat. The law does this by guaranteeing to each person – no matter how clever or how powerful she might be – a sphere of personal sovereignty over her own body and property. Private law rules of property, tort, etc, perform this basic function: they ensure that each person may decide for herself precisely how she would like to use her body and property and they prohibit others from interfering in these decisions. Although we might be tempted to impose our views on others – on the grounds that our views are morally superior to theirs – the Kantian ideal of equality before the law precludes that option. It is up to each person to heed the call of morality when exercising her own jurisdiction; the law's role is simply to ensure that each person is in a position to do so for herself. The point is that when we are concerned with the allocation of individual sovereignty among free and morally equal persons, the only appropriate normative standard is the equality of all persons' claims to sovereignty, and therefore we are committed to an allocation that gives everyone precisely the same claim as everyone else.

But, of course, an arrangement made up only of private claims of sovereignty over our bodies and property is not self-sufficient. We come quickly to see the need for public power when we recognize the limitations of a system made up only of private rights. We live in a world that is imperfect in at least two different ways. First, the world is imperfect in contingent but quite predictable ways: resources are scarce and some people may be so desperate for the necessities of life that they become totally dependent on the charity of others; and we live in a world where some people will succumb to the temptation to interfere in the affairs of others by stealing their property, injuring their person, etc. In the face of these realities, it is not enough for us simply to insist that we are entitled to our individual claims of sovereignty regardless of the conditions of others. But no one has the private right to take from the rich to give to the needy because this would undermine the rich person's claim to be the one who controls what happens to himself and to his property. And no one has the right to use force to prevent crime or to bring wrongdoers to justice because this would involve (at a minimum) interference with the offender's freedom of movement. And so on.

We live in an imperfect world in another sense too. That is, there are certain necessary features of our world that also give rise to problems with an allocation of private rights. We need a public power to determine the precise scope of our rights claims because the grounds of our claims do not precisely specify the extent of the particular rights claim; we also need a public power to adjudicate disputes as between private actors because there will be questions that cannot be answered precisely even by people of good will simply by examining the underlying normative claims; and we need a public power to establish and maintain public modes of communication so that individuals who occupy particular spatial locations may interact freely with those who are not their immediate neighbours.[14] Something is needed to do all these things (and more) simply in order to secure our equal claims of sovereignty themselves. For our claim of sovereignty is a claim of *right* – it is a claim that others are obligated to respect on pain of denying their own individual sovereignty – so it must be part of a system that is itself a necessary condition for the possibility of everyone's claim of individual sovereignty.[15]

Since all these measures are necessary simply in order to secure the conditions for us all to enjoy sovereignty over our own affairs, we have no grounds for complaint when we find that our individual sovereignty appears to be infringed by them.[16] The only problem that remains is who could have the standing to actually

[14] Private roads do not solve this problem, for they leave us at the mercy of private whims of the road's owners.

[15] I am deeply indebted to Arthur Ripstein's careful treatment of Kantian right in his recent book: A Ripstein, *Force and Freedom: Kant's Legal and Political Philosophy* (Cambridge, MA, Harvard University Press, 2010). Since my restatement of the basics of the Kantian position is extremely brief, it is sure to introduce short cuts and inaccuracies here and there. My point here is only to give a sense that there is a different way to think about equality before the law that is relevant to a number of doctrinal problems in criminal law.

[16] The parallel between the structure of justified infringement here and the one we find in many post-war constitutional models such as the German *Grundgesetz*, the European Charter of Human Rights and the Canadian Charter of Rights and Freedoms is not a coincidence; for they, too, are best understood in

carry out these tasks that are so necessary to the preservation of our individual sovereignty. If some private party took it upon herself to do so, her conduct would appear to be just another imposition of someone's private will on others. No matter how noble her motives, a private actor simply does not have the standing to make decisions about how to sacrifice individual claims of sovereignty for the sake of securing the conditions of individual sovereignty generally. Because these tasks must be performed in order for us to enjoy our equal claims of sovereignty, but no private party has the standing to perform them, the Kantian account posits a public actor that may do these things in the name of us all collectively.

Public power is a solution to these many problems that must arise under a system made up only of private parties with their private rights because it introduces a new sort of actor who can speak in the name of the system as a whole. Public authorities may interfere with the freedom of individuals in ways that private parties may never do because they stand in a different sort of relationship with us. When another private party tries to tell us how to run our lives, he is simply imposing his will on us from the outside. But when a legitimate public authority acts, it is, in an important sense, *us* collectively deciding how *we* shall act so as to secure the conditions of *our* individual sovereignty. It is for this reason that a public authority may expropriate private property for a public purpose (such as making public roads that allow private parties to move about without having to ask the say-so of their neighbours) even though it would be a clear violation if a private party were to do the same thing. And this is why a public authority may use force to punish a criminal wrongdoer (by imprisoning him or fining him, for example) even though private parties are strictly prohibited from doing anything like this. And this is why a public authority may extract money from the wealthy through a system of income tax and redistribute it to those who are in need even though would-be Robin Hoods are strictly forbidden from doing the same thing. Public authorities are entitled to do all these things (and much more) but private parties are not because of their different standing. I, as a private party with my own preferences and interests, have no business interfering in the affairs of others, for this would undermine that other person's claim of sovereignty over his own body and property. But a public authority that speaks in the name of all and acts for the purpose of securing the necessary pre-conditions for everyone's individual sovereignty may do so because it is not alien to us in the same way. When the public authority acts, it does not undermine the equal standing of all private parties before the law; it simply allows us to act collectively in order to set in place the pre-conditions for the individual sovereignty of all.

From the idea of the law securing the maximum freedom for each individual to make decisions for herself consistent with the same claim for others, we have come to the conclusion that there must be a public authority in place to ensure the preconditions of that sort of individual freedom. But now, it seems that we

terms of a Kantian account of public power. This is perhaps most explicitly the case in the recent German constitutional case striking down the German air safety law. For a broadly Kantian take on this case, see my 'The Constitution of Criminal Law' in *Criminal Law and Philosophy* (forthcoming).

have introduced a sort of inequality of status between officials and private citizens that is objectionable to the Diceyan view of things. But even that is not quite right. In fact, we have not introduced an inequality of status between two classes of *people* – officials and private citizens. Rather, we have only introduced a distinction between two different sorts of *grounds of decision-making authority* – the authority to decide certain questions for oneself and the authority to decide certain questions on behalf of all. One and the same person will be called on to exercise each sort of power on different occasions. When a public official is off duty at home, she is subject to the same limits as the rest of us: she is free to decide her own private matters pretty much as she would like, but only as concerns her own body and property. But when she arrives at work to make decisions on behalf of all in matters that alter the legal status of the bodies and property of others, the public official must do so in such a way that her decisions can be thought of as genuinely *public* decisions made on behalf of all. The sorts of reasons that she may consider are sharply limited; her decision-making process when deciding what to do on the basis of that limited set of reasons is also subject to demands of reasonableness and fairness as between competing private interests. And, insofar as it is possible, she must excuse herself whenever her own private interests are at stake in order to avoid any appearance that she might surreptitiously be making her decision on the basis of her own private reasons rather than on the basis of the limited set of reasons that are open to her to consider as a public official.

That is – contrary to the Kafkaesque image sometimes invoked by the opponents of the Kantian ideal of faceless bureaucrats being given licence to decide the fates of hapless private citizens just as they please and then being granted immunity even from the ordinary courts of private law and criminal law – the Kantian ideal actually *raises* the standards to which we are held when exercising public power by adding a further level of accountability. If we are purporting to exercise a public power, the Kantian account scrutinises not only our conclusions, but also the process through which we came to those conclusions. Even good answers may be rendered illegitimate if they were brought about in the wrong way. For then, they would be private decisions – albeit ones that just happened to come to the same conclusions that would have been reached by a process of public decision-making. But because only public decisions may justifiably interfere with the private rights of others, such decisions are treated as invalid and conduct that follows from it will not usually be recognised as justified.[17] So, on the Kantian account, the mere fact that an individual holds a particular public office should not insulate him from liability in tort or criminal law. If his conduct was not in accordance with the principles of public law, then it must be attributed to him as a private party[18] – and he

[17] For reasons that go beyond the present context, the law sometimes treats these acts as legally void and sometimes, it treats them as merely voidable.

[18] Although the individual may be held liable for his conduct that goes beyond the scope of his public power, this does not preclude Crown liability, as well. Such liability, however, must be based on the failure of officials to exercise due care in supervising the rogue official, rather than on the grounds that the rogue officials was in fact acting on behalf of the state. Thanks to Hamish Stewart for drawing my attention to this point.

must be held accountable as a private party for that conduct according to the same standards as all other private citizens. In short, the point of difference between the two positions is not that the Diceyan ideal holds everyone equally accountable, but that the Kantian ideal grants public officials immunity from liability in tort or criminal law for their acts. Rather, it is that when we hold individuals accountable in tort or criminal law for their conduct, the Kantian account adds a second level of scrutiny to those acts purportedly made in the name of the system as a whole.

C Coda

The difference between the two conceptions of equality before the law turns out to be quite far-ranging and crucial for a number of doctrinal and normative issues. According to the Diceyan ideal, there is nothing particularly special about the work of public servants. What makes a police officer a police officer, on this account, is little more than his pay cheque: he is paid to do (and may be obligated to do) certain things that he would be permitted to do anyway. The aspect of this story that proponents of the Diceyan account like to emphasize is that police officers are not privy to any special treatment – they are held accountable in criminal law in precisely the same way as the rest of us. But the obverse of the same story is the recognition that there is nothing special about the public provision of certain services: nothing of principle would be lost if we were to privatize all public functions: policing, prisons, even the military. Of course, advocates of the Diceyan position might suggest that there are pragmatic reasons for keeping some of these services in public hands, but they would not have any objections in principle to our doing so. I have argued elsewhere[19] that there are important reasons of principle to object to what Paul Verkuil calls 'outsourcing sovereignty'[20] – but they are reasons that are extremely difficult for the Diceyan account to articulate.

[19] M Thorburn, 'Reinventing the Night-Watchman State?' (2010) 60 *University of Toronto Law Journal* 425. Alon Harel has set out a powerful argument of principle against the privatization of prisons in A Harel, 'Why Only the State May Inflict Criminal Sanctions: The Case Against Privately Inflicted Sanctions' (2008) 14 *Legal Theory* 113. See also: A Harel, 'The Vices of Institutional Instrumentalism' (2009) 42 *Israel Law Review* 464. Harel nicely draws the distinction between two quite different issues, both of which are at stake here: (1) whether some things can only be done *in the name of the people* (rather than in our own private name); and (2) whether those thing done in the name of the people may be done *by public officials on the government payroll.* In my own writing, I follow Harel in drawing this distinction, as well. But for present purposes, however, it is important only to see that these issues of public and private are important in a number of different areas of current debate.

[20] P Verkuil, *Outsourcing Sovereignty: Why Privatization of Government Functions Threatens Democracy and What we can do about it* (Cambridge, Cambridge University Press, 2007).

III THE TWO IDEALS IN CONTEMPORARY CRIMINAL LAW DOCTRINE

So far in this chapter, I have not directly engaged any of the standard questions of criminal law theory. I have begun by setting out two ideals of equality before the law because I believe that some important disagreements about the rationale and the structure of criminal law are rooted in a deeper disagreement about how to understand this ideal. In this section of the chapter, I will consider a few key legal doctrines – particularly concerning criminal law justification defences – to see if they fit better with the Diceyan or the Kantian understanding of the ideal of equality before the law. I do so with some trepidation. For although some of the most important writers in the history of English law have recognized the importance of the public–private distinction that lies at the heart of the Kantian account, there are just as many who insist that it is alien to the spirit of the common law. On the one hand, no less of an authority than Maitland and Pollock's *History of English Law* states that the 'division of law into "public" and "private" . . . seems eminently well suited to be among the first outlines of any institutional work on modern law'.[21] On the other hand, however, John Allison has suggested in a recent book that the distinction between public law and private law is 'a continental distinction in the common law'[22] – a foreign transplant that sits uneasily with much of the structure of English law. As hostile as Allison surely is to the public–private distinction that is so important to the Kantian ideal of equality before the law, however, we should note that even he recognizes that it has *in fact* taken root in the common law. His concern is simply that we have not thought systematically about how the introduction of this distinction will affect almost every aspect of the system. He quotes Atiyah and Summers's ecological metaphor to explain the point, as follows:

> [T]he ecological ramifications [of a transplant] must be fully considered. For example, English lawyers and politicians who advocate the introduction of a constitutional Bill of Rights in England, with some power of judicial review, must become aware of the political ramifications and implications of such a move. These could, for example, bear upon methods of judicial selection, the styles of legislative drafting, and a complete reappraisal of the relative values of certainty and justice in the individual case.[23]

[21] F Pollock and FW Maitland, *The History of English Law before the Time of Edward I* vol 1 (first published 1895, Cambridge University Press, 1968 with an introduction by SFC Milson) book 2, ch 1, 230.

[22] JWF Allison, *A Continental Distinction in the Common Law: A Historical and Comparative Perspective on English Public Law* (Oxford, Oxford University Press, 1996). In making his argument, however, Allison notes that there has been support over the years for both sides in this debate. He notes (at 7–8) that Blackstone, for one, was a supporter of the public–private distinction in English law.

[23] PS Atiyah and RS Summers, *Form and Substance in Anglo-American Law: A Comparative Study of Legal Reasoning, Legal Theory, and Legal Institutions* (Oxford, Oxford University Press, 1987) 426–28.

One point that is beyond question, however, is that criminal law theorists have not taken the time to consider the implications of this distinction. Gardner is surely right when he writes that '[i]t does not seem to me that theorists of the Anglophone criminal law are particularly prone to relying on this distinction, or even to mention it, in carving up justification defences'.[24]

What, then, is the place of the Kantian ideal of equality before the law in the criminal law doctrine of the English-speaking world – particularly the distinction between public law and private law that lies at its heart? Nothing of principle turns on this question, of course. Even if the common law world has spurned the Kantian idea of equality before the law altogether, this does not in itself say anything about the moral force of this ideal. But my concern is not merely to present a detached normative argument about what the structure of our criminal law ought to be; I am also interested in providing a compelling normative reconstruction of our present doctrine. In this section, I shall consider some of the more important doctrinal areas where criminal law doctrine clearly shows an inclination toward one ideal or the other.

A The Kantian Ideal in the Common Law

In an earlier article,[25] I presented an account of justification defences that was (implicitly) an argument in favour of thinking about criminal law in terms of the Kantian understanding of the ideal of equality before the law. In that article, I presented many of the examples I shall outline here as evidence that we can make the best sense of the structure of (almost all) justification defences if we think of them as recognizing that the person claiming the justification was acting in the name of the state. Because I have already presented most of these examples elsewhere, I will keep my discussion of them here quite brief. I shall focus on four areas of Anglo-American criminal law doctrine[26] where the Kantian ideal seems to fit much more neatly than the Diceyan alternative. First, I will consider the much-noted failure of the criminal law to grant justifications for a great deal of conduct that we would take to be morally justified, all things considered.[27] If criminal law doctrine was truly committed to the Diceyan conception of equality before the law, this disconnect would be grounds for serious criticism of the present doctrine. Secondly, I will consider the ways in which the law grants some deference to the decisions of public officials in their judgement as to what is the justified way to address certain sorts of situations.[28] Thirdly, I consider the 'state

[24] Gardner, 'Justification under Authority' (n 8) 97.

[25] See Thorburn, 'Justifications' (n 2).

[26] Since this is a volume dedicated to Canadian criminal law theory, I should add that Canadian criminal law doctrine follows the same pattern except where noted below.

[27] This is a point made (to quite different effect) by Mitch Berman: M Berman 'Justifications and Excuse: Law and Morality' (2003) 53 *Duke Law Journal* 1. But this point has been made many times over the years.

[28] This is what Gardner calls my 'split authority thesis' in his 'Justification under Authority' (n 8) 74.

action doctrine' according to which the constitutional rights set out in the US Bill of Rights and the Canadian Charter of Rights and Freedoms are protected only vis-à-vis the conduct of public actors, but not private citizens. (Although this is not strictly speaking a criminal law doctrine, it is nonetheless important for my claim. For we should keep in mind that my claim about the nature of the ideal of equality before the law is not limited to criminal law; it is just that I am focused for present purposes on its implications for criminal law doctrine.) Finally, I will consider the ways in which private parties, insofar as they are entitled to claim justification defences at all, are generally treated as public officials of last resort who may claim a justification only when no duly authorised public official is able to do so.

i The Disconnect between Criminal Law and Morality

The disconnect between the demands of the criminal law and those of morality are well known. Much to the chagrin of those who would like to ignore the law's demands and simply 'do what's right', we find that the law is not very interested in our freestanding moral arguments about the moral justifiability of our conduct. This is true in a wide variety of contexts. Homeless squatters were denied a justification of necessity for their occupation of unused public housing in the well-known case of *Southwark London Borough Council v Williams*;[29] individuals who engage in minor acts of civil disobedience to prevent what they take to be serious wrongdoing by the government are similarly denied a justification for their actions;[30] and, of course, those who take it upon themselves to punish wrongdoers are treated as criminal vigilantes. In all these cases and many more, the criminal law treats us as vigilantes – no matter how powerful our moral arguments might be – they have no force simply because we do not have the *standing* to make decisions about the bodies and property of others.

Defenders of the Diceyan ideal might try to argue that the law's failure to mirror the structure of justification in morality more broadly is simply a result of the failure of law generally to live up to our ideals for what it might be. This is the line, by and large, that Gardner takes. As an exclusive legal positivist,[31] he insists that the law confers authority on individuals to make moral choices which, once made, have the force of law. But since we are dependent on the choices of individuals to make law in these areas, it is predictable that the law will be mistaken here and there. But this does not seem to be a sufficient account of the disconnect

[29] *Southwark London Borough Council v Williams* [1971] 2 WLR 467, 467 (Denning MR).

[30] See eg, *United States v Schoon* 971 F 2d 193 (1991 9th Cir).

[31] Gardner emphasizes this aspect of his work in 'Justification under Authority' (n 8) 73–74, as follows: 'As an exclusive legal positivist, I am slightly taken aback to be facing the complaint that I do not place enough emphasis on the role of authoritative determination in giving content to the law at the point of its application to particular cases'. On the nature of exclusive legal positivism – and the difference between exclusive and inclusive legal positivism, see eg, WJ Waluchow, *Inclusive Legal Positivism* (Oxford, Oxford University Press, 1994).

between law and morality that we see here. Whereas the Kantian ideal provides a deep normative account as to why it is right for courts to deny claims of justification in cases such as these (a sentiment that courts seem to endorse), the exclusive legal positivist account seems to suggest that courts should be rather embarrassed at being forced to deny such claims of justification. But courts in fact show few signs of any such embarrassment. Instead, they insist that the relevant question is not what is morally the right thing to do, but rather whether it is up to private parties to make decisions that are for public bodies to decide on behalf of us all.

ii The Split Authority Thesis

The converse of the law's disregard for private citizens' efforts to take the law into their own hands is its willingness to defer to the judgement of public officials about a number of difficult normative issues. Where the relevant public authorities have decided on a certain course of action – say, the imposition of a new form of taxation or the expropriation of private property for public use – this is generally regarded as legally justified so long as the decision was arrived at in the right way by the appropriate decision-makers, even if the decision they came to was incorrect (as judged by our best moral lights). This is not only true of high-placed officials making decisions about taxation and expropriation policy, but of lowly justices of the peace who grant search warrants, arrest warrants, wiretap warrants, etc and even beat cops who must exercise their judgement in deciding whether the use of force is justified to make an arrest or to prevent the commission of an offence.

Of course, once again, exclusive legal positivists such as Gardner could argue that this phenomenon, too, is simply a result of the law's conferral of decision-making authority on some people and not others. But that doesn't quite capture the nature of the situation either. For, once again, courts seem to be quite unashamed at the deference they grant to public officials and their determinations of what the justified course of action is in a particular case. There is little sense that courts are enforcing morally wrong rules. Instead, most court judgments seem to express the sense that it is appropriate for public actors to make these decisions for the community as a whole (often infused with language of deference to the will of the people), and it is not up to the courts to second-guess their decisions.

iii State Action Doctrine

In the North American common law world, we have been forced by our constitutional jurisprudence to recognize the difference in legal standing of public actors and private ones. If nothing else, it is clear that the protections of the Canadian Charter of Rights and Freedoms and the American Bill of Rights protect us from violations of those rights through 'state action' rather than 'private action'. The difference, however hazy in its application,[32] plays a crucial role in regulating police conduct on this side of the Atlantic. Wrongful arrests, for example, are subject to constitutional scrutiny when executed by someone who can be taken to be acting in the name of the state but not when executed by a private party acting in her own name.[33] Of course, the state action doctrine is not strictly speaking a criminal law doctrine. Nevertheless, its centrality to constitutional jurisprudence – and to criminal procedure jurisprudence in particular – makes clear that the public–private distinction is at the heart of the American and Canadian legal orders.

iv Bureaucratic Hierarchy in Justifications Doctrine

An aspect of justifications doctrine that has not been fully appreciated is the two ways in which the law prioritizes the claims of public officials over those of private citizens. First, we find that criminal codes throughout the English-speaking world increasingly are conferring special justifications on public officials that are simply unavailable to private citizens. Further, even the old familiar justification defences that are available to police officers and private citizens alike (such as arrest without a warrant and the use of force to prevent the commission of an offence) are in fact structured according to a sort of bureaucratic hierarchy. In practice, private citizens are almost entirely precluded from using coercive force whenever it is open to them to seek the protection of a police officer. According to this logic, the ground on which private citizens may claim justification defences is not simply their right as citizens or as legal persons. Rather, they do so only as public officials of last resort. That is, just as beat police officers are usually required to defer to the judgement of their superiors within the bureaucratic hierarchy wherever possible, so too ordinary citizens defer to police officers when they claim to be acting with a criminal law justification. Their only ground of justification, it seems, is that they are acting as state officials of last resort *pro tem.*

B The Diceyan Ideal in the Common Law

In an article written in reply to my earlier work on this topic, Gardner has suggested that the structure of criminal law justification defences is best understood according to the Diceyan conception of equality before the law.[34] In making his

[32] See CL Black, 'State Action, Equal Protection, and California's Proposition 14' (1967) 81 *Harvard Law Review* 69, 95 (describing state action doctrine as a 'conceptual disaster area'). See also, H Friendly, 'The Public-Private Penumbra – Fourteen Years Later' (1982) 130 *University of Pennsylvania Law Review* 1289, 1290 (stating that Black's characterization of the state of state action doctrine is 'even more apt today'); E Chemerinsky, 'Rethinking State Action' (1985) 80 *Northwestern University Law Review* 503, 503–04 (stating that '[t]here still are no clear principles for determining whether state action exists').

[33] *R v Lerke* [1986] 67 AR 390 (Alberta CA).

[34] Gardner, 'Justification under Authority' (n 8).

argument, he points to three specific doctrinal areas as evidence of the Diceyan commitments at work in the criminal law doctrines of the English-speaking world. First, he suggests that consent is a broad power that sometimes operates as a justification and sometimes as a negative element of criminal offences. Secondly, he argues that the law of self-defence is clearly concerned with the private right of individuals to act in their own defence, rather than granting them the limited right to act in the state's name. Thirdly, he points to the fact that most of the justifications available to police officers (such as lawful arrest) are also available to private citizens – suggesting that the difference between police officers and private citizens is simply their source of pay.

i Consent

Gardner is typical of most criminal law theorists today in his insistence that consent operates sometimes as a negative element of some offences and sometimes as a distinct justification defence. And, like most criminal law theorists today, his reason for saying this is that he believes that this is how consent operates in ordinary moral life outside the criminal law context. He argues that in cases where the moral reasons against engaging in a certain course of action are negated by the presence of consent (as in consensual sexual relations),[35] consent operates as a negative element of the offence; but where consent only provides new countervailing reasons in favour of permitting a course of conduct but does not negate the reasons against (as in consent to bodily assault), it operates as a justification defence.

Gardner's defence of his position here is little more than a citation to the notoriously unclear case of *R v Brown*[36] for the proposition that consent is sometimes held to have the role of justification. But that is neither a clear statement of the law in the English-speaking world on this point, nor does it engage the deeper point about how one might understand consent to assault to operate. For our task is to provide a rational reconstruction of the law of consent in criminal law as a whole. And surely one plausible way to understand the law's many limits on the power to consent to bodily injury is that the law must be able to conceive of a person's consent as pursuing some genuine purpose of his own by doing so – say, playing a contact sport, engaging in physically intense sexual relations, etc – rather than simply granting a licence to someone else to abuse his body. And if that is the case, then we come back to the conclusion that legally valid consent – even to assault – is simply an exercise of each person's sovereignty over his own body and property. Conduct that is undertaken with consent is not an interference with another's sovereignty (because it is simply carrying out the wishes of the person who is sovereign over his own body) and therefore it is not in need of justification.

[35] MM Dempsey and J Herring, 'Why Sexual Penetration Requires Justification' (2007) 27 *Oxford Journal of Legal Studies* 467.

[36] *R v Brown* [1993] 1 AC 212 (HL).

ii Self-defence

Gardner's critique of my account of self-defence is multifaceted, but the point that is of interest to us here is his insistence that the law of self-defence simply does not fit my description of it. In short, he argues that self-defence is a permit the law grants to citizens qua private individuals (and not qua public official *pro tem*) to use necessary and proportionate force to defend themselves from attack. Now, it must be admitted that Gardner's is clearly the orthodox position here among criminal law theorists working today. Most people assume that everyone is entitled to act in self-defence against a wrongful attack simply because it is clearly morally justified to do so. But it is not nearly so clear that this is the doctrinal position. Modern courts do not often discuss whether a criminal justification of self-defence is a private claim or a public one, but earlier sources such as Coke and Blackstone suggest that even self-defence is best understood as a public claim.[37]

My view on self-defence is unorthodox even to the point of appearing paradoxical. Surely, one might think, our right to use force to protect our own lives from deadly attack is not dependent on the delegation of the power to do so from the state; if it were dependent on this delegation of power from the state, individuals might be prohibited absolutely from using force in self-defence.[38] Of course, it would be a monstrous state of affairs if individuals were required by law to submit to a wrongful deadly attack, but my account does not allow this possibility either. Although I argue that the criminal law justification of self-defence has its normative ground in the delegation of a state power, it would be wrong for the state to foreclose the use of force in self-defence to private citizens. The *reason* why it would be wrong on my account, however, is crucial. Prohibiting the use of force by private citizens in self-defence is tantamount to condemning certain innocent individuals to death at the hands of their attackers. And this is an exercise of public power that, like the decision to execute innocent persons, could not possibly be legitimate.

iii Arrest

The third area of criminal law doctrine that Gardner focuses on is the law of arrest by police officers and by private citizens. The central point for present purposes is Gardner's treatment of what is colloquially referred to as a 'citizen's arrest' and its different standards from arrest by a police officer. Gardner correctly points out

[37] According to Blackstone, otherwise prohibited conduct such as killing is legally justified only insofar as it is undertaken to pursue one of the state's own purposes: the court-ordered killing of someone sentenced to death, killing that is necessary to apprehend someone resisting arrest and killing to prevent a serious crime such as murder or rape: W Blackstone, 'Commentaries on the Laws of England' (1765–1769) 178–82. Edward Coke, too, makes clear that private conduct such as self-defence is justified only insofar as it further the state purpose of law enforcement. See Edward Coke, 'The Third Part of the Institutes of the Laws of England' (1644) 55.

[38] Thanks to Hamish Stewart for raising this objection.

that the law seems to impose a standard of correctness on non-police officers who make arrests: if they believe on reasonable grounds that the person they are arresting has committed an indictable offence but this reasonable belief proves wrong, they may be liable in tort for kidnapping or battery and although they will likely escape criminal liability, this is on grounds of excuse, and not justification.[39] Gardner's doctrinal point here is an important one – and a clear indication that the structure of the criminal law does not fit my normative reconstruction of it in all places. If the law followed my own Kantian account of the law of arrest as the exercise of a public power, we should expect that citizens and police officers alike should be entitled to act on the basis of reasonable beliefs. One possible explanation for this feature of our law is our reluctance to private citizens taking the law into their own hands (and a correctness standard on matters of citizen's arrest would go a long way to deterring would-be vigilantes). But another equally plausible explanation is the possibility that there are important lingering influences of the Diceyan account of equality before the law at work here.

IV CONCLUSION

In this chapter, I have argued that there is an ideal at work in much of criminal law doctrine – indeed, in much legal doctrine generally – that is usually ignored. But this, I believe, is much to the detriment of criminal law theory, and legal theory generally. For when we ignore some of the most basic, albeit implicit, commitments in our way of thinking about the legal system, we often foreclose even thinking about alternatives. And in this case, I believe that this has done criminal law theory a great disservice. Over the past hundred or so years, the English-speaking world has come to recognize that public law plays a crucial – and quite distinct – part in the legal order. It simply makes no sense to treat the actions of public officials as though they were the actions of private parties. It is generally understood that public actors carrying out public functions are subject to public law requirements of fairness, reasonableness and so on in ways that private actors simply are not. Further, in constitutional orders such as Canada and the United States, the distinction between public and private action is crucial to an understanding of the scope of constitutional rights and the protection they afford to citizens. Criminal law theory has gone on for many years without taking these developments elsewhere in the law into consideration.

[39] Gardner, 'Justification under Authority' (n 8) 92.

2

Individual Emergencies and the Rule of Criminal Law

FRANÇOIS TANGUAY-RENAUD*

I INDIVIDUAL EMERGENCIES AND CRIMINAL LAW: AN INTRODUCTION

Human behaviour and the incidence of harm tend to be closely related, and societies often feel the need to regulate this nexus stringently. In the words of Stephen Morse:

> Human beings are injurious and all too often lethal to themselves and others. Surely more people have been killed and injured by the acts of others and themselves than by natural disasters. Only toxic microbes are as dangerous as people. All civil societies, including the least developed, therefore create numerous public and private socializing institutions and practices to cabin the injurious propensities of their members.[1]

Criminal law is one of these institutions of social control. It is often hailed as 'the primary instrumentality for preventing people from intentionally or recklessly harming one another'.[2] In many societies, the institution's ambitions are even wider, and criminal law seeks to prevent behaviour that negligently, sometimes even accidentally or 'strictly', causes harm. However, Morse reminds us, restraining practices and techniques such as criminal law 'are never foolproof: All fail sometimes, often disastrously'.

When criminal law fails to prevent armed attacks, rape attempts, kidnappings, arsons or violent burglaries, the resulting situation is often one of emergency for those facing the predicament. In such situations, often unforeseen, individuals typically face great risks of harm and need to react urgently if harm is to be averted or minimized. More often than not, the law is unable to provide any (further) assistance. The situation may be too extraordinary for the law to assess its

* I wish to thank Antony Duff, John Gardner, Stuart P Green, Michael Moore, James Stribopoulos, Victor Tadros and Malcolm Thorburn for comments and discussions.

[1] SJ Morse, 'Neither Desert nor Disease' (1999) 5 *Legal Theory* 265, 267.

[2] J Feinberg, *The Moral Limits of the Criminal Law Volume 1: Harm to Others* (Oxford, Oxford University Press, 1987) 31.

specificities accurately and provide helpful guidance *ex ante facto*. If it is in a position to provide such guidance, it may then be unable to convey it in time and reliably enough to those who need it. In fact, in many sudden emergency situations, legal officials may be in no position to provide any meaningful support whatsoever, direct or indirect, to those in the predicament. Natural emergencies can also constrain the law in similar ways. Consider the case of the hiker who, caught in a storm, must break into a cabin if he is to save his life. Such examples pave the way to the general puzzle I want to address in this chapter. If the rule of (criminal) law is to be contrasted with the rule of people by themselves,[3] that is to say, with anarchy, to what extent is it an achievable and desirable ideal given the inescapable reality of emergencies?

To be more precise, criminal law, because it seeks to regulate human behaviour by affecting the circumstances of human actions, has to grapple with reasons for action that may compete with it, such as emergencies. Some theorists have sought to explain law's position – and a fortiori criminal law's position – in relation to competing reasons by remarking that law claims for itself absolute and legitimate authority to regulate all forms of human behaviour or, in other words, purports to exclude from the range of available reasons for action all reasons that conflict with it. In Joseph Raz's useful terminology, law claims to be a system of 'protected reasons': reasons to act or refrain from acting in certain ways, which concurrently serve as second-order reasons – exclusionary reasons – not to act for conflicting reasons.[4] Now, to genuinely claim or purport entails that one strives to realise what one claims or purports. The law, by virtue of its claim to have authority to regulate all forms of human conduct, ought to endeavour to ensure that those to whom its guidance is directed can find out what it is and act accordingly. There exists a relative consensus on how it can, generally speaking, best strive to achieve this: laws should be clear, consistent, open, prospective, general and stable; legislative and executive action should be governed by laws with those characteristics; and there should be accessible courts which have review powers over the implementation of the aforementioned principles. But that the law needs to be capable of guiding the behaviour of its subjects does not necessarily mean that it can, or should, aim to do so absolutely – that is to say, in all instances – or at least that it can and should always seek to guide human behaviour according to all the desiderata outlined above. At the risk of stating the obvious, criminal law should seek to provide guidance that is legitimate, in the sense of being morally justified. In this chapter, I want to explore to what extent it can do so in situations of individual (as opposed to more generalized and disordering) emergencies, which people confront in their 'non-official' (some might say 'private') capacities.

[3] This impersonal formulation of the ideal of the rule of law – understood in opposition to the 'rule of man' (which I formulate gender-neutrally as the 'rule of people') – can be traced back to Aristotle, *Politics* 1287a.

[4] J Raz, *Practical Reason and Norms* 2nd edn (Oxford, Oxford University Press, 1990) 141–46, 150–51; J Raz, *The Authority of Law* (Oxford, Oxford University Press, 1979) 17–19.

First, I survey the main conflicting theoretical positions on how criminal law ought to contemplate and provide for its own potential failure in the face of individual emergencies. After exploring the normal justification of the law's authority and defending the endurance of morality in the face of emergencies, I then argue that when the de facto authority of the state is generally not in question, the criminal law's answers to possible emergency-related failures must not take the form of full *ex ante* disclaimers of competence. Rather, the criminal law may seek to engage its subjects while remaining acutely aware of the limits imposed on its authority and ability to provide guidance due to the exigencies of the situation. It may do so by granting them practical latitude when they would be morally justified in infringing general criminal law guidance. I go on to contrast such grants of latitude with other forms of leniency and concessions that criminal law may make to emergency responders, but which are not linked (or linked in the same way) to the normal justification of its authority. Throughout, I seek to make the case that whenever the rule of people is contrasted with the rule of law in the context of emergencies, it is the rule of rational people responsible for their choices and actions that is first and foremost at issue. This realisation, I contend, has some important bearing on how the criminal law should treat individuals in emergency predicaments. As a means of contextualizing my analysis, I conclude by contrasting it briefly with challenges that more generalized emergencies may pose for the law.

II HOW CRIMINAL LAW OUGHT TO CONTEND WITH INDIVIDUAL EMERGENCIES

A The Theoretical Camps

Scholars have recently produced an appreciable body of criminal law theory literature discussing the implications of individual emergencies for the fabric of Anglo-American criminal law. Whereas these writings never systematically define nor explain what emergencies are, most theorists agree that urgency-induced necessity – understood in a non-goal dependent, categorical sense – is a central dimension of the concept. Human beings *qua* rational creatures unavoidably encounter a wide range of rational pressures in the course of their life. One way of differentiating such pressures is to systematize them on a linear axis with urgency as the variable, keeping all else (such as the seriousness of the consequences that might result if the emergency is not appropriately addressed) constant. While some pressing situations necessitate an immediate reaction, time is less of the essence in others. The difference is often one of degree, but can also be cast in stark terms for the sake of clarity of exposition. Contrast the following two examples: (1) A pedestrian is violently attacked by a mugger who attempts to kill her. She finds herself constrained to counter-attack in self-defence, and kills her assailant in the process. (2) A caring father concerned with alleviating the constant pain experienced by his twelve-year-old daughter who, in addition to being quadriplegic, suffers from a severe and degenerating form of cerebral palsy and has the mental capacity and autonomy of a four-month old baby, kills her out of mercy.[5] Both the pedestrian and the father face predicaments which, in ordinary language, could be described as 'pressing'. However, one significant difference between them is that the pedestrian's opportunities to avoid serious harm are highly time-constrained. She has virtually no time to deliberate her reaction, she may have no reasonable chance to call for help (let alone involve the police or other official channels), she may have no reasonable prospect of fleeing, and so on. On the other hand, the father has more latitude when considering action. His daughter suffers, but her condition is unlikely to worsen significantly in the span of a moment. In both daily conversation and theoretical discourse, the distinction is often underlined by referring to situations of the first kind, and not of the second, as 'emergencies'.

Many theorists recognise that emergency situations may have important ramifications for norms in general – they often focus, as will I, on prescriptive rules – and, more particularly, for the law. Others dispute this claim, and identify with the 'acoustic separation' school of criminal law theory. According to this school of thought, the law ought, in an emergency, to give *ex ante* guidance on when ordinary citizens may, for example, justifiably kill or harm others, or steal or destroy somebody else's property.[6] Like in any other (non-emergency) case, it is then for judge or jury to decide whether that legal guidance was followed. One of the major weaknesses of this school of thought is that it tends to ignore the pressures exercised on the criminal law's guidance ability in emergency situations. Because he is not confronted with an emergency, the father in the previous example could, at minimal cost to his daughter, seek the guidance and assistance of the law and request a court order.[7] Expecting the same kind of behaviour from the person unjustifiably attacked on the street would no doubt be both unreasonable and impractical. She has virtually no time to deliberate her reaction, let alone an opportunity to seek official assistance, if she wants to avoid or minimise the harmful consequences of the assault.

One might retort that although the criminal law can only be of little assistance at the time of the emergency, its *ex ante* directives may prepare, or 'socialise', indi-

[5] Those were roughly the facts of the high profile Canadian case *R v Latimer* [2001] 1 SCR 3 (SCC). Note that in this case, the court explicitly refuses to characterize the predicament as one of 'necessity' or 'emergency'.

[6] Indeed, according to the main adherents of this theoretical current, justificatory criminal defences are 'rules of conduct' for the law's subjects. On the other hand, excuses are 'rules of adjudication' directed at judges and juries, eg, M Dan-Cohen, 'Decision Rules and Conduct Rules: On Acoustic Separation in Criminal Law' (1984) 97 *Harvard Law Review* 625, 637–39; PH Robinson, 'Rules of Conduct and Principles of Adjudication' (1990) 57 *University of Chicago Law Review* 729, 740–42.

[7] In many jurisdictions, if he judges that the suffering of his daughter is such that action should not be unduly delayed, he could further request that the court proceedings be fast-tracked. Compare: *Re A (Conjoined Twins)* [2000] 4 All ER 961 (CA).

viduals by making it persistently clear how they must behave when such situations arise. The problem with this line of argument is that it fails to acknowledge that criminal law guidance is typically 'an approximation, by rule, of a principled understanding of wrongful conduct. It states the normal case of wrongdoing, but fails to account accurately for wrongdoing in the extraordinary cases that arise under conflict and under the pressure of circumstances'.[8] For example, whereas taking somebody else's property without her consent may be, all things considered, wrong in the normal course of events, this may not be the case in emergency circumstances where other typically available opportunities for harm avoidance are absent. If legal rules are understood as entrenched generalizations of what behaviour is justified, they will inevitably be under-inclusive and over-inclusive from time to time (in relation to their underlying justifications).[9] Thus, general criminal law guidance may be quite an ineffective and inappropriate way of regulating individual emergencies.

Realizations of this kind have led a number of theorists to argue that criminal law ought to deal differently with (at least some) emergencies. It ought to make extra space for the individual to assess how to act. This is the assumption on which I intend to proceed. However, even among the theorists who share my assumption, views diverge as to how and to what extent the criminal law ought to create such extra space. At one end of the spectrum, some argue, rather implausibly, that the criminal law should recognize that there are circumstances of individual emergency that the law is entirely incompetent to regulate. Accordingly, it should holistically suspend its application to them. The thought, it seems, is that certain individual emergencies challenge the very possibility of legal guidance, so that prosecutions for failure to abide by it while the emergency exists should not even be considered. As one author puts it: 'It makes no sense to try to compel people to behave like civilised individuals when the minimum requirements of civilization are lacking'.[10] Admittedly, in the context of discussions of *individual* emergencies, such claims tend to be limited to a narrowly defined set of extreme cases, where people are reduced to the bare needs of survival and are cut off from access to the 'civilized world' – for example, castaways in lifeboats or spelunkers trapped in caves, without food and at the point of starvation. Yet, even with respect to such extreme cases, the argument that the criminal law ought to disclaim *all* jurisdiction seems like an overkill. Even if one agrees that some legal constraints make little sense when one is starving and desperate, many other constraints clearly remain appropriate. To take an obvious example, castaways and trapped spelunkers on the brink of starvation should not exploit the opportunity to rape or inflict avoidable harm on each other.

[8] GP Fletcher, 'The Nature of Justification' in S Shute, J Gardner and J Horder (eds), *Action and Value in the Criminal Law* (Oxford, Clarendon Press, 1993) 177.

[9] For a good recent discussion of this age-old point, see F Schauer, *Playing by the Rules: A Philosophical Examination of Rule-Based Decision-Making in Law and in Life* (Oxford, Clarendon Press, 1991) chs 2–3.

[10] A von Hirsch, 'Review Essay: Lifeboat Law' (1985) 4 *Criminal Justice Ethics* 88, 91.

Certainly, disclaimers of competence in favour of individuals are not unheard of in the criminal law context. Consider the case of outlawry in those societies that used to recognize such an absence of status. In English medieval times, to take a concrete example, an outlaw was one who, because of his bad acts, had been banished from society and placed outside the protection of the law. By declaring someone an outlaw, the state was acknowledging its inability to punish someone who had violated its laws, and was thereby disclaiming its competence to punish him in favour of any of his victims, the victims' families, a posse or, for that matter, anyone who might want to join in. An outlaw was fair game, which explains the maxim: 'Let them be answerable to all, and none to them'. That said, outlawry does not exist anymore in England,[11] just as resort to wholesale disclaimers of competence has, for reasons akin to those mentioned above, generally been abandoned by modern criminal justice systems.

Still, not all disclaimers of competence need to be indiscriminate as between actions. George Fletcher, for example, argues for a much more circumspect jurisdictional account of the proper treatment of individual emergencies by the criminal law. His focus is exclusively on actions that individual emergencies make imminently necessary:

> [In necessity cases], the imminence requirement expresses the limits of governmental competence: when the danger to a protected interest is imminent and unavoidable, the legislature can no longer make reliable judgments about which of the conflicting interests should prevail. Similarly, when an attack against individuals is imminent, the police are no longer in a position to intervene and exercise the state's function of securing public safety. The individual right of self-defence kicks in precisely because immediate action is necessary. Individuals do not cede a total monopoly of force to the state.[12]

According to Fletcher, because the government is generally incompetent to decide reliably in advance who shall bear the costs in a situation where the time frame is extremely short, the harm potential high and particulars often unpredictable, it must acknowledge its limitations and allow individuals to make that decision for themselves. If, nonetheless, it decides to provide guidance, its capacity to police it is also likely to be significantly curtailed, at least *ex ante facto*. Therefore, it is the individual in the predicament, not the government or the criminal law, who is positionally (more) competent and ought to have the authority to make decisions within the parameters prescribed by the situation of imminent risk. To that extent, the rule of law should give way to the rule of people by themselves. As per the age-old saying, necessity – but only necessity (and, Fletcher would add, 'imminent' necessity) – knows no law.

One might here agree with Fletcher that the criminal law is less competent in situations of imminent necessity, but argue that its incompetence does not come – or does not solely come – from its inability to make the appropriate decision or

[11] As reiterated in the case of *Cross v Kirby The Times* (5 April 2000).

[12] GP Fletcher, 'Domination in the Theory of Justification and Excuse' (1996) 57 *University of Pittsburg Law Review* 553, 569–70.

to police it effectively. Instead, one might contend, the law's incompetence in situations of emergency stems from its inability to convey effectively its decision to the individual in the predicament. Although the nuance is interesting, both positions are really two sides of the same coin: whether the law is incompetent to decide and police, or incompetent to make its guidance heard, it is incompetent. This affirmation is consistent with Fletcher's contentions that the core of the individual emergency *problématique* rests with 'the proper allocation of authority between the state and the citizen'.[13] For the sake of clarity, I will refer to this view as the 'political view'.

I will refer to it as a political view since, although Fletcher's account is clearly more morally circumspect than its wholesale disclaimer cousin, it is not morally driven. He locates it explicitly in 'the domain of political rather than moral theory', and refrains from integrating it upfront with a consideration of the overall morality of individual emergency responses.[14] According to another view, to which I will refer as the 'moral view', the criminal law need not surrender its rule in the face of individual emergencies. In many such cases, it remains competent to engage the individual, but might need to do it differently from the way it usually does. This is the position espoused by theorists like Jeremy Horder, who writes that: 'It is not reasonable to expect citizens to do more, in such extreme and exceptional situations, than follow the guidance of morality, in the expectation that they will, ex post facto, be vindicated at law'.[15] As I stressed earlier, the law generally purports to exclude from its subjects' practical horizons all reasons for action which conflict with it, and to replace them with its own guidance. However, as I also suggested, in cases of individual emergencies, the criminal law is unlikely to be able to replace other considerations consistently and reliably. Theorists like Horder argue that one alternative open to the law in such situations is to allow its subjects to rely directly on morality. Whereas non-legal social conventions may, like the law, become unreliable sources of guidance in times of emergency,[16] it is almost a truism that one always ought to act morally, even in the face of an emergency. Although an anarchist attitude vis-à-vis the law and social conventions is – irrespective of its rightness or wrongness – intelligible, amoralism is not. Morality is binding on us ultimately, irrespective of who we are, what we feel about it and the predicaments in which we find ourselves. Of course, different moral considerations from those that are

[13] ibid 570.

[14] ibid. Although Fletcher engages the relationship between emergency responses and criminal law in a much more morally-nuanced manner in other parts of his work, his approach always rests on strong political theory groundings. As he argues elsewhere, 'the criminal law addresses the state's authority to intervene in people's lives', so that 'authority must first be justified as a matter of political theory before one turns to the criteria, including perceptions of morality, that might enter into the use of the state's power'. GP Fletcher, *The Grammar of Criminal Law: American, Comparative, and International: Volume One: Foundations* (Oxford, Oxford University Press, 2007) 154.

[15] J Horder, 'Killing the Passive Abuser: A Theoretical Defence' in S Shute and AP Simester (eds), *Criminal Law Theory: Doctrines of the General Part* (Oxford, Oxford University Press, 2002) 286.

[16] This is not to say that in situations where the law is hopelessly unreliable, social conventions may never be of assistance. However, because emergencies are situations that typically throw uncertainty into our social norms, their reliability is, mutatis mutandis, as open to question as the law's competence.

otherwise applicable may sometimes prevail in emergency situations, but morality itself does not cease to apply or go awry, despite arguments to the contrary by a number of theorists. I shall bracket this point for the moment, and return to it in more detail in the next section.

What I seek to emphasize at this stage is that, by permitting *direct* reliance on morality within defined parameters, the law may aspire to engage more optimally with those facing emergencies. In the pressure of the moment, it does not leave them to behave according to their whims, but invites them to exercise moral judgement. In the process, it avoids distorting the complex rational conflicts that they might be forced to confront, while retaining the authority to review their conduct ex post facto and hold them accountable for unreasonable mistakes and excesses. Of course, as Horder remarks, the law may, and sometimes will, choose to refrain from inviting individual moral assessments in emergencies with larger moral and political implications than can possibly be accounted for by a person acting alone.[17] However, as I will discuss further below (II.C.ii: Some Clarifications and Cautionary Remarks) such a decision will always be at risk of being tagged as harsh, illegitimate or immoral, and even of being generally disobeyed by morally-abiding individuals, when it is indeed too inflexible.

From a rule of law perspective, an apparent advantage of the moral view is that it seems to stand up for the law's authority in situations in which the political view would mandate surrender of its authority to the individual. Who is right? I believe that the moral view provides a sounder and more complete explanation. Yet, both views have some truth to them and, in my view, the divide between them is rather artificial. In the next section, I will argue that the two approaches should be understood as converging or, better, as emanating from a single concern, namely, the legitimacy – and here, pace Fletcher, I mean the moral legitimacy – of the law's authority.

B Legal Authority and Individuals' Moral Universe

i Preliminary Remarks – One: The Normal Justification of Law's Authority

To be able to identify which model accurately reflects how criminal law ought to contend with individual emergencies, one point is worth reaffirming at this preliminary stage. As I already suggested, legal systems seek to position themselves, or mediate, between the reasons that apply to their subjects and the subjects themselves, by providing guidance via protected reasons for action – that is, reasons for action which concurrently exclude conflicting reasons – in the form of duties, rules and so forth. In Raz's terminology, every legal system claims for itself, at least in principle, all-encompassing authority to mediate between people and reasons for action that it does not itself provide. Such a claim, adds Raz, is by its

[17] J Horder, 'On the Irrelevance of Motive in Criminal Law' in J Horder (ed), *Oxford Essays in Jurisprudence Fourth Series* (Oxford, OUP, 2000) 177–84, 187–88.

very nature a claim to possess *legitimate* authority.[18] The question that must then be asked is when the law's claim is, all things considered, legitimate. In other words, when are the law's subjects justified in following its guidance, and when is the law justified in issuing directives to guide their behaviour?

A first consequence of this characterization of authority is that, to be legitimate, the law must be in a position to make a practical difference to the behaviour of its subjects by, for instance, extricating them from coordination problems and 'Prisoner's Dilemma' type situations. For this to be so, the law must have a significant degree of de facto authority over people, in the sense of actual power over them and obedience by them. Otherwise, it does not have what it takes to act as a practical authority, let alone a legitimate one. However, Raz's main point is deeper. The law's authority is normally legitimate (*qua* justified) when its subjects are more likely to comply with the reasons that ought to govern their behaviour by following the law's directives than by trying to follow those reasons directly. This might be the case when the law has greater expertise or superior knowledge, a distinctive capacity to solve coordination problems or strengthen our resolve to act as we ought to, or simply because it has better moral judgement. This is Raz's 'normal justification thesis', on which I intend to rely.[19]

While controversial, Raz's account of the normal justification of authority has been widely influential, and rightfully so. It is precise, powerful and a great advance over previous efforts. Theorists do not hesitate to celebrate it as part of the best recent work on authority.[20] More specifically for my purposes, the normal justification thesis sheds light on the fact that, although law is sometimes praised for its symbolic or expressive value, its role is first and foremost instrumental. Law *qua* practical authority needs to serve its subjects: it needs to guide them in ways that are likely to make things better for them. If it is not to become dead letter, it must seek to help them decide better which actions are right for them than if they acted solely according to their own lights. As Raz argues, the justification of law's authoritative guidance in any given case normally depends on how well it performs in this regard. Thus, the normal justification thesis provides us with a framework for understanding the *instrumental limits* of law. When the law is ill-placed to make things better for its subjects, it may be unjustified in seeking to do so, at least in its usual authoritative fashion. Individual emergencies are a case in point. As I suggested earlier, the law may be particularly ill-placed to seek to assist its subjects in its usual way in emergency circumstances, due to its inability (and the inability of those acting on its behalf) to move fast and effectively enough. The normal justification thesis provides us with a useful platform from which to understand how law, and a fortiori criminal law, ought to provide for this type of predicament.

[18] J Raz, 'Authority, Law, and Morality' in *Ethics in the Public Domain* rev edn (Oxford, Oxford University Press, 1994) 215ff.

[19] For an early formulation and defence of the thesis, see J Raz, *The Morality of Freedom* (Oxford, Oxford University Press, 1986) 53.

[20] eg J Waldron, 'Authority for Officials' in LH Meyer, SL Paulson and TW Pogge (eds), *Rights, Culture, and the Law: Themes from the Legal and Political Philosophy of Joseph Raz* (Oxford, Oxford University Press, 2003) 45.

ii Preliminary Remarks – Two: Individual Emergencies and the Status of Morality

As another preliminary matter, I also want to address the view (which I left unarticulated and undefended in the last section) that morality as a guide to action does not cease to be reliable and to apply in the face of emergencies. Although this claim might seem obvious to some, it is not to others, and underlies an important discomfort surrounding the concept of morality. A parenthesis seems important at this point to clarify the implications of my affirmation for the discussion that follows.

a The Challenge

'*Erst kommt das Fressen, dann kommt die Moral*' ('Grub first, then morality') wrote playwright Bertolt Brecht at the end of the second act of *The Threepenny Opera*. In other words, one might argue – when the avoidance of serious harm is at stake, perhaps paradigmatically in cases of individual or more generalized emergencies threatening one's preservation – moral considerations take a back seat or are altogether suspended. This view has had many philosophical incarnations over the centuries. For example, in a famous passage in chapter 15 of *Leviathan*, Thomas Hobbes argues that when adherence to the 'laws of nature' would be disastrous, then 'all bets are off':

> The laws of nature oblige *in foro interno*; that is to say, they bind to a desire they should take place: but *in foro externo*; that is, to the putting them in act not always. For he that should be modest, and tractable, and perform all he promises, in such time, and place, where no man else should do so, should but make himself a prey to others, and procure his own certain ruin, contrary to the ground of all laws of nature, which tend to nature's preservation.[21]

It is noteworthy that some people dispute interpretations of Hobbes's work according to which he believed that moral considerations could be suspended altogether. They argue instead that Hobbes thought that morality could sometimes become all permissive *in foro externo* for the sake of self-preservation, without ever lapsing. They cite as evidence his first and fundamental law of nature 'that every man, ought to endeavour peace, as far as he has hope of obtaining it; and when he cannot obtain it, that he may seek, and use, all helps, and advantages of war'.[22] No doubt, the line between the view that morality can become all permissive in the face of severe emergencies and the view that moral considerations may be altogether suspended is quite thin. Yet, some contemporary theorists seek to avoid any such source of confusion and endorse the latter claim in no equivocal terms. James Griffin, for example, writes that 'Not even morality, to my mind, applies universally to moral agents regardless of conditions: for example, it does

[21] As Hobbes goes on to specify, 'the science [of the laws of nature], is the true and only moral philosophy'. T Hobbes, *Leviathan* (Oxford, Oxford University Press, 1996) 105.
[22] ibid 87.

not apply if conditions get desperate enough – *sauve-qui-peut* situations'.[23] Views like these point to a deep question about the status of morality when its constraints are severely disadvantageous. Are they sound?

My argumentative strategy will be twofold and more or less indirect. First, I will argue that whereas some conceptions of morality make the view that morality may lapse or go awry intelligible, others do not. I will then seek to spell out my reasons for defending the latter in the context of this chapter, thus clarifying my claim that morality applies consistently, both inside and outside emergency predicaments.

b Jurisdictional and Non-jurisdictional Conceptions of Morality

Although not widely discussed, the definition of morality has great significance for moral theory in general, and for my argument in particular. Insofar as definitional and other forms of conceptual accounts are partly concerned with boundaries, seeking to clarify the notion of morality is inevitably relevant to the debate over the scope of its applicability. Is morality something that can cease to apply to us, lapse, or go awry?

Some theorists conceive of morality's reach as limited. For example, Bernard Williams refers to it as a 'peculiar institution', a 'special system, that demands a sharp boundary for itself'.[24] Others speak of the intelligibility of 'an extra-moral world'.[25] Such representations allow theorists to speak of morality in terms of its jurisdiction, bounds and branches – GEM Anscombe, for example, speaks of '*law* conception[s]' of morality.[26] For these theorists, morality may conceivably fall short. It may compete and lose out in jurisdictional conflicts with normative systems that are at variance with it, be they legal, religious or conventional. It may intelligibly 'fail to apply' or 'run out' in the face of non-moral (or extra-moral) considerations. Morality, Williams tells us, is not the be-all and end-all of normativity or rationality. It may make mistakes and be criticized, defied, even ridiculed for it. It may omit important nuances, it may be overly unclear, it may be too demanding and occupy fields from which it should keep away. In fact, Williams goes on to assert, we may be altogether 'better off without it'.[27]

Griffin's position, perhaps less radical, can be understood in a similar light. For him, morality is ill-suited to guide us in emergency situations where our survival is imminently at stake. 'It is', he writes, 'perfectly reasonable to go on saying that moral principles apply universally, that is, to us all simply in virtue of our being

[23] J Griffin, 'First Steps in an Account of Human Rights' (2001) 9 *European Journal of Philosophy* 306, 325 (fn 19). See also D Gauthier, *Morals by Agreement* (Oxford, Oxford University Press, 1986) for an interpretation of Hobbes's work that is overtly sympathetic to the view that morality can cease to be applicable.

[24] B Williams, *Ethics and the Limits of Philosophy* (London, Routledge, 2006) 7, 174.

[25] eg T Nardin, 'Emergency Logic: Prudence, Morality and The Rule of Law' in VV Ramraj (ed), *Emergencies and the Limits of Legality* (Cambridge, Cambridge University Press, 2008) 97.

[26] GEM Anscombe, 'Modern Moral Philosophy' (1958) 33 *Philosophy* 1, 5.

[27] Williams, *Ethics* (n 24) 174, 180, 196.

moral agents (*that is, given that morality applies at all*)' (emphasis added).[28] Whereas we may be unable to do away with morality within its proper sphere of jurisdiction, we ought to recognize that this sphere is not absolute and that morality is sometimes outright inapplicable, most notably in *sauve-qui-peut* situations. Echoes of Brecht and Hobbes's positions permeate these remarks. Whereas, according to Hobbes, morality – that is, the aggregate normative system of all laws of nature – always obliges *in foro interno*, it may not be a complete and unfaltering guide to action. Like Brecht seems to imply in his play, morality's jurisdiction as a guide to action is fundamentally limited by considerations of self-preservation. Thus, in reaction to Tom Sorell's observation that 'much of everyday bourgeois morality could seem pointless if the emergency were imminent enough, enveloping enough, and final enough', potentially giving rise to 'moral black holes',[29] these theorists would likely have a common reply. In such situations, they would say, morality is simply the wrong guide, or no guide, to action. People ought to ensure their own survival (or preservation) before seeking to act morally towards others.

Some theorists espouse a drastically different picture of morality. According to them, there are no moments, spaces or situations in human history from which morality is absent or can be suspended – the way we might, for example, suspend civil liberties in a time of civil war. On this view, morality has no doctrine of jurisdiction setting out the conditions of its applicability. It simply refers to the true, or valid, reasons that people have – reasons that apply to whomever they address and whose scope is determined by their content.[30] It applies to all agents capable of understanding it and binds them come what may, irrespective of their interest in it. Morality in this sense is sometimes described as the 'art of life'. It cannot be criticized, defied or ridiculed for omitting important nuances, for being overly unclear, for failing to provide adequate notice or for being too demanding or overreaching. It adapts itself perfectly to all imperfect situations with which it deals, be they ordinary or exceptional in nature. For example, when an individual faces an emergency, the urgency of the situation typically restricts the opportunities for avoiding serious harm which are available to her. As a result, she may have undefeated reasons to act in certain ways which would not otherwise exist. To account for such predicaments, morality adapts its requirements and makes justifications available in circumstances where they would not otherwise be. Hence, one is sometimes morally justified in burning part of a neighbour's field to contain an expanding forest fire, in killing in self-defence or in engaging even more disquieting behaviour. Of course, in various circumstances, given moral reasons may be defeated – overridden or excluded – by others. Morality, as I have just said, is not inflexible. There may also

[28] Griffin, 'First Steps' (n 23) 325 (fn 19). In his earlier work, Griffin seems to acknowledge that the issue of jurisdiction is not as clear-cut as my account might make it seem. For example, he writes that 'when it comes to the terribly hard choice between morality and survival', prudential reasons may 'run, without boundary, into moral ones'. Remarks of this sort may be taken to point to the second, non-jurisdictional understanding of morality that I introduce below. See J Griffin, *Well-Being: Its Meaning, Measurement, and Moral Importance* (Oxford, Oxford University Press, 1986) 160–62.

[29] T Sorell, 'Morality and Emergency' (2002) 103 *Proceedings of the Aristotelian Society* 21, 26.

[30] eg J Raz, 'Incorporation by Law' (2004) 10 *Legal Theory* 1, 2–3.

be situations of moral dilemma where all reasons for action and corresponding courses of conduct are defeated, and only moral excuses remain available against allegations of blame. But morality as a whole is never ousted.[31] For these non-jurisdictional theorists, an argument to the effect that it can would be unintelligible.

Such theorists would likely make a very different diagnosis of Sorell's observation that 'bourgeois morality' sometimes seems pointless in emergency situations. They might concede that from the point of view of individual psychology, morality's hold on us may *appear* to lessen or lapse in the face of an emergency. Depending on the extent to which our rational capacity is impaired by events, such a perception may be excusable, or even, in some radical cases, evidence of our unfitness to be judged morally responsible for actions perpetrated under its influence. However, such a concession does not amount to an admission that morality sometimes does not apply; it is simply a recognition that our perception of reality is sometimes pathologically altered. Morality, these theorists would insist, has no jurisdictional limits. It never withers away or retreats in ways that create moral black holes. Of course, they might add, there may be situations where 'bourgeois morality' seems pointless even to the fully rational agent. However, this is only because 'bourgeois morality' is a misrepresentation of morality, and often clings on to the sclerotic illusion of moral inflexibility – for example, to the idea that stealing is always unjustifiable, even in the face of an emergency. Consider the case of the unemployed poor. When such people have adequate alternatives to stealing – they receive sufficient charity, they are supported by adequate social security systems and so forth – the conflict between survival and reasons to respect the property of others may only be partial. On the other hand, when no such alternatives are available to them and their survival is imminently at stake, the conflict may become complete and its resolution in one sense or the other inescapable. In such situations, stealing may turn out to be an undefeated course of action. Food may then come first, yet, pace Brecht, come first in a morally acceptable way.

c Why Adopt a Non-jurisdictional Account of Morality?

The distinction between the two understandings of morality, just described, parallels JL Mackie's contrast between morality in the narrow and the broad sense. If morality in the broad sense incorporates and, where necessary, assesses the relative force of all the reasons for or against doing anything, morality in the narrow sense includes considerations from a limited range – that is, considerations regarding the protection of 'the interests of persons other than the agent and which present themselves to an agent as checks on his natural inclinations or spontaneous tendencies to act'.[32] Such a conception allows us to think of morality

[31] On defeated and undefeated reasons for action, and their relationship to justification and excuses, see J Gardner, 'Justifications and Reasons' in AP Simester and ATH Smith (eds), *Harm and Culpability* (Oxford, Oxford University Press, 1996).

[32] JL Mackie, *Ethics: Inventing Right and Wrong* (London, Penguin Books, 1977) 106–07.

as a specialized body of considerations that may be systematized and segregated from others. Thus, it also allows us to conceive of certain zones that are free from morality, or of moral outlaws. Morality in the broad sense does not allow for this type of reasoning.

In this chapter, I rely on the second (or broad) understanding of morality explained above. I opt for it because, inter alia, I want to emphasize that reasons of self-preservation often do not fill the whole domain of the rationality of action, even in extreme circumstances. Reasons of self-preservation may not render other reasons for action inapplicable in the way that the first (or narrow) sense of morality might allow. Consider the following phenomenological example. When an individual is constrained to kill an innocent aggressor to preserve his life, he often experiences some measure of regret, that is, of retrospective horror at what he was capable of. This is not just the horror of having witnessed something unpleasant, or the horror of having been in danger oneself. It is the horror of the agent, the 'what have I done', which we may all experience at some point in our life, even in circumstances of unusual and enormous pressure. This type of regret can be explained by the fact that morality is not absent from, or inapplicable to, such situations. There are forceful reasons other than reasons of self-preservation weighing against the killing – reasons of justice, humanity, and so forth. The agent who acts contrary to these reasons leaves behind what we may call a moral residue, which constitutes an object of regret. He may well have been justified in not following these reasons because they were defeated, were supererogatory, or because they and the reasons for self-preservation coexisted while remaining undefeated in virtue of their incommensurability. Be that as it may, he faces a dilemma triggered by the existence of forceful and conflicting reasons, applicable in a way that sits awkwardly with jurisdictional, survival-centric accounts of morality. A similar tension would likely arise if, say, an agent failed to come to the rescue of others, who were left to a horrible fate, to ensure his own survival. In the words of Tzvetan Todorov:

> Matters of conscience are not at all rare in extreme situations, and their very existence attests to the possibility of choice, and thus of moral life. One might flee such dilemmas because they entail that one freely choose an evil, albeit a lesser one perhaps that might have existed in the absence of choice. They cannot always be avoided, however.[33]

On the basis of the passages quoted in the previous section, Hobbes, unlike Griffin, might be able to account partially for such rational conflicts and regret owing to his distinction between what may oblige *in foro interno* but not *in foro externo*. A possible interpretation of this feature of his argument is that morality remains applicable in extreme situations, but that one should not listen to its guidance when deciding how to act. However, even if we grant the relevance of this distinction, Hobbes's overall account remains deficient. Like Griffin's account, it is deficient to the extent that, although self-preservation may be an

[33] T Todorov, *Facing the Extreme: Moral Life in the Concentration Camps* (London, Phoenix, 2000) 36.

important value or good in the realm of action, it is often not the only important value or good (even in extreme circumstances).[34] Many people are prepared to sacrifice their lives, not only for others, but for the sake of other-regarding principles, and it is far from clear that such behaviour is irrational. Even in the Nazi death camps, where the breakdown of social expectations approximated something like a state of nature, there were many examples of resolute commitment to reasons and norms that defy the survival-centric outlook. For example, an Auschwitz survivor could conclude after all the horror that 'at no time was my survival at the expense of anyone else and I had no justifiable reason to feel guilty of not acting in a human manner even in the "darkest" days of persecution'.[35] The example of a Polish priest who, in the nightmare of Auschwitz, volunteered to swap places with an innocent individual the Nazis had decided to execute, is also to the point.[36]

What could Hobbes and Griffin say of these people who put considerations of justice or charity above their own survival? I am not sure that they could, in all consistency, add anything very enlightening (taking it for granted that it is not helpful to say that they are irrational because these other considerations are 'inapplicable'). Hobbes and Griffin might try to say, along with some historians and sociologists, that people trapped in settings like concentration camps are usually dominated by the drive to individual survival, and that cases of altruism and principled action are merely anomalies that confirm the rule. However, as I hinted above, a more careful scrutiny reveals a significantly more complex reality. As Jorge Semprun, a Buchenwald survivor, remarked:

> In the camps, man becomes that animal capable of stealing a mate's bread, of propelling him toward death. But in the camps, man also becomes that invincible being capable of sharing his last cigarette butt, his last piece of bread, his last breath, to sustain his fellowman.[37]

The broad understanding of morality introduced above allows for a more nuanced explanation of the demands that morality places on us in such situations and, consequently, of how we may justifiably behave. As Anna Pawelczynska, another Auschwitz survivor, observed:

> [T]he Ten Commandments did not disappear [in the camps]; they were simply reinterpreted. Murder, for example, could be a moral [*qua* justified] act if it kept an assassin from carrying out cruel and vicious assignments. Bearing false witness could become a virtuous act if it helped save human lives. To love one's neighbour as one loved oneself was perhaps an excessive demand, but to avoid harming him was not.[38]

[34] Note that one should not make the converse mistake of thinking that moral considerations in the narrow sense are necessarily finally authoritative in situations where self-preservation is not at stake.

[35] K Hart, *I Am Alive* (London, Corgi, 1974) 153.

[36] This example is reported in CAJ Coady, 'Hobbes and "The Beautiful Axiom"' (1990) 65 *Philosophy* 5, 15.

[37] J Semprun, *The Long Voyage* (London, Weidenfeld and Nicolson, 1963) 60.

[38] Todorov, *Facing the Extreme* (n 33) 36, citing A Pawelczynska, *Values and Violence in Auschwitz: A Sociological Analysis* (Berkeley, University of California Press, 1979).

An understanding of morality that is non-jurisdictional and flexible, a morality that does not run out and does not get entangled in webs of overly rigid obligations, can account for Pawelczynska's observations. It is also an understanding that provides a perspicuous counterpoint to law. Within the sphere of jurisdiction it claims for itself, law is often understood as a system of rules – or prescriptive generalisations – that are inflexible, to the extent that they do not always make the exceptions and nuances they should make to accord with their underlying justifications. By definition, as I remarked before, rule-based generalizations are somewhat over-inclusive and under-inclusive. Morality, in the broad non-jurisdictional sense in which I shall now use the term, never is. It always applies to whomever it addresses and never goes awry.

It might here be relevant to mention the theoretical possibility of dire emergencies – sometimes referred to as supreme moral emergencies – that could subvert the very foundations of morality itself. Consider the case of a widespread nuclear war, which would bring into being a world in which survivors lapse into a bestial condition in order to survive in an environment in which nothing usually deemed necessary for human flourishing remains. It may be accurate to think of such an alien world as 'extra moral' or as a world in which morality is no better than obsolete as a means of practical guidance and behavioural appraisal. My point, though, is that such ultimate emergencies should clearly not be thought of as paradigm examples. It would also be inadvisable to treat them as such for the purpose of elucidating the relationship between morality and emergencies – especially relatively discrete individual emergencies. As a result, I shall not dwell on them any further.[39]

C More or Less Isolated Individual Emergencies and Criminal Law: Solving the Puzzle

With such theoretical tools and clarifications in hand, I now want to take a fresh look at the criminal law's relationship with individual emergencies. I want to focus on states of affairs in which such emergencies are inevitable facts of people's lives, but in which the *de facto* authority of the state is generally not in question. Such conditions prevail in most societies under modern conditions, where there is relative social stability. In many such states, the criminal law, at least in its *mala in se* dimension, is commonly regarded as giving general effect to some morally important reasons which exist independently of it – for example, reasons against murdering or harming others, or in favour of respecting others' property. But the criminal law does more than simply enforce pre-existing reasons of this kind, because their exact scope and force are controversial and uncertain. It can and often does serve as an authority that solves coordination problems by specifying

[39] For my take on supreme moral emergencies as only one extreme and non-paradigmatic type of public emergencies, see F Tanguay-Renaud, 'Making Sense of "Public" Emergencies' (2009) 8 *Philosophy of Management* 31, 47–50.

in more certain terms legal rules which reflect these reasons.[40] In terms of the normal justification thesis, the criminal law is justified in so proceeding when its subjects are more likely to conform to morality by following the coordinating rules than by determining their behaviour according to their own lights. In some cases, the criminal law may also be justified by the fact that it has a sharper moral judgement than us, especially when it is in a better position to account for all the relevant reasons that apply to us. More importantly, given that human beings are often weak-willed, the criminal law may also be justified on the ground that it helps strengthen our resolve to do what we ought to do, by appealing to our fear of sanctions. How, then, should the criminal law contend with more or less isolated individual emergencies?

i Individual Emergencies and the Legal Subdivision of Moral Labour

It should now be apparent that if the criminal law, when it attempts to give effect to pre-existing reasons (or to craft new reasons) in its rules, fails to account for significant moral nuances and to give individuals the leeway that morality gives them, it risks making it harder for them to comply with the reasons that otherwise apply to them (or at least being completely unhelpful). This point is meant to be general, but emergencies are paradigmatic scenarios. In emergency situations, deliberation time is typically so scant, opportunities to avoid harm so restricted, the stakes so high and unexpected, that if the law fails to recognize morally justified alternatives and erects authoritative rules that are too inflexible and exception-less, it risks undermining its claim to legitimacy.[41] For example, the criminal law should not seek, as part of claiming a monopoly over the legitimate use of physical force, to impose an overly strict variety of pacificism that makes no allowance for any interpersonal recourse to force – as necessary and proportionate as it may be – or that curtails such recourse by means of excessively rigid 'immediacy' or 'retreat' requirements.[42]

[40] If, in its *mala in se* dimension, the criminal law sharpens existing reasons by making them more precise and appealing, it also strives, in what academic commentators have termed its *mala prohibita* or 'regulatory' dimension, to sharpen morality in a more radical way. *Mala prohibita* criminal law seeks to solve moral problems by creating *new* reasons for action in the form of legal rules, reasons that would not exist but for the law, eg, the criminal law sometimes imposes labelling requirements to ensure safe food consumption by all. Note that whenever the law creates a new reason, this reason is subject to the same kinds of conflicts as any other reason. Therefore, although I have organized my discussion around *mala in se* criminal law, *mala prohibita*, which is merely an extension of the *mala in se* problem, does not fall outside its scope in any significant way.

[41] Here, a consequentialist might add that if the criminal law's subjects know it to reflect morality at least roughly, they may be, if only ever so slightly, more inclined – some might say, more conditioned – to act justifiably in the expectation of ex post facto vindication. However, retributivist and expressivist conceptions of criminal law would reject even this minimal consequentialist assumption, insisting instead that agents can be expected to act in accordance with morality even if criminal law norms do not act as explicit incentives.

[42] Compare: St Augustine 'Letter 47, to Publicola' W Parsons (trans) in RJ Deferrari (ed), *The Fathers of the Church: Volume 12* (New York, Fathers of the Church, 1951) 230: 'In regard to killing men so as not to be killed by them, this view does not please me, unless perhaps it should be a soldier or a

Does this line of argument reminiscent of the moral view introduced earlier entail that we should espouse it as the correct view? In other words, should criminal law account for its *ex ante* ineptitude in times of individual emergencies by expecting no more than direct reliance on morality? One might object that I have stacked the cards in favour of the moral view by assuming that the criminal law seeks to give effect to moral reasons and solve moral problems. Could we not say, along the lines of the political view, that, since the criminal law is often incompetent to assist its addressees when they are confronted with individual emergencies, it should simply move out of the way? To borrow Michael Ignatieff's formulation of the claim: 'If laws are rules, and emergencies make exceptions to these rules, how can their authority survive once exceptions are made?'[43] I believe this challenge to be somewhat artificial (at least with respect to relatively discrete individual emergencies). It is concordant with the normal justification thesis to say that general criminal law regulation can remain legitimately authoritative in the face of individual emergencies, *so long as* it makes enough space for individuals in the predicament and bystanders to assess the various reasons that apply to them and act according to morally undefeated ones. In other words, to remain legitimately authoritative in emergency situations (assuming, for the sake of argument, that it is otherwise legitimate, which it may not be), the criminal law may be well advised to grant some latitude of action to those who are confronted with them – not absolute latitude, but moral latitude.

In some ways, such subdivision of moral labour in favour of individuals confronted with emergency predicaments may be thought to be similar to other types of subdivisions of legal jurisdiction that can be implemented to bolster the law's legitimacy – for example, between the legislature, the judiciary and the executive (as well as within it). What I mean by this analogy is that, like in these other types of cases, the issue is both political and moral. On one hand, it is to be settled by the relevant state organs in consideration of, inter alia, the law's ability to provide assistance. On the other, it is intrinsically linked to the moral legitimacy of the legal rules to which the state gives shape. When the criminal law provides practical latitude to its subjects, they are typically allowed to act on various moral considerations that the law would otherwise pre-empt. Given the law's limited competence in times of emergency, such an approach may sometimes be the only morally legitimate alternative available to it. That said, insofar as no rational agent is ever exempt from morality (even when confronted with emergencies), private emergency responders are not left to behave according to their whims. At the very least, they remain subject to their predicament as moral agents, and the law may elect to judge them in this light – some might say, 'on the merits' – ex post facto.

John Gardner explains the subdivision of moral labour point in this way:

public official. In this case, he does not do it for his own sake, but for others or for the state to which he belongs, having received the power lawfully in accord with his public character'.

[43] M Ignatieff, *The Lesser Evil: Political Ethics in an Age of Terror* (Edinburgh, Edinburgh University Press, 2005) 25.

> So far as the criminal law is concerned all reasons in favour of performing the criminalised action are defeated by virtue of the law's unquestionable and all-embracing authority. It means that one is left with no automatic access to any justificatory considerations, however powerful they may be apart from the law. What the law does, which nevertheless creates a role for some justificatory defences, is to provide us with cancelling permissions to perform, under certain specified conditions, the actions which it criminalises.[44]

In other words, the criminal law may choose to create gaps – that is, justificatory defences – in its mandatory *qua* exclusionary guidance through which some conflicting emergency reasons are, within certain parameters, admitted as legally acceptable reasons for action. It is then up to individuals confronted with emergency predicaments to assess the comparative weight and structure of the said reasons, and to decide whether and how to act on them. Their discretion will often involve matters of considerable moral importance given the latent force of the underlying reasons that led to criminalizing the acts in question in the first place. For example, even if legally and morally permissible, the killing in self-defence of an assailant acting under duress remains the killing of an undeserving individual, and burning a neighbour's house as a necessary means of forestalling the devastating progression of a forest fire may well harm her considerably. Yet, to avoid distorting illegitimately the reasoning of emergency responders, the criminal law will often leave such dilemmas to them. Indeed, from the legal point of view, the person who finds herself outside the predicament – that is, outside the parameters of the justificatory defence as set by the law – remains subject to the direct authority of the criminal law and its prescriptive prohibitions. However, the person inside the predicament is granted some practical latitude to decide for herself how to act. To take once again the example of self-defence, in many jurisdictions the criminal law will defer to the decisions of self-defenders about whether to defend themselves and to what extent, insofar as they stay within the legally determined yet morally-sensitive limits of a necessary and proportionate response.[45]

ii Some Clarifications and Cautionary Remarks

At this stage, some important clarifications and cautionary remarks seem apposite. First, it is true that the recurrence and predictability of a given type of emergency may, sometimes, allow the criminal law to develop some expertise or coordination ability that enables it to provide and enforce clear and legitimate *ex ante* authoritative guidance via its general rules. Consider, for example, legal

[44] Gardner, 'Justifications and Reasons' (n 31) 116–17.

[45] In many legal systems, the criminal law goes further and grants practical latitude not only to people themselves in emergency predicaments, but also to third parties or bystanders who witness emergencies and are in a position to provide assistance. I believe that such cases can be understood in a similar light. Insofar as they involve additional complexities, which they sometimes will, I bracket them until another day. I also bracket questions related to the legitimacy of positive duties of emergency assistance that the criminal may impose on third parties.

guidance about the point at which doctors, who have the option – sometimes repeatedly – of extracting organs from one patient to save the life of many others, are justified in doing so.[46] In such morally intricate settings as the provision of emergency healthcare, the law may sometimes be able to set reliable *ex ante* parameters, convey guidance effectively through rules, and lead its addressees to better conformity with reason than if they acted urgently according to their own lights (even if they did so with the best of intentions). Nonetheless, the previous discussion teaches us that the criminal law should refrain from omitting to recognize justificatory latitude, except when it genuinely assesses that to do so is likely to facilitate better compliance with reason. Whenever it errs, the law runs the risk of being branded harsh and illegitimate, and to be systematically disobeyed by even the most morally-abiding citizens.

Consider the case of a poor and racially segregated neighbourhood situated in an otherwise stable state. Tensions run high. Racially motivated attacks are frequent, and self-defence is often perceived as retaliation, engendering an escalation in acts of violence. In this scenario, emergencies are relatively unsurprising and recurrent, and self-defensive responses to them may have wide-ranging implications – for example, growing loss of faith in state protection mechanisms and increased risks of riots and wide-scale violence. Yet, it is questionable whether the criminal law could legitimately omit to vindicate genuine acts of self-defence, even if it thus sought to send out a message. Conviction, followed by executive pardon, might be an appropriate response to the morally complex case of the doctor who indefensibly yet genuinely – some might even say, admirably – tries to save many by killing one. However, the conviction and stigmatisation of a morally justified self-defender would most likely amount to an abuse of authority by the law. When deciding which justification defences to recognize, legal systems may have some limited room to manoeuvre. They ought to consider their competence alongside all other reasons that militate for or against grants of practical latitude, such as prior wrongdoing on the part of the individual in the predicament, the quality of the various alternatives available to him, potential significant ramifications for society as a whole, etc. That said, most modern criminal law systems do acknowledge the legitimacy-related need for at least basic individual emergency latitude in the form of justificatory defences, such as self-defence and necessity. And so should they.

My second set of cautionary remarks regards my earlier suggestion that the subdivision of moral labour in the context of criminal law justifications may, in some ways, be similar to governmental separations of powers and administrative forms of delegation of authority. It is important to be conscious of the limits of this analogy. Contrary to what some theorists assert, it does not follow from the fact that the criminal law grants practical latitude to private emergency responders in the context of justification defences, that these individuals 'stand in the shoes of' or 'act as if they are' public officials, or that they otherwise claim to be

[46] I borrow this example from Horder, 'On the Irrelevance of Motive' (n 17) 180–82.

acting in the name of the state.[47] This questionable position seems to take roots in a recurrent yet exaggerated interpretation of Max Weber's assertion that the mark of the state is its successful claim of a monopoly on the legitimate use of physical force within a territory – a monopoly that implies that other associations or individuals may only use physical force insofar as they are permitted by the state to do so.[48] A thorough discussion of the problematic aspects of Weber's assertion would distract from the focus of this chapter and will have to await another day. However, I want to offer some grounds for doubting that it warrants the conclusion that individual emergency responders, such as self-defenders, are somehow necessarily acting on behalf of the state when granted a legal justification.

Bernard Williams once provocatively wrote that 'the securing of order, protection, safety, trust, and the conditions of cooperation' is the first question of political theory, and that the modern state presents itself as its solution. However, he also argued that, in order to retain basic legitimacy, the state must refrain at all times from becoming part of the problem.[49] Much of modern political theorizing has been concerned with the question of how far the state can legitimately go to ensure that the said social conditions prevail. In other words, at which point does the state become part of the main problem it exists to solve? Surely, there comes a point where it has done enough, and where doing any more by way of regulation, taxation, policing, punishment and so forth, would tip the balance of legitimacy. At that point, for the state to do any more would simply be too invasive, exploitative, manipulative, terrorizing or the like. Now, notice that, if the state pursues its foundational aims with enough restraint to remain legitimate in Williams's terms, there will inevitably always remain opportunities for legitimate individual uses of force that it should not pre-empt or take over. For example, since a legitimate state will no doubt refrain from obliterating its citizens' humanity by continuously surveilling and controlling their every movement and environment, emergencies, in the form of attacks or natural threats that would render the use of force morally justifiable (say, as self-defence or necessity), will unavoidably remain distinct possibilities. Thus, a state, or at least a state that aspires to legitimacy, should not strive nor claim to monopolise *all* legitimate uses of physical force.[50]

[47] See especially M Thorburn, 'Justifications, Powers, and Authority' (2008) 117 *Yale Law Journal* 1070, 1126 and ch 1, p 17, in this volume. See also St Augustine 'Letter to Publicola' (n 42) 230. Compare: Y Lee, 'The Defense of Necessity and Powers of the Government' (2009) 3 *Criminal Law and Philosophy* 133, 143.

[48] See M Weber, 'Politik als Beruf' in *Gesammelte Politische Schriften* 5th edn (Tübingen, Winckelmann, 1988) 505–06. Thorburn explicitly grounds his analysis in Weber's claim in his 'Criminal Law as Public Law' in RA Duff and S Green (eds), *Philosophical Foundations of Criminal Law* (Oxford, Oxford University Press, 2011) 36, fn 31.

[49] B Williams, *In the Beginning Was the Deed* (Princeton, Princeton University Press, 2005) 3–4.

[50] Raz reminds us of this additional feature of the legitimacy of state governance in his discussion of the normal justification of authority, when he emphasizes that, to be legitimate, the law's authority must not only meet the normal justification thesis, but be exercised in a way that does not excessively curtail the independence or autonomy of its addressees. See J Raz, 'The Problem of Authority: Revisiting the Service Conception' (2006) 90 *Minnesota Law Review* 1003, 1016–20. Of course, the point in the text is more broadly applicable and extends to other means of state monopolization, such

It may be that Weber had a weaker claim in mind.[51] Remember that he does not deny that non-state associations and individuals may be able to resort to force legitimately. His claim, though, is that they may only do so with the permission of the state. Now, in legitimate states where the rule of law prevails, the state only permits what is permitted by law. So perhaps Weber's claim about the monopoly on the use of force is not to be taken literally as a claim to a monopoly on the use of force, but as a claim to a monopoly on the authoritative determination of the permissibility of the use of force; after all, all legal systems by their very nature claim to be comprehensive and to monopolize the authoritative determination of everything. Yet, one may ask, does the law really claim to monopolise the authoritative determination of the permissibility of *all* uses of force? In legal systems with which I am familiar, it certainly does not explicitly make this claim across the board. For example, it does not regulate the permissibility of my decision to cut myself with a knife or to lift a heavy box. It sometimes even explicitly denies having interest in some uses of force against others, such as trifling ones, as exemplified by the oft-cited legal maxim *de minimis non curat lex*. Instead, the legal regulation of force seems to be focused on *certain* uses – namely, those that may hinder social life, such as violent retaliation, coercion and killings or serious inflictions of harm to others. The standard rejoinder to this line of argument is that even when the law is silent over a given matter, this silence is itself permissive. The law, it is said, necessarily permits whatever it does not prohibit, so that it really permits or prohibits all uses of force. This claim may well be accurate. However, it only passes the buck to the notion of 'legal permission' which, as I began to suggest earlier, simply entails that the subject of the permission is not pre-empted by law to make moral determinations himself or herself – including about the use of force – and to act for non-legal (moral) reasons.

Admittedly, there are various kinds of legal permissions, and my last claim that permission merely entails non-interference by the law may be most obvious where the law permits a given use of force by omitting to say anything about it. What about cases in which permissions are explicitly given by the law, like when it recognizes that resort to force in self-defence is justified? In such cases, legal silence is insufficient, but only because the permission is set against a backdrop of prohibitions, including the prohibitions on murder, wounding and assault. Beyond that difference, criminal law justifications function just like silent permissions by affording practical latitude to individual actors. They are not, as the theorists whom I am challenging argue, power or authority-conferring norms.[52] They do not operate like, for example, the criminal law rules which, in various jurisdictions, empower justices of the peace to authorize arrests and searches. That is, they do

as state coercion. Accordingly, my reference to the criminal law 'failing' to prevent individual emergencies at the beginning of the chapter should be read as assuming that there will be occasions where, all things considered, it may not legitimately seek to prevent them.

[51] Compare: R Nozick, *Anarchy, State, and Utopia* (Oxford, Blackwell Publishing, 1974) 23–24.

[52] Perhaps with the exception of the defence of consent, as explained in J Gardner 'Justification under Authority' (2010) 23 *Canadian Journal of Law and Jurisprudence* 71, 75–83.

not confer any public or state-related normative powers or authority on their beneficiaries to change anyone's normative position. Thus, whereas the law may grant some latitude of action to self-defenders to sustain the legitimacy of its general claim to authority, they do not necessarily exercise legal (or state) authority when self-defending. I say 'necessarily' because legal powers and legal permissions to infringe criminal law duties sometimes come together harmoniously, like in the case of police officers who, in numerous jurisdictions, perform forceful warrantless arrests of recalcitrant individuals that are at once legally valid and justified. However, the relationship between the two kinds of norms is merely contingent.

So, like Fletcher yet contra others like Thorburn, I believe that the state does not have a total monopoly on the legitimate use of force per se.[53] I also do not think, this time contra both Fletcher and Thorburn, that justified private resort to force in emergencies is best understood as a question of allocation of authority. Insofar as they are legally permitted to act directly for moral reasons in emergencies, private individuals need no special type of authority to do so, let alone any state authority. This conclusion is comforting since, as I argued, there are lines past which legitimate states must inevitably restrain their control and authoritative guidance of individual uses of force, and many private emergency responses take place beyond them.

Be that as it may, it remains the case that the comparison between public-law-style delegations of state authority and the practical latitude afforded to individuals through criminal law justifications can focus our attention on non-negligible complexities and borderline questions relative to the legal treatment of the latter. In countries with common law traditions, and also to a large degree in civilian jurisdictions, talk of subdivision of competence usually goes hand-in-hand with talk of ex post facto judicial review. Such talk usually includes discussion of the ambit of legally-conferred discretion, as well as of various standards of judicial scrutiny that may be applicable in different contexts. Could it be that individual emergency responses that, in some way, infringe general criminal law guidance may also appropriately be reviewed according to different standards – which may, like in the public law context, vary according to role-based expectations, expertise, the nature of the interests at stake, unusual circumstances, and so forth? Thinking of the ex post facto review of individual emergency responses in terms of varying standards of scrutiny opens the door to an investigation of why it is in fact the case that, in most jurisdictions, the criminal law chooses to recognize, in addition to justifications, related defensive claims such as excuses. When facing an emergency, a person will sometimes overstep the limits of the practical latitude

[53] Thorburn sometimes seems to concede the point partially when admitting that there may be 'fundamentally private' emergency justifications for otherwise prohibited resort to force. However, his conception of the dividing line between the public and the private is rather obscure, insofar as he really thinks there is one, eg, it is unclear why he thinks that resort to force in self-defence or in burning down a building to create a firebreak is intrinsically public, while a necessary blood transfusion to an unconscious patient by a doctor is best explained as fundamentally private. This conclusion is especially puzzling in light of the fact that the provision of healthcare is regarded by many as a public good. See Thorburn, 'Criminal Law as Public Law' (n 48) 32–36.

afforded by the criminal law. Consider, for example, cases of excessive self-defence, some excusatory cases of duress or cases in which one reasonably but mistakenly assumes that an emergency exists and reacts as if it did. Even when unjustifiedly wrongful in the sense of exceeding the practical latitude granted by the law, such emergency responses may still be judged 'reasonable' by a reviewing court and, thus, not criminally blameworthy or deserving of punishment. Of course, since these other pleas, like justifications, lead, when successful, to full or partial exculpation and not, like power-conferring norms, to findings of legal validity, analogies between judicial review of the two can only be imperfect. However, they do help us see that justification defences may not be the only defences relevant to emergency predicaments. Thus, for the sake of completeness, it now seems important to take some time to situate these other possible pleas in relation to the argument of this chapter.

D Criminal Law Latitude beyond All-things-considered Justifications

i Two Types of Latitude with a Perplexing Borderline

I suggested before that when the criminal law grants us a justification in recognition of its inability to facilitate our compliance with reason, it grants us *practical* latitude – that is, latitude to act in ordinarily prohibited ways, for certain reasons. I contended that, insofar as its contours are sufficiently morally sensitive, such latitude can allow the criminal law to retain legitimacy in the face of individual emergencies. However, since, in emergencies, time is scarce, opportunities to assess and weigh epistemic particulars tend to be limited, and emotions typically run high, people's ability to assess correctly and respond fittingly to reasons for action may be negatively impacted. As a result, emergency responders may wrongfully exceed the bounds of legally-recognized practical latitude, yet do so in ways that are quite understandable in the circumstances. Indeed, insofar as they still manage to act in ways that meet the minimum expectations of virtue and skill that befit their relevant role(s) in society, a strong case may be made that the law should also recognize it and refrain from blaming, censuring or punishing them for their unjustified criminal deeds. In other words, in addition to its grants of practical latitude, the criminal law may afford us some *interpretive* latitude. It may recognize that unjustified wrongdoers sometimes deserve to be judged, within reason, in accordance with their incorrect epistemic and emotional interpretations of the world. In lawyers' terms, one may say that questions of legal justifications are questions of law – that is, the law should relax its claim of authority and not hold this or that action to be unlawful – whereas questions of interpretive latitude are questions of fact – that is, facts should not be treated as they are/were, but as how, within reason, they were interpreted. This distinction is traditionally referred to in criminal law and criminal law theory circles as the distinction between justifications and excuses.

For example, the German Criminal Code (*Strafgesetzbuch*) recognizes both a defence of 'necessity as justification' and a defence of 'necessity as excuse'. The first permits limited infringements of criminal law prohibitions for certain emergency reasons:

> Whoever, faced with an imminent danger to life, limb, freedom, honor, property or another legal interest which cannot otherwise be averted, commits an act to avert the danger from himself or another, does not act unlawfully, if, upon weighing the conflicting interests, in particular the affected legal interests and the degree of danger threatening them, the protected interest substantially outweighs the one interfered with. This shall apply, however, only to the extent that the act is a proportionate means to avert the danger.[54]

'Necessity as excuse', on the other hand, provides extra leniency for what 'could be expected [of the agent] in the circumstances'.[55] This second defence does not affect the wrongful character of the impugned action, which remains 'unlawful,' but, if successfully-invoked, negates the agent's liability to be condemned and punished for it. Likewise, the German Code recognises a defence of 'necessary defense' that negates the 'unlawfulness' of resort to force when one is 'required to avert an imminent unlawful assault from oneself or another,' and a defence of 'excessive necessary defense' for situations in which 'the perpetrator exceeds the limits of necessary defense due to confusion, fear or fright'.[56] Like necessity as excuse, excessive necessary defence only negates the perpetrator's liability to be condemned and punished. It does not create any permissive gap in the law's general guidance, and what the perpetrator did is still deemed legally wrong, all things considered.

Legal systems sometimes seem to blend the two forms of latitude. In Canada, for example, one central feature of the 'justification' of self-defence is that the self-defender 'believes, on reasonable grounds, that he cannot otherwise preserve himself from death or grievous bodily harm'.[57] Such legal formulations lead some theorists to insist, misleadingly, that the uniquely appropriate standard of appraisal for claims of justification must be 'one of reasonable belief at the time rather than correctness'.[58] To repeat, such insistence on an epistemically-grounded standard of reasonable belief – for example, what a self-defender reasonably, even if mistakenly, believed to be an attack as well as a necessary and proportionate

[54] *Strafgesetzbuch*, s 34 (Germany), online: www.iuscomp.org/gla/statutes/StGB.htm#32 (English translation provided by the German Ministry of Justice).

[55] ibid s 35.

[56] ibid ss 32–33. Interestingly, unlike in most other jurisdictions and, arguably, morality, proportionality is not recognized as an element of the justification of necessary defence in German law. For an explanation, see GP Fletcher, *Rethinking Criminal Law* (Oxford, Oxford University Press, 2000) 861–62.

[57] Criminal Code RSC 1985 ch C-46 s 34(2)(b). The standard of reasonable belief also applies to two of the three elements of the defence of necessity as it is recognised at common law in Canada – namely, reasonable belief in the existence of an imminent danger or peril as well as in the absence of legal alternatives. Unlike self-defence, though, that defence is deemed to constitute an excuse, and solely an excuse. See the discussion in *R v Perka* [1984] 2 SCR 232 (SCC), as well as specifications in *R v Latimer* [2001] 1 SCR 3 (SCC).

[58] Thorburn, 'Justifications' (n 47) 1110.

response – as opposed to a correctness standard – for example, whether there actually was an attack and whether the self-defender's response was in fact necessary and proportionate – obliterates an important distinction. It denies the difference between a legal permission to infringe criminal law norms for given reasons for action and within given limits, and a recognition that, although an action exceeded these parameters and was therefore criminally wrongful, it still was not blameworthy. Such theoretical conflation should be avoided since it obscures fundamentally different ways in which criminal law may tailor its rule to address various types of rational pressures that emergencies (and possibly other thorny situations) may impose on us – with, on one side, sudden variations in our actual reasons for action and, on the other, hasty belief formation given a (perceived) need to act quickly, or fearful and anxious reactions in the heat of the moment.

At this point, one may interject that the story about criminal law grants of practical and interpretive latitude as I have told it so far is still too simplistic. One may ask: what about situations in which people reason impeccably, given the available evidence, yet end up interpreting the world incorrectly and acting wrongfully? How should the criminal law treat such individuals, assuming that they respond fittingly to reasonably-formed beliefs which, if they had been truly reflective of the state of the world, would have tracked undefeated, legally-permitted reasons for action? By speaking generically of *excusatory* interpretive latitude, I analogized such cases to those in which people's practical reasoning is distorted by, for example, strong yet perfectly understandable, emotional outbursts. Certainly, there are similarities and instances of significant overlap between the two types of scenarios. However, is there not a distinctively justificatory aspect to the impeccable, yet erroneous, reasoning cases which demands that they be categorized separately? I want to go back to my earlier discussion of legitimate authority to put forward a reason why I think there is such a reason to distinguish them.

I initially spoke of the need for legal grants of practical latitude in emergency situations in relation to the normal justification of authority. The idea, as I presented it, is that the criminal law should grant us justificatory latitude when it is unable to reliably help us comply with reason better than if we acted according to our own lights. Note, however, that it is unclear whether, for Raz's normal justification thesis to be satisfied, the law's rational advantage needs to be epistemically-ascertainable at the time of action, or whether it is sufficient that the law turns out after the fact to have better captured what we ought to do. The tension is at its starkest in cases where relevant facts (and thus reasons) are unknowable even in principle at the time of action – that is, unknowable by anybody, including the law – but where the law happens to have pre-empted them accurately in its guidance (as confirmed ex post facto). In such cases, the law could not say that it was better placed than anybody else to facilitate conformity with reason at the time of action, yet, as it turns out, its guidance was in line with reason and following it would have been rationally/morally helpful. When evaluating people's conduct ex post facto in such circumstances, should the criminal law consider recognizing justificatory latitude since it could not know better than them how to act at the time of action, or should it merely make excusatory concessions since, as it turns out, people would have complied with reason better by deferring to it?

This ambiguity may be thought to wane in cases where a detached observer could have known the relevant facts at the time of action, given the evidence available, yet no one in the epistemic position of the agent in the predicament could have. In such cases, one may say, the law could at least in principle have known the relevant facts in advance. The problem here is that the law is no omniscient god. It is a human artefact whose epistemic potential is finite and susceptible of error in exigent circumstances, just like that of individual human beings. Thus, while, in these latter cases, the law *may* have known better than emergency responders who failed to abide by its guidance, it would be ill-placed to demand of them a kind of rational perfection that *no one* in their specific epistemic position – that is, in the same circumstances, with the same relevant incapacities – could possibly achieve.[59] Furthermore, one may wonder, in relation to many exigent and particular cases, how likely it really is that the law would in fact know better.

The additional category of *evidence-relative* justification has recently been suggested to account for legal grants of latitude in situations where, except as a matter of sheer luck, a correct epistemic interpretation of the world would either be impossible in principle, or from the position of the interpreting agent.[60] This additional category aims to mark the conceptual middle-ground between cases of all things considered, reason-relative justifications – some prefer the expression 'fact-relative' to highlight more starkly the distinction with the evidence-relative domain – and cases of excusatory latitude afforded for merely belief-relative or, say, emotion-relative misapprehensions of the world. Approaching the question from the perspective of the normal justification of law's authority helps explain why this further theoretical distinction is itself justified.

ii Emergency Concessions to Human Frailty?

Now, even if we move away from questions of legitimate legal authority into the territory of outright interpretive latitude, important emergency-related complexities remain for criminal law theorists. From the beginning of this chapter, I have been discussing emergencies in terms of their impact on us as rational, self-determining beings. I also assumed that appropriate criminal law responses – be they fact-relative or evidence-relative justifications – should be treated as

[59] Of course, cases not involving actual emergencies may also fall in this perplexing category. Situations of hostage-taking in which secluded individuals are told that they might be killed 'sometime in the future', or prolonged patterns of domestic violence that make it psychologically impossible for someone to know better than they actually know are often cited as examples. Hence, the reluctance of many legal systems to retain 'imminence' or 'immediacy' requirements for criminal law defences which might cover such scenarios. See, eg, the decisions of the Supreme Court of Canada in *R v Lavallée* [1990] 1 SCR 852 and *R v Pétel* [1994] 1 SCR 3.

[60] See especially V Tadros, *The Ends of Harm: The Moral Foundations of Criminal Law* (Oxford, Oxford University Press, 2011) ch 10. For a relevant discussion highlighting the need for conceptual refinement in this theoretical area, see also RA Duff, *Answering for Crime: Responsibility and Liability in the Criminal Law* (Oxford, Hart Publishing, 2007) ch 11.

solutions to problems internal to rationality. Some leading theorists argue that the further type of criminal law latitude to which I referred under the rubric of 'excuses' should also be understood in rationalistic terms.

Their contention takes roughly the following shape. Unlike someone who claims a fact-relative or an evidence-relative justification, someone who claims an excuse does not claim that her behaviour was reasonable in the sense of being deserving of practical latitude. She concedes that her actions were unreasonable in the practical sense, but claims that they were nonetheless reasonable in a secondary sense. She may claim, for example, that she was acting in the grip of an emotion that was rationally appropriate in the circumstances – such as fear of something genuinely fearful, or anxiety in the face of a sudden, unfamiliar, and genuinely unnerving situation – and that a person of reasonable firmness in her position might have been motivated, and have reacted, in the same way. She may also make a similar claim about actions taken on the basis of erroneous beliefs too hastily acquired, even allowing for emergency circumstances, but so acquired because of generally appropriate cognitive or affective attitudes. Consider, for example, the army officer who is sufficiently hot-headed to be able to motivate her troops and succeed in battle, but whose otherwise morally desirable attitude sometimes leads her to fail to make the kinds of checks she should ideally make, and to appraise evidence as carefully as she should. The contention, I take it, is that claims of excuses are best understood as paradigmatically grounded in a variety of important *reason-sensitive* ways of apprehending the world that, regrettably but understandably, sometimes distort our apprehension and handling of reasons for action and lead us to unjustified wrongdoing.[61] In other words, excuses are often understood as legal (and moral) means of accounting for the understandable complexities and trappings of our lives as rational creatures, which cannot solely be explained in terms of reasons for action or impeccable epistemic appreciations.

Much research remains to be done about the structure of excuses and the type of latitude that ought to be legally provided qua excusatory. In this chapter, I can only gesture towards some of the many directions that related research should take, in a way that allows me to clarify some remaining aspects of the relationship between emergencies and the rule of criminal law. Indeed, there is another school of thought about excuses that does not account for emergencies, their impact on us and the appropriate response of the criminal law with the same emphasis on rationality. In a recent assertion of this view, William Wilson writes that

> reasons theory has little to say concerning the significant constitutive role played by human frailty in certain key defences. Sometimes our behaviour, though it is not grounded in reason, is afforded an excuse precisely because it issued out of the kind of external crisis which can lead even reasonable people to act unreasonably.[62]

[61] For specific defences of this general claim, see DM Kahan and MC Nussbaum, 'Two Conceptions of Emotions in Criminal Law' (1996) 96 *Columbia Law Review* 269 and J Gardner, 'The Logic of Excuses and the Rationality of Emotions' (2009) 43 *Journal of Value Inquiry* 315.

[62] W Wilson, 'The Filtering Role of Crisis in the Constitution of Criminal Excuses' (2004) 27 *Canadian Journal of Law and Jurisprudence* 387, 394–95.

As I already suggested, insofar as it is construed sufficiently broadly so as to include the different tools that humans have to track and follow reasons – from beliefs, to emotions, to attitudes, to moods and so forth – it is untrue that reasons theory has little to say about human limitations in the face of emergencies. But the frailty to which Wilson is referring is of another type. It is not the frailty of human rationality, but a kind of human frailty that exposes us to becoming less human in times of crisis.

Why less human? As Thomas Nagel famously argued, the responsible human self – who *we* are – seems to disappear if we focus on the influence of what is not under our control.[63] Aren't our inclinations, capacities, and temperament, the kind of problems and situations we face, the way our actions and projects turn out and the way we are determined by antecedent circumstances, all a matter of luck or, in other words, dependent on uncontrollable causes foreign to the self? It is control that makes us the human beings that we are, and control 'consists in the proper functioning of the person's rational faculty, the proper functioning of the person's ability to recognise and respond to reasons'.[64] Put differently, it is above all our ability to recognize and respond appropriately to the normative aspects of the world – ie reasons – which constitutes us as beings capable of making a difference within it (agents), as opposed to purely passive embodiments of luck (patients). It should come as no surprise that Aristotle remarked over two millennia ago that, together with speech, this ability is the main faculty that, in its most developed form, differentiates us from other animal and vegetal life forms.[65]

A metaphorical way of characterizing Wilson's view is to say that, according to him, emergencies or 'crises' often turn us into (less human) animals largely dependent on their uncontrolled surroundings and, at best, able to reason only to serve given ends such as basic survival. Such a condition is to be understood in opposition to that of (more human) animals who are extensively rationally active within the world, to the point of reasoning about their own ends and nurturing appropriate attitudes and emotional dispositions that assist them in negotiating the complexities of life. For Wilson, behaviour performed while in the former condition is the main type of behaviour that the criminal law ought to excuse, because excuses find their roots in crises, and crises tend to induce that sort of condition. In his own words, 'It is only in response to crisis that it is plausible to claim that our actions are not authentically ours or, if authentically ours', that they are 'not actions for which, as decent self-respecting human beings, we should own up and take responsibility'.[66]

When appraising our reactions to emergencies, the criminal law ought to be careful not to prematurely dehumanize us in such a way, for the simple reason that, pace Wilson, we often remain responsive to reasons while facing such situations. If anything, it is a question of respect for human dignity and agency. Take

[63] T Nagel, 'Moral Luck' in *Mortal Questions* (Cambridge, Cambridge University Press, 1979) 36.
[64] See further J Raz, *Engaging Reason* (Oxford, Oxford University Press, 1999) 76.
[65] See especially his *Politics* 1253a7ff and *Rhethoric* 1355b1ff.
[66] Wilson, 'The Filtering Role of Crisis' (n 62) 389.

the example of coercive threats *qua* emergencies which ground the defence of duress *per minas* ('by threats') – a defence which Wilson does not shy away from discussing in dehumanizing terms.[67] It might be possible to conceive of coercive threats which might have such a radical impact on us that, if they were uttered to us, would lead us, or some of us, to lose complete touch with reason. However, if such threats and such reactions to them are conceivable, they no doubt constitute the rare exception. Coercion operates through the coercee's own appreciation of his reasons for action, and consequently, the more a threat undermines his rational capacities, the less effectively he can be coerced.[68] Think also of the countless examples of Jews deciding appositely (and often courageously) to escape, resist, help and save one another in Nazi concentration camps. If one, if not the most horrifically threatening and generalized emergency situation of the last century did not necessarily break detainees' 'human spirit' and remove their capacity to answer to reason, then Wilson's position, which seems to start from a contrary assumption, likely misses the mark.

Then again, by how far does it really miss the mark? Even so-called reasons theorists are likely to admit of the possibility of emergency scenarios which, quite literally, drive us pathologically insane and lead us to be much less, if at all, rational. Think, for example, of some individual reactions to dangerous phobias, or of emergencies that lead at least some of us to 'lose it' completely out of psychotic anxiety.[69] What makes these people *reasons* theorists, though, is that they are simultaneously likely to insist that, although conceivable, such cases are clearly abnormal. According to them, only in the rare and radical situations in which reasons do not have any grip on us do we cease to act as responsible (*qua* response-able) human beings. Although grounded in a praiseworthy ambition to recognize human agency insofar as it is present, this position may itself be too inflexible.

Here are some grounds for doubting its wisdom. On one hand, some oft-neglected though common and eminently rational emergency responses are not responses for which we are responsible. I am referring here to responses for which we are hardwired, and thus, in respect of which we are not active, but passive. For example, we are hardwired to be alert to certain dangers and react to them instinctively and without deliberation, as we react to fire or to sudden movement in our immediate vicinity. Insofar as such reactions lead us to commit what would otherwise amount to wrongdoing, they should not be exculpated on the basis of their reasonableness (or at least primarily so) but, more fundamentally, because they

[67] ibid 406, 410, 414.

[68] Derek Parfit makes the point cogently and succinctly in his 'Schelling's Answer to Armed Robbery' example, in addition to demonstrating why a pre-commitment to act irrationally when faced with threats may sometimes be rational. D Parfit, *Reasons and Persons* (Oxford, Clarendon Press, 1984) 12–13.

[69] Consider the example of Winston Smith who, in chapter 5 of George Orwell's *Nineteen Eighty-Four*, is confronted by his tormentor O'Brien with his worse fear, rats. 'For an instant', Orwell narrates, 'he was insane, a screaming animal'. Because of his phobia's hold on him, Winston Smith hardly appreciates the reasons that apply to him. To the extent that he does, his appreciation is all but reliable, and leads him to betray his greatest love and commitment.

are actions for which we are not responsible. On the other hand, it may also be that even when an emergency response is generally driven by a cognitive and/or affective reason-sensitive assessment of the situation, the responder partially loses touch with reason in the process of responding. Human capacity for rationality is often not an all or nothing affair, as demonstrated by children of different ages or people with mental disabilities who are capable of appreciating and responding appropriately to some aspects of the world, but not others. Something similar might be true of some otherwise responsible emergency responders – say, of self-defenders who, in the heat of the moment, partially 'lose it' and go a little further than required with their use of defensive force. Although they may have undefeated reasons for resorting to force in the first place, and the reactive emotions they are experiencing may be appropriate, I doubt whether such responses are always fully responsible and best explained in such rationalistic terms. In other words, it may be that the borderline between excuses and denials of responsibility is not as tight as some make it to be, and that some excuses are best understood as hybrid grants of interpretive latitude and concessions to human frailty in Wilson's sense.[70] To repeat, though, I believe that the criminal law should refrain from conceding that emergencies undermine our responsibility when they do not. This may mean that when our responses are predominantly responsible, the criminal law should treat them as if they fully were, and stick to the language of excuses as opposed to that of denials of responsibility. That said, much more work would be required to flesh out this suggestion fully.

E Criminal Law Defences, Vagueness and Adjudication

For some readers, my last set of comments will have brought to the fore a general discomfort that they have with the distinctions drawn so far. Pointing out that many legal systems do not draw these distinctions as finely (or even at all), and prefer to spell out the defences they recognize in vague and broad terms of 'reasonable' or 'involuntary' behaviour, they may question the wisdom of such a detail-oriented discussion. After all, isn't the criminal law too blunt a tool to try to make distinctions that are so fine-grained? Wouldn't it be better if it simply focused on being as lenient as necessary to account for all the scenarios discussed above, however it chooses to do so? Phrased in this way, the objection is rather inconsequential as it assumes that we already know what criminal law latitude and concessions are sufficient and why, which is what my inquiry was in part trying to establish. The objection also disregards without any explanation the possibility of differences in legitimacy that follow from the criminal law's efforts (or lack of effort) to treat its subjects in terms that accurately reflect their predicament – be it as actors that are responsible or non-responsible, fact-relatively or evidence-relatively justified, or merely excused criminal law infringers.

[70] For an important first stab at this question, see J Horder, *Excusing Crime* (Oxford, Oxford University Press, 2004) chs 2–4.

This is not to say that there is no legitimate space for vagueness and indeterminacy in the formulation of criminal law defences. On the justificatory side, for example, they enable the law to ensure that individuals are provided with sufficient practical latitude. So when legal systems recognise, inter alia, a justification of 'necessity' or 'lesser evils', they often frame it in terms of an indeterminacy of aims, which allows criminal defendants to invoke a wide range of undefeated moral reasons that give rise to genuine necessity. Since such reasons – that is, undefeated reasons of necessity that have not been anticipated – can always arise, the defence provides, when available, important latitude relative to criminal prohibitions. It is noteworthy that rule-of-law objections on the ground of vagueness have no basis here, since justifications are gaps in the law's authoritative guidance of individuals, as opposed to exercises of such authority. Their role is to provide moral latitude, not to provide guidance.[71] On the excusatory side of the spectrum, defences are even less connected to any such objections in that, at most, they provide interpretive, not practical, latitude. Fletcher first hinted at this general point over three decades ago, when he wrote that the distinction between criminal offences and defences 'might bear on the analysis of permissible vagueness in legal norms'.[72] Ironically though, he did not integrate his analysis with the theory of authority nor with any meaningful discussion of morality. Doing so allows us to see more clearly why his distinction matters, and why legal categories may at times suitably be left more elastic with respect to defences than with respect to authoritative, guidance-oriented definitions of legal wrongs.

Admittedly, the criminal law does provide some authoritative guidance through its defences. It authoritatively instructs judges and juries to exculpate criminal defendants who have acted within their confines. That being said, some vagueness is still not a problem at that level since rule-of-law considerations do not apply with the same stringency to the law's guidance of judges and juries as it does to its guidance of ordinary individuals. That is, while the law should be especially careful not to ambush its addressees when breach of its guidance may lead to serious adverse normative consequences like criminal censure and punishment, adjudicators face no such prospect within the confines of their role. In fact, vagueness may even assume special importance at the time of adjudication, in a way that is once again related to the normal justification of the law's authority – this time, over adjudicators themselves. Given the factual subtleties involved in many emergency responses (as well as, arguably, other situations not explored here in which claims of justifications or excuses may plausibly be made), and given the fallibility

[71] Of course, insofar as one is aware of them, prior judicial pronouncements on similar cases and statutory delineations may influence one's deliberations, but it remains that someone who successfully claims a fact-relative (or evidence-relative) justification must actually have been motivated to act for a permitted reason for action (or undefeated reason for belief in the form of evidence). Mixed motives will often constitute no bar to such claims, but only insofar as the individual in the predicament has actually acted for at least one relevant undefeated reason. On this last point, as well as on the possibility of mixed motives in the context of excuses, see F Tanguay-Renaud, 'Understanding Criminal Law through the Lens of Reason' (2010) 16 *Res Publica* 89, 93–94.

[72] Fletcher, *Rethinking Criminal Law* (n 56) 555.

of evidence gathering and production in the criminal process, adjudicative guidance that is too clear, precise and uncompromising in respect of defences may lead to the conviction of innocents who, in fact, did fulfil their conditions of applicability. Liberal legal systems erect a presumption of innocence and impose a general burden of proof beyond reasonable doubt on the prosecution to try to avoid such grave errors. Formulations of defences allowing for some margin of appreciation on the part of adjudicators may provide another line of defence against them.[73]

So, while the categories of fact-relative justification, evidence-relative justification, excuse – and to some extent denials of responsibility – are important to understand the full intricacies of the relationship between individual emergencies and the rule of criminal law, there is at least one plausible reason why legal systems may choose not to always adhere to them perfectly. However, since, in liberal legal systems, presumption of innocence and burden of proof beyond reasonable doubt are already in place to satisfy that reason, its existence does not undermine my analysis. It simply contextualizes it further.

III CONTRASTING GENERALIZED EMERGENCIES

To conclude, let me reiterate that, in this chapter, I did not seek to address more generalized and disordering emergencies, such as civil wars, violent revolutions or widespread natural disasters. In addition to confronting vast arrays of people in the form of countless individual emergencies, such situations often constitute emergencies for the law itself, and a fortiori for the criminal law. When, for whatever reason, a generalized emergency undermines a legal system's de facto authority to the extent of rendering it largely inefficacious, it challenges that legal system's very existence and continuity. HLA Hart famously conveyed the point by insisting that disregard for the rules of a system may be so complete and protracted 'that we should say, in the case of a new system, that it had never established itself as the legal system of a given group, or, in the case of a once-established system, that it had ceased to be the legal system of the group'.[74] Hart's point applies as much to collapsing *anciens régimes* as to governments forced into exile, hopeless insurgencies and so on. A legal system that is not by and large efficacious in a given community is not the legal system of that community. It is not competent to be such a system and, at best, it only purports to be. Morally speaking, it cannot aspire to make individuals more likely to comply with the reasons that apply to them by asserting a power to disseminate sounder expertise and judgement, or to solve coordination problems, because it altogether lacks that power.

[73] I am referring here to both the use of vague terms like 'reasonable' and the law's insistence that emergency responders are not required to assess their predicament 'to a nicety' (*R v Baxter* (1975) 27 CCC (2d) 96, 111 (Ontario CA)) or with a 'jeweller's scale' (*Reed v Wastie* [1972] Crim LR 221 (DC)).

[74] HLA Hart, *The Concept of* Law 2nd edn (Oxford, Clarendon Press, 1994) 103.

Therefore, in extremely disordering emergency circumstances, the political view, perhaps even in its wholesale disclaimer guise, may assert itself: the criminal law may be outright incompetent to regulate individual behaviour. It may not even be able to defer efficaciously to morality.

What one must grasp here is that legal retreat in relatively generalized emergencies will often be a question of degree.[75] The point may seem trite but widespread emergencies may not incapacitate, or have incapacitated yet, the whole of the legal system. When anticipating such extreme scenarios (or in the midst of grappling with them), the law may choose to devise counter-emergency strategies to pre-empt disintegration of its efficacy and legitimacy, as well as to protect the people it normally seeks to guide. Historically, it has sometimes tried to do so in the form of extraordinary 'martial law', 'war', 'emergency powers' or 'emergency management' measures, or simply through ordinary statutory guidance.[76] The law may also acknowledge that it would be partly incompetent by anticipatorily announcing the extent to which it would disclaim competence were certain emergency circumstances to arise.[77] It may even plan for its own general suspension. As noted by John Finnis, 'Sometimes [. . .] the values to be secured by the genuine Rule of Law and authentic constitutional government are best served by departing, temporarily but perhaps drastically, from the law and the constitution'.[78] In some such circumstances, other juridical orders, such as international criminal law, may then try to assert themselves to fill the juridical void.

These further questions are clearly important. With respect to them, however, the argument of this chapter should not be seen as anything more than a useful point of departure for further inquiry.

[75] This point is too often neglected. For a recent example of such neglect, see M Hildebrandt, 'The Indeterminacy of an Emergency: Challenges to Criminal Jurisdiction in Constitutional Democracy' (2010) 4 *Criminal Law and Philosophy* 161, 177.

[76] For an interesting discussion of the second type of approach, see eg, SP Green, 'Looting, Law, and Lawlessness' (2007) 81 *Tulane Law Review* 1129.

[77] Such a rationale might, in part at least, explain why murder can only be committed under 'the Queen's peace' under the common law of England. Those who kill enemy combatants in wartime need not argue that they did so for the defence of the realm – or for other lawful reasons – because the offence of murder simply does not extend to their actions. Their argument has already been anticipated in the shape of the prohibitory norm, by means of an exception.

[78] J Finnis, *Natural Law and Natural Rights* (Oxford, Clarendon Press, 1980) 275. Conversely, a legal system may also seek to assert retroactively authority which it did not have throughout a generalized emergency. Consider, eg, the Nuremberg trials. Individual defences such as self-defence, necessity and duress may then once again be recognized effectively and, perhaps, retroactively.

3

The Wrong, the Bad and the Wayward: Liberalism's Mala in Se

ALAN BRUDNER*

I INTRODUCTION

A normative theory of criminalization seeks a principle or set of principles for identifying conduct that a political authority ought to forbid on pain of punishment. I say 'ought to' rather than 'may' because a normative theory of criminalization differs from a theory of constitutional limits on penal legislation. A theory of limits guides a court's decision as to whether a political authority may restrain a person's liberty to act in a certain way and, if so, for what reasons and under what means-related constraints. Such a theory, however, leaves unanswered the question regarding what types of conduct a political authority has a duty to restrain given the ends for the sake of which its authority is recognized. That question too has juridical import, for conduct that a political authority has a duty to criminalize is conduct that a court ought to mandate the lawmaker to criminalize on petition from a qualified applicant.[1] Also unexamined by a limits theory is the strength of the state's duty in different contexts. When (if ever) is the state's duty to criminalize unqualified and when is it a duty to criminalize only if no better or equally effective means of right-vindication, prevention or instruction are available? A theory of criminalization should fill these gaps.[2]

* A version of this chapter was presented as the 'Harry Street Lecture on Public Law' at the University of Manchester (October 2010). Previous drafts were also presented at the Osgoode Hall Law School Conference on 'Rethinking Criminal Law Theory' (September, 2010); the Cambridge University Public Law Discussion Group (November 2010) and the Oxford University Jurisprudence Discussion Group (November 2010). I owe special thanks to Benjamin Berger, John Gardner, Nigel Simmonds, Victor Tadros and Malcolm Thorburn for helpful comments.

[1] Normally restrictive standing rules have been relaxed in such contexts; see eg, *Minister of Justice of Canada v Borowski* [1982] 130 DLR (3rd) 588.

[2] Philosophers writing on criminalization have typically posed only the 'may' question. See JS Mill, *On Liberty* (Indianapolis, Liberal Arts Press, 1956) 3; J Feinberg, *The Moral Limits of the Criminal Law Volume 1: Harm to Others* (New York, Oxford University Press, 1984) 3; D Husak, *Overcriminalization* (Oxford, Oxford University Press, 2008) 82.

Insofar as they seek principles for identifying conduct that a political authority ought to proscribe given the ends for the sake of which it is recognized, theories of criminalization will yield different principles depending on the assumptions they make about the final end of political authority. Those who view political authority as justified only as directing its subjects to virtue will recommend a criminal code quite different from those who see it as justified only as a means to physical security and comfortable living. Still, assumptions need not be arbitrary. Provided they are part of the public culture shared by the citizenry to whom the theory is addressed, rational persuasion is possible.

I shall take the view of the late liberal tradition of political philosophy that the final end of political authority is the realized dignity of the human individual, and I shall work towards the principles of criminalization best aligned with that theory of what political authority is for. I will not defend here the theory of political authority that puts human dignity at its centre, for that is a project by itself. Rather, I will only elaborate the implications of that theory for how we should go about identifying criminal conduct.[3] Criminal conduct, from this viewpoint, is conduct antithetical to human dignity. This chapter's burden is to distinguish and connect various conceptions of dignity and to identify corresponding ways conduct can oppose it. The different ways conduct can oppose dignity are criteria for identifying criminal conduct.

Of course, not all conduct typically proscribed by the liberal state is conduct antithetical to dignity. The state may and does regulate all sorts of activity affecting the public welfare but having no bearing on dignity. It may, for example, regulate market activity in the interest of efficiency, resource use in the interest of conservation, behaviour in public places in the interest of preventing common nuisances and so forth. However, the conduct prohibited under regulation is not generally viewed as criminal conduct. It is conduct that is penalized as contravening a statute, not conduct that is punished as violating a public norm existing apart from statute. So, if we take as the liberal state's final end the realization of the human individual's claim to dignity, then conduct antithetical to dignity may be said to distinguish the class of crimes or *mala in se* from the class of infractions or *mala prohibita*.[4] In this chapter, however, I say nothing further about the latter. My aim, rather, is to derive a set of criteria for identifying conduct that a political authority whose end is individual dignity ought to proscribe on pain of punishment.

[3] For a defence of this chapter's premise, see A Brudner, *Constitutional Goods* (Oxford, Oxford University Press, 2007) 1–15, 38–49.

[4] Within *mala prohibita* I would include conduct that, while immoral, is not inherently unlawful (because not against human dignity) but only becomes unlawful when prohibited. Cruelty to animals is an example. A state whose end is human dignity has no juridical duty to prohibit such conduct, though it has a moral reason to prohibit it and may do so.

II THREE PRINCIPLES OF CRIMINALIZATION

For many years the liberal position on criminalization was the one famously set forth by John Stuart Mill. It was that 'the only purpose for which power can be rightfully exercised over any member of a civilised community, against his will, is to prevent harm to others. His own good, either physical or moral, is not a sufficient warrant'.[5] Of course, Mill did not mean that harm to others was a sufficient condition of criminalization, for he was a utilitarian who believed that harm to others – from economic competition, for example – might be justified by greater benefits overall.[6] Still, he thought it was a necessary condition. Moreover, not all hurts or losses counted as legally relevant harms. The disgust one feels at the thought of another's private conduct could not count in the social calculus, for otherwise one's moral independence to pursue the good as one sees it might be subordinated to a different opinion or taste.[7] Only harms or risks of harm to interests ascribable to all human beings could be admitted on the scales, for only such harms could be said to lower quality of life objectively.[8] Examples are harm to bodily integrity, to physical and emotional health, to the liberty to pursue ends of one's choice, to the secure possession of things rightfully acquired and, of course, to life itself as well as to the resources needed to sustain it.

With these qualifications incorporated, the harm principle might be formulated as follows. Conduct may be prohibited on pain of punishment only if the conduct causes or risks harm to the humanly important interests of others, and only if that harm is not outweighed by the social benefits the conduct brings, and only if criminalizing the conduct is necessary for its prevention and would not cause as much or greater harm than the conduct left alone would cause. So stated, the harm principle is – and was meant to be – protective of liberty and uncongenial to criminalization. It was advanced at a time when the criminalization of conduct harmless to others was justified either on religious grounds or by appeal to widely-shared but philosophically untested moral sentiments. The harm principle was liberalism's weapon against the vestiges of theocracy and the tyranny of the moral majority. In this essay, however, I argue that offences hitherto thought to rest on religion or positive morality and that the harm principle would exclude can be defended on liberal grounds. Still, I don't argue for jettisoning the harm principle. Rather, I argue for reinterpreting it as one of several principles that are generated by a more comprehensive principle of liberal criminalization – one that I call the dignity principle.

[5] Mill, *On Liberty* (n 2) 9.
[6] ibid 96.
[7] ibid 85.
[8] Mill restricts relevant interests to those which may be considered rights; see *On Liberty* (n 2) 95–96. See also J Raz, 'Autonomy, Toleration, and the Harm Principle' in R Gavison (ed), *Issues in Contemporary Legal Philosophy* (Oxford, Clarendon Press, 1987) 327, 331–33.

The harm principle has lately come in for damaging criticism from liberal legal theorists.[9] Several writers have argued that the principle is both too narrow and too broad to map our strong intuitions about what is and what is not criminal conduct. It is too narrow in that it cannot capture intentional interferences with the free exercise of choice that might not inflict or risk harm and that might even benefit the person interfered with. Consider, for example, a physician who, against the will of a dying patient who wishes to live but who has an irrational fear of needles, injects the patient with riskless and life-saving medication. In a liberal society, this beneficial action is an assault, because it violates the individual's right to decide for his body as he chooses. Or suppose someone enters my home when I am not there, steals something I never knew I had, and removes all traces of his having been there so that I never become aware of his entry. Where is the harm in that burglary?

The point of those examples is that the harm principle cannot account for harmless wrongs. Now, it is true that not punishing such conduct might lead to more assaults and burglaries of the harmful variety, and so one might think that the harm principle can justify punishing harmless wrongs as a deterrent to harmful ones.[10] But that is not necessarily so. Any diminution of deterrence that might result from not punishing a harmless wrong could be compensated for by more certain prosecutions of, and more severe punishments for, the harmful variant of that wrong. If the deterrent loss could be neutralized, then punishing harmless wrongs to deter harmful ones curtails liberty more than is necessary for harm prevention, and that is a violation of the harm principle. So the harm principle is too narrow in that it could condemn as inefficient harm prevention the criminalization of harmless wrongs.

A defender of the harm principle might fall back on the argument that the meddlesome physician and fastidious burglar have harmed an *interest* in self-rule and in property, respectively, so that the harm principle can reach their conduct.[11] However, this reply will not do, for it ignores a distinction between agency and interests that the very idea of an interest in self-rule or property presupposes. By imputing to the victim an interest in self-rule and property, we show that we mean by 'interest', not a passing or idiosyncratic desire of this individual, but an abiding inclination widely shared among the members of the life species to which this individual belongs. However, only a being capable of freely choosing the ends its bodily motion or possessions will serve could have an interest (in that sense) in

[9] A Ripstein, 'Beyond the Harm Principle' (2006) 34(3) *Philosophy and Public Affairs* 215–46; H Stewart, 'The Limits of the Harm Principle' (2010) 4(1) *Criminal Law and Philosophy* 17–35.

[10] J Gardner and S Shute, 'The Wrongness of Rape' in J Gardner, Offences and Defences (Oxford, Oxford University Press, 2007) 1–32. The authors argue (at 29–30) that punishing harmless wrongs can satisfy the harm principle if not punishing them would have the effect of making others' lives worse. But given the authors' convincing argument that harmless rape is 'pure rape', a violation of 'the right to sexual autonomy', one wonders why we should care any longer whether criminalizing it satisfies the harm principle. Does a pure rape become punishable only if an impurity is added to it?

[11] Feinberg viewed "harmless" wrongs as harms to the liberty or proprietary interest invaded; Feinberg, *The Moral Limits of the Criminal Law* (n 2) 35.

ruling its body and possessions in accordance with its choices; and so the capability must be prior to the interest. This means that an interest in self-rule or property is an interest *of* an agent, a predicate of a subject. But then someone's interfering with another's freedom of choice cannot be reduced to harming an interest in self-rule or property without collapsing the priority of agency that makes an interest in self-rule or property possible. Instead, we must view the interference as an independent wrong against the subject to whom we ascribe interests – one that consists in treating it unfittingly as an object and that would exist even if no interest of the individuated subject were harmed. Thus, if, eccentrically, the patient had no interest in self-rule, or if he were a masochist who enjoyed being reduced to an object, the physician's action would be a wrong without a harm.

If the harm principle is too narrow in one sense, it is too broad in another, for it can proscribe harming or risking harm to others even though the risk was accepted by the person harmed, as in a consensual fist fight. With the exception of death or very serious bodily harm, tort law regards harm the risk of which was accepted by the victim as a harm without a wrong – and yet the harm principle would proscribe it more broadly than tort law would remedy it. Take, for example, the case where one of the combatants in a consensual fist-fight has goaded the other into agreeing to fight. Such a person is morally blameworthy for the harm he inflicts despite the victim's consent; and so the usual paternalistic worry about disallowing a defence of victim consent need not stand in the way of a straightforward application of the harm principle. After all, the liberal injunction against proscribing harm to self is not violated by punishing the combatant who blamably harmed the other. Even if the harm-doer were morally innocent, the harm principle could still approve a law punishing him for engaging in a consensual fight in order to prevent the wider disturbances to which such fracases might lead.[12]

The problems besetting the harm principle as a principle of criminalization have led some to put forward instead a 'sovereignty principle'.[13] According to this principle, a liberal state ought to proscribe conduct that interferes with the freedom of persons to act as they please within the domain (their bodies and acquired things) over which their choices rightfully rule even if such conduct is harmless. Conversely, a liberal state ought not to proscribe exercises of free choice that are consistent with the equal freedom of others to act on their choices just because the conduct risks or happens to inflict harm. The sovereignty principle thus condemns the conduct of the interfering do-gooder and the fastidious burglar, while generally leaving alone the person whose application of force was consented to. True, there are limits to the effectiveness of victim consent as a defence to an accusation of wrongdoing; for example, someone's consent to another's killing her is legally ineffective to exculpate the killer of murder. However, this example

[12] *R v Jobidon* [1991] 2 SCR 714.
[13] Ripstein, 'Beyond the Harm Principle' (n 9) 215; the term is taken from Mill, *On Liberty* (n 2) 13.

does not embarrass the sovereignty principle, for the principle itself generates the limit. One cannot effectively consent to homicide because one cannot treat as an optional interest the very freedom whose foundational status in a liberal legal order explains why consent normally absolves from wrongdoing.

Nevertheless, the sovereignty principle is also inadequate as a stand-alone principle of criminalization in a liberal polity. This is so because it generates a narrowly tort-centred view of crime according to which crimes are that species of trespass to the person or property distinguished by the presence of a criminal level of fault – intention or recklessness, however understood. Thus the conduct element of the crime is paradigmatically limited to conduct constituting a civil wrong. This is not to say that the sovereignty principle cannot countenance crimes outside the paradigm case. It can – for the following reason. The liberty and property rights the sovereignty principle protects are realized only through enforcement agencies and adjudicative institutions. Therefore, it is also a crime under the sovereignty principle knowingly to interfere with the impartial working of the administration of justice and to evade one's duty to share its fiscal burden. Still, this is a tort-centred view of criminal conduct, because interferences with liberty and property form the core of criminality, from which all other criminal conduct radiates. On this view, conduct that does not directly or indirectly engage the right against interferences with liberty and property cannot be criminalized.

What, it may be asked, does the tort-centred view of criminality leave out that a full liberal theory of criminality would want in? In a word, harm. While inflicting or risking harm is neither necessary nor sufficient for criminality, still, some kinds of harming intuitively seem eligible for criminalization even where the sovereignty principle is not violated. Below, I discuss a few examples in some detail. Here, I simply mention an obvious one: consensual transactions in harmful narcotics one cannot consume temperately. While controversy exists as to whether the use of harmful narcotics is properly criminalized, the unlicensed *distribution* of harmful drugs is almost universally punished with severe deprivations of liberty even though no usurping of another's rightful sovereignty over his body or possessions is involved, either directly or indirectly. It is punished, presumably, because it gravely harms others' capability to exercise moral independence in directing their lives.[14]

If neither the harm principle nor the sovereignty principle taken alone seems an adequate principle of criminalization, where do we turn? Of course, we could say that a liberal theory of criminalization generates two principles – a harm principle and a sovereignty principle – and leave matters at that. But that conclusion would hardly be satisfying. If the tort-centred view of crime cannot reach the public evil of drug trafficking and if the harm principle cannot capture the wrong of harmless trespass, then combining them to produce a desired result is mere ad hocery. Furthermore, neither the sovereignty principle nor the harm principle

[14] There is, of course, a respectable harm-based argument for decriminalizing use and treating addiction as a public health concern for which the regulated dispensation of drugs is a better solution.

reaches conduct that is also universally and uncontroversially punished as a crime, usually by the severest penalty available in a legal system.

I mean the conduct called treason. One kind of treason – sometimes called high treason – can be brought within the harm principle or even within the penumbra of the sovereignty principle. It consists in levying war against one's country or giving aid and comfort to an enemy of one's country. Such conduct risks harm to national independence, and, insofar as it involves the subversive acting out of a unilateral judgement about one's government's illegitimacy, such conduct also impliedly opposes the idea of a civil order within which alone sovereignty rights are realized. However, this initial thought sits uncomfortably with the existence of a less serious form of treason consisting in the disclosure of the military or scientific secrets of one's country to a foreign country, whether or not that country is an enemy.[15] This kind of treason cannot be brought within the sovereignty principle because it does not imply a maxim opposed to civil order; nor can it easily be brought within the harm principle, because no risk of harm to institutions is required nor is any consideration given to whether disclosure of the information was likely to produce more cosmopolitan benefit than domestic harm. What second degree treason seems to target is disloyalty to one's country pure and simple – seeking to benefit another country at the expense of the interests of one's own, however slight that interest. In doing so, this lesser form of treason illuminates the nature of high treason as well, revealing it as a crime, not of sedition against civil order in the abstract, but of aggravated disloyalty to *this* civil order in particular. But while unreachable by either the sovereignty or the harm principle, treason is conduct that a political authority ought to criminalize for reasons I spell out below. To reach this kind of conduct, one needs to invoke a third principle of criminalization, which I call the community principle.

A unified liberal theory of criminalization will integrate within a coherent account of criminal conduct the sovereignty principle, the harm principle and the community principle. So far, I have merely foreshadowed these principles with inconclusive appeals to intuition and common practice. I must now derive them from a properly theoretical account of criminal conduct for a liberal polity. In what follows I sketch the outlines of such an account, the main points of which can be summarized as follows.

The question for a liberal theory of criminalization is one about the duties of a liberal political authority toward its subjects. One must ask: what conduct does a liberal political authority have a duty to outlaw given the ends for the sake of which its authority is recognized? Here I assume that the final end of a liberal political authority is the legally realized dignity or end-status of the individual agent. The argument for this view was first articulated by Rousseau. Giving legal

[15] The Espionage Act 18 USC s 793 criminalizes the gathering or disclosure of information respecting national defense with intent either to injure the US or to benefit a foreign (not necessarily enemy) nation. 'Treason' is limited by Art 3 of the US Constitution to levying war against the US or giving aid and comfort to an enemy. In Canada, assisting an enemy is high treason, whereas divulging military or scientific secrets to a foreign state is treason; Criminal Code RSC 1985 ch C-46 s 46.

reality to the human being's claim to dignity must be the liberal state's justifying end, because that is the only end for the sake of which free agents can recognize state authority without loss to the independence that is theirs prior to authority.[16] So, a liberal state has a duty, on whose discharge its valid authority depends, to outlaw (or, if possible, otherwise prevent) conduct antithetical to human dignity. There are, however, several conceptions of what confers dignity on the human individual, and each of these conceptions generates its own principle for determining what conduct is inconsistent with dignity. The several principles are not, however, competitive; rather, they complement one another and, in doing so, they form a whole whose unifying idea is the political life sufficient for dignity. No principle taken alone suffices for dignity, yet each is necessary and together they are jointly sufficient. So we will have a plurality of principles of criminalization united under the idea of a political life sufficient for dignity. If one wishes a name for the overarching principle of criminalization suggested by this theory, we can call it the dignity principle.

III DIGNITY AS FORMAL AGENCY

Let me now distinguish three specific conceptions of dignity, beginning with what I take dignity as a general concept to mean. By dignity I mean a quality or attribute of a being distinguishing it from the realm of instrumental values – that is, from everything that can be a means for another's purpose without also being an end for others. So a being with dignity, as Kant famously argued, is one that cannot exist solely as a means. Such a being bears a final worth or end-status obliging all those capable of obligations to respect it as an end, at least by forbearing from forcing it to serve their own desires or goals.

According to a tradition of political theory beginning with Rousseau and Kant, a human individual possesses dignity in that sense by virtue of its capacity for free choice – that is, for not being determined to act in accordance with laws of nature. Because the human individual can reject outright the motivations supplied by natural instinct, it follows that, when it acts pursuant to a biological end, it does so not out of natural necessity, but out of its own free choice to adopt the biological end as the aim of its action. And this possibility of free choice confers dignity on the human individual because it reveals a self that, as necessarily presupposed in the choice of all optional ends, is itself a necessary, universal and objective end. Whatever particular values human agents choose to pursue, they necessarily act for the sake of the self that chooses, and so the self is an end unconditioned by preference or cultural opinion. And an unconditioned end commands unconditional respect. Thus, whatever one might think of the character in whom the capacity for free choice is individuated, one must respect the capacity itself by

[16] JJ Rousseau, *The Social Contract and Discourses*, trans GDH Cole (London, Dent, 1968) 12.

forbearing from interfering with its exercise so long as its exercise respects the same capacity of other agents.

I call this view of what confers dignity on the human being the formal agency conception of dignity. Let me specify the kinds of conduct this conception of dignity considers wrong as an offence to dignity and that are therefore eligible for criminalization. By 'conduct eligible for criminalization' I mean (in this section) conduct that requires only a culpable mind to be conduct that a state ordered to human dignity ought to criminalize. The kind of conduct that requires only a culpable mind to be conduct that a state ordered to human dignity ought to criminalize is conduct that unjustifiably infringes free agency's right to respect (wrongful conduct). A state recognized for the sake of human dignity has a duty to criminalize willful right-infringements because such actions give force to a principle which, if valid, would mean that human beings as such are without dignity. Specifically, these actions embody a claim of special dignity entitling the claimant to treat other agents as means. They therefore deny the end-status involved in free agency that a state recognized for the sake of human dignity is duty bound to realize. A state that did not practically oppose this denial would be one that, contrary to its duty, allowed it to stand.[17]

The conception of dignity as formal agency generates what I earlier called the sovereignty principle of criminalization. Because dignity inheres only in the self's capacity for free choice, the kinds of conduct that can offend dignity and that are thus wrongful are correspondingly confined to those that negate freedom of choice by subjecting the will to the laws of physical force. Conduct is wrongful and therefore eligible for criminalization if, without justification, it destroys the capacity for free choice by destroying the life it requires, if it applies physical force to an agent so as to prevent an exercise of the capacity in voluntary motion, or if it interferes with the capacity by coercing (by threats of wrongful force) the agent's choice of ends. So wrongful killing, battery, assault and forcible confinement are the core kinds of conduct upon which the formal agency conception of dignity builds criminal conduct.

What about interferences (entries, takings) with the things one has publicly manifested a will to control? Certainly, takings of things in one's bodily possession are applications of force to the body that are eligible for criminalization under the narrow compass of wrongs described in the previous paragraph. They are batteries or assaults. But what about takings of things – or entries upon land – that one has physically acquired by means that publicly signal an intention to control but that are not attached to one's body?

For the formalist framework, the dignity the self can reasonably claim inheres in its being an end necessarily presupposed in the choice of all relative values and

[17] A civil remedy may restore wrongdoer and victim to equal dignity, but the willful wrongdoer implicitly denied the normative force of equal dignity, and nothing in the civil remedy answers his challenge. Only by visiting upon the willful wrongdoer the rightless condition that his conduct implied does the state demonstrate the nemesis of his claim of special dignity and so vindicate equality as the sole basis of valid dignity claims. I discuss this at greater in length in A Brudner, *Punishment and Freedom* (Oxford, Oxford University Press, 2009) 45–55, 76–80.

in its thus being a final end – that for the sake of which all action is performed. Its being a final end, however, implies that entities lacking the capacity for free choice and therefore lacking end-status are rightfully means for free agents. But then once something is actually reduced to a means by action signalling an intent to control it, the thing rightfully belongs to the self that reduced it; for it now embodies and realizes that self's end-status vis-à-vis the thing. Because end-status becomes objectively real in possessing the thing, the thing is objectively *for* the end that possessed it. Hence its belonging to the self is now conceptually independent of the physical act of continuing possession. If, therefore, someone takes it, fraudulently acquires it, or enters it without permission, he converts to himself an embodiment of another's dignity; and since dignity is real only as realized, he does something inconsistent with the reality of another's dignity. Accordingly, unconsented-to takings of things and entries into land or buildings acquired by another are actions eligible for criminalization under the formalist framework as theft, fraud and criminal trespass. Similarly, unconsented-to damage to things in another's rightful possession is proscribable as criminal mischief if (and only if) the damage is connected to an interference with ownership – that is, to a trespass.

Such, then, are the core crimes of the formal agency framework. They can be boiled down to trespass to the person and trespass to property. As already intimated, however, the formalist framework also criminalizes conduct outside the core that nonetheless indirectly engages the dignity of the freely choosing agent. Because realized dignity requires legislative, executive and adjudicative institutions that work reliably and impartially, it is a crime under a legally institutionalized formalist framework to interfere with the fair working of these institutions, to evade shouldering one's share of their fiscal burden, to disobey or otherwise show disrespect for a court, or to rebel, or incite rebellion, against the public authority.

The upshot is that the formalist conception of human dignity yields a criminal code only a tree conservationist could love. A thin conception of the bearer of dignity generates a correspondingly slim criminal code. Consider the kinds of conduct to whose criminality the formalist framework is blind but whose place in the criminal codes of liberal legal orders is beyond dispute.

First, one cannot derive from the formalist framework the offence of criminal negligence causing bodily harm or damage to property. This is so because formalism protects only the relation of self-rule and ownership of things; it does not protect the agent's welfare as such, for it understands by welfare nothing but the satisfaction of subjective preferences no dignified end may (outside contract) be coerced to promote. Even the agent's interests in life, health and bodily integrity are treated as contingent preferences; for if these interests are just natural interests, and if the capacity for free choice is a capacity to detach oneself from interests given by nature, then one's attachment to these interests is optional and subjective. So, provided one does not apply physical force to the agent or impede its free movement or coerce it by threats of wrongful force or usurp its sovereignty over its rightful possessions, one may act in the world in utter disregard for the likely impact of one's action on the health, bodily integrity, or material resources of others.

No doubt, careless disregard causing harm to the body or to possessions damages things over which the agent is sovereign and can, in the extreme case, render sovereignty unreal. A king whose country has been destroyed is a king of nothing no matter whether the destruction was by invasion or by a border state's accidental release of toxic gas. Still, non-trespassory harming is not something the formal agency paradigm can view as wrong. If the harmdoer's action does not impliedly usurp the victim's sovereignty, then the harm caused is only harm to the victim's resources; it is not the material sign of a challenge to his *ownership*. Outside trespass, therefore, such harm can be regarded as a setback to welfare and nothing more. But formalism recognizes no entitlement (outside contract) to another's concern for one's welfare, and so it recognizes no duty of care breach of which causing harm could be wrongful. Nor can formalism see the criminality of conduct that, independently of an assault, recklessly threatens harm without causing it – for example, impaired or otherwise dangerous driving, reckless handling of explosives and so on.

Secondly, one cannot derive from the formalist framework the criminality of blackmail. The blackmailer, after all, does not sway his victim by threatening him with an action that formalism considers wrong. Such a threat would be coercive and hence reachable by formalism as robbery or assault. Rather, the specific difference of blackmail is the lawfulness of the threatened action. If the blackmailer's information is true, he is at liberty to disseminate it, and yet blackmail can be committed by threatening to divulge the truth. Accordingly, the blackmailer's threat can just as well be characterized as an offer to sell his liberty to divulge the information for a price the victim may or may not think is worthwhile. True, the blackmailer puts his victim to a choice between evils that did not exist apart from the blackmailer's proposal. Rather than taking advantage of a prior situation of need, he himself creates it; and so his action may be said to interfere with another agent's power to act from ends it authors and values. But formalism recognizes no right to act from self-valued ends, only a right to act from ends one freely chooses.

Thirdly, one cannot derive from formalism the crime of trafficking in narcotics. Assuming fully consensual transactions, the harm produced by this practice is inflicted by nothing the formalist framework can view as wrong. It might be argued that abetting addiction makes one accessory to another's wrong of destroying the dignity involved in his freedom of choice, analogous to abetting suicide. But no, the freedom of choice foundational to formalism is too metaphysical to be negated even by physical addiction. Assuming an awake self-consciousness, an 'irresistible' impulse is for formalism always an extremely powerful impulse one did not resist, though one could have; for the free will is just the capacity to resist.

It is natural to ask why – given the poverty of formalism's intellectual resources to account for obvious crimes – one should pay any regard to it. Surely, one might object, the few crimes that it can account for are also explicable within theoretical frameworks with far more explanatory power because built on more robust conceptions of the self and of the kinds of conduct that can offend its dignity. Why, then, should we bother with a framework that is based on so impoverished a conception of the self?

The simple answer is that the formalist paradigm, while insufficient for dignity, is a necessary part of a life complete in dignity because it guarantees to the human being what no other theoretical framework can. Specifically, it guarantees a partner capable of recognizing dignity. Let me explain.

An adequate theory of what confers dignity on the human being must identify not only something that can plausibly *claim* dignity, but also something whose dignity-claim can possibly be validated as real, for unrealizable claims are mere conceits or fantasies. On this score, the poverty of formalism's conception of the self turns out to be *richesse*, because that conception generates a criterion of dignity so undemanding as to let all agents in. All that formalism requires for dignified status is the capacity for free choice. Any more discriminating criterion – one that, for example, made living well or living autonomously the badge of dignity – would create a distinction between those who had achieved the status and those who had not, the former an aristocracy, the latter an inferior class. But an aristocracy has privileges relative to its subordinates; it cannot have rights in relation to them, because subordinates cannot deliver the independent recognition of a dignity-claim that validates the claim as a right. Dignity-claims require addressees who are equal to, and independent of, the claimant, for only such addressees are free others qualified to validate the claim by recognizing it. So, valid dignity-claims can exist only among free and equal agents. The formalist framework, precisely because of its thin conception of the bearer of dignity, ensures what more robust conceptions cannot – namely, the equal dignity of human beings and hence the possibility of rights as publicly valid claims to dignity. But since rights so understood are essential to dignity, the formalist paradigm that alone generates them is essential to a life sufficient for dignity.

That said, it is also the case that the formalist self is too frail to carry on its own the dignity it claims, and a diagnosis of its weakness will point to a more robust self whose dignity can be denied by more ways than trespass.

IV DIGNITY AS REAL AUTONOMY

If the capacity for free choice were a sufficient basis of dignity, then an agent who, to avoid the less desirable option of starvation, freely chose to enter into a contract of employment under which, in return for subsistence, she provides sexual services to third parties procured by the employer would do nothing incompatible with her dignity. Yet such a relationship involves the non-reciprocal use of one person's life for another's ends that we call exploitation. By exploitation I mean to include, besides outright slavery (where the exploited are rightless), a condition where one human being lives exclusively for the sake of the self-projected ends of another, who does not reciprocate service to any self-projected end of the first. By a self-projected end I mean one that is not adopted immediately from nature but that is chosen on deliberation as to what pursuits and activities would give point to one's life. Thus a pimp might provide a wage to his prostitute and might be enjoined from doing to her what formalism views as wrongs against her dignity; but if the pimp provides nothing beyond what is necessary to sustain the prostitute's life, and if the prostitute's waking life is spent toiling for the pimp's projects, then the prostitute's life is a means to her employer's self-projected ends and not to her own. She thus lives solely for another's purposes – and this quite compatibly with the dignity resting on freedom of choice. Within the formalist framework, as Hegel and Marx taught, there is no norm against the exploitation of labour within the context of voluntary, limited-term contracts.

The fact that, under formalism's criterion of dignity, one's existence could be unilaterally a means for another's ends shows that the criterion of dignity must be redefined so as to rule out this possibility. That is to say, the very end-status of the self that orders the formalist framework demands a move towards a conception of dignity richer than the formalist one, since formalism cannot criticize a relation in which an agent voluntarily chooses unilaterally to live for another agent rather than starve, beg, or steal.

The permissibility of labour exploitation is ruled out by a definition of the human being's *full* dignity as depending, not only on a capacity for free choice, but also on the realized potential (contained in this capacity) for living one's life in accordance with ends one autonomously projects. This conception of dignity envisages a self richer than the formalist one, for the self now embraces the life plan it deliberatively sets for itself as well as the scheme of ends belonging to this plan. The self is now conceived, not simply as an agent, but also as a moral subject – as an agency that generates goals and commitments, orders them into a scheme of priorities and strives to embody them in a life reflecting its own authorship. The moral subject's dignity consists in its realizing this ideal of an autonomous life. So, on this criterion of dignity, respect for end-status includes not only respect for the capacity for free choice, but also *concern* for another's realization of his potential for living from self-authored ends insofar as this is compatible with concern for the realization of one's own projects. And a public authority recognized for the sake of dignity will now have an obligation not only to protect liberty against interferences, but also to promote the autonomy of all its subjects.

The autonomy conception of full dignity generates the harm principle. This is so because the autonomy conception yields for the first time a public conception of harm that the legal order can recognize without forcing dignified ends to serve others' particular aversions. Under the formal agency conception, harm consisted in setbacks to subjective preferences. Since any value could be rejected by the free will, all were optional; none were values necessarily common to agents and so no setbacks to those values could be punished compatibly with the end-status of agents. Under the autonomy conception of dignity, by contrast, there are common goods because autonomy is a goal one has to achieve, and its achievement requires material supports – life, bodily integrity, health, property, a good reputation – in short what we can call agency goods. Public harms are harms to agency goods. They are setbacks to interests in things everyone needs to form and live out a self-authored life plan. So a public authority whose end is full dignity has a duty to prevent such setbacks whether or not the source of the threat is a trespass.[18]

In this context, however, the state's duty to prevent harm to agency goods is not an unqualified duty to criminalize consciously harmful or risky conduct involving no right-infringement; for criminalization is only one means of prevention, and the formalist right to liberty demands that it be resorted to last. Here the duty to prevent is a duty to outlaw only if no means less restrictive of liberty would be effective.[19] Within the real autonomy paradigm, conduct eligible for criminalization is conduct a liberal state ought to criminalize subject to that condition and to the requirement of culpable mind. So, unauthorized possession of dangerous objects (weapons, burglary tools) is conduct eligible for criminalization, as is drunk or otherwise dangerous driving. So too is the unlicensed distribution of addictive substances that take control of one's life and that cannot be consumed temperately. These kinds of conduct cannot be called wrong, for they infringe no one's right; nonetheless they are bad in a legally relevant sense because they threaten the conditions of attaining the good – real autonomy.

In the formalist paradigm, no free agent had a coercive duty of care for the welfare of another, because welfare signified nothing but the satisfaction of subjective preferences. Thus, provided one did not trespass on another's rightful domain, one could act in the world in total disregard for the impact of one's action on another's health or material resources. In the real autonomy paradigm, this is no longer the case. Because full dignity depends on one's having the resources to pursue a self-valued life plan, a being with end-status has a right to another agent's care for its agency goods insofar as this right is compatible with the other's legitimate concern for realizing her own projects. Reconciling a legal duty of care for another's agency goods with appropriate self-regard is the burden of the civil law of negligence, which limits the duty of care through the concepts of a foreseeable victim, unreasonable risk and harm within the ambit of the wrongful risk. If harm-causing negligent conduct is performed with knowledge of the unreasonableness of the risk, then it signifies a claim of liberty unbounded by the rights of others to reasonable care and therewith a practical denial of the human dignity the right embodies. A state recognized for the sake of human dignity has a duty to oppose that practical denial by denouncing it as criminal negligence.

Further, the problem that blackmail posed for the formal agency conception of dignity is resolved by the autonomy conception. Whereas free choice is exercised

[18] For a similar derivation of the harm principle, see Raz, 'Autonomy, Toleration, and the Harm Principle' (n 8) 326–31.

[19] This qualification does not apply where law vindicates rights, for if intentional right violations were not as a rule punished, the denial of rights implicit in such conduct would be left unanswered.

whether the agent considers the course chosen good for him or merely the lesser evil, autonomy is realized only through shaping one's life in accordance with self-valued ends. And so if a being with end-status has a qualified right to another agent's concern for the material conditions of its autonomy, then it has a qualified right against another agent's directly subverting its autonomy by imposing a choice between evils it did not previously face. The qualification concerns the values the blackmailer must threaten. Not just any imposed choice of evils counts as blackmail, for otherwise the offeror's liberty would be hostage to what the offeree considers unacceptably bad. Rather, the offeror must impose a choice between evils that are objective in the sense that they involve the loss of an agency good – for example, 'your wealth or your reputation'. Because the wrong consists simply in imposing on a moral subject a choice between objective evils, it is irrelevant whether the evil threatened would be a wrongful act by the blackmailer.

V DIGNITY IN COMMUNITY

The autonomy conception of dignity criminalizes much that the formal conception cannot, but it still cannot reach conduct that is proscribed without much fuss by almost all liberal legal orders of the twenty-first century. Because this framework sees full dignity as inhering in the realized potential for living according to self-authored ends, it has no intellectual resources for criticizing the content of aims autonomously chosen. While recognizing agency goods as material supports for the autonomous life, the real autonomy framework recognizes no specific commitments or relationships as being a constitutive part of the dignified life for all moral subjects, however variable their life plans might otherwise be; and so it cannot regard some ways of life as richer or poorer in dignity than others. Thus, provided the moral subject commits no wrong against other moral subjects and threatens no harm to their agency goods, it may pursue whatever life plan it chooses, even if that plan includes having sex with animals, sex for money, incestuous sex with consenting adults, or many wives.

Nor can the formal agency or real autonomy conceptions of dignity recognize loyalty to country as a constitutive element of the fully dignified life; and so they cannot see the crime in acts of disloyalty threatening no harm to the state's legal and political institutions. Certainly, they cannot see the crime in relatively harmless acts of disloyalty meant to advance the cause of human dignity globally – those of Daniel Ellsberg or Anat Kamm, for example. No doubt the autonomy framework regards citizenship of some state as necessary to dignity because citizenship is political self-rule rather than subordination to another. Hence, interfering with the activities of citizenship – for example, by intimidating voters or engaging in electoral fraud – is conduct the autonomy framework can reach. However, this framework cannot regard loyalty to a *particular* country as a necessary part of the fully dignified life; for it, a patriotic life is merely one life choice among others, neither better nor worse than a life of cosmopolitan indifference to one's country. Accordingly, the autonomy paradigm cannot see the crime in acts of disloyalty to one's country threatening no harm to institutions supportive of autonomy or likely to produce more cosmopolitan benefit than domestic harm.

Now, if the rights and entitlements generated by the formal agency and real autonomy frameworks sufficed for dignity, then conduct that neither paradigm could see as wrong or bad would be unreachable by a public authority whose end is dignity. Criminalizing such conduct would thus itself be a wrong to free persons, for it would entail punishing people for adhering to ways of life that are simply different from the paths chosen by the social majority. Disapproval of the conduct could spring only from one's contrary preferences and opinions; it could not be articulated with public reasons all dignity claiming beings could accept. As a consequence, all morals offences would be creatures of what Herbert Hart called 'legal moralism' – the embodiment in law of critically untested moral prejudice.[20]

Yet the frameworks discussed so far provide an insufficient realization of dignity for the following reason. Together, these frameworks generate what is necessary for the realized dignity of human individuals considered as generic agents and moral subjects. They realize a dignity claimed on the basis of a capacity for free choice and a potential for real autonomy, which capabilities group diverse individuals under the categories of Agent and Moral Subject within which their differences are erased. These frameworks do not, however, acknowledge the worth of determinate characters. By determinate character I mean that unique organization of natural gifts, inclinations, habits, memories, past deeds, aims, convictions, commitments, etc that bears a proper name. Determinate characters obtain recognition as having special worth in marital or quasi-marital relationships, in families, in civil associations and through the public honours bestowed by a particular country on its patriots and heroes. However, neither the dignity resting on the capacity for free choice nor that inhering in realized autonomy captures the rational importance of the determinate individual. According to these conceptions of dignity, the determinate individual has no importance.

Is the recognized worth of the individual character necessary for the life sufficient for dignity? Earlier, we showed that a system of entitlements geared to realized autonomy is a necessary supplement to a system of rights ordered to formal agency by showing how, left to its own resources, the formalist framework could countenance a relationship (there, of labour exploitation) inconsistent with the agent's end-status, which was its own fundamental principle. Something along the same lines can be shown here.

If individuals have moral worth only as undifferentiated capacities for free choice and potentials for real autonomy, then I have a legal and moral duty always to treat beings with these features as equal in worth, showing no favouritism for myself or for my close kin regardless of circumstances. Thus, in a conflict between

[20] HLA Hart, *Law, Liberty and Morality* (New York, Vintage, 1963) 6.

an innocent stranger's life and that of my own or a close family member's, I may not be excused from criminal liability or from moral blame for preferring myself, my wife, or my child at the other's expense. For example, I would have no legal defence for killing someone who I know is involuntarily posing an imminent threat to my life – a sleepwalker, let us say, who sees me as a wild beast and is about to shoot me – even if I could not stop him otherwise. Since he is an innocent, the formalist right of self-defence, a right only against wrongful threats (those bearing on one's dignity), has no application. Moreover, since our lives are of equal worth, no other reason justifies my preferring my life to his. And since no dignity principle has yet emerged to excuse an unjustified killing, I am defenceless. I might be pardoned for murder at the discretion of the political sovereign or have my sentence mercifully reduced, but I would not have a right against being punished. Nor would I have a moral excuse for saving my own child rather than two who are not my own when I cannot do both. I must be inhumanly impartial towards the worth of human lives, treating my life and that of my intimates as having no more importance for me than they would have for a disinterested observer or judge.

The inability of the formalist and real autonomy frameworks to countenance partiality to self or to one's own in such situations is a problem for them. This is so because the fundamental end for both frameworks is the dignity of the *individual* human being, and yet both end up valuing the individual for generic human capabilities in which his or her individuality is effaced. Thus, the realized worth of the agent and moral subject implies the insignificance of the determinate individual whose dignity was supposed to rest securely on its agency and real autonomy. We see this aporetic outcome in several settings: in distributive justice schemes that, purporting to respect the separateness of persons, allow rewards to their natural advantages only to the extent justified by the collective welfare; in public health insurance schemes that prohibit a private option on egalitarian grounds though people die waiting for treatment; and in the jurisprudence of necessity and duress, where self-preference in kill-or-die scenarios is looked upon as 'frailty', to which the law may or may not condescend.

This does not mean, however, that the frameworks based on universal agency must be jettisoned in favour of one ordered to the recognition of particularity. These frameworks are essential to a life sufficient for dignity, for they alone provide a system of universal rights and entitlements based on generic human capacities – a system that cannot exist except among agents who are free and equal irrespective of where their loyalties lie and above all disparities of station or character. We know what life would be like without such a system. Whereas the state that confirms the dignity of metaphysical subjects and nothing more is a universal idea of reason juxtaposed to the diversity of living cultures, those that confirm the worth of determinate characters are particular, local and real. This means that, without a system of universal rights based on generic human capabilities, outsiders are juridically defenceless against domination by the local communities in whose midst they find themselves. Taken as exhaustive, a framework ordered to the recognition of particularity entails a chauvinistic regard for family, tribe and nation, the primacy of which entitles each to enslave the different.

Accordingly, the two frameworks discussed so far require supplementing, not replacing, by one ordered to loyalty to one's own. The public life sufficient for dignity protects the sovereignty rights of free agents, secures the agency goods of moral subjects and fosters the relationships within which the worth of determinate characters is validated – families, civil associations and political community. And so now we come to the reason why a political authority whose end is the full dignity of the human individual ought to criminalize treason.

Because the life sufficient for dignity is possible only within a political community that enforces sovereignty rights, protects agency goods against harm and promotes associations wherein determinate individuals are valued, the political community that fulfils these requirements also fulfils the kind of being who claims dignity and desires its reality. Such a community is thus a common good, not a burdensome imposition on an agent conceived as morally self-sufficient. Therefore, each member can acknowledge a special attachment to the particular political community that fulfils all its dignitary needs, while the political community can reciprocally value the member's patriotic allegiance as that which confirms the community as an end and realizes it as a living unit distinct from others. Because the life sufficient for human dignity is life within a political unit requiring the loyalty of its members to exist as a unit, a public authority committed to dignity has a duty to educate humanitarians to become patriots by outlawing disloyal actions without regard to whether their cosmopolitan benefits would outweigh harm to the national interest.[21]

So understood, the law of treason belongs to a class of what may be called signpost laws. A signpost law is instructive rather than repressive; it points 'this way' to the life sufficient for dignity. Signpost laws have a unique function. Whereas formalist law vindicates personal sovereignty rights and autonomy law prevents harm to agency goods, signpost laws guide determinate characters towards relationships constituent of the life sufficient for dignity. They do this by warning them away from seductive alternatives unproductive of dignity, while (treason aside) punishing only those who would normalize the alternative by practising it in the public domain.

Most signpost laws deal with sexual and family life. A public authority whose end is the life sufficient for dignity has a duty to guide its citizens into the kind of private relationships within which a human being's claim to worth as a determinate character can be satisfyingly validated. These relationships evince the same form of mutual recognition between equals that underlies valid right claims among free agents, but here the parties to the relationship are living characters rather than metaphysical subjects. A political authority ordered to full dignity has a duty to announce the relationships that, conforming to this pattern, are worth

[21] It follows that the duty to criminalize disloyalty to country is conditional on the country's deserving loyalty.

validating for characters and that it will therefore publicly recognize as alone generating enforceable entitlements and obligations. And it has a duty to manifest disapproval of relationships that, while imitating worth-producing ones, fail to evince the form of mutual recognition between free and equal selves that can alone generate valid worth claims. Sex between a human being and an animal can never validate a human being. Sex for money validates no one's special worth. Erotic relationships between close relatives fail to validate characters because family members are generally preferred for their being family members, not for their characters, or at least the non-discerning affection diminishes the value of any discerning one; in short, objective confirmation of one's worth as a character must come from the unbiased choice of one who begins as a stranger. Polygamy too is dysfunctional from the standpoint of worth validation because one who unilaterally recognizes the special worth of another not only suppresses her self-worth, but also fails to deliver a satisfying validation to her spouse; while an arrangement allowing everyone to have multiple spouses generates special worth for no one. Committed homosexual relationships, by contrast, involve the mutual recognition of equals no less than do committed heterosexual ones.[22]

However, when sexual offences are put on an instructive footing, the duty to enact such offences weakens, for there is no logical necessity for state education to take the form of criminalization and punishment. What we can say is this. Given its duty to guide characters toward worth-validating relationships, the liberal state has a duty (subject to a further qualification I'll mention in a moment) to prohibit 'wayward' conduct unless there exist better or equally effective means of discharging its background duty to guide. In the case of adult incest and polygamy, for example, it may be enough for the state to refuse to solemnize or otherwise recognize such unions without punishing the few who harmlessly and consensually practice polygamy or incest. This is a question for prudential judgement in specific cultural circumstances.

Because a public authority ordered to the fully dignified life must respect the moral independence of its members, it can never enact a signpost law for the benefit of characters without regard for constraints that protect the moral subject's freedom to pursue the good as it sees it. Moral paternalism is out of bounds for a liberal state – even for one that has progressed from neutrality vis-à-vis ways of life to a commitment to the ways constituent of the life complete in dignity. The type of constraint may vary with the kind of law. In the case of bestiality and

[22] A law forbidding adultery (disloyalty to spouse) is also a signpost warning married individuals away from conduct incompatible with a relationship whose exclusivity and elevation above transient passion are what make it worth validating. However, adultery is more complicated than other morals offences, because it sometimes (when the parties to the extra-marital relationship are in love) indicates that the married relationship the adultery law seeks to protect has ceased to be worth validating and that the partnership ought to dissolve. At the same time, however, marriage ought not to dissolve, for the family is an institution giving reality to the worth of determinate characters only insofar as it is secure. A law stigmatizing all adulterers regardless of circumstances would unfairly lump together those caught in this dilemma with those whose infidelity is motivated by an appetite for sexual variety; while a law singling out only those disloyal to a good marriage would call for judgements no outside observer could make. For this reason (and perhaps others), adultery is best left to natural punishment.

incest laws, the balance between expressive disapprobation and moral autonomy is struck by enforcing the law passively (no roaming or intrusive vice squads) and with token penalties, in the case of prostitution laws by prohibiting only public solicitation, in the case of anti-pornography laws by zoning the public display and in the case of polygamy laws by exempting from punishment those for whom consensual polygamy is a matter of conscience. Accordingly, it does not follow from the liberal injunction against moral paternalism that the state may not legislate a view of suitable relationships and reserve public spaces for the relationships it endorses. Provided it defends its view with public (dignity) reasons, a liberal state may favour certain kinds of relationship on perfectionist grounds. What it may not do is punish people for harmlessly acting out errant views in private, where there is no danger of the anomaly's crowding out the norm.

VI CONCLUSION

Liberal theories of criminalization tend to be either intellectually rigorous but one-sided or many-sided but lacking in rigour. Mill's theory derives from a comprehensive understanding of the good, yet his harm principle fails to reach harmless conduct inconsistent with the person's sovereignty over its body and possessions. Kant's theory proceeds from a systematic conception of the right, yet his sovereignty principle cannot reach consensual transactions subversive of the autonomous life nor even negligently caused setbacks to welfare. And neither theory will hold up a 'dead-end' sign to guide people away from harmless relationships between consenting adults unproductive of dignity. Efforts to reach all conduct that seems intuitively wrong, bad, or wayward yield a plurality of principles but typically lack a unifying theory.

A theory of criminalization drawn, as this one is, from Hegel's philosophy of law reconciles system with many-sidedness. The key idea is that of a plurality of normative systems, each ordered to its own conception of human dignity and yielding its own principle of criminalization, yet mutually complementary within the political life sufficient for dignity. Here a sovereignty principle, a harm principle and a community principle cohere within a whole governed by a dignity principle. The result is a reconciliation of foes even Isaiah might have thought improbable. In the life sufficient for dignity, Kant dwells with Mill, Hart lies down with Devlin and Hegel leads them.

4

Obscenity without Borders

LESLIE GREEN*

I GLOBAL PORNOGRAPHY

Digital technologies are changing our lives. For example, we can now more easily publish, access, read and collect essays about obscenity law. No need for a trek to the library, you can do it all from the comfort of home and late into the night, if that is where your inclinations take you. Alas, the same goes for the *targets* of obscenity law. No need for a furtive trip to the bookshop or video store, to say nothing of that relic of another century, the Adult Movie Theatre. You can get it online. You can even become a producer. A video camera, a subject, a laptop and an internet connection are all you need. But while you are at it consider that something else has become a lot easier too. You can also become a criminal. A lot of explicit material online – no one knows how much – is obscene in some jurisdiction or other. One mouse-click could amount to the offence of 'accessing' forbidden material; a second click could be 'possessing' or even 'making' pornography. The law will presume you know what is forbidden and what is not. Its presumptions might surprise you. What can be lawfully made, distributed and viewed in a public library in Niagara Falls, New York can bring criminal penalties and the harshest of stigma if accessed in the privacy of a home in Niagara Falls, Ontario, just across the bridge.[1] And don't think yourself safe if you block all images to the computer. Text is forbidden as well, for instance when it can be construed as counselling certain sex offences. Maybe before reading any further you ought to hire a lawyer.

Whether these or other obscenity offences can be justified is famously controversial. The arguments are almost painfully familiar. On the one hand, prohibiting words or images that could shape attitudes might help prevent serious wrongs:

* Thanks to Chris Essert, Denise Réaume and François Tanguay-Renaud for illuminating criticisms.

[1] In Canada, but not in the United States, child pornography need not represent actual children: purely imaginary representations, including cartoons, computer-generated images, etc are all banned, and it is an offence to 'access' them online, whether or not one goes on to 'possess' them: Criminal Code RSC 1985 ch C-46, s 163.1(6), (7). Contrast 18 USC § 2256(8); and see *Ashcroft v Free Speech Coalition* [2002] 535 US 234.

cleaning up the moral environment might reduce sexual assaults, sex discrimination, sexual exploitation and even sex-neutral forms of indignity and brutality. On the other hand, such prohibitions come at a cost to our collective interest in free expression and our individual interest in personal liberty; they open doors to official petty-mindedness, stupidity and abuse; they intentionally harm those convicted. It may be reckless to trade assured costs for merely speculative benefits. Perhaps when important rights are at stake we shouldn't even be engaged in such accounting. Or is it artificial to think of this as a collision between rights and goals? Could there not be rights on both sides of the equation and might we not be derelict if we did not try to minimize the overall violations? Others say worries about rights and results are misplaced: the main job of criminal law is to send a loud and clear message that some things are just wrong. They have opponents who agree with the principle but caution that before we fire up the denunciation-machine we should have a credible explanation of why the conduct in question *is* wrong. That will not be difficult when we are thinking of things like forcing people to participate in the production or consumption of obscene materials, or subjecting them to exploitation when their participation is willing. But those are normally prohibited by other criminal and regulatory offences. Moreover, if there is a further obscenity-specific wrong that needs denouncing should we not first find out whether that could be accomplished in other, less hazardous, ways?

Any justification for the law of obscenity would have to resolve these issues and others. This chapter hardly addresses them. Its ambition is limited. It identifies particular features of obscenity in a digital environment and explores how far some influential views about their significance hold good. The results will be relevant to many of the debates just mentioned though they may not settle them. Even so, they take us to some interesting, and under-examined, moral and conceptual problems about obscenity.

The features I have in mind are these:

(a) Accessibility

Obscene materials are now as available as an internet connection. In the absence of censorship and filtering, what is available to people in Toronto and Teheran would be more or less the same. Once published online, the original creator's control over further dissemination of the material is in practice limited. In the absence of effective age-verification or other means of access-control any image or text available to adults will be available to minors. It will also be available at any time: the online shop has no closing hours. It is these dimensions of wide accessibility that suggest we live in a world of obscenity without borders.

(b) Affordability

A lot of pornography is produced for profit, a point sometimes thought to have moral relevance. The internet has certainly created new opportunities in the business and increased total output. That has probably driven down prices. What is more, a large quantity (if not proportion) of online pornography is available at zero price: it is a free good. Some comes as a loss-leader to induce purchases; some is commercial material freely shared, often in violation of copyright. But alongside this there is also homemade and not-for-profit material including what we might call 'auto-pornography', explicit pictures of the very person posting them, made public not to enrich but to entice or to indulge exhibitionist fantasies.[2] The emergence of cheap and free pornography has effects of different sorts. As the price of an ordinary good falls more tends to be consumed; here, more consumption may be worse consumption. On the other hand, the wider variety of genres makes it rash to generalize about the intentions with which obscene materials are made or circulated.[3] If it is correct that pornography produced as a commercial venture merits less protection, it is relevant that there is also a lot of pornography produced or disseminated for other reasons.

(c) Variety

Because the barriers to entry in this market are so low, niche interests are easily served. Most tastes are probably catered for, and it must by now be obvious even to the least inquisitive that the range of human sexual appetites is astonishing. What is more, the internet not only provides a means of serving minority pleasures, it provides a means of connecting those who enjoy them. Just as the tiny group of people who share a passion for the (tiny) repertoire for the baroque *flûte d'amour* can finally link up, so too can the (tiny?) group of men who are aroused by scenes of genital piercing. Online, there is something for everyone.

Taking all that into account, where do things stand obscenity-wise, post-internet? Getting worse? Getting better? Possibly just different? Off hand, it would seem that there are vectors operating in several directions and their sum will be hard to figure. This becomes evident when we give weight not only to the changes commonly reckoned as negative, but to those we might consider positive. The internet makes pornographic materials available; it makes attacks on those

[2] A borderline genre, current among some youth, is 'sexting' – sending their friends and acquaintances salacious messages or naked pictures of themselves. These too risk falling afoul of obscenity laws: M Brunker, '"Sexting" Surprise: Teens Face Child Porn Charges' (15 Jan 2009) *MSNBC.COM*, online: www.msnbc.msn.com/id/28679588/. For a discussion see DT Sacco, R Argudin, J Maguire and K Tallon, 'Sexting: Youth Practices and Legal Implications' (Cambridge MA, Berkman Center for Internet and Society at Harvard University, 2010).

[3] Eric Barendt asserts, 'Almost all [pornography] is written simply to make money. Its publishers have no intention of communicating information or opinions. While even the shabbiest politician wants his audience to believe what he has to say or to vote for him, a porn merchant simply wants consumers to purchase his wares. As far as he is concerned they can throw them away afterwards': E Barendt, *Freedom of Speech* (Oxford, Oxford University Press, 2005) 360. I know of no evidence that 'almost all' online material is made simply to make money. In any case, Barendt's analogy is inexact. The *shabbiest* politician is the one who simply wants voters to elect him; he doesn't care whether they believe anything he says in his manifesto, and as far as he is concerned they can throw it away afterwards. Sound principles of free expression protect his venal speech as well as his disposable manifesto.

materials available, too. There are pornographic websites; there are Men-Against-Pornography websites. There are websites where one can report to the authorities the websites one finds objectionable. Justice Stevens put the point romantically, but not inaccurately:

> Through the use of chat rooms, any person with a phone line can become a town crier with a voice that resonates farther than it could from any soapbox. Through the use of Web pages, mail exploders, and newsgroups, the same individual can become a pamphleteer.[4]

While the internet makes obscenity more available and affordable, it does the same for pornography that adults can lawfully purchase, including adults whose isolation or circumstances offer them little other access to sexual pleasure. In cyberspace people with frightening fetishes can now connect with others; so can the young lesbian in Pond Inlet, Nunavut who thinks she is The Only One. Reflection on this might leave us hesitant or ambivalent: the liberty to produce or consume sexually explicit materials can produce both bad and good; some of the bad comes part and parcel with the good; in the digital media it may be difficult for the law to find a reliable or fair way to separate them.

Ambivalence has not been the main reaction of contemporary writers, however. Rae Langton's confidence is more typical:

> Now, with the growth of the internet, pornography has become almost mainstream. Policies for which there was, and officially is, consensus, have gradually been eroded with the ubiquity of pornography. Material is increasingly violent and non-consensual. There is more child pornography. Back then [before the Internet], the question was whether some people could have the option of having pornography. Now we are in the world of pornography, unless we opt out. Pornography invades every web-accessing household that has not the will and resources to block it.[5]

This, Langton claims, is the moral reality of obscenity without borders, yet philosophers and lawyers continue to argue as if the issue is whether a civilized society can tolerate *Hustler* or *Freshmen* or, more fantastically, *Fanny Hill* or *The Well of Loneliness.* The history of obscenity law includes causes and campaigns that were disastrously misguided, but if Langton's assessment is correct those are barely relevant to thinking about how we should now respond to the invasive and dangerous material all around us. She thinks that what we actually encounter online is worse than ever and that it tends to cross every barricade we set up.

A second line of thought focuses not on the borders that obscenity breaches, but on the borders that demarcate obscenity. In all legal systems with which I am familiar, whether something is criminally obscene turns on whether it violates

[4] *Reno v American Civil Liberties Union* 521 US 844 (1997).

[5] R Langton, *Sexual Solipsism: Philosophical Essays on Pornography and Objectification* (Oxford, Oxford University Press, 2009) 19–20. Langton uses 'pornography' as a stipulative term narrower than the ordinary concept of pornography. I have argued against the stipulation elsewhere: L Green, 'Pornographies' (2000) 8 *Journal of Political Philosophy* 27. In the present chapter, 'obscenity' means sexually explicit materials potentially subject to criminal sanction and 'pornography' means what it ordinarily means.

certain community norms. In the United States these norms are primarily local ones. Back in 1995, Dennis Chiu suggested that, 'Since the Internet lacks meaningful geographical boundaries, the "contemporary community standard" is misplaced'.[6] The essential idea is that it is anachronistic to devolve on local communities the power to determine what counts as obscene when these communities are all virtually connected and are becoming more alike: a national standard would be more sensible. On the timeline of the internet, 1995 was the Mesozoic Era. But this issue has not been settled in the aeons that followed. Courts and commentators remain perplexed about what constitutes the criterial 'community' for the purposes of defining obscenity and unsure what its standards are.[7] Pamela Paul offers a diagnosis: she thinks the globalization of pornography has left these norms as vaporous as the ether:

> The Internet has thoroughly internationalized the world of pornography so that to speak of international borders with regard to production and tastes is increasingly meaningless. Americans consume Japanese *manga* (cartoon) pornography and gaze at nude photos of Dutch women. Russian woman are virtually exported around the world . . . Men in Canada can visit the brothels of Bangkok from the comfort of their home offices.[8]

Now this is a difficult passage to construe. Is Paul troubled by the loss of indigenous erotic cultures? I doubt it. (Why should a broadening of Americans' interests to include foreign erotica and women be a matter for regret, let alone prevention?) I shall assume that what she really finds alarming is that the arrival of Japanese sex cartoons (and everything else) on the doorstep not only undermines the distinctiveness of local norms, it encourages a permissive free-for-all. And this tends to spread. Global markets require colonization by the class whose interests they serve. As *The Communist Manifesto* puts it, the bourgeoisie 'must nestle everywhere, settle everywhere, establish connexions everywhere'.[9] In the anti-obscenity manifestos, it is pornographers who are represented nestling, settling and establishing connections everywhere with the result that, morally speaking, 'all that is solid melts into air'.[10]

Well, there is no doubt some exaggeration in all that, but it does capture a prevalent fear. It is a fear with consequences. In addition to renewed calls for a crackdown, it has inspired two trends in obscenity law.[11] The first is the addition

[6] DW Chiu, 'Obscenity on the Internet: Local Community Standards for Obscenity are Unworkable on the Information Superhighway' (1995) 36 *Santa Clara Law Review* 185, 211–17.

[7] In *Ashcroft v ACLU* 535 US 564 586 (2002), a plurality of the US Supreme Court held the 'contemporary community standards' test is still relevant. For doubts and discussion see B Boyce, 'Obscenity and Community Standards' (2008) 33 *Yale Journal of International Law* 299.

[8] P Paul, *Pornified: How Pornography is Damaging our Lives, our Relationships, and our Families* (New York, Times Books, 2005) 59.

[9] K Marx and F Engels, *Manifesto of the Communist Party*, ch 1.

[10] ibid.

[11] I am not here suggesting this is their aim. Langton is officially agnostic on the merits of criminal prohibitions on obscenity (*Sexual Solipsism* (n 5) 119) and, at points anyway, Paul seems to declare herself opposed to them (*Pornified* (n 8) 256). If this is so, it becomes hard to understand what argument these authors think they are having with 'liberals'. A liberal view is not one that considers

to the general prohibitions on obscenity of further bans on particular content thought to be virulent in digital transmission. Child pornography offences are now pretty much universal, and in some places legislation or judicial interpretation have also singled out other materials for attention, for example, what is in the UK called 'extreme pornography'. A second change bears on the locus of prohibition. Now that obscene images and text easily cross national boundaries, the law tries to stop them where they are consumed, including in libraries, business offices and private homes. Thus there has been a shift in attention from the supply-side to the demand-side and a greater emphasis on consumption offences ranging from simple possession all the way down to crimes of merely accessing or viewing texts or images.[12] Taking consumers as the main target has a tactical advantage for prosecutors: it cuts through jurisdictional problems (since the place in which the materials were made or sold is often beyond the reach of the local police and courts). It also resonates with the popular hypothesis that one can throttle production and demand for something considered harmful by criminalizing its consumption – by 'shutting down the market', as the slogan has it.

So these anxieties about the loss of borders are not just theoretical; they had, and continue to have, practical effects. How far they are based in reality turns on empirical questions we cannot resolve here. We might, however, hope to make progress on some theoretical issues that arise in their wake. I am going to focus on two prompted by anxiety about borders. I will start with the concern just outlined: that the permeability of borders adversely affects the character of community norms relevant to obscenity. Then I return to the question of whether the fact of greater availability amounts to a wrongful invasion of public or private space. In both cases the story turns out to be more complex than the critics allow.

II BORDERS OF OBSCENITY

As long as we have a concept of obscenity it will have borders. There will, for example, be features that roughly divide the obscene from the ugly and the obscene from the silly. But no one is fretting about the possibility that we might lose our concept of obscenity; they are concerned that what has for long been a constituent of its borders in law, that is, a test based on a certain kind of community standards, is becoming unworkable or incoherent. We will face this issue in section III. Here, I deflect a threshold objection that would limit the relevance of that discussion. An express community standards test for obscenity is distinctive of American law, and so is the idea that the relevant standards are local ones. Are Chiu, Paul and others fixated on a parochial problem of American doctrine? They

pornography morally benign; it is one that holds that people should have the liberty, free from criminal and other serious sanctions, to produce and use (some) pornography.

[12] For some pertinent worries about the English scheme, see J Rowbottom, 'Obscenity Laws and the Internet: Targeting the Supply and Demand' [2006] *Criminal Law Review* 97.

are not. Even places that do not have an express community standards test nonetheless rely on community standards in the determination of what is obscene.

The law's idea of obscenity is not the ordinary one that extends to obscene violence, obscene wealth and obscene government cuts.[13] If the law is troubled by any of this it is not under the heading of obscenity. The only obscenity that matters to law is the sexual sort: mainly artifacts within the province of what used to be called 'hard core pornography'. Chiu's mention of local community standards refers to the way that province was demarcated in *Miller v California*, where it was held that an artifact is criminally obscene only if an average person, considering it as a whole, would find that it pruriently describes or depicts sexual conduct in a patently offensive way as judged by 'contemporary community standards'.[14] These standards are both temporally-limited ('contemporary') and socially-limited ('community') because they are determined by what people have thought, said and done about pornography. This marks them as positive norms, in this case communal norms whose existence depends on the practice of a group of people over some stretch of time and in some place or context.[15] Not all norms are like this. In addition to positive norms there are non-positive norms that do not similarly depend on human actions and decisions. Here is one: 'From premises of the form "*if p then q*," and "*p*," infer "*q*."' That is a norm of logic or, perhaps, of reasoning. Its existence does not depend on common practice and if anyone should ask, 'Who laid down that norm?' or 'When did it come into force?' we would answer, 'Don't be silly; it's not that sort of norm'.[16]

There are non-positive norms also in morality. HLA Hart called these norms of 'critical' or 'ideal' morality in order to distinguish them from the norms of 'social morality' actually practised in a particular group.[17] It is, of course, a standard feature of a society's practised morality that, according to itself, it ought morally to be practised (though it may contain toleration norms of the form 'we should not compel people to practise all of our norms that ought to be practised'). 'Never torture people', is a norm of critical morality. This norm is valid because it is supported by sound moral reasons, not because it is generally practised and not, in my view anyway, because someone laid it down. It could come to be widely

[13] The *Oxford English Dictionary* gives, in addition to 'Offensively or grossly indecent; lewd', and 'Offending against moral principles, repugnant; repulsive, foul, loathsome', '. . . (of a price, sum of money, etc) ridiculously or offensively high': *Oxford English Dictionary* 3rd edn (Oxford, Oxford University Press, 2009) online: ezproxy.ouls.ox.ac.uk:2277/Entry/129823.

[14] More exactly, '(a) whether "the average person, applying contemporary community standards" would find that the work, taken as a whole, appeals to the prurient interest; (b) whether the work depicts or describes, in a patently offensive way, sexual conduct specifically defined by the applicable state law; and (c) whether the work, taken as a whole, lacks serious literary, artistic, political, or scientific value'. *Miller v California* 413 US 15 (1973) (internal citation omitted) building on *Roth v United States* 354 US 476 (1957).

[15] Exactly what is required for a norm N to be communally practised in S is a complicated matter. At a minimum it includes a substantial degree of non-coincidental use of N by members of S to guide or assess their own conduct or that of others. That loose statement skates over thorny issues in general jurisprudence, but it will be adequate for present purposes.

[16] People did notice it and name it ('*modus ponens*') but those are not acts of norm creation.

[17] HLA Hart, *Law, Liberty and Morality* (Stanford CA, Stanford University Press, 1963) 17–24.

practised, and that would be a good thing. Many norms of critical morality should be practised as social norms, but they do not disappear from the moral horizon if they are not. Unlike the inference-norm and the torture-norm, the obscenity-norm set out in *Miller* is positive and practice-dependent: it was not only noticed but laid down in that case and then applied on many other occasions. Like any positive norm, the *Miller* norm could disappear from the legal horizon. Chiu thinks it should disappear by repeal since he considers it ill-adapted to a world of obscenity without borders. It could also disappear in a different way, by falling into disorder or disuse. Paul presumably thinks something like that is a result of the fact that distinctions among tastes and attitudes have become 'meaningless'. If it is senseless to say that something is regarded as out of bounds around here, and if obscenity still exists, then it must be demarcated in some other way. If that is correct, legislators and courts are certainly keeping up a brave face, for such norms remain key to the law's notion of obscenity in the US and elsewhere.

Consider the work of Canadian courts struggling to construe Parliament's ban on materials whose dominant characteristic is the 'undue exploitation of sex'.[18] Many interpretations have been offered over the years but none of them has detached obscenity from communal norms. In the *Towne Cinema* case, for example, Chief Justice Dickson said

> it is a standard of *tolerance*, not taste, that is relevant. What matters is not what Canadians think is right for themselves to see. What matters is what Canadians would not abide other Canadians seeing because it would be beyond the contemporary Canadian standard of tolerance to allow them to see it.[19]

This is not the same as the *Miller* test, but it is sensitive nonetheless to community norms. Canadians might be able to abide other Canadians seeing prurient materials that have no redeeming value at all. *Patent offensiveness* and *intolerability* pick out different properties. However, *intolerability* does not draw the line at the sort of images or texts that it would be proper or reasonable to tolerate, but at what Canadians would not abide others seeing. Perfectly tolerable materials, morally speaking, can be banned under that test – Canadians might actually be unwilling to put up with them. Hence, contrary to what that court thought (and perhaps hoped) a tolerability test is not necessarily more generous than one based on taste. That depends on whether members of the community tend to be more or less censorious of others than they are of themselves. (The 'revisors' who administered the *Index Librorum Prohibitorum* thought it permissible to read books themselves they thought it intolerable for others to see. Their standard of taste was more liberal than their standard of tolerance.)

The role of communal norms lies near the surface of *Miller* and *Towne Cinema*; sometimes it is buried deeper below. In the widely-discussed case of *R v Butler*, the

[18] 'For the purposes of this Act, any publication a dominant characteristic of which is the undue exploitation of sex, or of sex and any one or more of the following subjects, namely, crime, horror, cruelty and violence, shall be deemed to be obscene'. Criminal Code s.159 (8).

[19] *Towne Cinema Theatres Ltd v The Queen* [1985] 1 SCR 494 [34].

Canadian court held that consensually produced and consumed material can be criminally obscene if it is 'degrading and dehumanizing' – and it can be degrading and dehumanizing (and thus 'undue' in its exploitation of sex) 'not because it offends against morals but because it is perceived by public opinion to be harmful to society, particularly women'.[20] The court seemed to think that reference to harm-perception removes communal norms from the picture – perhaps that is why Justice Sopinka said that no longer would anything be held obscene merely 'because it offends against morals'. But this is misleading. To insulate obscenity from communal norms, the test would have to be not what is 'perceived by public opinion' to be harmful but what is harmful. 'Harm' is itself a moral notion, and public opinion's view of what is harmful is part of its positive morality. If the law was trying to track actual harm then public perceptions, legislative proclamations, values formally expressed in our institutions and so on, would count less, or at any rate differently, than they now do.[21]

My final specimen is from the UK.[22] The Obscene Publications Act 1959, provides by section 1(1) that 'an article shall be deemed to be obscene' if 'taken as a whole' it 'tends to deprave and corrupt persons who are likely . . . to read it'. Here, it is not enough for material to offend or to be thought intolerable or degrading, it must tend to deprave or corrupt (which can include worsening the depravation and corruption of those already depraved and corrupted). This is, again, a different standard and a different criterial audience (those likely to read it). Yet we still see the force of communal norms as soon as we ask what it is to be *depraved or corrupted.* The works of Ayn Rand ostentatiously glorify the vices of selfishness and greed and in doing so tend to deprave and corrupt those likely to read them. Their publishers would never be charged let alone convicted in English courts. Why not? Have the courts read Mandeville and been persuaded that private vices can be public virtues? Unlikely. The explanation is obvious. The courts know that selfishness, greed, etc are in England not regarded as vices of the relevant kind; they are not taken to constitute the kind of depravity the community cares about in this context, and the law attends to what the community actually cares about. Britain's recent experiment with obscenity law continues this well-entrenched tradition. The 2008 Criminal Justice and Immigration Act adds a new offence that includes possession of 'extreme pornographic images', defined as those which might reasonably have been thought to have been produced principally for sexual arousal and which realistically portray any of a list of acts that are also 'grossly offensive, disgusting or otherwise of an obscene character'.[23] It is too early to

[20] R v Butler [1992] 1 SCR 452.

[21] I am not denying that actual harm may be dependent on the existence of positive norms. My point is that this ruling failed to exclude the sort of dependence that allows harmless material to be counted as obscene. This is obscured by the court's tendency to defer to Parliament on the question of what is harmful and then to equate that with some aspect of 'public perception'.

[22] Obscene Publications Act 1959, ch 66; Obscene Publications Act 1964, ch 7.

[23] Here is the list: '(a) an act which threatens a person's life, (b) an act which results, or is likely to result, in serious injury to a person's anus, breasts or genitals, (c) an act which involves or appears to involve sexual interference with a human corpse, (d) a person performing or appearing to perform an

know how often the courts will have to determine what is grossly offensive or disgusting. That inquiry may be eclipsed by the list of prohibited images. But when they do need to determine it they will apply communal norms. There is so much social morality built up around these notions that to launch a free-ranging inquiry into what is really offensive or truly disgusting would be a major departure. I am not saying that the courts lack the power to set off on it or that it would be wrong for them to try. The concepts of harm, offence, disgust, prurience, or tolerability might all become untethered from communal norms. But to this point they have not, and that is precisely why pundits, politicians and philosophers are so concerned about the effects of digital media on those norms.

III WHY AND HOW COMMUNITY STANDARDS MATTER

So obscenity as the law understands it is bounded by community norms. These norms are said to be threatened. We need to get clear about how that could happen. We also need to get clear about why it might matter. For is it not true that to use the criminal law merely to enforce communal norms, without regard to their merits, is an objectionable form of legal moralism? It was sensitivity to that objection that led Justice Sopinka to reassure Canadians that the courts would not be enforcing popular moral standards if they judge what is obscene by relying on what Canadians perceive to be harmful. That was incorrect. But our argument to that conclusion might seem to suggest that obscenity is *inevitably* moralistic in the present pejorative sense. If so, we might be relieved to read that there are no longer any community norms to be enforced. It cannot be denied that such norms may be immoral or pointless, and that those who violate them may, as far as that violation goes, have done nothing wrong.[24] Yet we deliberately treat people convicted of obscenity offences as if they are wrongdoers, as if their conduct is not merely unconventional but actually immoral. To treat those whose conduct is morally innocent as wrongdoers is to wrong them. It is a 'lying imputation of their responsibility and guilt'[25] and the stigma and hard treatment meted out to them is not a penalty but a wrong.

The assumption that obscenity law *must* be moralistic is too hasty. There are ways of using communal norms that attract this objection and ways that do not. On the standard view, a legal moralist is one who holds that the criminal sanction should be used in order to uphold the actual moral standards of a community, as such, without regard to their content, whether or not they are sound, just or wise.

act of intercourse or oral sex with an animal (whether dead or alive)': Criminal Justice and Immigration Act 2008, s 63. Acts of type (a) are, of course, commonly and realistically portrayed in films, computer and video games and so on. The Act prohibits possession of such images only if they occur in pornography.

[24] I am bracketing how far everyone has a duty to obey a legally valid but morally unacceptable law. That is a further question.

[25] A Quinton, 'On Punishment' (1954) 14 *Analysis* 134, 137.

This idea has long been out of favour, and not only among liberals.[26] When popular, it allowed much sexism, homophobia, prudishness and superstition into the law. Legal philosophers associate that sort of moralism with the views of the English judge Patrick Devlin.[27] The reasons Devlin gives for enforcing community standards through criminal law (for instance, that it is necessary in order prevent social disintegration) are pretty unconvincing.[28] Whether his arguments are actually meant to sustain the conclusion that there is value in conformity as such is open to doubt.[29] Be that as it may, there are ways to account for the place of positive communal standards in the law, including the law of obscenity, that are not moralistic in the sense endorsed by (or pinned on) Lord Devlin.

First, there are reasons flowing from the requirements of legality and the functions of law. If we are going to presume that people know what is forbidden then considerations of fairness and the rule of law suggest we ought not to let the law's idea of obscenity stray too far from what a subject of ordinary integrity and intelligence might be able to figure out on his own, without specialist guidance. One of the places subjects look for assistance with that is in what is commonly practised in their society. (This is the root of the law's frequent appeals to 'common sense' standards in various areas.) Secondly, if we are going to charge officials with administering authoritative decisions, they need some way to identify what those require that does not involve deliberation about the merits of the issues that those decisions purport to resolve.[30] These two forces are constant in the life of the law. They explain its obsessive attention to positive standards to determine what the law is and also its tendency to look first to positive *non-legal* standards when necessary in applying and interpreting the law. Of course, law has other functions too – for one thing, it needs to settle disputes that authority has left open. But even here judges who acknowledge they are breaking fresh ground often hasten to claim that they are doing so by applying standards that have some social, if non-legal, foundation.[31]

[26] A liberal case is argued in Hart, *Law, Liberty and Morality* (n 17); but for a note of (partial) agreement from a non-liberal perspective see R George, *Making Men Moral* (Oxford, Oxford University Press, 1995) 51–60.

[27] P Devlin, *The Enforcement of Morals* (Oxford, Oxford University Press, 1965).

[28] Hart, *Law, Liberty and Morality* (n 17).

[29] Devlin says that 'the moral judgements of a society' are *not* determined by the quantity of support, but by judgments of 'the reasonable man', the 'man in the street' and, most interestingly, 'the man in the jury-box': *The Enforcement of Morals* (n 27) 38–39. While some of these might just be proxies for a concordance of opinion, his favorite jury metaphor is different. It is that the relevant norms are only those whose breach would, after discussion, unanimously engender 'intolerance, indignation, and disgust': *The Enforcement of Morals* (n 27) 40. There is a difference between nearly instinctual feelings of indignation and disgust and the feelings that would arise *after discussion* in a certain *hypothetical* (jury-style) situation. The latter may have no roots in existing social morality, hence the room for doubt about the extent of Devlin's moralism.

[30] For one influential argument to this conclusion, see J Raz, 'Authority, Law and Morality' in his *Ethics in the Public Domain: Essays in the Morality of Law and Politics* rev edn (Oxford, Oxford University Press, 1994) 210–37.

[31] Here is a typical example: 'The court must apply positive law. But judges' sense of the moral answer to a question, or the justice of the case, has been one of the great shaping forces of the common law. What may count in a situation of difficulty and uncertainty is not the subjective view of the judge but what he reasonably believes that the ordinary citizen would regard as right': *McFarlane and Another v Tayside Health Board* [1999] 4 All ER 961, 977–78 (Lord Steyn).

There is also a second reason for thinking that the presence of communal norms in obscenity law may not be a symptom of moralism. The law's aim may not be to secure conformity to those norms. I will assume that it would be moralistic for the law to require conformity to social morality as an end, without regard to its merits. In this case, what I am going to call the *primary* legal norm requires compliance with a communal norm and such compliance is what the authorities aim to achieve. The primary norm P appears before the exclamation mark below:

(1) P: Let no one breach CN!

This seems to be what people have in mind when they say it is moralistic to compel conformity to social morality *as such*. But this is not the only possible set-up. It may be that the authorities do not aim at producing conformity to CN, not as an end and not as a means either. They may intend to produce conformity to a *non-positive* moral norm because and to the extent they take it to be sound. To do that, they enact a positive legal norm that provides for incentives, clarity and other supports for the primary non-positive norm. It may also be that other conduct, here and now, constitutes or counts as or expresses conformity to the primary legal norm. For example, we want people to respect others and, here and now, sticking out one's tongue at them is a sign of disrespect. Assume this is true only because that gesture has settled into a communal norm with that meaning. (That gesture could just as well have been a sign of respect.) Thus, we get something like this:

(2) P′: Let no one disrespect others!*
*L: Breach of CN constitutes disrespect for others.

Notice that CN no longer appears before the exclamation mark: it is not the primary norm. What the issuer of directive P′ wants to achieve is that people should refrain from disrespecting others; as far as that is concerned it is neither here nor there to them that CN is involved. As it happens, however, CN helps specify what counts as disrespect here and now. Thus it appears after the asterisk in the *dependent* norm L, the complete function of which can only be understood in conjunction with the primary norm.[32] So we have two ways of looking at things. According to (1), the law treats breach of communal norms itself as a genuine wrong and it justifies this in moralistic terms. According to (2) it does not: CN gets its relevance only through its relationship to P' and the explanation for its presence has nothing to do with an interest in producing conformity to the widely or fervently held CN. It is simply a modality of avoiding disrespect for persons, which norm is enforced not because it is widely or fervently held, but because it is thought sound.

The payoff of the analysis is this. A directive like (1) is very vulnerable to whatever destabilizes CN. In the limiting case, where communal norms have really become evanescent or meaningless, it is pointless to aim at greater conformity to

[32] Here the secondary norm stands in a constitutive or expressive, not instrumental, relationship to the primary norm. I am adapting the term 'dependent norm' from H Kelsen, *Pure Theory of Law* (M Knight trans, Berkeley University Press, 1967) 54–58.

them. But in a situation like (2) that does not follow. Even without CN we still have a primary norm to conform to: we are to show no disrespect. (I offer this merely as one plausible example of the sort of thing non-moralistic obscenity laws might aim it; there are others as well.) Not being able to rely on CN, disrespect must now be differently specified. It will have to rely on whatever resources we get out of the concept of respect itself together with other relevant positive and non-positive norms to help specify it. What might those include? If there is conduct that would almost inevitably be counted as disrespectful in any society of people recognizably like ourselves, then it would be reasonable to regard it as disrespectful even if, as things stand, it not actually regulated by communal norms. This may be the realm of the universally obscene. So we can imagine an obscenity law that is not moralistic and that does not rely heavily on social morality to determine what is obscene. Even if community standards were under threat in the way Paul and others imagine, the law of obscenity could remain in working order.

None of this proves that actually existing obscenity law is not objectionably moralistic – quite a lot of it obviously is. Maybe it would be just as well if it fell into demise. Be that as it may, there is really no good reason to think we are facing a demise of communal norms in this area. It does not follow from the claims about internationalization and homogenization. Communal norms about what is harmful, or offensive, or depraved are not formed only by changes in the attitudes of pornography users *to pornography*; they depend also on their attitudes to other things. After all, these notions are widespread in moral thought and are shaped by many influences, including the views of friends, the press, preachers, politicians and many others offering normative guidance of one sort of another. And while norms are not honored *in* a breach, they are reinforced by critical responses *to* a breach, including the responses of those who apply and enforce the law. We are nowhere near a situation of private, let alone official, indifference to breaches in obscenity law, especially the law regulating things like child pornography or extreme pornography.

Talk of the meaninglessness of community standards is surely a hyperbolic way of complaining about some kind of decline in those standards. The community norms as shaped by the internet may be worse norms; people's loyalty to sound primary norms may be eroding. The increased availability of pornography might lead to further objectification of women; increases in consumption might destroy capacities for intimacy; its greater variety might include horrific tales and images that incite brutality. The claims are familiar and, as I forewarned, will not be examined here. I do, however, want to say something about the conjectural processes of 'mainstreaming' or 'normalizing' that play important roles in many of the causal stories on offer.

What someone has posted or made available online is no better evidence of what we take to be normal or mainstream than what someone has painted on a wall as graffiti; either may be unnoticed or unwelcome. More relevant is what people are searching for online. There is evidence that our communities are energetically searching for materials that could well be unlawful, and some have argued that this as an indication of what we are collectively prepared to permit or tolerate, or even what we regard as acceptable.[33] That too is a wild leap. All we can securely infer from this is that people search for the kind of thing they want to find: as Anscombe says, 'the primitive sign of wanting is trying to get'.[34] But people sometimes want things they feel or know it is wrong to want, and they can certainly want things that many *others* feel it is wrong for them to want. The Google search is a bit like the Ring of Gyges, whose power to render the wearer invisible revealed what people would do when freed from the supervision of social morality. It is a poor guide to the content of social morality, or to the degree of compliance with it when still under its supervision.

Perhaps the thought about normalization imagines only a looser connection. There does seem to be at least a rough relationship between the statistical deviancy of conduct and our willingness to believe in its moral deviancy, prominent in the familiar tendency – highly resistant to argument – that associates what is statistically normal with what is normal in an ideal sense. (Hence the old riposte: 'Heterosexuality isn't normal; it is just common'.) Discovering that some sexual scenarios are more commonly desired, at least in fantasy, than is generally acknowledged may have an effect of this kind. One of the results of the Kinsey reports was to make people realize, or at any rate believe, that sexual conduct previously considered so weird as to be non-existent is not so rare. In the revelations about the prevalence of oral sex and of homosexual conduct this may have had some influence on social morality. One wild flower on a hillside might look like a weed, but a whole drift of them looks like a garden. Still, this sort of normalization is far from guaranteed, and it does not always go unchallenged. (When some people noticed the drift of wild flowers, they hauled out the legislative lawnmower.)

All this is so much speculative sociology. The possibilities identified do however suggest that a greater amount of pornography online, or a greater variety in what is represented, or even its increased use, does not inevitably produce worse or more permissive norms. Nor does a shift in communal norms show that the community has been left without any norms in this area, or that it would be wrong or pointless to give weight to the (new) local norms. If the relevant norms are more homogeneous among communities than they used to be we can still sensibly ask 'what are the rules around here?' It only means that when we do ask it we are likely to get similar answers in different places. There may be sound objections to a situation in which people are highly mobile and yet held to unpredictably variable local standards. If anything, the homogenization of local community standards ought to mitigate these worries, not exaggerate them.

[33] For instance, in 2010, the marketing tool Google Insights showed that out of a possible 100 points, the normalized annual score for the search string '*free teen porn*' among all Canadian searchers was 76 out of 100 and the string '*mobile teen porn*' was among the top trending searches, up 180% over the year. For the suggestion that this sort of evidence ought to be put to juries, see S Creasy, 'Defending against a Charge of Obscenity in the Internet Age: How Google Searches can Illuminate *Miller's* "Contemporary Community Standards"' (2009–10) 26 *Georgia State University Law Review* 1029, 1052.

[34] GEM Anscombe, *Intention* (Oxford, Blackwell, 1957) 68.

IV BORDER SECURITY

So much for anxiety about the borders of obscenity itself; I turn now to the worry that pornography slips past every border control. As I noted in section I, this is thought to be a consequence of its availability, including current difficulties of effective control over access. I say 'current difficulties' because these matters change quickly. It is now rarely true that 'a person doesn't need to look for pornography, it just pops up'.[35] Nor is it really true that 'Pornography invades every web-accessing household that has not the will and resources to block it'.[36] There is always some host who invites it in and, nowadays, the resources to rescind that invitation are readily available and easily deployed. But there is no denying that some slips through.

What makes this slippage intolerable? The underlying point is that freedom of expression and personal liberty (what Mill calls the 'liberty of tastes and pursuits') are bilateral. People should be free to use pornography and also free not to use it, at their option. This is the basis of Langton's complaint that, 'Back then, the question was whether some people could have the option of having pornography. Now we are in the world of pornography, unless we opt out'.[37] It is *freedom from* pornography that is allegedly losing ground. I do not think we should interpret this as the sort of vulgar libertarianism that regards all border-crossings as appropriate points for veto or compensation. We have learned to tolerate junk mail, intrusive billboards, overheard phone conversations and noisy church bells. In many of these cases opting out is not even an option. What is it about unwelcome pornographic imagery that makes it different, that suggests that the proper response is either impermeable borders or outright prohibition? It is often asserted to be exceptionally harmful. I have mentioned but not here tested some arguments said to support that assertion. However, what about the influential idea that such texts or images are intolerable because they are radically *indecent*? In an awkward passage in *On Liberty*, JS Mill writes,

> there are many acts which, being directly injurious only to the agents themselves, ought not to be legally interdicted, but which, if done publicly, are a violation of good manners, and coming thus within the category of offences against others, may rightly be prohibited. Of this kind are offences against decency; on which it is unnecessary to dwell, the rather as they are only connected indirectly with our subject, the objection to publicity being equally strong in the case of many actions not in themselves condemnable, nor supposed to be.[38]

As I said, some argue that the availability of pornography is not injurious only to the agent himself; they contend that it is, or could possibly be, harmful to

[35] Paul, *Pornified* (n 8) 208. This is a remark by one of her informants.
[36] Langton, *Sexual Solipsism* (n 5) 19–20.
[37] See n 5.
[38] JS Mill, *On Liberty* in *Collected Works* (London, Routledge, 1963–91) vol xviii 295–96.

others by a variety of routes. But even if those arguments fail there remains the question whether it might nonetheless constitute a public indecency and thus fall under Mill's principle. Exactly what principle is that? Does Mill want to say that all serious violations of good manners are or could be harmful to others? That might follow from a version of what Joel Feinberg calls the 'offence principle'.[39] There are few constraints on what might cause grave offence to someone or other. People can become hot under the collar at the bare knowledge that others think or privately act in a way they find repugnant; public displays make them incandescent. It seems unlikely that most of those who are outraged by the availability of online pornography spend much time viewing it. It is the knowledge that it is freely available that they react to.[40] On this account, they are victims of serious offence, but protecting people from that leaves liberty vulnerable to the thin-skinned.

We should be hesitant to take Mill's argument as endorsing the offence principle. Not only is it starkly in tension with his professed harm principle, it is hard to see how enough scope for liberty survives it. Mill insists that we should not only tolerate but encourage conduct that takes people outside their comfort zones. He thinks that liberty must have this amplitude if it is to contribute to human development and progress and, ultimately, to general utility.

We have to hand, however, a better interpretation of the indecency argument, one based on the second role for communal norms as set out in section III. In some cases, a public violation of good manners may express contempt for, or constitutes a violation of, a primary norm that is not itself a directive to conform to the dictates of good manners. In this regard, it is suggestive that what Mill says is not that violations of manners become harmful whenever they are sufficiently *offensive to* others. He says that when committed in public certain otherwise innocent acts can violate manners and thus become 'offences *against* others'. Here, indecency strikes at others through the secondary norms that help fix what counts as a violation of a sound primary norm, such as the duty to respect people. This explains how a friend of personal liberty might consistently be an enemy of offensive wrongs.[41]

In the law, obscenity offences are not normally classed as a subset of indecency offences, but they do have overlapping justifications; they also share a special

[39] 'It is always a good reason in support of a proposed criminal prohibition that would probably be an effective way of preventing serious offense (as opposed to injury or harm) to persons other than the actor, and that it is probably a necessary means to that end . . .': J Feinberg, *Offense to Others* (Oxford, Oxford University Press, 1985) 1.

[40] As far as one can tell from her book, Pamela Paul's views about pornography are based on her reactions to what informants with bad experiences told her, together with a small survey that asked people about their views of the matter. We learn, for instance, that 'Four in ten eighteen- to twenty-four-year-olds believe pornography harms relationships between men and women . . .' (Paul, *Pornified* (n 8) 199). Among youth identifying as politically conservative this belief rises to a majority. (*Pornified*, 246) We learn nothing about the sort of pornography they had in mind, nor why their belief is correlated with their political views nor, importantly, whether it is true.

[41] For a related view see AP Simester and A von Hirsch, 'Rethinking the Offense Principle' (2002) 8 *Legal Theory* 269.

interest in sex, sexual organs and sexual activity. Why this obsession, given that so many other public violations of good manners can bring about offensive wrongs and yet are tolerated by the law? Part of the answer is that the law is wrong to be quite this obsessed with sex. Another part is that for us the sexual realm is one with a special connection to the intimate, so some degree of particular attention is warranted. Intimacies are a special locus of value and depend on the security of boundaries between what is shared (only) among intimates and what is generally available. We need to be able to choose the time of, place for and participants in our intimacies. This is at risk when an innocent act – say, consensual sex between adults – is performed in public. We do not want to confront people having sex in the aisles of the supermarket, not because that is peculiarly offensive, but because in co-opting us into an intimate context it is an offence *against* us. This is not to say that sexual conduct is only ever licit in private; that depends on the character of the conduct and on the extent to which it is capable of co-opting others into intimacy. It is essential to some homosexual conduct (kissing, for example) that it be permitted not only in the privacy of the home, but in public, even where many find it intolerably offensive. This is one of those cases where the long-run prospects of liberty require that people be coaxed and even pressured out of their comfort zones, a case where 'get over it' is the right response to public opprobrium.

When we think of unconsented engagement with pornography we will want to keep such distinctions in play. We will also need to keep clear about what sort of thing we have in mind, how significant the engagement is and what it takes to avoid it. Some cases are minor – glimpsing a pornographic magazine when buying one's newspaper or noticing a sex website when online. In most cases the answer here is to move on. Other encounters are far from minor. When they are repeated, or occur in contexts that one need not or cannot easily avoid (pin-ups in the office, or in the next locker at the gym) we may have a case for limiting liberty, whether by some kind of zoning or in serious cases by recourse to discrimination law, the law of sexual harassment and so on. Insofar as obscenity law has any role here, it will be an ancillary one.

Is there anything to be said in general about unconsented encounters with internet pornography? One thing that can be said is that on some dimensions it is actually *less* intrusive than its ancestors. To begin with the obvious: not everyone is online, and not all the time and when they are, the normal state of affairs is that they rarely see pornography (and even more rarely unlawful obscenity) unless they are looking for it. It is often remarked that in the internet world the nuisance aspect of obscenity is attenuated because the connection between distributor and consumer is narrowly drawn. The fibre optic cable and pair of copper wires deliver obscene material from one computer to another in ways that produce less direct fallout than did earlier forms of distribution.

Matters are very different if the ubiquity of obscene materials imposes greater risks of non-consensual *use.* We cannot afford to be delicate here. The standard use for pornography is, as Catherine MacKinnon rightly says, as 'masturbation material'.[42] That is not a use that can occur non-consensually merely by noticing pornography online or by reflecting on the fact that others are noticing it. Masturbation does not stand to online pornography as breathing stands to second-hand smoke. To get a case where people are made to use pornography without their consent we need to consider more awful scenarios, the most alarming of which involve people being forced into making pornography, or being forced into sex by users of pornography, or being forced in the context of unforced sex to use or watch the use of pornography. These are all serious wrongs that should be, and are, prohibited by law. Again, however, they are not prohibited by the law of obscenity, and if we repealed all obscenity laws they would still be offences.

We cannot leave this point without mention of a different possible downside to the privatization of consumption. At the point of access and especially use, pornography is less subject to informal social control than are other potentially risky things. Because its typical use is not only private but also *secret*, it is less easy to regulate by the informal social control of communal norms. Compare that with alcohol consumption. Persistent drunkenness is a vice; but it is worse persistently to get drunk alone than it is with friends. There are two reasons for this. A drink, or several, shared among friends blends pleasures of the palate with social disinhibition and community. That is why we call the participants 'social drinkers'. It is also relevant that the social drinker is subject to the supervision of social norms, be they as informal as a Friday night at the local or as exacting as a sherry party at the vice-chancellor's (to say nothing of wine drinking at Plato's *Symposium*). This is not true, or anyway less true, of pornography. (I hasten to add that I am not here advocating a pornographic parallel to social drinking.) So while digital delivery can reduce the nuisance and offensive wrongs of pornography it may give rise to new concerns about the abuse of self. Paul tells us that the internet 'is frequently referred to as the crack cocaine of pornography'.[43] If there is truth in that, we might worry that obscenity law is pornography's equivalent of the war on drugs. Violence strikes me as an unkind approach to any addiction. It is also often a pointless one.

V CONCLUSIONS

Like every medium that was at its inception blamed for moral decline – the printing press, the radio and especially television – the digital media are a mixed affair. Digital delivery has made pornography, including the subclass that amounts to obscenity, more available, more affordable and more variable than it ever has been. But suggestions that all this adds up to the evanescence or irrelevance of

[42] C MacKinnon, *Only Words* (Cambridge MA, Harvard University Press, 1993) 17.
[43] Paul, *Pornified* (n 8) 215.

borders are not plausible. The relevant community norms, including the norms about what counts as obscene, have possibly changed, though in what direction is unclear. In any case, unless the law of obscenity takes as its primary aim the enforcement of those norms, even dire scenarios envisioning an end of communal norms need not undermine either the law or the concept of obscenity. Other resources sustain it. Nor is it correct to think that online pornography is always more invasive than its ancestors. Many of its nuisance aspects have been attenuated with private delivery and although secret, and perhaps greater, consumption may bring other problems, a proliferation of offensive wrongs is not among them. Finally, non-consensual encounters with pornography are one thing, non-consensual use of pornography another. The law has resources to respond to the latter without relying on obscenity crimes. Whether it has the will to do so is an important question, but also a different one.

PART I

Rethinking the Philosophical Foundations of Substantive Domestic Criminal Law

B

New Perspectives on Exculpation

5

Understanding the Voluntary Act Principle

ANDREW BOTTERELL*

I. INTRODUCTION

The *actus reus* of a criminal offence typically consists of a number of elements. These elements may include the circumstances in which the so-called prohibited act takes place, together with any proscribed consequences. They may also include doctrines concerning factual and legal causation. According to the orthodox view of the *actus reus* requirement, however, criminal liability must in addition depend or be based on a voluntary act. For simplicity, I will call this the 'Voluntary Act Principle': criminal liability must be based on a voluntary act.

This principle has been articulated in a number of different ways. The Supreme Court of Canada, for example, has said that a 'fundamental principle of the criminal law is that no act can be a criminal offence unless it is performed or omitted voluntarily';[1] that an act 'must be the voluntary act of the accused for the *actus reus* to exist';[2] and that 'there can be no *actus reus* unless it is the result of a willing mind at liberty to make a definite choice or decision'.[3] On this view, the presence of a voluntary act is a necessary condition for criminal liability. Consequently, where there is no act, or where there is an act that is not performed voluntarily, there can be no criminal liability.

Something like the Voluntary Act Principle plays an important role in criminal law theory and doctrine; indeed, according to the Supreme Court of Canada it is 'a principle of fundamental justice that only voluntary conduct – behaviour that is the product of a free will and controlled body, unhindered by external constraints – should attract the penalty and stigma of criminal liability'.[4] All the same, the principle remains the subject of debate. There are at least two reasons for this: first, because the criminal law sometimes imposes liability in the absence of an

* Many thanks to Dennis Klimchuk and Carolyn McLeod for comments on a previous version of this chapter, and to Victor Tadros, my commentator at the 'Rethinking Criminal Law Theory' conference, for his extremely helpful questions and criticisms.

[1] *R v Stone* [1999] 2 SCR 290, 301.

[2] *R v Théroux* [1993] 2 SCR 5, 17.

[3] *R v King* [1962] SCR 746, 749 (Taschereau J).

[4] *R v Ruzic* [2001] 1 SCR 687 [47].

act; and second, because it remains controversial just what it means for an act to be performed voluntarily. There is therefore some reason to question whether the Voluntary Act Principle constitutes a fundamental principle of criminal law. All the same, the principle is surely gesturing towards something important about the necessary conditions for criminal liability. My goal is what follows is therefore to indicate what I think is right and what I think is wrong about the Voluntary Act Principle and to make some suggestions about how I think the principle should be interpreted and understood.

In broad outline, the chapter proceeds as follows. As indicated above, the Voluntary Act Principle has two components. The first part, *the act component*, claims that criminal liability can be imposed on an accused only for the performance of an act. The second part, *the voluntariness component*, claims that criminal liability can be imposed on an accused only for the *voluntary* performance of an act. I will argue that both components of the Voluntary Act Principle are in need of amendment. I will first indicate why I think the act component of the Voluntary Act Principle is in tension with the criminal law's own conception of the necessary conditions for criminal liability, and suggest a relatively simple fix. I will then argue that what is really at work in the voluntariness component of the Voluntary Act Principle is not so much voluntariness but rather what some authors have called the *practical agency condition*. In making my argument I will appeal to Harry Frankfurt's hierarchical account of the will in the hopes of illuminating what it means for an action to *belong to* an agent, and thus, what it means for an agent to be responsible for something she has done.

II. THE VOLUNTARY ACT PRINCIPLE

Let me begin with the claim that the Voluntary Act Principle is false because the criminal law sometimes imposes liability on an accused in the absence of an act. There are three familiar sorts of cases in which this can be seen to occur: in the case of omissions; in the case of possession offences; and in the case of attempts.

Consider first omissions. It is uncontroversial that criminal liability is sometimes imposed not for positive acts, but rather for failures to perform an act where there is a legal duty to do so. Section 219 of the Criminal Code[5] defines criminal negligence as follows:

> 219. (1) Every one is criminally negligent who
> (a) in doing anything, or
> (b) in omitting to do anything that it is his duty to do,
> shows wanton or reckless disregard for the lives or safety of other persons.

Although section 219 does not itself impose criminal liability on an accused (it merely defines what counts as criminal negligence), section 220 – Causing Death

[5] Criminal Code RSC 1985 ch C-46.

by Criminal Negligence and section 221 – Causing Bodily Harm by Criminal Negligence, do. Thus, an accused could be found guilty of causing death by criminal negligence if he showed wanton or reckless disregard for the lives of safety of others in omitting to do something that he has a legal duty to do, and where that omission was a significant contributing cause of the death of another human being.[6] In such a situation there is no act such that the accused is being held criminally liable for doing *it*. Rather, the accused is being held criminally liable for *failing* to act when he was under a duty to do so.[7] This seems to be in direct tension with the Voluntary Act Principle.

Consider next possession offences. According to section 4(3)(a) of the Criminal Code,

> 4.(3)(a) a person has anything in possession when he has it in his personal possession or knowingly
> (i) has it in the actual possession or custody of another person, or
> (ii) has it in any place, whether or not that place belongs to or is occupied by him,
> for the use of benefit of himself or of another person.

Again, although section 4(3)(a) does not itself impose liability – there is no Criminal Code offence of having something in one's possession – certain offences are offences because an accused has a prohibited thing or substance in her possession. For example, section 4(1) of the Controlled Drugs and Substances Act[8] (CDSA) states that, except as authorized under the regulations, no person shall possess a substance included in Schedule I (for example, opium and its derivatives), II (for example, cannabis and its derivates), or III (for example, amphetamines and their derivates) of the CDSA. But again, there is no particular act that an accused must do or perform in order for her to be found criminally liable under section 4(1) of the CDSA. She must simply have in her possession a prohibited substance. And as defined, the concept of possession does not require that the accused *do* any particular thing.

Interestingly, the Model Penal Code (MPC) suggests otherwise. According to it, possession is an act 'if the possessor knowingly procured or received the thing possessed or was aware of his control thereof for a sufficient period to have been able to terminate his possession'.[9] Commentators have noted, however, that this provision makes dubious sense. As Douglas Husak puts it, '[t]he state of affairs in which I possess my socks is not an act, and this state is not magically transformed into an act simply because I procured my socks knowingly'.[10] Just as calling a tail

[6] For the Supreme Court of Canada's most recent treatment of the offence of criminal negligence causing death, see *R v JF* [2008] 3 SCR 215.

[7] See, eg, *R v Instan* [1893] 1 QB 450; *People v Beardsley* 113 NW 128 (1907) (Supreme Court of Michigan); *R v Miller* [1982] 2 All ER 386 (HL); *R v Kirby* [2004] 245 DLR (4th) 564 (NWTSC). See also Criminal Code s 215, Duties of Persons to Provide Necessaries.

[8] Controlled Drugs and Substances Act, SC 1996, ch 19.

[9] MPC, §2.01(4).

[10] DN Husak, 'Rethinking the Act Requirement' (2006–07) 28 *Cardozo Law Review* 2437, 2440. See also DN Husak, 'Does Criminal Liability Require an Act?' in RA Duff (ed), *Philosophy and the Criminal Law: Principle and Critique* (Cambridge, Cambridge University Press, 1998).

a leg does not turn dogs into five-legged animals, calling the possession of a thing an act does not transform a non-act into an act. So we are again left with the conclusion that possession-based offences are in prima facie tension with the Voluntary Act Principle.

Finally, consider attempts. Although the issues are complicated, it is arguable that when an accused is found liable for attempting to commit a criminal code offence there is no legal requirement that there be a voluntary *act*. Rather, the presence of a particular state of mind, namely the specific intention to perform the prohibited act in question, will sometimes suffice for the imposition of criminal liability.[11] As the Supreme Court of Canada put it in *R v Ancio*:

> [B]ecause the crime of attempt may be complete without the actual commission of any other offence and even without the performance of any act unlawful in itself, it is abundantly clear that the criminal element of the offence of attempt may lie solely in the intent.[12]

As a result, attempts also make trouble for the principle that criminal liability must be based on a voluntary act. For *Ancio* seems to stand for the proposition that an accused may be found liable for attempting to commit a criminal code offence for nothing more than having a particular intent. And that seems to run counter to the Voluntary Act Principle.[13]

III. AMENDING THE VOLUNTARY ACT PRINCIPLE?

An argument can therefore be made that criminal liability need not be imposed on an accused based on the performance of a voluntary act.[14] Again, this is because the criminal law appears to recognize forms of liability-attracting behaviour that do not depend on the presence of an act at all.

Various responses suggest themselves. One could argue that the exceptions are indeed exceptional, and thus, that the central role assigned to the Voluntary Act Principle in criminal law theory and doctrine remains unaffected.[15] Alternatively, one could argue that the apparent exceptions to the Voluntary Act Principle are merely apparent, and that reflection on what the act component of the Voluntary Act Principle in fact requires will show that omissions do not constitute counterexamples to it. I would like to spend a bit of time discussing this second option.

The MPC is potentially instructive here. According to it, the fundamental predicate for all criminal liability is that '[a] person is not guilty of an offense unless his

[11] *R v Ancio* [1984] 1 SCR 225; *R v Logan* [1990] 2 SCR 731.

[12] *R v Ancio*, ibid 247.

[13] But see H Stewart, 'The Centrality of the Act Requirement for Criminal Attempts' (2001) 51 *University of Toronto Law Journal* 399.

[14] See M Moore, *Act and Crime: The Philosophy of Action and its Implications for Criminal Law* (Oxford, Clarendon Press, 1993) 6.

[15] This is, in part, Moore's strategy; see *Act and Crime*, ibid ch 2.

liability is based on conduct that includes a voluntary act or the omission to perform an act of which the accused is physically capable'.[16] The key word here is 'includes'. The idea underlying the MPC's inclusion requirement is two-fold. First, there is the idea that many acts that give rise to criminal culpability are what might be called 'complex acts', where complex acts contain as proper parts simpler acts. Second, there is the idea that even where a complex act is done involuntarily, it may include as proper parts other acts that are done voluntarily. So, for example, Bert's setting fire to his kitchen might have been done involuntarily: he fell asleep and the rice that he was preparing caught on fire. But the involuntary behaviour that constitutes Bert's setting fire to his kitchen may have included, upstream, one or more acts that were within Bert's power to do or not do. For example, Bert could have refrained from taking the cold medicine that he knew would make him drowsy; or he could have remained in the kitchen to watch over his rice rather than lying down on the sofa in another room. On this view, in other words, it may be appropriate to impose liability on Bert given that his otherwise involuntary behaviour included a voluntary act.[17]

Moreover, it pays to note that there seems to be judicial authority in Canada for the claim that criminal liability can be imposed for involuntary behaviour so long as there is a voluntary act that is appropriately 'upstream' of the involuntary behaviour. Consider by way of illustration *R v King*.[18] Mr King had visited his dentist to have two teeth extracted, and was given sodium pentothal as an anaesthetic. After regaining consciousness, the attending nurse warned Mr King not to drive until his head was 'perfectly clear'. Mr King replied that he intended to walk and left the dentist's office, although he later reported remembering no such conversation. Mr King got into his car and while driving became unconscious. His car ran into the rear of a parked automobile. He was charged and convicted of driving a motor vehicle while his ability to do so was impaired by a drug, contrary to (then) section 223 of the Criminal Code. In the Supreme Court of Canada, however, it was held that Mr King should not be found guilty of impaired driving on the grounds that (i) he 'became impaired through no act of his own will' and (ii) he was not aware of, and could not reasonably be expected to have known about, the intoxicating effects of the anaesthetic. However, as Ritchie J went on to say,

> a man who becomes impaired as the result of taking a drug on medical advice without knowing its effect cannot escape liability if he became aware of his impaired condition before he started to drive his car just as a man who did not appreciate his impaired condition when he started to drive cannot escape liability on the ground that his lack of appreciation was brought about by voluntary consumption of liquor or drug.[19]

[16] MPC, §2.01(1) and explanatory notes, 213.

[17] For an interesting discussion of the conditions under which it may be appropriate to impose criminal liability on an accused for an involuntary act that is brought about in the right way by voluntary behaviour, see D Klimchuk, 'Aristotle on Intoxication and Liability' (2003) 20 *History of Philosophy Quarterly* 225.

[18] *R v King* (n 3).

[19] ibid 764. See also *R v Jiang* [2007] 220 CCC (3d) 55 (BCCA).

It is natural to interpret this passage as standing for the proposition that where a voluntary act causes, 'brings about', or is part of the prohibited conduct, liability may be imposed notwithstanding the fact that the prohibited conduct is involuntary.

Compare *King* with *R v Shaw*.[20] Mr Shaw was driving his car when he suddenly fainted. His car left the road and hit a tree, killing two of his five passengers. At trial Mr Shaw was acquitted of the (then) Criminal Code offence of Causing Bodily Injury.[21] On appeal, however, the Court held that there was evidence that Mr Shaw had suffered such fainting episodes in the past, and concluded that while he may not have been aware of the nature of these episodes he was certainly aware of the danger that might result were he to suffer from such an episode while operating a motor vehicle. It therefore ordered a new trial. In reaching this conclusion the Court reasoned as follows:

> Those operating motor cars must be impressed with the terrible danger there is, not only to the passengers and themselves, but to others using the highway when one subject to attacks such as these does not refrain from driving cars at all. The drunken driver is dangerous; even more dangerous is the man who is afflicted as Shaw was, and who is subject to fainting spells or periods of unconsciousness.[22]

Again, it is natural to gloss this as follows: those who are, or have reason to be, aware of a potentially debilitating condition and who voluntarily drive cars are liable for any injuries or damage caused as a result of the sudden onset of the condition in question notwithstanding the fact that any injuries or damage are directly caused by involuntary behaviour.

King and *Shaw* might therefore appear to suggest that liability can be imposed on an accused for involuntary conduct so long as that involuntary conduct includes a voluntary act as part of its etiology. However, *Shaw* in fact makes trouble for the most natural understanding of 'includes'. On this understanding (involuntary) behaviour C includes (a voluntary) act A if A occurred *where* C took place (spatial inclusion), or if A occurred *when* C took place (temporal inclusion). The problem with *Shaw* is that the voluntary act in question – choosing to operate a motor vehicle knowing that one is afflicted by fainting episodes – is neither spatially nor temporally included in the prohibited act of causing bodily injury. It is not spatially included because that voluntary act did not occur *where* the prohibited conduct occurred; and it is not temporally included because that voluntary act did not occur *when* the prohibited conduct occurred.

[20] *R v Shaw* [1938] OR 269 (CA). For similar cases, see *People v Decina* 138 NE 2d 709 (1956) (NYCA); *Buckley v Smith Transport* [1946] OR 798 (CA); *Roberts v Ramsbottom* [1980] 1 WLR 823 (QBD); *R v Jiang*, ibid.

[21] RSC 1927 ch 36, s 284.

[22] *R v Shaw* (n 20) 271.

IV. THE VOLUNTARY CONDUCT PRINCIPLE

What then is left of the act component of the Voluntary Act Principle? Not much, it might be thought. We seem to have a range of exceptions to its scope – omissions, attempts and possession-related offences – and it is not obvious how to retain the act component of the *actus reus* requirement without doing violence to its theoretical and doctrinal underpinnings. But I also think that a relatively simple fix is available.

The fix I have in mind can be found in the MPC and in some of the Supreme Court of Canada's jurisprudence. According to this fix, what is important for the act part of the *actus reus* requirement is not so much the presence of a positive *act* but rather the presence of *behaviour* or *conduct* for which the accused can be held responsible. So I suggest that we replace talk of acts with talk of conduct, yielding what I will call the 'Voluntary Conduct Principle': criminal liability must be based on voluntary conduct.

This requirement is explicit in the MPC's requirement that '[a] person is not guilty of an offense unless his liability is based on conduct that includes a voluntary act or the omission to perform an act of which the accused is physically capable'.[23] Similarly, it seems clear that the Supreme Court of Canada had a more expansive conception of the *actus reus* requirement in mind when it said that '[i]t is a principle of fundamental justice that only voluntary conduct . . . should attract the penalty and stigma of criminal liability'.[24] The category of conduct is broader than that of action in the sense that things other than positive acts may nonetheless count as forms of conduct. A shift from talk of acts to talk of conduct will therefore take care of some of the problems raised for the Voluntary Act Principle by cases of liability for omissions and liability for possession. For while neither omissions or possession can be said to be acts, it does not seem implausible to call them forms of conduct, since they do seem to be ways in which people behave.

The idea underlying the Voluntary Conduct Principle is thus that individuals ought to be held responsible for some of the ways in which they behave, or better, *conduct* themselves. It is clear that the word 'conduct' can function both as a verb and as a noun. We say that Smith conducted himself honourably, but also that Smith's conduct was honourable, and in ordinary circumstances there is no reason to prefer one manner of speaking to the other. But in the context of discussions concerning the *actus reus* of criminal offences, it seems to me to be preferable to focus on the manner in which Smith conducts himself. For in focusing on Smith's conduct, rather than on how Smith conducts himself, we risk concluding that there must be some *thing* done by Smith that deserves our attention, where what we ought to be focusing on instead is simply the manner in which Smith

[23] MPC, §2.01(1).

[24] *R v Ruzic* (n 4) [47].

behaves, whether this includes a positive act or a (mere) failure to do what he was required to do.

Still, it might be objected that adopting the Voluntary Conduct Principle threatens to do more harm than good.[25] In brief, the worry is that even if we can preserve the spirit of the Voluntary Act Principle by calling omissions a form of conduct, this can be done only at the expense of rendering the *conduct* element of the revised principle redundant in any analysis of whether it is permissible to hold a person criminally responsible. In other words, if everything – that is to say, both things we do, that is, actions, as well as things we don't do, that is, omissions – can in principle count as forms of conduct, then it would seem that the *conduct* component of the voluntary conduct principle is explanatorily idle; what seems to be doing all the work is instead the *voluntariness* component.

While there is something to this objection, it seems to me to be a mistake to conclude that introducing talk about conduct renders the conduct component of the voluntary conduct principle unnecessary. First, the claim is not that any and all omissions are in principle subject to criminal sanction. An omission will only give rise to criminal liability if it constitutes a failure to perform a duty imposed by law and as the law imposes limits on when omissions can give rise to criminal liability, it follows that there are identifiable boundaries to the sort of conduct in which the criminal law will take an interest.

Second, it pays to ask why we have an act or conduct requirement in the first place. Paul Robinson sets out some possible reasons for the requirement.[26] According to Robinson, the presence of an act requirement serves to bar punishment for un-externalized thoughts, attempts to provide objective confirmation that the intention of the accused existed, helps to provide a time and place for the occurrence of an offence, and places limits on the government's ability to define and introduce new criminal offences. It may be that the act requirement does these things imperfectly. Still, the idea that an omission to perform a duty imposed by law might give rise to criminal liability also seems to satisfy these requirements to varying degrees. No doubt, liability for omissions is the exception rather than the rule, and positive duties imposed by law are small in number and narrowly defined. All the same, because we can identify a similar rationale for why criminal liability might be restricted both to positive actions and to omissions to perform duties imposed by law, it is not unreasonable to group them together under the heading of 'conduct'. Or so I claim.

[25] Thanks to Victor Tadros for raising the following objection.

[26] P Robinson, 'Should the Criminal Law Abandon the *Actus Reus-Mens Rea* Distinction?' in S Shute, J Gardner and J Horder (eds), *Action and Value in Criminal Law* (Oxford, Clarendon Press, 1993).

V. VOLUNTARINESS

At this point I turn to discussion of the voluntariness component of the Voluntary Conduct Principle. The standard view is that the link between prohibited conduct and criminal liability should be provided by the requirement of voluntariness: an accused is liable for prohibited conduct only where that conduct is engaged in *voluntarily*. (Equivalently: where prohibited conduct is engaged in involuntarily, an accused is not liable for that conduct.) But what does it mean to engage in conduct voluntarily? The traditional view, which is found in the work of John Austin, is broadly speaking causal in nature, holding that a (voluntary) act is a muscular contraction or bodily movement that is caused in the right way by a volition or act of will.[27] As Austin put it:

> [T]he only objects which can be called acts, are consequences of Volitions. A voluntary movement of my body, or a movement which follows a volition, is an *act*. The *in*voluntary movements which are the consequences of certain diseases, are *not* acts. But as the bodily movements which immediately follow volitions, are the only ends of volition, it follows that those bodily movements are the only objects to which the term 'acts' can be applied with perfect precision and propriety.[28]

In a similar vein, Oliver Wendell Holmes remarked that '[a]n act, it is true, imports intention in a certain sense. It is a muscular contraction, and something more. A spasm is not an act. The contraction of the muscles must be willed'.[29] More recently, Michael Moore has defended a broadly similar position.[30] There is an enormous literature on the concept of voluntariness and I will not say much about it except to point out the obvious, namely that concept is contested. HLA Hart, for example, famously argued that Austin's view suffered from a fatal defect, namely that 'its account of human action is really nothing more than an outdated fiction – a piece of eighteenth-century psychology which has no real application to human conduct'.[31] According to Austin, an agent performs an act when she wills that certain muscular contractions occur. Hart's main complaint was that this was simply false: a person does not act when she desires that a certain bodily movement or muscular contraction occur. When, wanting to quench my thirst, I reach for a glass of beer, I do not desire a particular muscular contraction; I desire simply *to drink my beer*.

What Hart offered in place of Austin's causal account of voluntariness was what might be called a *purposive* account of voluntariness: a person acts involuntarily

[27] J Austin, *Lectures in Jurisprudence* 5th edn (London, John Murray, 1885).

[28] ibid Lecture 18, 414.

[29] OW Holmes, *The Common Law* (Boston, Little, Brown, and Company, 1881) 54.

[30] See Moore, *Act and Crime* (n 14); M Moore, *Placing Blame* (Oxford, Oxford University Press, 1997) ch 6. For other defences, see JG Murphy, 'Involuntary Acts and Criminal Liability' (1971) 81 *Ethics* 332; KW Saunders, 'Voluntary Acts and the Criminal Law: Justifying Culpability Based on the Existence of Volition' (1987–88) 49 *University of Pittsburgh Law Review* 443.

[31] HLA Hart, 'Acts of Will and Responsibility' in *Punishment and Responsibility* 2nd edn (Oxford, Oxford University Press, 2007) 101.

where the acts that he performs 'are not subordinated to the agent's conscious plans of action: they do not occur as part of anything the agent takes himself to be doing'.[32] (I call this account *purposive* because it focuses on the *purposes* for which actions are performed, rather than on mental states (of will, or of volition) that *cause* those actions.) Hart concluded that the 'single fundamental defect' that is present in cases of involuntary conduct is 'a man's lack of conscious control over his muscular movements'.[33] On this view, no criminal liability may be imposed on an accused where the accused lacked (conscious) *control* over the liability-creating conduct.

More recently, Husak has articulated a version of this same sort of view.[34] According to Husak,

> [w]hat is important to our theory of criminal responsibility . . . is not action itself, but rather the control that actions typically presuppose. In other words, our reason for wanting to include an act requirement in criminal law is because we care about control. It is easy to see why this concern would lead (or mislead) us into believing that an act should be needed for liability. Paradigmatically, our acts are under our control, while our non-acts are not under our control.[35]

Similarly, Michael Corrado remarks that the essence of the voluntary act requirement 'is that the actor must have been able to avoid choosing to break the law. She must have been able to control her choice'.[36] And in a judicial context, Doherty JA comments as follows in *R v Luedecke*, a case involving the defence of automatism:

> A person who is unable to decide whether to perform an act and unable to control the performance of the act cannot be said, in any meaningful sense, to have committed the act. Nor can it be appropriate in a criminal justice system in which liability is predicated on personal responsibility to convict persons based on conduct which those persons have no ability to control.[37]

The control requirement is attractive, and much good work has been done to articulate and defend it. All the same, it seems to me that as a gloss on the voluntariness component of the *actus reus* requirement it cannot be correct. That is because there appear to be cases where although an individual lacks the appropriate sort of control over her conduct we are nonetheless inclined to hold her responsible for what she has done, this on the grounds that in an important sense the actions over which she lacked control were all the same *her* actions. In order to describe and explain such cases, however, I need to introduce some terminology.

[32] ibid 105.
[33] ibid 106. But see his comments at 255–56.
[34] Husak, 'Rethinking the Act Requirement' (n 10).
[35] ibid 2454.
[36] M Corrado, 'Is there an Act Requirement in the Criminal law?' (1994) 142 *University of Pennsylvania Law Review* 1529, 1557.
[37] *R v Luedecke* [2008] 93 OR (3d) 89 (CA) 107.

VI. FRANKFURT'S HIERARCHICAL ACCOUNT OF THE WILL

I begin with Harry Frankfurt's distinction between first and second-order desires.[38] According to Frankfurt, first-order desires are desires of the form 'X wants to ϕ', where 'X' is a variable ranging over persons and 'ϕ' is a variable ranging over actions. So, for example, my desire for a drink of water or my desire to lose weight count as first-order desires. Not all first-order desires are created equal, however. Some first-order desires are idle in the production of behaviour while other first-order desires are causally implicated in one's actions. For example, although I might desire to lose weight, I might also order desserts whenever they are offered to me. As a result, my desire to lose weight may not actually move me to act on it. It is what we might call a *mere* desire. An *effective* first-order desire, on the other hand, is a first-order desire that 'moves (or will or would move) a person all the way to action'.[39] And according to Frankfurt a person's *will* is the set of that person's effective first-order desires.

By way of comparison, second-order desires are desires of the form 'X wants to want to ϕ'. By way of illustration, I may not in fact desire fruit for dessert; but I may all the same *desire* that I desire fruit, since again I might want to lose weight. Conversely, I may not desire to desire salt, since my physician has told me that increased sodium intake can lead to high blood pressure; all the same, I do desire salt, since it makes my food taste better. Like first-order desires, second-order desires come in varying degrees of strength. In particular, second-order *volitions* are desires about what sort of *effective* first-order desires I want to have, and so are desires about what sort of will I want to have. According to Frankfurt, freedom of the will is a function of the relation between effective first-order desires and second-order volitions. When I am capable of bringing my effective first-order desires – my will – into conformity with my second-order volitions, my will is said to be free. I enjoy free will, in other words, just in case I am free to have the will I want to have:

> It is in securing the conformity of his will to his second-order volitions . . . that a person exercises freedom of the will. And it is in the discrepancy between his will and his second-order volitions, or in his awareness that their coincidence is not his own doing but only a happy chance, that a person who does not have his freedom feels its lack.[40]

Frankfurt illustrates what this amounts to by means of a comparison between two kinds of addicts: an unwilling addict and a willing addict. Both addicts are hopelessly addicted to drugs, and are powerless in the face of their addictions. The

[38] H Frankfurt, 'Freedom of the Will and the Concept of a Person' (1971) 68 *Journal of Philosophy* 5. For critical discussion of Frankfurt's views on the will, see G Watson, 'Free Agency' (1975) 72 *Journal of Philosophy* 205 and the papers collected in S Buss and L Overton (eds), *Contours of Agency: Essays on Themes from Harry Frankfurt* (Cambridge MA, MIT Press, 2002).

[39] Frankfurt, 'Freedom of the Will', ibid 8.

[40] ibid 15.

unwilling addict, however, while hating his addiction and struggling against it, in the end always succumbs to it. Thus, when he takes drugs he is not acting freely because his will – his effective first-order desires – is not the will he wants to have. There is an important sense, in other words, according to which the unwilling addict is not responsible for his drug taking behaviour or conduct, and this is because he does not identify with that behaviour or conduct; it does not reflect the will he wants to have.

The willing addict, on the other hand, is perfectly happy with her addiction. She too is powerless in the face of her addiction, but unlike the unwilling addict, were her addiction to wane or weaken she would take steps to reinstate it. Her will is not free because she is not free to have the will she wants to have, but the will she has is in fact the will she wants to have. In consequence, when the willing addict takes drugs she is responsible for her conduct in part because it reflects the will she wants to have. Had she not *identified with* or *endorsed* her will – or, as I will sometimes say, had she not *embraced* her will – she would not be responsible for conduct that flows from it.

As an aside, Frankfurt's current view is that what makes an agent responsible for his will is best understood in terms of *wholeheartedness.* An agent is wholehearted with respect to his will

> when there is in him no endogenous desire to be volitionally different than he is. Although he may be unable to create in himself a will other than the one he has, his will is free at least in the sense that he himself does not oppose or impede it.[41]

More to the point, an agent is wholehearted with respect to a feeling, attitude, desire, or intention when he is 'fully satisfied that they, rather than others that inherently (ie, non-contingently) conflict with them, should be among the causes and considerations that determine his cognitive, affective, attitudinal, and behavioral processes'.[42] To say that an agent is satisfied (with his will) is therefore to say that the agent enjoys a state of satisfaction with the condition of his self. The key idea is that unlike identification or endorsement – which seems to require an active stance on the part of an agent – satisfaction simply involves the absence of restlessness or resistance.[43]

However, while getting clear on the relationship between identification, endorsement, wholeheartedness, and satisfaction is philosophically important and worthwhile, it does not seem to me to affect the point developed above. For even on Frankfurt's revised view the willing addict is wholehearted in her will, since there is no division in her will, no desire to be volitionally different than she is. So again, even on Frankfurt's revised account of what it means to be responsi-

[41] H Frankfurt, 'The Faintest Passion' (1992) 66 *Proceedings and Addresses of the American Philosophical Association* 5, 11. See also H Frankfurt, 'Identification and Wholeheartedness' in *The Importance of What We Care About* (Cambridge, Cambridge University Press, 1988). For a useful discussion of these and other concepts, see C Calhoun, 'Standing for Something' (1995) *Journal of Philosophy* 235.

[42] Frankfurt, 'The Faintest Passion', ibid 12.

[43] ibid.

ble for one's will, although the unwilling addict's will is not free, his will remains his own.

Let me return to the willing and unwilling addicts. Because they are in the grip of their addictions both addicts lack control over their effective first-order desires, and so lack control over their wills. Nonetheless, it seems clear that the willing addict is responsible for her conduct in a way in which the unwilling addict is not. The willing addict's conduct flows from the will she wants to have, but over which she lacks control; consequently, she lacks free will. All the same, she is responsible for taking drugs notwithstanding the fact that she cannot control her drug taking behaviour. (As Frankfurt puts it, somewhat paradoxically, the willing addict's will is not free; but when she takes drugs the willing addict does so freely and of her own free will.)[44] This suggests that that control requirement misses something important about the relationship between conduct and responsibility. For there seem to be situations where an individual is responsible for performing certain actions or engaging in certain forms of behaviour even though she lacks the appropriate sort of control over that conduct.

With this in mind, consider again Doherty JA's remark that '[a] person who is unable to decide whether to perform an act and unable to control the performance of the act cannot be said, in any meaningful sense, to have committed the act'.[45] According to the account just described, this claim is arguably false. For although the willing addict is in the relevant sense unable to control her drug taking acts it is misleading to say that she did not commit them. Much the same can be said about Austin's remark that '[t]he *in*voluntary movements which are the consequences of certain diseases, are *not* acts'. Again, it may be true that such movements are not acts over which an agent has control; all the same, it does not follow that such movements are not acts for which the agent is responsible.

On the view sketched above, therefore, an individual is responsible for her conduct only if it flows from a will she embraces, a will she wants to have.[46] If this is correct, then there is an important sense in which *agency* rather than *control* is what is at issue in the voluntariness component of the *actus reus* requirement: where an individual is responsible for certain conduct it follows that she embraces the will from which certain conduct flows. And this can be true even if she lacks control over her will. For simplicity, call this the 'Willed Conduct Requirement':

[44] Frankfurt, 'Freedom of the Will' (n 38) 19.

[45] *R v Luedecke* (n 37) 107.

[46] Frankfurt also discusses the concept of a *wanton*, an individual who, because she lacks second-order volitions, is indifferent with regard to which first-order desires constitute her will. Wantons are therefore creatures for whom the issue of freedom of the will simply does not arise; wantons therefore lack freedom of the will 'by default' (Frankfurt, 'Freedom of the Will' (n 38) 15). This might be thought to make trouble for the view I am sketching since if it is possible for a wanton to engage in criminal conduct, we would surely want to hold her responsible for her actions notwithstanding the fact that she lacks second-order volitions and so lacks the ability to act freely and of her own free will. Although the issues are complex, I suspect that some wantons might indeed be relieved of responsibility for their actions, while others might not be; much will depend on the extent to which the wanton is commandeered or buffeted by her first-order desires. For an interesting discussion of this issue, see M Oshana, 'Wanton Responsibility' (1998) 2 *The Journal of Ethics* 261.

criminal liability must be based on conduct that flows from a will that the accused embraces.

Note that the Willed Conduct Requirement articulates a *necessary* condition for criminal liability. It does not say that merely embracing one's will makes one responsible for all actions that flow from that will. If I wholeheartedly endorse my epileptic seizures I do not automatically become responsible for all the consequences of those seizures simply because they flow from a will that I embrace. (All the same, it might be appropriate to hold me responsible for those consequences if I engage in conduct C knowing that I am susceptible to epileptic seizures, and knowing that if such seizures occur while engaged in conduct C, certain proscribed consequences might result; recall again *R v Shaw.*)[47] If, however, I do not embrace the will from which my seizures flow, then according to the Willed Conduct Requirement I cannot be held responsible for the consequences that flow from that will, or from those effective first-order desires that are implicated in the production of the proscribed conduct. And this is because the conduct cannot properly be attributed to me; it is not mine.

VII. AN OBJECTION

Before continuing, let me briefly discuss one objection.[48] It often happens that, having performed an action, an individual wishes she had done otherwise. In short, it often happens that an agent regrets what she has done. But it is a short step from here to the claim that when an agent regrets what she has done she fails to embrace the will from which her actions flow. And this suggests that when an agent regrets what she has done she cannot be held responsible for it. But this cannot be quite right.

There are two sorts of cases worth considering. In the first, an individual regrets what she has done after she does it. This presents no problem for the Willed Conduct Requirement, however, since according to it what is important is the agent's relationship to her will at the time at which she acts. The fact that she later comes to regret or second-guess her actions does not mean that they were improperly attributed to her at the time at which she performed them.

Let me turn now to the second – and more difficult – sort of case. The sort of case I have in mind arises when an individual *at the time at which she acts* regrets what she is about to do. Most of the time the fact that an agent regrets what she is about to do is neither here or there. But in some cases the fact that she experiences regret might be relevant to whether she ought to be held responsible for what she is about to do. However, the thing to note is that it is not the presence of feelings of regret that is doing the explanatory work, but rather the circumstances giving rise to those feelings. In cases where an agent's will is overborne by threats by

[47] *R v Shaw* (n 20).

[48] Thanks to Dennis Klimchuk for drawing my attention to this issue.

another person (duress) or by dangerous natural circumstances (necessity) we may be prepared to recognize an excuse. But we do this not because the agent does not like what she is about to do. Rather, we do this because we think that due to the circumstances (of duress or necessity) in which the agent finds herself her will has been overborne by external factors. And this seems to me to be another way of saying that in such circumstances the will from which the agent's behaviour flows is not a will that she embraces, that is, that the Willed Conduct Requirement is not met.

VIII. THE PRACTICAL AGENCY CONDITION

The general picture sketched above shares certain similarities with what Vincent Chiao has recently and helpfully called the *practical agency condition*.[49] According to the practical agency condition, an agent is not responsible for the consequences of her conduct unless those consequences were caused or constituted by the agent's conduct *qua* practically rational agent.[50] Chiao suggests that in cases involving sleepwalking or automatism, for example, agents are excused because 'their will is in some sense not implicated in the crimes they commit'; as a result,

> they fail to be practically rational agents insofar as they do not have, one might say, *executive* self-control. In other words, we conceive of such agents as being in some way commandeered, as having their agendas set by something or someone else.[51]

Chiao further remarks that

> [t]he radical dissociation between the agent's sense of self and the relevant conduct calls into question this agent's ability to set his own ends . . . and this may call into question whether such individuals can be seen as practically rational agents such that prosecuting them for harms committed in that state is justified.[52]

Dennis Klimchuk has said something similar. According to Klimchuk, actions performed under conditions of duress or necessity are excused 'because they are performed in circumstances which conspired to compromise the defendant's capacity to choose his or her course of action, and hence compromised his or her autonomy'.[53] As a result, the reason '[w]e do not punish those who act involuntarily [is] because their actions resist imputation to them. Their agency, so to speak, is not implicated in their doings'.[54]

49 V Chiao, 'Action and Agency in the Criminal Law' (2009) 15 *Legal Theory* 1.

50 ibid 16.

51 ibid 18.

52 ibid.

53 D Klimchuk, 'Moral Innocence, Normative Involuntariness, and Fundamental Justice' 18 *Criminal Reports* (5th) 96, 102. Hints of the practical agency requirement can also be found in M Shaffer, 'Scrutinizing Duress: The Constitutional Validity of Section 17 of the Criminal Code' (1997–98) 47 *Criminal Law Quarterly* 444, especially 457.

54 ibid.

It should be clear, given what I have said above, that I am sympathetic to the shift away from a control requirement in favour of a requirement based on practical agency, since the latter requirement seems to me to make better sense of what it is that makes an agent responsible for his conduct. The problem I have with the account of the practical agency condition given by Chiao and Klimchuk is that it seems to mis-describe what is going on in certain situations where reason and control come apart. Consider again the willing addict. There seems to be a straightforward sense in which the agency of the willing addict is *not* implicated in her drug taking behaviour. This is because she takes the drugs not because she wants to do so – although she is in fact happy enough to do so – but rather because she lacks authority over her effective first-order desires. This is what it means, in part, to be an addict. Because according to the practical agency condition the willing addict lacks executive control over her behaviour, it would seem to follow that she is not responsible for her drug taking behaviour. All the same, although the willing addict seems to lack executive self-control, and so fails to meet the practical agency condition, it seems to me that she is nonetheless responsible for what she does. She lacks executive self-control because she is not capable of controlling her drug taking behaviour in any meaningful sense, but she is responsible for her drug taking behaviour because she endorses and identifies with that behaviour, and with the will that gives rise to it.

To be fair, Klimchuk's main concern in the article from which I quoted was not to explain what it means for behaviour to be imputable to an agent, and Chiao himself suggests that Frankfurt's hierarchical account of the will might be helpful in understanding what it might mean to enjoy executive control.[55] Moreover, I admit that intuitions about the willing addict and other similar cases may vary. For example, it could be argued that the reason why the willing addict is responsible for taking drugs is precisely because she is *not* being commandeered or having her agenda set by something or someone else. After all, given that the willing addict is delighted by her condition and identifies wholeheartedly with it, isn't this what prevents her lack of control over her will from negating her responsibility? All the same, it seems to me that there is a distinction to be drawn between lacking executive self-control because one cannot control one's will (a characterization that applies to the situations of both the willing and unwilling addict) and lacking executive self-control because one's will is not one's own (a characterization that applies to only the unwilling addict). Although the issues are complex, it seems to me that the latter analysis is preferable. Moreover, if the present proposal is on the right track, then the Supreme Court of Canada ought to say more about why 'only voluntary conduct – behaviour that is the product of a free will and controlled body, unhindered by external constraints – should attract the penalty and stigma of criminal liability'.[56] As we have seen, what it means for conduct or behaviour to be voluntary – to be the product of a free will – is open to dispute.

[55] See Chiao, 'Action and Agency' (n 49) fn 46.
[56] *R v Ruzic* (n 4).

This is illustrated by the fact that although the unwilling addict's will is not free, his behaviour is done freely and of his own free will.

Before concluding this section, let me briefly address one potential worry. The worry is this: isn't this precisely the sort of causal account that Hart so decisively refuted? Recall Hart's main criticism of Austin: because Austin misrepresented what it was for something to be an act, he also misrepresented what it was for someone to perform an action. According to Hart,

> [t]he simple but important truth is that when we deliberate and think about actions, we do so not in terms of muscular movements but in the ordinary terminology of actions. Of course muscular movements are involved in all such actions; but that does not show either that we are aware of them before action or that we have a desire for them.[57]

However, as Murphy has pointed out, Hart's rejection of Austin's account seems to rest on a conflation of two separate claims: (1) that the difference between a voluntary act and an involuntary act is a *causal* difference; and (2) that acts are to be analyzed as movements of the body or as muscular contractions.[58] Hart's arguments go to the truth of (2). But even if Hart was right to reject (2), it does not follow that he was right to reject (1) – although it may show that the causal antecedents proposed by Austin were not of the right sort.

This observation is important because the practical agency condition seems to combine both causal and purposive accounts of agency and responsibility. It is causal since it suggests that what causes an agent to perform an action can be relevant to determining whether a particular action is attributable or imputable to that agent *qua* practically rational agent; but it is purposive since it is interested in the sorts of mental states – for example, executive self-control – that accompany action. But this seems to me to be no objection to the practical agency condition since as Murphy has pointed out, and for all Hart has argued, a causal account of agency may still be possible.

To summarize, I have indicated why I think the practical agency condition is an improvement on the control condition, and I have suggested that the practical agency condition is best understood in terms of identification with, or endorsement of, one's effective first-order desires, or will. On this view, when an agent embraces her will she is responsible for those desires that constitute her will, and for any conduct that flows from them. Again, this yields what I have dubbed the Willed Conduct Requirement, which holds that criminal liability must be based on conduct that flows from a will that the accused embraces. In the vast majority of cases an agent will embrace her will when she is in control of it, or when conduct or its consequences was imputable to her *qua* practically rational agent. But as I have tried to show, in some cases it may make a difference to responsibility in general, and criminal liability in particular, which view we adopt; and in those cases it seems to me that the Willed Conduct Requirement better reflects what is at issue when we are trying to determine whether a particular action is attributable to an agent.

[57] Hart, 'Acts of Will and Responsibility' (n 31) 102.

[58] See Murphy, 'Involuntary Acts and Criminal Liability' (n 30) 337.

IX. TWO FINAL OBSERVATIONS

What is the practical upshot of the practical agency condition understood in the way in which I have suggested? I will make two observations.

First, return to *King* and *Shaw*. In *Shaw*, liability was imposed on the accused because in the opinion of the court, he was aware that his medical condition could lead to danger were he to drive. Thus, regardless of whether he could have chosen not to drive, his decision to drive was something with which he freely identified: he was aware of the risks involved and proceeded in the face of those risks. In *King*, liability was not imposed because the accident causing conduct was not imputable to the accused. The effective first-order desire that lead to Mr King's impaired driving, therefore, was not really his own, and it is this fact that negated liability. There are, of course, situations where it is not clear what we ought to say. Suppose an individual is in the grip of kleptomania, and is powerless when it comes to stealing. Should this fact excuse him from criminal liability on the grounds that the *actus reus* of theft has not been made out? Or suppose a paedophile argues that although he absolutely detests his behaviour, he is powerless to alter or interfere with his effective first-order desires to have sexual relations with young children: should that make a difference as to whether criminal liability ought to be imposed? These are difficult questions and much will depend on whether kleptomania and paedophilia, for example, are properly grouped with addictive forms of volitional impairment, on empirical facts about the nature and causes of addictive behaviour, and on whether addicted individuals are in fact powerless in the face of their addictions.[59] So one practical upshot of the practical agency condition understood along the lines I have suggested may be, in some cases, a renewed focus on empirical matters.

Second, the criminal law distinguishes what might be called *physical involuntariness* from what has been called *normative involuntariness.* If Alice pushes Bert into David, Bert's application of force to David was physically involuntary; thus, Bert did not commit the *actus reus* of assault. If on the other hand Alice pushes Bert into David because Charlie put a gun to her head, then Alice's application of force to Bert was normatively involuntary; thus, Alice may be excused for assaulting Bert. Physical involuntariness has traditionally been thought to go to the *actus reus* of a criminal offence while normative involuntariness has been thought to go to the *mens rea.* Thus, the defences of duress[60] and necessity[61] have been character-

[59] For interesting discussions of the relationship between addiction and criminal liability, see G Watson, 'Excusing Addiction' (1999) 18 *Law and Philosophy* 589; RJ Wallace, 'Addiction as Defect of the Will: Some Philosophical Reflections' (1999) 18 *Law and Philosophy* 621; and DN Husak, 'Addiction and Criminal Responsibility' (1999) 18 *Law and Philosophy* 655. For exploration of the concept of volitional impairment see G Watson, 'Volitional Necessity' in S Buss and L Overton (eds), *Contours of Agency: Essays on Themes from Harry Frankfurt* (Cambridge MA, MIT Press, 2002).

[60] *R v Ruzic* (n 4).

[61] *R v Perka* [2001] 1 SCR 687.

ized as excuses on the grounds that individuals who act in such circumstances act in a normatively involuntary manner, and thus lack the requisite *mens rea.*

The present view suggests, however, that physical involuntariness and moral involuntariness have much in common. This is because both involve at a certain basic level a lack of agency.[62] What precludes an agent from being responsible for her actions in both sorts of cases has to do with the fact that they flow from a will that she does not embrace. In the first case described above, the will that led to Bert's performing what would otherwise be an assault on David came from without. The will in question was Alice's, and so was not one that Bert embraced. In the second case, while the intentional states that caused Alice to push Bert into David came from within, they too were not intentional states that she embraced. So again, there was dissonance between her actions and her will. Thus, a second practical consequence of the present view may be a reassessment of the relationship between physical and normative involuntariness, and of those excusing conditions that make appeal to such concepts.

X. CONCLUSION

My goal in this chapter has been a modest one: to get clearer about the content and contours of the Voluntary Act Principle. I have suggested that the principle can be usefully modified along two dimensions: first, by enlarging the scope of the act component to include conduct; and second, by focusing, in the context of what I have been calling the voluntariness component, on the relationship between an agent and her will. My discussion of this latter issue is congenial to what some have called the practical agency condition, the idea that in order for an agent to be responsible for her conduct, that conduct must be attributable to her *qua* practically rational agent, and encourages a renewed focus on the relation between an agent and her will, as well as on the ways in which that relation may bear on the question of what, if anything, she can be held responsible for.

[62] For an argument along similar lines, see Klimchuk, 'Moral Innocence, Normative Involuntariness' (n 53).

6

Mental Disorder and the Instability of Blame in Criminal Law

BENJAMIN L BERGER*

In this contribution to a volume about 'Rethinking Criminal Law Theory', my purpose is to examine the law of mental disorder in a way that reconnects the philosophical and theoretical study of the criminal law to the social functions played by the criminal justice system. I want to examine the criminal justice system as a repertoire of symbolic and rhetorical moves that pursue certain goals and serve certain functions within society at large. Philosophical inquiry into the logic of the criminal justice system and the systematic exploration of the theory of responsibility and criminalization serve an indispensible role in the study of the criminal law. This chapter, however, seeks to pivot the theoretical focus somewhat, with a turn to the role that the criminal justice system, and in particular criminal responsibility, plays in society's self-management.[1] Central to my project is a claim that the law – not solely the criminal law – is consistently engaged in a more or (usually) less self-conscious process of strategic display, concealment, emphasis and elision that has as its goal the maintenance of certain assumptions felt to be crucial to the smooth operation of society.

An important tool in this social function of law is the reification of distinctions or boundary lines. These reified distinctions take up residence in our minds as being the basis for natural categories, such that the law appears as simply epiphenomenal. Some such categories are aesthetic in nature (in Kant's sense of involving conceptions of space and time) whereas others are sociological or normative. Concepts of jurisdiction, for example, fall in the aesthetic category, whereas dividing lines created by the concept of harm are more normative in nature. The edges

* I am grateful to James Stribopoulos and François Tanguay-Renaud for organizing the conference on the philosophy of criminal law at which this piece was first presented. I benefitted greatly from the comments of the participants in the conference, particularly the response by Susan Dimock. As always, I am grateful to Gerry Ferguson and John Borrows for their comments and suggestions and I owe thanks to Claire Truesdale and Emily Lapper for their invaluable research assistance on this project.

[1] Outstanding in this vein of inquiry is work such as D Garland, *Punishment and Modern Society: A Study in Social Theory* (Chicago, University of Chicago Press, 1990); MD Dubber, *The Police Power: Patriarchy and the Foundations of American Government* (New York, Columbia University Press, 2005); L Farmer, *Criminal Law, Tradition, and Legal Order* (Cambridge, Cambridge University Press, 1997).

of these categories are liminal conceptual spaces and, therefore, both crucial and dangerous areas for the law. It is at these borders that disruptions are most vigorously defended against; it is also here that we can glimpse the often-unacknowledged stakes of maintaining these distinctions and categories.

We have seen both the importance of reified categories and the sociologically illuminating nature of their disruption in the academic exploration of the private/public divide. In the context of gender inequality the division of the private and public has served as a buttress supporting the intricate architecture of the division of the social and the legal, for fear that the collapse of the two would imperil the gothic majesty of law's independence from social inequality.[2] One could trace a reappearance of this particular border, and its contestation, in the contemporary debate over the meaning of legal secularism, wherein the public and private have reappeared as legal categories important to the social management of religious diversity.[3] One could equally train one's attention on the belief/conduct divide as another reified distinction serving to police the borders essential to secularism.

These symbolic and rhetorical functions of the law cannot be uniformly treated as illusions to be dispelled by clearer or sharper visions gifted to society by legal theorists. Some such assumed categories ought to be destabilized, their borders disrupted. Others are valuable conceits on which the system of modern public and private law depends and by means of which it can achieve just and salutary ends. Whether a given distinction is better characterized as one or the other is a matter for reform-based arguments. What can always be said, however, is that these categorical distinctions – these repertoires of symbolic and rhetorical moves – are markers for the legal system serving certain broad social and structural ends, markers for law doing social work.

This chapter is concerned with one such division within the criminal law, how it is defined and the social role that this definition has in shoring up our defences against an instability intrinsic to crime and social breakdown. This border is the line between those criminally responsible for their acts and those deemed not criminally responsible by reason of mental disorder (NCRMD).[4]

Much theory working within the logic of the criminal justice system[5] notes the extremely high threshold for a finding of NCRMD, often critiquing it for failing to take account of certain diseases of the mind that ought to bear on a sense of

[2] See, eg, SB Boyd (ed), *Challenging the Public/Private Divide: Feminism, Law, and Public Policy* (Toronto, University of Toronto Press, 1997); J Fudge, 'The Public/Private Distinction: The Possibilities of and the Limits to the Use of Charter Litigation to Further Feminist Struggles' (1987) 25 *Osgoode Hall Law Journal* 485.

[3] See, eg, BL Berger, 'Law's Religion: Rendering Culture' (2007) 45 *Osgoode Hall Law Journal* 277; A Shachar, *Multicultural Jurisdictions: Cultural Differences and Women's Rights* (Cambridge, Cambridge University Press, 2001).

[4] Although there is wide variation in the way in which this category is labelled in various legal systems and in the scholarly literature, in this chapter I will assume the Canadian terminology of 'not criminally responsible on account of mental disorder', or 'NCRMD'.

[5] In PW Kahn, *The Cultural Study of Law: Reconstructing Legal Scholarship* (Chicago, University of Chicago Press, 1999), Kahn refers to this mode of theorizing as 'auto-theory', which he defines as 'attempts to justify legal rules from within the legal culture' (at 103).

whether criminal responsibility is fairly ascribed to the individual. Although I will provide grist for this critique by exploring and amplifying the serious under-inclusiveness of the category of NCRMD, this chapter essentially begins after this critique has been levelled. Instead of turning to the issue of reform, however, I turn to the question of '*why*'? Given the gap between what we know about certain mental disorders that seem to speak to key components of criminal responsibility, on the one hand, and what the criminal law will recognize as interrupting the assignation of guilt, on the other, why does the threshold for a finding of not criminally responsible by reason of mental disorder remain so high in Canada and other related jurisdictions? What we find is a doctrine that, viewed in light of certain facts about mental disorder, displays a remarkable degree of estrangement from its own principled foundations; and in exploring the question *why*, I argue that the law of mental disorder is a uniquely valuable point of insight into a key function of the criminal justice system at large – the channelling of and containment of blame.

There is an abiding instability in the criminal law. To recognize the key role of social and political contributors to crime would complicate to the point of structural paralysis the question of assigning guilt and responsibility; and, in some real way, we need our criminals to expiate our social sins of callous disregard for social dislocation and deep societal inequality. This, I argue, is a function of the criminal justice system at large, not unique to the issue of mental disorder; it is, however, uniquely well exposed in this area of criminal jurisprudence. The interaction of criminal responsibility and mental disorder offers a particularly valuable window into the elisions of responsibility that take place in the criminal justice system. So, at the end of the day, *why* is the threshold for mental disorder (NCRMD) so high? I argue in this chapter that it is so in order to protect our capacity to use the criminal justice system as a means of channelling and containing blame. Might this be reformed? Perhaps, but to do so would require facing a deep instability in the criminal law.

This chapter will begin by examining the threshold for NCRMD, using the Canadian case as the touchstone, and looking to certain theories of mental disorder defences that could serve as plausible accounts for this boundary between the criminally responsible and the mentally disordered. Drawing from the social science literature I then look at the expanding gap between what we know about mental disorders that would appear to bear on the central conditions for criminal responsibility and what the criminal law seems willing to recognize. The chapter then considers what would be required to close this chasm and the political and social impossibility of doing so given what we ask of the criminal justice system. I turn, finally, to what this teaches us about the social function of the law of mental disorder and, more broadly, findings of guilt in the criminal justice system.

I THE CONCEPTUAL STRUCTURE OF NCRMD

In their classic article on the law of insanity, Joseph Goldstein and Jay Katz capture the pivotal but fraught position of the defence of mental disorder in the theory of criminal law. They explain, simply, that '[n]o device haunts the criminal law and clouds the values it seeks to re-enforce more than "insanity" as a basis for relieving persons of criminal responsibility'.[6] The defence of mental disorder has bedevilled the criminal law for centuries and has been the subject not only of substantial doctrinal and theoretical debate, but of marked change over its history. For much of Anglo-Canadian criminal law history the defence operated as a straight exemption, entirely withdrawing the insane accused from the reach of the criminal justice system. The modern variant of the defence now seeks to split concepts of guilt and responsibility in some manner, whether by declaring the accused guilty but not responsible or, as in Canada, designating the accused not criminally responsible on account of mental disorder and channelling that individual into a forensic psychiatric process.[7]

In so doing, the mental disorder defence is a uniquely valuable vehicle for thinking about certain basic theoretical assumptions that inform the criminal justice system. The defence operates by identifying some flaw or disruption in a human faculty or aspect of human nature that interrupts the assignation of responsibility for an otherwise criminal act. Other doctrines in the criminal law – defences such as necessity, duress, and provocation – ultimately gesture in a similar direction, but none drives so directly at the nature of the human mind and none is so suggestive of a theory of the feature of human nature that supports the weight of criminal responsibility. Daniel Robinson points to this theoretical dimension of the defence as the basis for its interest among criminal law theorists, explaining that

> lurking behind the insanity defence is a nest of disturbing questions about the very foundations on which the rule of law has been built, foundations that stand as a veritable theory of human nature, a theory about the determinants of significant human actions; about the power to control and constrain behavior that is otherwise impelled by powerful motives and feelings; about the uniformity of the criteria adopted in establishing such centrally relevant conditions as competence, reasonableness, fairness, coercion, duress, negligence, injury.[8]

[6] J Goldstein and J Katz, 'Abolish the "Insanity Defense" – Why Not?' (1963) *72 Yale Law Journal* 853, 854.

[7] Goldstein and Katz argue that it is a mistake to view the modern mental disorder doctrine as a defence to criminal liability, arguing instead that it is designed 'to define for sanction an exception from among those who would be free of liability', ibid 865. They provocatively explain that 'the insanity defense is not a defense, it is a device for triggering intermediate restraint', ibid 868.

[8] DN Robinson, 'Madness, Badness, and Fitness: Law and Psychiatry (Again)' (2001) 7 *Philosophy, Psychiatry & Psychology* 209, 209.

To tease apart the internal theory animating the defence of insanity is an exercise in isolating something essential about the conditions for responsibility. Criminal law scholars have generated compelling accounts of plausible theoretical bases for the defence that could provide it with coherence and philosophical integrity. The thesis of this chapter, however, is that the law of mental disorder *as lived* does not honour such theoretical lines; indeed, my core assertion is that whatever theory of human nature or agency might inspire the defence (and I am interested in and open to a number of theses circulating in the literature), the controlling influence on the law of mental disorder is the criminal law's sociological function in containing and laundering blame.

A first step in building this argument must turn back to a brief sketch of the doctrine of the defence of mental disorder, identifying its salient features. On the strength of this foundation we can erect certain plausible theoretical accounts of what aspect of human nature is being addressed by the law of mental disorder.

The *M'Naghten*[9] rules cast as prominent a shadow in Canada as they do in other parts of the common law world. The Canadian law of mental disorder was substantially revised in 1991 by means of a raft of legislative amendments to the Criminal Code. One feature of the new legislation was the shift from language of 'insanity' to 'mental disorder'. No doubt the key change was in disposition. Rather than an accused being found not guilty by reason of insanity, at which point the accused would be held at the pleasure of the Lieutenant Governor,[10] an accused who is declared NCRMD is now moved through a disposition hearing before a review board comprised of legal and psychiatric experts who decide on the appropriate treatment and control option, a decision driven largely by assessments of dangerousness.

Despite these far-reaching amendments, the heart of the mental disorder test remained largely unchanged, turning on a definition of mental disorder and the two classic 'branches' or 'arms' of the *M'Naghten* test. In setting out the core of the substantive test, section 16(1) of the Criminal Code states that

> no person is criminally responsible for an act committed or an omission made while suffering from a mental disorder that rendered the person incapable of appreciating the nature and quality of the act or omission or of knowing that it was wrong.[11]

The words 'a mental disorder' in section 16 of the Criminal Code are defined as 'a disease of the mind' and the courts have given this concept an expansive construction. Courts have emphasized that reference to a 'disease of the mind' is not a delegation to psychiatric authority – the term is a legal one, to be defined and applied by judges.[12] The Supreme Court has put very few restrictions on what can

[9] *M'Naghten's* Case [1843] 8 ER 718 (HL).

[10] In *R v Swain* [1991] 1 SCR 933, the Supreme Court of Canada held that this disposition was unconstitutional.

[11] Criminal Code RSC 1985, c. C-46. Section 16(2) establishes a presumption that people do not suffer from mental disorders and imposes a persuasive burden on the party who seeks to rebut this presumption.

[12] *R v Simpson* [1977] 35 CCC (2d) 337 (Ont CA).

count as a disease of the mind or mental disorder, defining it as 'any illness, disorder, or abnormal condition which impairs the human mind and its functioning'[13] and excluding only 'self-induced states caused by alcohol or drugs, as well as transitory mental states such as hysteria or concussion'.[14] The meaning of 'disease of the mind' has increased in importance with the development of the law of automatism, serving as the boundary marker for what conditions are automatism 'proper' and those that are best understood as forms of mental disorder.[15] Yet even here developments in the Canadian jurisprudence on mental disorder have tended to expand the category, classifying as mental disorders any conditions that are 'internal', those that present a continuing danger and even those for which pure policy reasons suggest that a disposition hearing would be the best remedy.[16]

Focusing on mental disorder as opposed to claims of automatism, then, most of the work is done by the two branches – deciding whether a disease of the mind has rendered a person 'incapable of appreciating the nature and quality of the act or omission' or of 'knowing that it was wrong'. Canadian jurisprudence has established that appreciating the nature and quality of the act involves a general ability to 'measure and foresee' the consequences of the act in issue,[17] making clear that 'appreciation' does not involve an emotional appreciation or require appropriate feelings[18] and that the 'consequences' that must be measured and foreseen are not the potential penal consequences for the accused – just the physical consequences of the act.[19] With respect to 'knowing that it was wrong', after some toing and froing, the Supreme Court has held that the defence will apply to a person who is unable to know that an act or omission was legally *or* morally wrong, judged on society's standards.[20] Importantly, the Court has emphasized that this capacity to distinguish between right and wrong is not an abstract or generalized capacity but rather the accused's ability to rationally apply standards of right and wrong in the situation in which he finds himself: '[t]he crux of the inquiry is whether the accused lacks the capacity to rationally decide whether the act is right or wrong and *hence* to make a rational choice about whether to do it or not'.[21]

Consider the salient features of what we might call the '*M'Naghten* paradigm' as reflected in the Canadian test for metal disorder. First, and perhaps most prominent, is the emphasis that these tests place on the capacity for practical reasoning and cognition. In the *M'Naghten* paradigm an accused's 'insanity *amounts* to his "defect of reason"'; 'cognition is recognized as determining of nonculpability and the final "two limbs" of the McNaughten Rules . . . reinforce the

[13] *R v Cooper* [1980] 1 SCR 1149, 1159.

[14] ibid.

[15] *R v Stone* [1999] 2 SCR 290.

[16] See *R v Stone*, ibid [218]. This last component of the definition of 'disease of the mind' shows the extent to which this area of law involves the dispositional tail wagging the substantive dog.

[17] See *R v Cooper* (n 13).

[18] *Kjeldsen v The Queen* [1981] 2 SCR 617.

[19] *R v Abbey* [1982] 2 SCR 24, affirmed in *R v Landry* [1991] 1 SCR 99.

[20] *R v Chaulk and Morrissette* [1990] 3 SCR 1303. This case reversed the decision in *Schwartz v The Queen* [1977] 1 SCR 673, which held that 'wrong' meant only illegal.

[21] *R v Oommen* [1994] 2 SCR 507, 518.

sole relevance of cognition'.[22] This highly rational and narrowly cognitive approach to mental disorder excludes certain conditions that would appear to bear on our sense of the justice of attributing criminal responsibility.[23] As commonly noted, this cognitive focus of the test excludes *volitional* impairments from the defence of mental disorder, as it does issues of emotional appreciation.[24] Furthermore, the threshold for disruption is a high one, requiring 'extreme cognitive impairments',[25] a test that is 'rarely met by even the most psychotic of defendants'.[26] Another prominent (and associated) feature of this approach to mental disorder is the exclusion of *emotional* appreciation from the measure of criminal responsibility. This exclusion draws the boundary around NCRMD in such a way as to remove the defence from those suffering extreme forms of personality disorder such as psychopathy or sociopathy. These various features of the doctrine yield a defence that is chiefly concerned with a narrow band of mental disorders; indeed, the defence is shaped in such a way as to be most responsive to and largely focused on extreme forms of paranoid schizophrenia that involve powerful delusions.[27]

Finally, an important feature of the defence of mental disorder is its dominantly binary nature. One either has those psychiatric features or deficits that preclude the attribution of criminal responsibility or one does not. To the extent that there may be a spectrum of mental disorder, such considerations are relegated to the sentencing phase, in which the law approaches such issues from a profoundly different perspective that gives attention to variations in degrees of responsibility foreign to the question of guilt or innocence.[28] Even in those jurisdictions that have a defence of diminished responsibility, those defences act as partial excuses only and are confined to specific offences.[29]

Using these features of the defence of mental disorder as we find it in the criminal law as a starting point, and sometimes a foil, theorists have attempted to

[22] N Eastman, 'Psychiatric, Psychological, and Legal Models of Man' (1992) 15 *International Journal of Law and Psychiatry* 157, 163.

[23] Although the Supreme Court of Canada briefly recognized emotional impairment as a relevant component of the first limb of the insanity test in *R v Cooper* [1980] 1 SCR 1149, and *R v Barnier* [1980] 1 SCR 1124, they soon resiled from that view in *R v Kjeldsen* [1981] 2 SCR 617, and *R v Abbey* [1982] 2 SCR 24. See G Ferguson, 'A Critique of Proposals to Reform the Insanity Defence' (1989) 15 *Queen's Law Journal* 135, 145.

[24] S Wilson and G Adshead, 'Criminal Responsibility' in J Radden (ed), *The Philosophy of Psychiatry: A Companion* (Oxford, Oxford University Press, 2004) 305.

[25] K Roach and A Bailey, 'The Relevance of Fetal Alcohol Spectrum Disorder in Canadian Criminal Law from Investigation to Sentencing' (2009) 42 *University of British Columbia Law Review* 1, 3.

[26] Wilson and Adshead, 'Criminal Responsibility' (n 24) 298.

[27] A review of the jurisprudence bears this out; the leading cases in which accused were successful in invoking the defence overwhelmingly concern those suffering from delusions associated with some form of paranoid schizophrenia.

[28] Indeed, Eastman, 'Models of Man' (n 22) argues that all matters of mental disorder would be best analyzed in the more nuanced context of sentencing rather than being confined by the binary logic of the guilt phase.

[29] See SJ Morse, 'Diminished Capacity' in S Shute, J Gardner and J Horder (eds), *Action and Value in Criminal Law* (Oxford, Clarendon Press, 1993). On this point Morse notes (at 250) that '[o]rdinary morality makes differential, excusing allowances on a sliding scale of diminished rationality, and in principle the law might do so as well'.

provide a principled basis for why it may be that we would relieve of criminal responsibility those who suffer from particular forms of 'disease of the mind'. These accounts are in search of the normative foundation for the jurisprudential defence, attempting to isolate that feature of the human being necessary to support the attribution of criminal responsibility. I want here to focus on two plausible broad accounts of why we might excuse or exempt offenders from criminal responsibility based on mental disorder.

The first, the 'reason-based account', closely tracks the doctrinal features outlined above. This account is based on the theory that criminal responsibility attaches to the subject's capacity for practical reasoning[30] – her capacity to bring rationality to bear on the situations that she confronts and using that reason-based assessment as a guide for her actions.[31] To the extent that an individual possesses this capacity, she is an appropriate subject for the attribution of criminal responsibility. Stephen Morse and Morris Hoffman provide a synoptic explanation of this account of mental disorder as a defence:

> The crucial normative question is whether it is unfair to blame and punish a defendant who meets the definitional elements of the crime, but whose rationality at the time of the offense was severely impaired. Rationality is the touchstone of responsibility, as the structure of criminal law itself indicates. All laws, criminal and civil, make sense and are functional precisely because they provide action-guiding reasons addressed to potentially rational creatures. . . . It is simply unfair to hold responsible, blame, and punish mentally disordered wrongdoers who are not morally responsible because they were not capable of being rational at the time of the crime.[32]

The 'simple unfairness' to which the mental disorder defence responds is the injustice of holding someone responsible for actions that are not a product of his reasoned decision-making. Indeed, Morse argues that, properly defined, instances of volitional impairment are really about defects of reason inasmuch as reason involves the capacity to conform one's behaviours with reasoned based assessments.[33] This view of mental disorder meshes with a general sense of moral responsibility, which Susan Wolf calls the 'reason view', whereby 'having responsible status depends . . . on a distinctive intellectual power, the power to exercise right Reason and to govern one's actions accordingly'.[34] Wolf notes that there is a degree of adaptability and learning inherent in this theory of responsibility whereby 'part of what it *is* to act in accordance with Reason is to be sensitive and responsive to relevant changes in one's situation and environment – that is, to be

[30] See SJ Morse, 'Craziness and Criminal Responsibility' (1999) 17 *Behavioral Sciences and the Law* 147, 155, where he explains, '[m]ental disorders affect practical reasoning primarily by producing crazy perceptions (hallucinations) and crazy beliefs (delusions) that give rise to grossly crazy reasons'.

[31] See Wilson and Adshead, 'Criminal Responsibility' (n 24) 298, in which the authors suggest that '[l]egal insanity has been seen as a cognitive matter, concerning reason, or rather lack of reason, and this should be seen in the context of the traditional legal view that reason controls behavior'.

[32] SJ Morse and MB Hoffman, 'The Uneasy Entente Between Legal Insanity and Mens Rea: Beyond *Clark v Arizona*' (2007) 97 *Journal of Criminal Law and Criminology* 1071, 1117.

[33] Morse, 'Diminished Capacity' (n 29) 270; Morse and Hoffman (n32) 1095.

[34] S Wolf, *Freedom within Reason* (Oxford, Oxford University Press, 1990) 71.

flexible'.[35] This, then, is one plausible account of the normative basis for the insanity defence, an account that might serve as the principled basis for explaining the boundaries of the defence of NCRMD – we do not punish those who suffer a disease of the mind that interferes with their capacity to reason because reasoning and conforming one's actions to the product of reason are the preconditions to moral responsibility.

Without in any way suggesting that the two are unrelated, I want to identify another theoretical account of the defence of mental disorder that emphasises different normative concerns as the basis for the defence. This is an 'agency/authorship-based account' that focuses on whether an act can be fairly attributed to an individual as the author of an autonomous and authentic human life. Robinson argues that the logic of the law includes an assumption of 'agentic power', which he describes in general terms as 'a state of competence sufficient to bring about or forbear from bringing about' a particular event.[36] As opposed to isolating *reason* as the human faculty that attracts responsibility, this account would focus instead on whether the act is a genuine expression of the individual's free and voluntary *will*.[37] Tadros draws out the theory of responsibility in this account when he explains that '[r]esponsible agents . . . are agents who can develop their lives autonomously in relation to the set of moral concerns that are central to the criminal law'.[38] It is this conception of responsibility that leads him to his character-oriented theory of mental disorder that would provide a defence to those who could claim that the act 'was not reflective of the agent *qua* agent'[39] – to the accused who could rightly claim 'it wasn't really me'.[40] There is no doubt a component of reason at play in this agency account, but the emphasis lies on self-authorship and the degree to which acts are a genuine expression of one's authentic will. Here Taylor's explanation of human agency is helpful. He places the capacity for 'strong evaluation' at the centre of what it means to be a responsible human agent, explaining that 'an agent who could not evaluate desires at all would lack the minimum degree of reflectiveness which we associate with a human agent, and would also lack a crucial part of the background for what we

[35] ibid 69.

[36] Robinson, 'Madness, Badness' (n 8) 210.

[37] See Roach and Bailey, 'The Relevance of Fetal Alcohol Spectrum Disorder' (n 25) 3: 'The justice system is premised on assumptions that people act in a voluntary manner that is determined by free will and that they can make informed and voluntary choices both with respect to the exercise of their rights and the decision to commit crimes'. See also R Cairns Way, 'The Charter, the Supreme Court and the Invisible Politics of Fault' (1992) 12 *Windsor Yearbook of Access to Justice* 128, 147: 'The criminal law is philosophically linked to the free-will model of human conduct which posits an autonomous agent who, by the exercise of a voluntary and informed choice, violates established behavioural norms. It is that choice which provides the moral justification for punishment'.

[38] V Tadros, *Criminal Responsibility* (Oxford, Oxford University Press, 2005) 135.

[39] ibid 332.

[40] ibid 322. See also L Reznek, *Evil or Ill? Justifying the Insanity Defence* (New York, Routledge, 1977) who argues for a character change-based account of the mental disorder defence. Reznek's central argument is that '[a] person is NGRI if and only if (1) he is suffering from a mental illness, and (2) the mental illness causes a change of moral character'. (11) For a critique of Reznek's arguments, see Robinson, 'Madness, Badness' (n 8).

describe as the exercise of will'.[41] On this account, the law of mental disorder is responding to those situations in which, owing to a disease of the mind, a given act cannot be fairly attributed to the autonomous will of an accused.

Needless to say, there are significant points of contiguity between these two accounts. The cleanliness of the distinction is not crucial. What matters is that these two accounts draw out different plausible sets of concerns that might form a conceptual foundation for a principled defence of mental disorder – a sense of responsibility constellated around the faculty of reason and one that focuses on the capacity to exercise an autonomous will. With a sense of the current state of the law and with these two sets of concerns in hand, I turn now to consider the state of our contemporary knowledge about the kinds of conditions that afflict substantial numbers of accused involved in the criminal justice system. What emerges is a yawning chasm between a conceptually coherent approach to mental disorder and the doctrinal defence with which we are equipped.

II THE TROUBLING PRESENCE OF MENTAL DISORDER IN THE CRIMINAL JUSTICE SYSTEM

The substance of our insanity defence has remained remarkably stable since the articulation of the *M'Naghten* rules in 1843. The core of the defence still turns on the presence of a disease of the mind with two possible branches of cognitive effects: incapacity to appreciate the nature and consequences of the act, or to know that the act was wrong. This stability in the legal doctrine stands in stark contrast to the degree of change in our appreciation of the incidence and nature of various psychological and developmental disorders afflicting those who find themselves involved in the criminal justice system. Whereas the shape of the mental disorder defence might have once enjoyed a degree of fit with social knowledge as to the facts of forensically relevant psychiatric conditions, there is mounting evidence that the legal test for mental disorder is inhospitable or even actively hostile to certain mental disorders found with surprising frequency in our growing penal population.

In focusing briefly on three such disorders and charting what we know about how they may affect criminal responsibility, my goal is not to critique the criminal law for using concepts foreign to or outdated within psychiatric knowledge, nor is it to tar the criminal law with the brush of being psychiatrically unsavvy. I take as important that the criminal law and psychiatry have different goals and functions that mean that the concerns and orientations of one may justifiably depart from those of the other. I am not concerned with identifying a gap between psychiatric knowledge and the defence of mental disorder. Rather, having identified two plausible accounts of the conceptual concerns endogenous to the criminal law

[41] C Taylor, 'What is Human Agency?' in *Human Agency and Language* (Cambridge, Cambridge University Press, 1985) 28.

that may inform the defence of mental disorder, in this section I wish to demonstrate that whatever view one adopts of why mental disorder ought to matter to criminal responsibility, the facts show a law disconnected from *its own* principled foundations. Whether one adopts a reason-based, agency-based or some mixed account of the theoretical basis for mental disorder, the situations that activate these concerns are far more widespread and complex than one would infer from watching the operation of the criminal justice system. The gap of interest to me, then, is that which exists between the defence of mental disorder and the facts relevant to the set of concerns that, on theoretical terms intrinsic to the criminal justice system, ought to matter to the assignation of criminal responsibility.

Foetal Alcohol Spectrum Disorder (FASD)[42] is perhaps the most widely discussed condition in relation to its effects on criminal liability. Evidence of the incidence of FASD in the criminal justice system is startling, suggesting that a minimum of 10 per cent[43] and up to 28 per cent[44] of those in Canadian carceral settings suffer from a significant form of FASD, compared with approximately one per cent in the general population.[45] Reversing the gaze produces an even more harrowing image: one study indicates that 60 per cent of those suffering from FASD find themselves in trouble with the criminal justice system and fully 50 per cent experience confinement.[46] Roach and Bailey observe that 'FASD is most often dealt with under the criminal law', noting that this is 'consistent with observations that the criminal justice system is being left to deal with more and more failures of social policy and the effects of mental illness, substance addiction, poverty, and despair'.[47] FASD is a developmental disorder with which children are born; it does not flow from choices made by the individual in his own lifetime. But is this the kind of disorder that ought to be of concern in the assignation of criminal liability? Consider the range of effects of FASD.[48] In addition to producing superficial abilities in and understanding of language and having adverse effects on attention and memory, FASD can have substantial impacts on an individual's capacity for adaptive behaviour and reasoning. Those suffering from FASD have difficulty understanding and conforming to standards of pesonal independence and social responsibility. Disturbingly, given the assumptions of the criminal justice system, they have difficulty learning from past experiences

[42] I will be using this term, cognizant of the fact that Foetal Alcohol Effects (FAE), Foetal Alcohol Syndrome (FAS) and other terms are in circulation.

[43] See Roach and Bailey, 'The Relevance of Fetal Alcohol Spectrum Disorder' (n 25) 8–9.

[44] DK Fast and J Conroy, 'Fetal Alcohol Spectrum Disorders and the Criminal Justice System' (2009) 15 *Developmental Disability Research Reviews* 250, 251.

[45] ibid 251. Fast and Conroy also report that approximately one quarter of youths in custody are diagnosable as suffering from FASD.

[46] See Roach and Bailey, 'The Relevance of Fetal Alcohol Spectrum Disorder' (n 25) 9.

[47] ibid 11.

[48] For accounts of the effects of FASD, see Fast and Conroy, 'Fetal Alcohol Spectrum Disorders' (n 44) 252–53; LN Chartrand and EM Forbes-Chillibeck, 'The Sentencing of Offenders with Fetal Alcohol Syndrome' (2003) 11 *Health Law Journal* 35, 36–43; and Yukon Department of Justice and Department of Justice Canada, 'The Path to Justice: Access to Justice for Individuals with Fetal Alcohol Spectrum Disorder – Conference Final Report' (Whitehorse, 17–19 September 2008), online: www.justice.gov.yk.ca/pdf/Path_to_Justice_Conference_Final_Report_FINAL_Eng.pdf.

and, in particular, connecting cause and effect. Combined with impairments in processing social cues, those with FASD can have difficulty appreciating the effects that their behaviours have on others and the seriousness of their actions.

In their survey of Canadian case law, Roach and Bailey show that although some courts have been willing to include FASD within the meaning of 'disease of the mind', claims of NCRMD have failed because of the very high standard for cognitive impairment imposed by the law. Yet FASD seems to strike at the heart of the sets of concerns that plausibly animate the law of mental disorder. From a reason-based perspective, one must be extremely troubled by the extent to which, with an inability to process social cues and a high degree of impulsivity, those with FASD who commit crimes can be said to be exercising the rational faculties consistent with assigning criminal responsibility. With a diminished appreciation of cause-and-effect, and an insensitivity to the impacts of their behaviours on others, FASD would seem to put into principled question the extent to which an individual is genuinely appreciative of the nature and quality of their acts or whether the act was wrong. At a basic level, people suffering from FASD may lack the capacity for flexibility and learning that Wolf argues is central to responsible reasoning. Matters are equally difficult from an agency-based perspective on why mental disorder is an important part of our law. The inability to learn from past actions and the diminished capacity for exercise of will found in the impulsivity strongly associated with FASD raise serious concerns about the extent to which those suffering from FASD are fairly considered autonomous authors of their actions. Note that in this respect, volition does, indeed, seem relevant to the conceptual foundations of mental disorder. Studies have noted that the linguistic and memory disruptions caused by FASD make the individual particularly susceptible to influence, suggestion and control, again raising red flags about agency. In short, despite the law's unreceptive posture towards such claims, from either a reason-based or agency-based perspective, the effects of FASD ought to severely complicate the attribution of criminal responsibility and, sadly, ought to do so for a substantial number of those addressed by the criminal justice system.

An equally complicating but less widely discussed mental disorder that also falls under the radar of our doctrinal defence is Autism Spectrum Disorder and, in particular, Asperger's Syndrome. Recent studies have addressed the forensic relevance of Asperger's Syndrome.[49] Evidence suggests that the incidence of Asperger's Syndrome is significantly higher among those involved in the criminal justice system as compared with the general population. Those suffering from Asperger's Syndrome often demonstrate a limited appreciation and understanding of both the emotional reactions of those around them and of interpreting

[49] See, eg, L Burdon and G Dickens, 'Asperger Syndrome and Offending Behaviour' (2009) 12 *Learning Disability Practice* 14; I Freckelton and D List, 'Asperger's Disorder, Criminal Responsibility and Criminal Culpability' (2009) 16 *Psychiatry, Psychology and Law* 16; BG Haskins and JA Silva, 'Asperger's Disorder and Criminal Behavior: Forensic-Psychiatric Considerations' (2006) 34 *Journal of the American Academy of Psychiatry and the Law* 374.

social cues.[50] Many show weakness in rational problem solving and the interpretation of the behaviour of others, particularly their emotional reactions.[51] Asperger's Syndrome can also produce a 'limited capacity to foresee the consequences of their behaviour'[52] and, under conditions of stress or if overwhelmed or confused, those with Asperger's Syndrome can respond with extreme impulsivity, sometimes leading to uncontrollable violent reactions.[53] Taking account of this melange of characteristics that can appear in those suffering from Asperger's Syndrome, one author squarely poses the question at the heart of this chapter's concern: 'if social conventions and connectedness are opaque to them how can they authentically appreciate that their actions are morally wrong'?[54]

Once again, Asperger's Syndrome does not tend to produce the narrow and acute form of cognitive disruption imagined in the law of mental disorder. Nevertheless, the effects of this condition cut across the sets of concerns with attributing criminal responsibility at the heart of both the reason-based and agency/authorship-based accounts of a mental disorder defence. If criminal responsibility trades on the individual's ability to rationally assess the concrete situation in which that individual finds herself, Asperger's disruption of one's capacity to read social cues, evaluate emotional reactions, foresee consequences and engage in problem-solving make it a forensically relevant condition. Similarly, it is not solely the high degree of impulsivity associated with Asperger's that impels one to seriously query the extent to which an act can be fairly ascribed to a person *qua agent* or author of one's own life; being deprived of the capacity to measure the consequences and emotional impact of one's actions radically destabilizes one's ability to say that a person's actions are a manifestation of one's character or authentic will.

Perhaps the most intriguing example of the estrangement of the doctrine of mental disorder from its own plausible theoretical accounts is found in the case of psychopathy.[55] The law has assiduously worked to exclude psychopathic personality disorders from the defence of mental disorder by marginalizing the role of

[50] Freckelton and List, 'Asperger's Disorder', ibid 18. See also, Haskins and Silva, 'Asperger's Disorder', ibid 378, where the authors trace this impairment of the ability to process social situations to a deficit in Asperger's patients' 'theory of mind'.

[51] See N Katz and Z Zemishlany, 'Criminal Responsibility in Asperger's Syndrome' (2006) 43 *Israel Journal of Psychiatry and Related Sciences* 166, 171–72: 'People with AS are unable to perceive other people's needs, desires or distress due to their inability to interpret correctly other people's behavior. . . . There is no understanding whatsoever on the AS subject's part of the implications and repercussions of their actions'. See also Freckelton and List, 'Asperger's Disorder' (n 49) 19; Haskins and Silva, 'Asperger's Disorder' (n 49) 382.

[52] Freckelton and List, 'Asperger's Disorder' (n 49) 31.

[53] ibid 31.

[54] JB Barry-Walsh and PE Mullen, 'Forensic Aspects of Asperger's Syndrome' (2004) 15 *Journal of Forensic Psychiatry & Psychology* 96, 106. See also Katz and Zemishlany, 'Criminal Responsibility' (n 49) 172, in which the authors explain that, for those suffering from Asperger's Syndrome, '[i]t is especially in the social sense that their judgement is deficient to a degree that inhibits their ability to understand that what they were doing was wrong'.

[55] Psychopathy is not a diagnostic category in the DSM IV-TR; Anti-Social Personality Disorder (ASPD), to which it is closely related, is a recognized condition.

emotional appreciation in the doctrinal test. Studies suggest that 65–75 per cent of the prison population suffer from Anti-Social Personality Disorder with fully 25–30 per cent diagnosable as psychopaths.[56] Famous nineteenth-century psychiatrist James Cowles Pritchard called psychopathy 'moral insanity' on the basis that he regarded psychopaths as 'truly insane and irresponsible for their actions who were not so intellectually disordered that they could be recognized as insane by the traditional criteria'.[57] Despite the legal insensitivity to psychopathy as disrupting criminal responsibility, contemporary research on the condition points to ways in which psychopathy strikes at the core of the principled preoccupations of both the reason-based and agency/authorship-based accounts of why mental disorder should matter to the criminal law. The deficits associated with psychopathy include those that bear on the emotional, cognitive/linguistic, motivational and executive function or capacity for decision-making.[58] In particular, the core of the psychopath's condition appears to be that whereas 'most individuals seek at least a balance between immediate gratification and long-term cost'[59] psychopaths are neurologically focused exclusively on immediate opportunities for gain or reinforcement. Some trace this inability to weigh immediate desire against extrinsic considerations to a malfunctioning in the seratonin-dopamine system,[60] but the essential forensically-relevant problem is that, when making behavioural decisions, psychopaths seem unable to consider factors outside the moment.

Schneider and Nussbaum ultimately describe the condition of psychopathy as an incapacity to 'encode and process moral issues in ways that would suggest moral appreciation of the situational issues that might guide their behavior'.[61] In contrast to the emphasis in *Oommen* on the accused's capacity to reason in a way that is responsive to the practical situation at hand, 'it can be argued that at least for acts of predatory violence, which are most characteristic of the psychopath, the psychopath cannot consider moral or legal wrongfulness when s/he is making the decision to attack, because their decision is overwhelmingly tuned to the immediate opportunity for gain'.[62] The psychopathic individual simply does not have access to knowledge of society's moral code – or indeed to other considerations – at the moment of committing the offence. Whether one holds up the capacity for meaningful reasoning as the key to criminal responsibility, or whether one emphasizes the ability to conform one's actions to one's character or strong evaluations, psychopathy should be of central concern to the defence of mental disorder.

Examining the nature and effect of two mental conditions virtually ignored by the criminal justice system, and one actively excluded from relevance, powerfully

[56] RD Schneider and D Nussbaum, 'Can the Bad be Mad?' (2007) 53 *Crim Law Quarterly* 206; see also E Viding, 'Annotation: Understanding the Development of Psychopathy' (2004) 45 *Journal of Child Psychology and Psychiatry* 1329.

[57] Schneider and Nussbaum, ibid 210–11.

[58] ibid.

[59] ibid 215.

[60] ibid.

[61] ibid 221.

[62] ibid 222.

suggests that the system is insensitive to conditions that nevertheless activate concerns at the heart of a principled account of why mental disorder should matter to criminal responsibility. Both the prevalence and the relevance of these conditions are far greater than one would discern from the daily workings of the Canadian criminal justice system. The picture painted is of a criminal law chronically detached from or comfortably ignorant of situations that raise serious concerns within the best accounts of the conditions for criminal responsibility. And this leads us to the question: 'what is the function of a criminal law doctrine so unconcerned with facts that bear on its own theoretical preoccupations?' The first step in beginning to answer this question is to consider what would be involved – practically and symbolically – if such conditions were taken seriously within the criminal law.

III WHAT IT WOULD MEAN TO TRULY RESPOND TO MENTAL DISORDER IN THE CRIMINAL LAW

The conditions that I have drawn out are not at the boundaries of the criminal justice system. They are not marginal or idiosyncratic phenomena. With figures as high as 25 per cent of those involved in the criminal justice system affected by FASD and 35 per cent suffering from some severe form of antisocial personality disorder such as psychopathy, we are looking here at a substantial component of the work done by the criminal justice system. These conditions drawn from a much larger possible list (including perhaps bipolar disorder and depression) would appear to directly engage concerns at the theoretical basis for the law of mental disorder. Yet the law of mental disorder fails to take meaningful account of these mental conditions, structurally excluding them by means of the combination of a narrow definition that disregards emotional and volitional considerations and a high bar requiring severe and obvious impairment of cognition. My claim is not, however, that the doctrine requires reform. Nor, indeed, do I mean to suggest that it would be preferable for a larger number of offenders to be drawn into our current NCRMD disposition and assessment scheme. The misfit of fact, theory and doctrine is, I suggest, irredeemable. Yet this very resistance to redemption through doctrinal reform offers a clue to a core purpose of the criminal justice system revealed by the law of mental disorder.

As a thought experiment, consider what it would look like for the defence to drop some of its doctrinal guards and to be more solicitous of conditions such as those I have canvassed – mental illnesses that raise legitimate concerns about the attribution of criminal responsibility.

There would be an obvious practical effect. The system would buckle under the weight of a new-found therapeutic task. Assuming, conservatively, that somewhere near 50 per cent of cases demanded some inquiry into the accused's appropriateness as a bearer of criminal responsibility, a system already creaking under the pressure of case overload and the complexity of contemporary trials would grind to a halt. The day-in, day-out practice of the courts would become substantially diagnostic, a task for which it is simply not equipped. Judges and juries would be commonly engaged in the detailed assessment of mental health issues. Furthermore, the resources devoted to the dispositional side of mental disorder – the review board system and forensic psychiatric services – would have to be vastly expanded (a need that is, in truth, already critical). These are practical difficulties. Yet they are suggestive of the structural unsuitability of the criminal justice system for taking seriously the relationship between mental health and criminal responsibility. More interesting – and more telling – for present purposes, however, are the communicative and symbolic effects were the law to take meaningful account of any but the narrowest band of extreme mental disorders.

These effects would be twofold and closely related.

First, a brooding instability would afflict the process of assigning individual blame and responsibility. Raising a question mark as to the responsibility of this broad swathe of accused would disrupt broad systemic comfort with the attribution of individual responsibility for crime. The criminal justice system is asked to take a moment of social breakdown and to introduce some reason, some order, into that moment of victimization by assigning responsibility to a single actor.[63] As it now stands, only limited exceptions to the binary verdict of guilty or not guilty are permitted. But consider the momentous shift in the communicative force and function of the criminal law should 35–50 per cent of accused raise serious questions as to whether blame is possible. This would be one symbolic consequence of a more porous law of mental disorder that was more responsive to its theoretical substratum of principled concerns – incapacity to stably assign blame to individuals.[64] Rather than answering the question 'is he to blame?' with a confident 'guilty' or 'not guilty', the system would be facing the radically different prospect of far more frequent answers in the faltering register of 'not applicable'. Many argue that a key communicative function of the criminal law is to reassert, by attributing blame, collective moral commitments regarding an ethic of responsibility for one's actions, the importance of control, and to paint a picture in which violence is a marginal and rationally-controllable phenomenon.[65] Craig Edwards suggests that, in pursuit of such goals, '[o]ur condemnation of [certain] conditions may be necessary to adequately express our moral values concerning violence, self-control, and social responsibility'.[66] On this view, maintaining the

[63] BL Berger, 'On the Book of Job, Justice, and the Precariousness of the Criminal Law' (2008) 4 *Law, Culture and the Humanities* 98.

[64] As Goldman writes, '[i]t is not possible . . . for the law to risk its capacity to judge and punish people by flirting too much with this view'. P Goldman, 'Law, Ideology and Social Causality' (1987) 12 *Queen's Law Journal* 473, 482.

[65] See especially Garland, *Punishment and Modern Society* (n 1) 249–76, in which Garland discusses punishment as a 'cultural agent' and J Feinberg, *Doing and Deserving: Essays in the Theory of Repsonsibility* (Princeton, Princeton University Press, 1970).

[66] C Edwards, 'Ethical Decisions in the Classification of Mental Conditions as Mental Illness' (2009) 16 *Philosophy, Psychiatry & Psychology* 73, 84.

communicative force of the norms embodied in the criminal law demands stability in the attribution of responsibility, a stability that might require disregard of factors that otherwise influence our sense of an individual's personal responsibility.[67] To drop the threshold on mental disorder would enervate the criminal justice system's capacity to serve this communicative role.

It bears noting that hand-in-hand with this enfeebled capacity to confidently assign individual blame would be the criminal justice system's involvement in the multiplication of victims. Consider the nature and aetiology of FASD. Met with an instance of victimhood, a system with an expanded defence of mental disorder would not only frequently be unable to comfortably assign blame to an individual; in the process it would transform the moment into the recognition of another, albeit different form of, victim – the mentally ill accused. The expansion of the doctrine of mental disorder would be associated with a destabilizing of the border between the categories of perpetrator and victim.

And this point brings us to the second and closely related communicative or symbolic shift that a 'rationalized' doctrine of mental disorder would produce: the haemorrhaging of blame. It is not just that blame would be more difficult to pin on offenders; rather, unpinned to the individual, it would circulate, touching social and political institutions broadly. It is not solely that it would be a more complex and uncertain affair to point the finger at the accused (the first effect). To take account of mental disorder in a manner consistent with the principled reasons why one might consider the defence to be crucial to issues of criminal responsibility would simultaneously point fingers at social, political and collective responsibility for crime. Embedded in each story of criminogenic mental disorder is a parallel, though generally buried, narrative about collective commitments to the distribution of resources to aid those suffering from mental illness, political will in emphasizing issues of treatment and prevention rather than the adoption of (genuinely sociopathic) 'tough on crime' models of attending to social breakdown, systemic marginalization of vulnerable communities and the stigmatization of mental illness. Patricia Backlar offers the scenario of a woman who pushes her baby off a balcony believing it to be a demon. After addressing the way in which the law might address the relationship between her delusions and her criminal fault, Backlar puts her finger on the point at issue:

> What if her psychotic episodes were *known* to be unpredictable and neither influenced by medication noncompliance or substance abuse? Should we hold others responsible? If she has a family are they, in some way, answerable? Could they have made sure that she was never left alone with her child? What about her mental health provider? Could he have made certain that she was protected and prevented from harming herself and

[67] Edwards explains: 'It may be that even if a violent criminal offender's temper and alcoholism was originally caused by factors outside both his and his parents' control, we must still apply a duty upon him to take an active and morally responsible role in seeking treatment for such conditions, or else we could not truly hold our prohibitions against violence as *moral* rules (as most offenders could lay claim to a rationality-impairing character flaw that motivated their conduct)' (ibid 84).

> others? And, what about her community – did her community play a part in this tragedy?[68]

With the focus diverted from the accused, that relentless gaze that searches for the locus of blame may well settle on decisions about the distribution of resources, community attitudes to mental health and failures in the political and social system that might have contributed to the coming about of this criminal act. The resulting finger-pointing would be warranted. Evidence suggests that it is not severe mental illness alone that leads to crime; rather, it is the *confluence* of mental health issues and social disadvantage that is predictive of legal involvement.[69] Of those accessing mental health services, it is those in receipt of social assistance and, most notably, those who are unstably housed who are most likely to become involved in the criminal justice system. The more seriously one takes mental illness in the criminal justice system, the more issues of collective, social and political responsibility for crime come into focus and the more suspect becomes our use of the criminal law to blame the individual accused. The issue can be fruitfully thought of as one of *standing* to blame.[70] If one understands blame as a relational or reciprocal in nature,[71] society's authority to call an accused to answer for a wrong committed might well be eroded when it becomes clear that, through systemic injustice, society has visited serious disadvantage and social wrongs on this person. By creating or sustaining unjust conditions that lead to crime, the state is complicit in and shares responsibility for the crime, making it unjust to blame the accused without also acknowledging and taking steps to remedy its own blameworthiness.[72]

This second symbolic effect – the haemorrhaging of responsibility for crime into society at large – may be most obvious in the case of FASD, where the incidence of this developmental disorder is inextricable from issues of poverty, marginalization and substance abuse. The high incidence of FASD in Canadian Aboriginal communities and its link to the political and social disregard for the historical and contemporary issues facing Indigenous communities stands as strong evidence of the point that I am making here.[73] Once the lid is opened on the possible lines of responsibility for crime, blame is difficult to contain and it becomes deeply uncomfortable and even unjust to myopically focus our collective attention – and the violence of the law – on the accused. In his discussion of

[68] P Backlar, 'Criminal Behavior and Mental Disorder: Impediments to Assigning Moral Responsibility' (1998) 34 *Community Mental Health Journal* 3, 7.

[69] CT Sheldon et al, 'Social Disadvantage, Mental Illness and Predictors of Legal Involvement' (2005) 29 *International Journal of Law and Psychiatry* 249.

[70] See RA Duff, 'Blame, Moral Standing and the Legitimacy of the Criminal Trial' (2010) 23 *Ratio* 123; RA Duff, *Answering for Crime: Responsibility and Liability in the Criminal Law* (Oxford, Hart Publishing, 2009) esp 175–193; V Tadros, 'Poverty and Criminal Responsibility' (2009) 43 *Journal of Value Inquiry* 391. For another relational theory of blame, see TM Scanlon, *Moral Dimensions: Permissibility, Meaning, Blame* (Cambridge MA, Belknap Press of Harvard University Press, 2008) ch 4.

[71] See Duff, *Answering for Crime*, ibid, and Tadros, 'Poverty', ibid.

[72] Tadros, 'Poverty', ibid 409.

[73] See Chartrand and Forbes-Chillibeck, 'The Sentencing of Offenders' (n 48).

stigma and status responsibility in the criminal law, Tadros offers a passage that is equal parts humane and harrowing and that bears directly on the point being made here:

> [P]erhaps a better explanation of the attempt to remove stigma from mental disorder is the suggestion that most of those with mental disorder are status-responsible. They are capable of participating fully in social and political institutions. However, it may be that some of those individuals are so capable only with the right kind of social support, the right treatment, and the right attitude of those around them. Where an individual lacks that social support, it may be that the proper stigma is not to be attached to the person with the mental disorder, but rather to the society that fails to create the conditions under which those with mental disorder can participate fully in our social and political institutions.[74]

To expand the defence of mental disorder in a way that would take account of those conditions that legitimately activate the concerns at the theoretical basis of the defence would demand precisely this set of questions, pointing to society's complicity in crimes committed by the mentally ill and exposing an instability in our collective standing to blame absent the acceptance of, and the adoption of meaningful steps to remedy, systemic contributions to such crime.[75] A symbolic effect of taking mental disorder seriously in the criminal law would be the distribution of blame for crime at a collective and political level – and, it seems, the last place that we want our blaming gaze to fall is on a mirror.

IV CONCLUSION: MENTAL DISORDER, BLAME AND THE SOCIAL FUNCTION OF THE CRIMINAL LAW

Looking at what would be involved in giving serious doctrinal regard to the facts about mental disorder that ought to be of theoretical concern provides clues as to the symbolic or rhetorical role of the law of mental disorder. In so doing, it also opens up a line of sight into some of the crucial but generally unacknowledged social functions of the criminal justice system.

I have thus far suggested that the restrictively designed keyhole through which successful defences of mental disorder must pass helps to preserve the systemic capacity to stably address the issue of individual blame and to assign individual responsibility. With only a limited and grudging concession to those most extreme cognitive disorders that would be impossible to disregard in their effect on criminal

[74] Tadros, *Criminal Responsibility* (n 38) 148–49.

[75] The need for the state to not only accept responsibility but take tangible steps to treat the mentally ill in a politically just manner is well explained by Tadros, 'Poverty' (n 70) in his discussion of blame in the context of gross economic injustice: '[i]n order adequately to accept responsibility for the crimes of the poor, the state would have to create the expectation that it would not act in such a way that it is complicit with similar crimes in the future. It could do this only by rectifying criminogenic economic injustice. If such a practice is possible at all, it is possible only at the point that an economically unjust state becomes just' (410).

responsibility, the system is able to get on with its work of assigning individual blame on largely stable footing. This preserves a communicative reaction central to the logic of the criminal law, one that responds to a moment of victimization and social breakdown with a re-inscription of social commitment to an ethos of personal responsibility for actions in the hospitable atmosphere of a strong presumption of free and rational human agency. This communicative moment also broadcasts a sense of violence as idiosyncratic and subject to rational control.

In so doing, our doctrines of mental disorder also prevent the spread of blame into larger political and social issues, despite the fact that such a critical turn to examine collective responsibility for crime and victimization is eminently warranted. In its selective and restrictive form, the under-inclusive doctrine of mental disorder serves as a mechanism for the elision of collective blame for a complex social problem, insulating society from the troubling self-criticisms and gestures to political and social responsibility that findings of NCRMD tend to produce.

In this, I suggest that the doctrine serves a rhetorical and symbolic function conceptually distinct from the theoretical concerns that ought to animate a defence of mental disorder. In all, I am essentially suggesting an anti-realist account of the defence of NCRMD.[76] Our doctrines of mental disorder have a function that is independent of any correspondence between the reasons that we would care about mental disorder as a matter of criminal responsibility and what we learn about the incidence and nature of responsibility-affecting conditions suffered by those in the net of the criminal justice system. Its force does not come from its referential quality; rather, it comes from its rhetorical and symbolic capacity to structure our response to crime in a way that serves certain social functions untethered to theories of responsibility. Understood in this way, the fact that certain mental impairments are under-recognized or ignored in our criminal law doctrine is lamentable and sometimes tragic but it ought not to be surprising. The law of mental disorder is not ultimately aimed at coherence with the theory of mental disorder as an exempting condition and the facts that bear upon it. The law of mental disorder is ultimately concerned with the channelling and containment of blame.

Mental disorder's role in stabilizing and containing blame shines through at an illuminating moment in Lawrie Reznek's study, *Evil or Ill*?[77] Having carefully developed an account of what he views as the proper conceptual foundations of the law of mental disorder, Reznek falls upon a 'moral paradox'.[78] Reznek's argument is that the insanity defence ought to turn on a character-based theory of responsibility whereby we excuse actions that are departures from the accused's moral character. Yet psychopathy poses a clear problem on this account. Reznek concedes that if one were to adopt this character approach to insanity, it would seem that the accused suffering from a personality disorder would also enjoy a

[76] On realist and anti-realist accounts of mental disorder and the criminal law see Wilson and Adshead, 'Criminal Responsibility' (n 24).

[77] Reznek, *Evil or Ill?* (n 40).

[78] ibid 309.

defence of mental disorder because 'he too has undergone a change in moral character'.[79] How does Reznek avoid this 'slippery slope'?[80] He argues simply 'we should conclude that those with personality disorders are responsible'.[81] He explains that '[w]e do this by arguing that psychopaths are not ill – we may judge that some condition is not a disease *if the political consequences of classifying it as a disease* are too costly' (emphasis added).[82] Following his theoretical account to its natural extension would introduce an untenable instability in the criminal law. '[W]e are better off', Reznek concludes, 'viewing psychopaths as evil and dealing with them in the penal system'.[83] Mental disorder is not tracking psychiatric knowledge; more central, however, to this paper is the fact that the doctrine of mental disorder seems unable to track its own theoretical foundations in theories of criminal responsibility. Mental disorder serves to veil the abidingly precarious nature of the assignation of criminal responsibility in favour of society's need for the communicative and social functions of ascribing guilt to an individual.

Although demonstrated through an analysis of the defence of mental disorder, my claim is that this is true of the criminal justice system at large. The law of mental disorder – and, in particular, the very high bar for meeting the defence – is simply a point in the law of criminal responsibility particularly well configured for use in exposing these aspects of the criminal law. The criminal justice system is a 'resource in signification',[84] a repertoire of symbolic and linguistic moves (with the most material of consequences) that serves certain key functions including the channelling of blame for social breakdown into the individual and the containment of blame in that single accused. The binary 'guilty/not guilty' that is the dramatic climax of the criminal justice system launders issues of responsibility. A key function of the criminal trial is to put the individual components of responsibility on strategic display while concealing the lines of collective, social and political responsibility that we are loath to confront.[85] One could have demonstrated this point with a close analysis of the treatment of domestic violence through the law of self-defence; the law of sexual assault and the manner in which it conceals issues of gender modelling of abiding and destructive purchase; or more generally the systemic elision of poverty and homelessness as a factor in criminal responsibility. The verdict of guilt not only reasserts a set of commitments around the norms expressed in the criminal law and an abstract commitment to an ethic of

[79] ibid.
[80] ibid.
[81] ibid.
[82] ibid.
[83] ibid.
[84] RM Cover, 'The Supreme Court 1982 Term – Foreword: Nomos and Narrative' (1983) 97 *Harvard Law Review* 4, 8. Cover's full statement is resonant for the law of mental disorder: 'Law is a resource in signification that enables us to submit, rejoice, struggle, pervert, mock, disgrace, humiliate, or dignify'.
[85] See Cairns Way, 'Invisible Politics' (n 37) in which the author complains of the manner in which the criminal law hides the complexity of allocating blame for crime, pointing specifically to the constitutionalization of subjective fault in the criminal law as 'marginalizing alternative, multidimensional and contextual assessments of fault, and reconfiguring the parameters of political debates about criminal responsibility' (178). See also Goldman, 'Law, Ideology' (n 64).

individual responsibility, it is a crucial move in helping us to wash our hands of complex, disturbing and politically volatile questions involving gender, poverty and – as I have focused on in this chapter – mental illness. The factors that influence criminal responsibility are selected from a far broader possible set; the doctrines are carefully crafted, not given. All is done with the criminal justice system serving certain communicative and pragmatic aims around the management of responsibility for social breakdown and victimization. The criminal justice system is a rhetorical resource for laundering blame in service of social ends.

In his study *A Grammar of Motives*,[86] Kenneth Burke sought to provide an answer to the question, '[w]hat is involved, when we say what people are doing and why they are doing it?'[87] In the first three quarters of this illuminating text Burke examines five terms – act, scene, agent, agency and purpose – that he claims are at the core of any account of why people are acting as they are: 'any complete statement about motives will offer *some kind of* answer to these five questions: what was done (act), when or where it was done (scene), who did it (agent), how he did it (agency), and why (purpose)'.[88] Yet in the latter stages of his attempt at setting out a general linguistic structure of the ways in which we assign and explain motives, Burke turns his attention to the issue of dialectics. In this section of the book Burke is seeking to demonstrate that there is a verbal, linguistic or dialectical reality at the base of a number of social and even classificatory phenomena. At the most general level, Burke defines 'dialectics' as 'the employment of the possibilities of linguistic transformation'[89] and identifies one of the key heads of the study of dialectics as being the study of merger and division. Ultimately, Burke argues that a principal form of linguistic transformation at play in social phenomena is the symbolic interplay between generalization (merger) and distinction drawing (division), to which he adds a third – the drawing of continuities. It is in the context of this discussion of merger, distinction and continuity in dialectics that Burke famously introduced his idea of the dialectic of the scapegoat.

The 'scapegoat mechanism', Burke argues, is a clear example of these three linguistic moves. The scapegoat is 'profoundly consubstantial with those who, looking upon it as a chosen vessel, would ritualistically cleanse themselves by loading the burden of their own iniquities upon it'.[90] There is a merger here, but the mechanism turns on the symbolic move of division 'in that its persecutors would alienate from themselves to it their own uncleanliness'.[91] Yet the expiating force of this alienation ultimately comes from a lingering form of continuity: '[f]or one must remember that a scapegoat cannot be "curative" except insofar as it represents the iniquities of those who would be cured by attacking it'.[92] Unrecognized as such by those involved in it, the dialectic of the scapegoat is a social process

[86] K Burke, *A Grammar of Motives* (Berkeley, University of California Press, 1969).
[87] ibid xv.
[88] ibid xv.
[89] ibid 402.
[90] ibid 406.
[91] ibid.
[92] ibid.

based in moves of symbolic and rhetorical transformation. It must be remembered that Burke is arguing for this symbolic and dialectic reality at the foundation of social phenomena that we might resist seeing in such terms. And it is at this point that Burke unexpectedly – and almost in passing – inserts a provocative example:

> Criminals either actual or imaginary may thus serve as scapegoats in a society that 'purifies itself' by 'moral indignation' in condemning them, though the ritualistic elements operating here are not usually recognized by the indignant.[93]

There is much in this sentence from Burke, and much that resonates with the argument that I have made in this chapter. His description of criminals 'either actual or imaginary' reminds us that the category of those who are given the label 'guilty' is not one that corresponds to a given reality; rather, it is one structured by rhetorical moves and symbolic needs. So it is in the law of mental disorder, and this chapter has sought to show that the doctrinal policing of the border between guilty and NCRMD is driven by a set of communicative interests and structural concerns quite severable from a coherent theory of insanity-based excuses. The reference to 'moral indignation' is a reminder of a key function of assigning criminal responsibility, which is to channel blame and mark the accused as the site for reaffirmation of norms of individual responsibility and the promise of reason over violence. And, finally, when Burke speaks of purification and the unrecognized ritualistic elements involved in marking a criminal, one can find a resonance with my argument that, whatever else it is also doing, the criminal justice system is a stylized mechanism with its own idols, priests – and, sometimes, sacrifices – for hiding from ourselves the possibilities of collective blame and our political and social sins.

[93] ibid.

7

Responsibility, Self-respect and the Ethics of Self-pathologization

ANNALISE ACORN*

I INTRODUCTION

John Gardner and Timothy Macklem make the claim that defences which deny responsibility on grounds of mental illness are the 'the least appetizing of all defences for a self-respecting person to offer'.[1] Gardner and Macklem maintain that self-respecting persons accused of a crime should ideally want to be able to give a rational account of their actions. 'They should prefer to have justifications for their actions, or failing that excuses, and should prefer not to have to fall back on their illnesses to furnish them with a defence'.[2] By claiming non-responsibility on grounds of mental illness, one excludes oneself from full membership in the

* I would like to thank the participants of the conference on 'Rethinking Criminal Law Theory' at Osgoode Hall Law School for helpful comments on an earlier draft of this chapter. I am particularly indebted to Susan Dimock, James Stribopolous and François Tanguay-Renaud. I must also thank John Gardner for many fascinating conversations on this topic while I was a Hart Fellow at University College and for his questions about an earlier draft. I fear, however, that I may still be playing Sir James to his Dorothea here – chiming in with 'Exactly!' when I haven't understood at all what he is meaning to say.

[1] J Gardner, *Offences and Defences* (Oxford, Oxford University Press, 2007) 274. Note that Gardner qualifies this statement with an 'all other things being equal' proviso. I think though that other things are almost never equal. The particular context of the English Homicide Act, 1957 which Gardner and Macklem are addressing with its pairing of the partial defence of diminished responsibility in s 2 and provocation in s 3, offers a unique setting in which an accused can conceivably, on the same set of facts, choose (with minimal regard to the consequences because the result of success of either defence is to drop the offence from murder to manslaughter) to slot themselves into provocation which affirms the accused's responsibility, or a defence of diminished responsibility which does not. It is the assumption of this chapter, however, that their claim about the threat to self-respect posed by defences which deny responsibility on grounds of mental illness has far reaching significance and cannot be confined to the narrow and possibly artificial context of ss 2 and 3 of the Homicide Act 1957 where there is at least theoretically no practical downside of choosing to cast oneself as mentally ill.

[2] Gardner and Macklem originally made these arguments in two articles. See J Gardner and T Macklem, 'Compassion without Respect? Nine Fallacies in *R v Smith*' [2001] *Criminal Law Review* 623 and 'No Provocation without Responsibility: A Reply to Mackay and Mitchell' [2004] *Criminal Law Review* 213. Most of what I'm referring to here is reprinted in Gardner's book and as this is a more accessible source I will cite to the book. Gardner, *Offences and Defences* (n 1) 276.

moral community of rational and accountable human beings. Conceding mental illness concedes an inability fully to participate in human life. Indeed, Gardner and Macklem go so far as to say that stigma *should be* attached to a verdict of diminished responsibility.[3]

Their critics, Mitchell and Mackay argue that Gardner and Macklem promote an ignorant and prejudiced view of mental illness. They write:

> Small wonder that defendants are reluctant to plead insanity when we encounter the kind of stigma which is being promulgated here. This not only perpetuates an unfortunate attitude to the mentally disordered but also relegates the interest in avoiding a murder conviction as being less important than what is referred to as a defendant's 'interest in being accorded their status as fully fledged human beings'.[4]

In response Gardner and Macklem underline the ways in which mental illness really is debilitating; really is an illness that everyone, including the mentally ill, can agree is something we would all be better off without. They write:

> Mentally ill people have often been persecuted, neglected, patronized, and treated as objects of mirth. Their woes have often been compounded by quack treatments, pointless incarcerations, and brutal 'care' regimes. They have often fallen victim to bizarre superstitions and prejudices. But one should not conclude from the fact that mentally ill people have been on the receiving end of so much baseness and stupidity that their mental illness should be regarded with equanimity. Mental illness is not like homosexuality or left-handedness, unobjectionable traits that do not need any remedy. Mental illness really is a kind of illness and illnesses by definition call for treatments and cures.[5]

The reply is masterful. Yet it seems somehow to bypass the crux of MacKay and Mitchell's critique. To say that mental illness really is something wrong does not answer the trickier questions of whether pointing to that illness to claim non-responsibility is demeaning or properly stigmatized.[6] People with AIDS, leprosy or learning disabilities all have something really wrong with them. It does not follow that these conditions lower them in dignity or standing. Some cultures take these defects as proper markers for stigma and others don't. Our culture is particularly concerned with eradicating the stigma formerly attached to such defects. So much so that even my calling such conditions defects may sound objection-

[3] See Gardner and Macklem, 'No Provocation' (n 2) 216 where they write 'we did not rely on the fact that stigma is attached to a diminished responsibility verdict. We claimed that stigma *should be* attached to it'.

[4] R Mackay and B Mitchell, 'Provoking Diminished Responsibility: Two Pleas Merging Into One?' [2003] *Criminal Law Review* 745, 757.

[5] Gardner, *Offences and Defences* (n 1) 275.

[6] It is not at all clear that everyone agrees even that it really is something wrong. We still retain some of the ancient reverence for the magic of mental illness that Foucault describes in *Madness and Civilization* (New York, Random House, 1988). Tim Burton's wildly successful film *Alice in Wonderland* released in 2010 stands as evidence of that reverence as he frames the action at the beginning and end with the line 'You're mad, bonkers . . . but I'll tell you a secret – all the best people are'. See A Rufus, 'Tim Burton's Alice in Wonderland: She's "Bonkers"' (4 March 2010) *Psychology Today*. Rufus writes: 'that early line lingers. Its presence at the start of a trendy new film by a cult-favorite filmmaker could be the motto of a new mental-illness pride movement'.

able. The question of whether mental illness demeans or lowers the person in dignity or standing is not adequately answered by the observation that it is something to be eradicated through treatment and cure.

Although I agree with Gardner and Macklem's view, I think their reply to Mitchell and Mackay lacks an acknowledgement and critique of what I will call the therapeutic persuasion; a cultural phenomenon that has radically altered popular conceptions of responsibility, mental illness and self-respect. If Mackay and Mitchell carry the day it is because their position is more in harmony with the late twentieth and early twenty-first century therapeutic discourse that deposes rational agency as the foundation of self-respect. Gardner and Macklem, by contrast, take rationality as the foundation of self-respect. This, in absence of a more direct attack on the therapeutic persuasion, rings anachronistic.

In what follows I articulate in more detail the sensibility of the therapeutic perspective and I offer a sketch of a critique of that sensibility and its influence on criminal conceptions of responsibility. I do this in an effort to support Gardner and Macklem's view. Though Gardner and Macklem might well reject such support, it seems to me their argument suffers from the absence of more detailed articulation and critique of the therapeutic persuasion and its assumptions about responsibility, mental illness and self-respect which are, I think, ultimately behind the kind of expansion of mental health based defences which Gardner and Macklem, in my view, rightly find objectionable.

I will elaborate and critique three crucial aspects of the therapeutic persuasion. First, I will discuss pathologization as a marker of inclusion in human community rather exclusion from it. Secondly, I examine the idea that proper and professional treatment of mental illness entails the utmost respect for the complex humanity of the individual patient. Thirdly, I will discuss the idea that the proper object of responsibility is not past action but future submission to self-improvement in therapy. In elaborating these aspects of the therapeutic persuasion I will try to demonstrate how acceptance of these elements of the therapeutic sensibility makes Gardner and Macklem's position seem unfair to the mentally ill. In sketching a critique of these ideas I hope to try to show why Gardner and Macklem ought still to prevail over Mackay and Mitchell.

To elaborate these ideas I will draw on two literary sources: Ken Kesey's *One Flew over the Cuckoo's Nest*, a mid-twentieth century look at mental illness, self-pathologization and responsibility not yet imbued with the therapeutic persuasion[7] and David Chase's HBO TV series *The Sopranos* (Seasons I and II), a text which I argue, stands on the edge of the new therapeutic conception of the worthy self and its relation to mental illness and embraces a new therapeutic ethic of self-pathologization.[8]

[7] Ken Kesey, *One Flew over the Cuckoo's Nest* (London, Picador, 1973). First published in 1962.

[8] David Chase, *The Sopranos* (HBO, 1999–2000).

II RESPONSIBILITY AND THE THERAPEUTIC PERSUASION

In the words of sociologist Eva Illouz, the therapeutic discourse

> promotes a self that is passive – in that it is defined by wounds inflicted by others – but is commanded to become highly active, in that it is summoned to change. It is highly responsible for self-transformation, yet it is not held morally accountable for its deficiencies. This split model of responsibility marks, I believe, a new cultural form of selfhood.[9]

This new form of selfhood ushers in a new ethics of self-pathologization. Under this model, the individual does good by seeking diagnosis and by taking responsibility for tackling their mental problems. Culpable irresponsibility lies in unwillingness to acknowledge ones pathologies and refusal to submit to the discipline of therapy, self-healing and emotional growth. Responsibility, under this model, is primarily future-directed. One is responsible for seeking clues to one's mental problems in the past, but one's primary responsibility is to work towards transformation of the self into the future.

This therapeutic narrative has increasingly expanded the territory of mental illness outwards to engulf much of human experience. The roots of the therapeutic persuasion are, of course, in Freudian psychoanalysis.[10] However, as Illouz explains, other influences have been at play in propelling the therapeutic narrative forwards. These have included changes in psychological theory that aligned it with American ideas about self-reliance and voluntarism,[11] an increase in professional authority of psychiatrists occasioned by the centrality of sexuality as a topic for public discussion,[12] the state placing unprecedented resources into psychological research and behavioural studies,[13] the ascendance of the psycho-pharmaceutical industry, the creation of the Diagnostic and Statistical Manual of Mental Disorders,[14] the insurance industry and other institutions' reliance on the DSM to make decisions about reimbursement, benefits and compensation,[15] developments in civil society such as feminism's critique of child abuse and Vietnam war veterans' lobbying for the category of Post Traumatic Stress Disorder.[16]

The result has been that a psychiatric understanding of the human personality has become normal both in the sense that most everyone is pathologized and that pathologization is good – a good first step towards greater mental and emotional health and a marker of hope for future self-realization. Here, self-respect is

[9] E Illouz, *Saving the Modern Soul: Therapy, Emotions and the Culture of Self-help* (Berkeley, University of California Press, 2008).
[10] ibid ch 2: 'Freud: a cultural innovator'.
[11] ibid 157–61.
[12] ibid 161–62.
[13] ibid 162–64.
[14] ibid 164–65.
[15] ibid 165–66.
[16] ibid 167–69.

enhanced rather than threatened by self-pathologization. The respectable self is no longer the rational self who takes responsibility for past action. The respectable self is one who acknowledges her own pathologies, is committed to greater awareness of their sources and is diligently active in relation to them under the direction of the psy-industry.[17]

The new therapeutic model of self uncouples the crucial link between rational agency and self-respect and forges new links between self-pathologization, responsibility for therapeutic hygiene and self-approbation. Under this new therapeutic model working on the self through psycho-therapy, psycho-pharmacology, or self-help; working to understand what is wrong with the self and striving to achieve greater conformity with models of health propounded by the psy-industry simply are that for which one is responsible. Such physic of the personality becomes the foundation not only of self-approbation, but of a new model of membership in the moral community.

Having sketched the basic outline of the therapeutic persuasion, let us now take a look at three of its component parts to examine how they purport to alter our assessment of whether denials of responsibility should be demeaning to an accused.

III PATHOLOGY AS INCLUSION

For Gardner and Macklem (and for Gardner in particular) rationality – the capacity to have and to give reasons for action – is what makes us distinctively human. Rationality is the foundation of a fully human life and of human dignity.[18] Because it impairs rationality, mental illness, unlike leprosy, AIDS or learning disabilities, is a defect in this crucial status-conferring attribute. The mentally ill then cannot be 'accorded status as fully fledged human beings'.[19] To claim impaired rationality is to exclude oneself from full membership in the human community. It is, therefore, demeaning.

The capacity to have and to give reasons for action is not especially important to the therapeutic understanding of the self. From the therapeutic perspective, not knowing why one did what one did, being subject to complex irrationalities buried in the subconscious, is endemic to the human condition. A capacity for an archaeology of the self directed towards greater knowledge of the mental injuries one has suffered displaces rationality as the distinctively human capacity. One seeks to understand the ways in which past injuries may have given rise to present illness. However, what is distinctively human is to acknowledge that one's actions are driven by irrational causes, to scrutinize one's past to uncover formative

[17] See N Rose, *Inventing Our Selves: Psychology, Power and Personhood* (Cambridge, Cambridge University Press, 1998).

[18] See Gardner, 'The Mark of Responsibility' in *Offences and Defences* (n 1) 177.

[19] Gardner, *Offences and Defences* (n 1) 274.

wounds and to work towards healing for the future. From within this therapeutic persuasion therefore, claiming impaired rationality and an inability to give reasons for ones actions does not demean.

Consider how Ken Kesey's novel illustrates the rationalist perspective that Gardner and Macklem embrace. In the opening scene we learn that our narrator Chief Bromden, the enormous half-blood Indian who has for years pretended to be deaf and dumb, sees himself as mentally ill. The first words of Bromden's story are, 'They're out there'.[20] This opening statement of paranoia is soon embellished with more delusional thoughts: 'I creep along the wall quiet as dust in my canvas shoes, but they got special sensitive equipment detects my fear'.[21] Though we are fascinated by the elliptical poetry of Bromden's voice we are discomfited by the intensity of our engagement with a narrator who is apparently so mentally ill.

The tension, however, is resolved during a crucial battle between the new inmate Randal McMurphy and Nurse Ratched. Calling Nurse Ratched on her pretended commitment to democracy, McMurphy makes a motion to allow afternoon TV so the men can watch the World Series. Twenty of the men – all those present at the group meeting – vote in favour of the change. But Nurse Ratched manoeuvres around the victory: 'There are forty patients on the ward, Mr McMurphy. Forty patients and only twenty voted. You must have a majority to change the ward policy. I'm afraid the vote is closed'.[22] McMurphy appeals to the absentees across the day room, the chronics, the acutes, those too much in the fog to have participated. He gets no support. Then he turns to the Chief. 'You Chief, what about you? . . . Chief you're our last bet'.[23] As Bromden slowly raises his hand he explains himself *to himself* in psychotic terms. He interprets McMurphy's influence, his energetic contribution to actions not just as the first, but as the physical, even mechanical, cause of his action. He reaches for familiar and seemingly comforting delusions about external control.

> It's too late to stop it now. McMurphy did something to it that first day, put some kind of hex on it with his hand so it don't act like I order it. . . . I can't stop it. McMurphy's got hidden wires hooked to it, lifting it slow just to get me out of the fog and into the open where I'm fair game. He's doing it, wires . . .
>
> No. That's not the truth. I lifted it myself.
>
> 'Twenty-one! The Chief's vote makes it twenty-one! And by God if that ain't a majority I'll eat my hat!'[24]

Bromden's line, 'No. That's not the truth. I lifted it myself' is arguably the climax of the book. In that moment Bromden rejects self-pathologization, takes responsibility and recovers self-respect. He recognizes his own self-explanation grounded in mental illness as both unappetizing and untrue. We see the moment as a triumph over the malevolent power of the psychiatric machine. By rejecting the idea

[20] Kesey, *One Flew over the Cuckoo's Nest* (n 7) 3.
[21] ibid.
[22] ibid 132.
[23] ibid 133.
[24] ibid 133–34.

that McMurphy is controlling his hand with wires, by taking not just responsibility *but credit* for his own actions, Bromden accepts and claims membership in a moral community. His rejection of self-pathologization is the first step towards his living a fully human life.

On the surface Kesey's target is the brutality of the psychiatric profession but what he ultimately takes aim at is the practice of self-pathologization. He does so largely on the ground that it is simply false. Bromden, along with many of the others on the ward is not mentally ill. They are responsible, rational men who have misguidedly adopted self-pathologization as a way out of the challenges of life. The way forward is for them to reject self-pathologization and have the courage to live as responsible agents and thus to restore self-respect.

Contrast the view of the ethics of self-pathologization that we see in *The Sopranos.* Much of the intelligence of this series lies in its articulation of ambivalence about the therapeutic persuasion. The series presents a dialectic between a conception of the self as respectable insofar as it takes responsibly for rationally chosen actions (a conception represented by the old rules of the Mafia) and a pathologized conception of the self which is deserving of approbation only insofar as it takes responsibility for therapeutic healing of the psychic wounds of the past and working towards healing (a conception represented by Dr Jennifer Melfi). Because we are most engaged with the project of New Jersey Mafia boss Tony Soprano's therapeutic journey, *The Sopranos* comes down tentatively on the side of the therapeutic persuasion and the self as presumptively pathological and respectable inasmuch as it takes responsibility not for past actions but for striving toward health in therapy.

After a battery of tests turns up no physical explanation for his losses of consciousness, Tony sees a psychiatrist. In their first meeting Dr Melfi tells Mr Soprano that his physical symptoms have psychological causes. He has been having panic attacks. When Soprano, who feels such a diagnosis would be demeaning, resists this explanation Dr Melfi reassures him that a panic attack is a 'legitimate psychiatric emergency'. Here we see the first glimpse of the possibility that Tony may fulfil his longings for social inclusion through 'legitimate' psychiatric diagnosis.[25]

As the therapy progresses we learn more about Tony's violent and confusing childhood, his mother's cruelty, his father's brutality and criminal lifestyle. We pity Tony's boyhood trauma. And we have both faith in and desire for his healing in therapy. We long for Tony to discover the key to his identity in the wounds inflicted by others and we pin our hopes on the possibility that he will become authentically active in the process of self-transformation. We want Tony to embrace a psychiatric self-interpretation. Tony, the protagonist with whom we identify, leads our reactions to the therapeutic discourse in his responses to arguments about responsibility and mental pathology as they are made by and for those around him.

[25] For a very interesting discussion of the legitimacy that can be conferred by mental diagnosis see S Brison, *Aftermath: Violence and the Remaking of a Self* (Princeton, Princeton University Press, 2003) 77–83.

Although Tony resists therapy for himself, his assent to the therapeutic persuasion begins in his relation to his underling Christopher Moltisanti. In episode eight 'The Legend of Tennessee Moltisanti' Christopher, an 'unmade man', is struggling with feelings of low self-worth. He's failing to write a movie script. He's dreaming of the ghost of a man he murdered. He's angry that his contributions to the business are unrecognized. As he sits staring at his computer and the empty beer cans and pizza boxes that litter his apartment he gets a call from Tony summoning him and telling him to pick up cannoli for the guys on his way. Christopher obeys, goes to the crowded bakery, takes a number, and waits, and waits, and waits. Finally, when it is his turn, another customer who appears to be a friend of the baker cuts in and in the ensuing altercation Christopher loses it and ends up shooting the baker in the toe.

When Tony finds out, he is enraged. 'We're under a microscope and I've gotta hear on the street you shot some fucking civilian in the foot because he made you wait for buns?' Every time Christopher tries to explain Tony screams 'Shut up!' Finally Tony lets Christopher speak. 'I don't know, Tony. It's like just the fucking regularness of life is too fucking hard for me, or something. I don't know'. Tony is moved by Christopher's existential despair and he begins to soften. He feels compassion for Christopher and begins to apply his newly acquired therapeutic discourse to his case. 'Look at you. I bet you're sleeping all the time, right?' Christopher tells Tony that he thinks he might have cancer. Tony replies, 'Does this word "cancer" pop into your mind a lot? A little bit? What?' Christopher looks puzzled. Tony continues, 'Well, I'm just thinking maybe you're depressed'. Christopher denies it but Tony presses the point. 'Maybe you got a uh seratonin problem, or whatever the fuck they call it'.

This scene too is climactic because here Tony's understanding of mental illness and responsibility changes. He tentatively sets aside his old ethical framework, the moral understanding that would see Christopher as guilty of a culpable loss of self-control and deserving of harsh punishment. Fellow-feeling, comingled with his own experience in therapy, inspires Tony to construct and accept a kind of diminished responsibility defence for Chris.[26] His compassion for Christopher, his identification with him as a human being, leads him not only to pathologize Christopher's behaviour, but to try to shield him from the belief that the pathology carries a stigma. He connects to Christopher as member of the moral community by offering a diagnosis.

We see the scene as a breakthrough because in the moment that Tony diagnoses Christopher he implicitly concedes his own pathology. We rejoice in Tony's adoption of the therapeutic persuasion in relation to Christopher because we believe it means that he is accepting the responsibilities of therapy for himself. Pathologization marks inclusion.

As we continue through the series we come to understand just how inclusive the move towards pathologization is. We find, for example that Dr Melfi also

[26] The facts of the case are not entirely different from those of *R v Smith* [2000] 3 WLR 654 (HL) discussed in Gardner and Macklem, 'Compassion' (n 2).

understands herself in pathological terms, submits herself to therapy and strives with her own psychiatrist, Dr Kupferberg, towards self-transformation. Like Russian nesting dolls, the therapist's has a therapist who has a therapist. Everyone is included in the distinctively human task of self-cure.

Submission to psychiatry no longer marks one as different. Mental illness is now on a continuum from schizophrenia to depression, from bipolar disorder to anxiety, from psychosis to relationship phobia and so forth. At the lower end of the spectrum virtually everyone can understand their own experience in pathological terms – we all experience anxiety, depression or obsession in one form or another. Once these shared experiences are understood as illnesses, everyone can get on board. We may still make a distinction between the floridly mentally ill and the elective patient who could function without therapy. But the potential to benefit from therapy is held in common. Pathology is good news. As one self-pathologizes one joins others on the road to recovery. We are all called upon to be good patients.

Moreover, not only is pathology the marker for inclusion, it is also the foundation of compassion. Seeing the other person as suffering from depression, anxiety or some other form of mental illness becomes the spark of fellow-feeling. Within the therapeutic persuasion our compassion extends on three distinct planes. We pity the psychic injuries that caused the illness, we pity the suffering of the illness itself and we pity the behavioural effects of the illness. Compassion is grounded in a judgement of non-responsibility.[27] They couldn't help it.[28]

From the view that mental pathology is and ought to be a fundamental spring of human compassion, Gardner and Macklem's view is bound to seem morally suspect. Indeed their title 'No Compassion without Respect' affronts the therapeutic persuasion at both ends: illness should be an important basis for compassion and submission to the therapeutic endeavour should be an important ground of respect. Here it is axiomatic that we should extend both compassion and respect to those who cannot give reasons for their actions due to mental illness but who recognize their need for and take on the responsibility of seeking improvement through treatment.

Gardner and Macklem do not want to be or to be seen to be unfair to the mentally ill. However, Mitchell and Mackay, with their commitment to broaden the scope of exculpation for the mentally disordered, seem to outscore Gardner and Macklem when it comes to caring about potentially vulnerable people accused of criminal offences.[29] In an effort to stay on side with the disadvantaged, Gardner and Macklem blame the severity of the law. They write:

[27] In Aristotle's discussion of pity in *The Rhetoric*he stresses the need to view the other as innocent in their own suffering in order to feel pity for them. See Aristotle, *The Rhetoric and the Poetics*, W Rhys Roberts and I Bywater (trans) (New York, Random House, 1954) 113 (Bk 2, Part 8, 1385b).

[28] For an interesting discussion of the challenges the expansion of the category of mental illness poses for law see SK Erickson, 'The Myth of Mental Disorder: Transsubstantive Behavior and Taxometric Psychiatry' (2008) 41 *Akron Law Review* 67.

[29] See however, Gardner and Macklem's rejoinder on this score in 'No Provocation' (n 2) 214 where they write 'the temptation to make the same kind of legal allowance for every kind of human disadvantage is a temptation that thoughtful believers in social inclusion should strenuously resist'.

> The more severe the penalty he faces the more a defendant is under rational pressure to find a way to secure his own acquittal. The point may come at which using a demeaning argument to get off the hook is reasonable. If so, it is the law that is being unreasonable. Its penalties should not be so severe that a defendant has no reasonable alternative but to demean himself in order to avoid incurring them.[30]

If Gardner and Macklem mean that legislatures should reduce penalties for offences like murder from life to, say, five years in prison so as not to pressure accused persons to put forward mental illness based defences then the argument is very problematic. As a policy for sentencing this would disregard all the usual factors like proportionality and deterrence. Another interpretation might be that Gardner and Macklem think that sentencing should reliably take into consideration an accused person's rational reasons for committing a crime, which though they may fall short of a responsibility-affirming defence, would nevertheless give us reason to feel compassion for the accused.[31] Instead of forcing accused persons to turn to mental illness-based defences as a last resort the sentencing hearing should be reliably responsive to any responsibility-affirming reasons for action that provide moral arguments for exculpation whether or not they fall within existing defences. [32]

Consider, for example, Bromden's murder of the lobotomized McMurphy. Though Bromden escapes from the ward after the murder we feel that were he ever to be tried he would, in his restored self-respect, distain an insanity defence.[33] He had reasons. 'I was only sure of one thing: he wouldn't have left something like that sit there in the day room with his name tacked on it for twenty or thirty years so the Big Nurse could use it as an example of what can happen if you buck the system'.[34] Bromden is rationally responsible for the killing but he has no responsibility-affirming defence. Though we find Bromden's act disturbing we affirm it, nonetheless. We see the psychiatrists as the real murderers of McMurphy.

Bromden's actions read more as an attempt to stop the desecration of his friend's corpse than as a culpable murder. Still, an insanity defence might well be rationally advantageous in Bromden's case.[35] The key moral philosophical objection to such a defence, however, must be that the defence would be untrue. The claim to non-responsibility would be simply false and the defence would be demeaning, at least in part, for that reason. Bromden would be asking for compassion on false pretences, casting himself as less of a person than he actually is.

[30] Gardner, *Offences and Defences* (n 1) 274–75.

[31] I am incorporating Gardner's understanding of defences as claims of responsibility. See 'The Gist of Excuses' in *Offences and Defences*, ibid 121.

[32] See J Ross, 'Autonomy vs A Client's Best Interests: The Defense Lawyer's Dilemma when a Mentally Ill Client seeks to Control their own Defense' (1998) 35 *American Criminal Law Review* 1343.

[33] Interestingly, however, after McMurphy has been through electroshock therapy, Bromden begins to view McMurphy as not responsible for his actions. Bromden sees McMurphy's assault on Nurse Ratched not as the result of mental illness, but as being externally controlled by the desires of the rest of the men on the ward. 'We couldn't stop him because we were the ones making him do it'. Kesey, *One Flew over the Cuckoo's Nest* (n 7) 303.

[34] ibid 307.

[35] On the terms of the novel Bromden was not committed.

Assuming the law ought to extend compassion and lenience to one such as Bromden, I do not see that it should do so by lowering penalties for murder at the outset to alter his cost-benefit analysis surrounding the insanity defence. Rather, perhaps, what is needed is some other way for the law to create opportunities for accused persons to explain the rational and responsible reasons for their actions. Perhaps our existing defences do not provide sufficient space for the kind of novelistic detail that would ultimately provide a better foundation for knowing when we ought to extend compassion and hence exculpation. Perhaps then, what Gardner and Macklem mean is that sentencing should at least be more flexible – if not more lenient in general – so that owning up to the truth, truth that might demonstrate rationally responsible yet morally defensible reasons for action, would be reliably more rationally advantageous to an accused than presenting false expert testimony about mental illness. This move might widen the scope for the court to look at the blameworthiness of the victim or of others in exculpating the conduct of the accused.

As we see from this example, one reason for rejecting the therapeutic perspective on this point is that mental illness is a false marker of inclusion; false because it asks people to understand themselves as defective when they are not. False because it encourages people to lie about themselves in order to be included in the ranks of the sick. It has only been through the artificial expansion of the category of mental illness beyond its true boundaries that the therapeutic persuasion has managed credibly to construct confession of mental illness as a marker of inclusion. Conceding mental illness and the impaired rationality it entails brings a person into solidarity with the rest of the human community committed to improvement through psychiatry. Self-pathologizing offers a way of repudiating action, avoiding moral accountability and at the same time affirming moral accord with the community.

The call to self-pathologize within the therapeutic perspective is much like the call to proclaim oneself a sinner within Christianity. One confesses a defect to be included. Being a sinner really is bad though it is also universal. Though Christianity is, in my view, misguided in encouraging this sin-based self-understanding, it is at least honest and above board about its own status as a religion and a belief system. Within Christianity, belief in God is logically prior to the confession that one is a sinner and the latter is of no use without the former. The therapeutic persuasion, by contrast, sets itself above religion as true science. It posits itself as an authority independent of belief. It acknowledges neither its ideological foundations nor the need for faith in the psy-industry. It promotes normative prescriptions for humanity and with its veneer of science shields those prescriptions from the ethical scrutiny to which religions, philosophies and other belief systems should been subjected. The therapeutic persuasion makes gods of psychiatrists and patients of the rest of us without ever articulating what it is we have committed to believing in beside the reality and ubiquity of illness.

IV THERAPY AS RESPECT

As we have seen, Gardner and Macklem argue that one cannot reason from the errors of brutal treatment of the mentally ill to the conclusion that treatment is itself an error. Nor can one reason from success in eliminating brutal treatments to the conclusion that mental illness is not something wrong. To need treatment is, for Gardner and Macklem, a bad thing and the mentally ill do need treatment.[36] What I want to explore here, however, is the way that shifts in our perception of the nature of treatment alters our judgement about whether mental illness is something wrong after all. The further question that I want to pose is: does our perception that treatment for mental illness is now both effective and respectful alter our moral evaluation of whether it is demeaning to deny responsibility on grounds of mental illness?

Peter Strawson's distinction between the reactive and objective attitudes in his essay 'Freedom and Resentment' is helpful here.[37] According to Strawson, if one takes the reactive attitude towards another, one engages with that other as a fellow human being. The reactive attitude is characterized by authenticity and participation as well as immediacy. It assumes responsibility. The objective attitude, by contrast, is reserved and strategic. The objective attitude views the other as less than responsible and seeks to get around the other rather than to engage with them. It is pedagogical or therapeutic or instrumental. Strawson writes,

> [t]o adopt the objective attitude to another human being is to see him, perhaps, as an object of social policy; as a subject for what, in a wide range of senses, might be called treatment; as something certainly to be taken account, perhaps precautionary account, of; to be managed or handled or cured or trained; perhaps simply to be avoided, though this gerundive is not peculiar to cases of objectivity of attitude.[38]

To take the objective attitude to another is to see them as one down. You view yourself as superior, both because you have the advantage of responsibility and because you are capable of playing them to achieve an end of your choosing. As Strawson explains:

[36] Gardner and Macklem note that their philosophical understanding of mental illness is broadly congruent with that of KWM Fulford. See 'No Provocation' (n 2) fn 16 referring to KWM Fulford, *Moral Theory and Medical Practice* (Cambridge, Cambridge University Press, 1989, reprinted 1995). Though admittedly the task is prohibitively difficult, Fulford's attempt at it is in my view excessive in philosophical complexity and disappointing in substance. What is dominant, however, is his faith in psychometric pharmacology as a cure for the misconstruing of reality that mental illness causes. The philosophical analysis is dominated by 'The case of Mr AB' discussed in the clinical preface (x–xi). Mr AB is a suicidal patient who believes or pretends to believe he has brain cancer. He is involuntarily admitted to a mental hospital and treated for depression and makes a full recovery on medication. I am distrustful of a philosophical understanding of mental illness that is derived from an example so sanguine about the effectiveness of psychotropic drugs.

[37] PF Strawson, *Freedom and Resentment and Other Essays* (London, Metheun, 1974).

[38] ibid 9.

> If your attitude towards someone is wholly objective, then though you may fight him, you cannot quarrel with him, and though you may talk to him, even negotiate with him, you cannot reason with him. You can at most pretend to quarrel, or to reason with him.[39]

Gardner and Macklem assume, I think, that treatment of mental illness entails the objective attitude. Defences grounded in mental illness are demeaning because they invite this objective attitude. An accused denies responsibility and at the same time concedes that he is not among those to be reasoned with. The accused asks the court to view him as an object of policy, as someone to be managed, cured, or treated.

What happens to this reasoning, however, when 'treatment' – which for Strawson was actually the source of a definition of the objective attitude – appears to have outgrown or transcended that stance of objectivity? To get a closer look at this question, we now turn to our literary sources to see how treatment might either entail or reject the objective attitude.

Ken Kesey's *One Flew over the Cuckoo's Nest* depicts the classic nightmare of the objective point of view. The therapist, Nurse Ratched, sees the men as objects to be managed.[40] She probes them with detachment and remains aloof from the emotional consequences of her therapeutic interventions. She experiments on them for their good as she sees it and denies them the status of fellow human beings.

The objective attitude is also in evidence in the manner of medication of patients. Nurse Ratched and the hospital staff combine professional expertise and self-interest to make unilateral decisions about psychometric drugs for the patients. The patients are the passive objects of professional manipulation. As one patient puts it 'We shall be all of us shot at dawn. One hundred ccs apiece. Miss Ratched shall line us all against the wall, where we'll face the terrible maw of a muzzle-loading shotgun which she has loaded with Miltowns! Thorazines! Libriums! Stelazines! And with a wave of her sword, *blooie!* Tranquilize us all completely out of existence'.[41] The medication is a form of annihilation and of course McMurphy is soon to be victim of the ultimate treatment; the lobotomy that guts his subjectivity completely.

Here brutality is an add-on to the presumptive humiliation of the objective attitude. The core lesson of the novel, however, is in line with Gardner and Macklem's view. No self-respecting person wants to be mentally ill at least in part because no self-respecting person wants to be managed by others instead of being one with whom others engage.

If we turn now, however, to *The Sopranos* we see very different conceptions about these attitudes and relations. The fact that Tony Soprano has a psychiatric problem does indeed mean that Tony needs to be managed and treated; probed in

[39] ibid.

[40] It's interesting that Strawson's 'Freedom and Resentment' and Kesey's novel were both published in 1962.

[41] Kesey, *One Flew over the Cuckoo's Nest* (n 7) 289.

uncomfortable ways for his own good. But therapy and treatment are no longer undertaken from a purely objective attitude and are consequently less demeaning. Dr Melfi does have the characteristic upper hand of the objective attitude in the sense that she elicits information from Tony and guides his reactions to his own revelations. The objective attitude here, however, is modified. The therapist participates with the patient in the process of transformation. They are both humbled to a joint project of helping the emergence of a healthier psyche. Though she uses her professional expertise on him she also is deeply, humanly, engaged with him. Indeed part of her job as therapist is to be humanly present to him; to take the reactive attitude toward him in a controlled way so that he can trust sufficiently in her 'being there for him' to become authentically engaged in his own cure. Dr Melfi's approach reflects the professional ethic articulated by psychoanalyst Jonathan Lear:

> [T]here is no form of clinical intervention – in psychology, psychiatry, or generally medicine – which pays greater respect to the individual client or patient. The proper attitude for an analyst is one of profound humility in the face of the infinite complexity of another human being.[42]

Tony does sometimes try to pull the therapist into un-withheld reactivity. In her rejection of Tony's sexual advance, his confession that he is in love with her, Dr Melfi retreats to a fully objective attitude to Tony and demeans him in the process. She pathologizes his feelings for her calling them a by-product of therapy. She reminds him that her kindness is part of his treatment. Tony continues to assume mutuality of the reactive attitude. He tells Dr Melfi that what she means is that she is not in love with him. Later when Dr Melfi is surprised by Tony's disclosure that he has a twenty-four year old girlfriend, he turns her therapeutic vocabulary against her: 'How are you doing with that?'

As the relationship progresses we see the objective attitude of the therapist as always modified by real human engagement. In the glimpses we get into Dr Melfi's relationship with her own therapist, Dr Elliot Kupferberg, we see just how deeply engaged she is, just how fully she participates in her relation with Tony. Indeed, Dr Kupferberg actually pathologizes her fully reactive attitude towards Tony, her unreserved engagement with him and prescribes a medication normally given to obsessive compulsives to treat her preoccupation.

In the therapeutic model, the patient gives over authority to the therapist. But again the model of authority here is significantly modified. Under the therapeutic model the hierarchy of therapist over patient is not merely consented to but is constituted by the patient.[43] The legitimacy of the authority of the therapist lies in the patient's position as arbiter over it. Interestingly, however, the patient's rejection of the therapist's authority never really counts as de-legitimating and is often seen as part of the therapeutic process.

[42] J Lear, *Open Minded: Working Out the Logic of the Soul* (Cambridge, Harvard University Press, 1998) 26.

[43] There is a mountain of literature on transference that is relevant here. For a start, however, see Lear, *Open Minded* (n 42) ch 4: 'An Interpretation of Transference'.

Consider further the difference here in the sensibility around psycho-pharmaceuticals. As Dr Melfi is writing a prescription for Prozac, she tells Tony, 'With today's pharmacology no one needs to suffer with feelings of exhaustion and depression'. Dr Melfi monitors the side effects carefully, and the threat the drugs pose to Tony's sexuality is a significant concern for her. When Tony complains that he can't get an erection (we know that has failed with his girlfriend Irina) Dr Melfi immediately registers her respect for the value of his virility and attempts in the most professional, non-humiliating way to determine whether Prozac is causing his impotence. So beneficent is the pharmacology that impairment of his extramarital performance would be prohibitive. If the drugs do not enhance his autonomy as he defines it, the therapist will concur in his rejection of them.

We are a long way now from the dictatorial prescriptions of Nurse Ratched. Authoritarianism has given way to collaboration; mind-numbing tranquilizers have been replaced with invigorating curatives; rigid hierarchies are now egalitarian partnerships. With this radical democratization of the treatment for mental disorder, self-pathologization no longer invites the objective attitude. Though the patient admits the need for treatment, the treatment respectfully engages him in the work of authentic self-realization.

Where treatment is perceived as a collaborative endeavour fully engaging both patient and professional in the quest toward self-actualization for the patient, submission to treatment is no longer perceived as acceptance of a one-down infantalized position. Irrationality and lapse of responsibility are perceived as distinctively human mysteries to be unravelled in the therapeutic journey. If the treatment for mental illness really is a wholly beneficent, respectful, engaged collaborative assistance with self-discovery, actualization, understanding and improvement, why not wish mental illness on yourself?

Of course, if treatment really is better now, if psycho-pharmaceuticals are now vastly more beneficial to patients[44] and if psycho-therapy really is undertaken from a place of humility and respect on the part of the professional, this is certainly better than treatment that aims to benumb and humiliate. However, by way of critique here we can get help from Foucault who famously argued that the therapeutic persuasion covertly brings people under institutional control by enlisting them in an apparently beneficent project of self-liberation.[45] The seductive power of therapy lies in its very respectfulness. Yet, despite this commitment to humility in the face of the patient's individuality, the therapist is still the authority over and therapy is still a kind of experimentation on the patient. In this sense the therapist remains qualitatively different from the friend.

[44] I confess to being very sceptical that this is the case. I am very much persuaded by the compelling contrary view put forward by R Whitaker, *Mad in America: Bad Science, Bad Medicine, and the Enduring Mistreatment of the Mentally Ill* (New York, Perseus Publishing, 2002); and *Anatomy of an Epidemic: Magic Bullets, Psychiatric Drugs, and the Astonishing Rise of Mental Illness in America,* (New York, Crown Publishing, 2010).

[45] M Foucault, *Discipline and Punish: The Birth of the Prison*, A Sheridan (trans) (New York, Vintage Books, 1979). 201. See also Illouz, *Saving the Modern Soul* (n 9) 4.

Apparent amelioration in the tactics of treatment should not therefore alter our sense that submission to treatment puts the person in the one down position. However beneficent the treatment, the patient still gives over a portion of his agency and self-authorship. Though not as bad as a lobotomy, being displaced as the primary authority over and author of ones own life still is something one ought not to wish on oneself. It is especially undesirable if we are at all sceptical about the moral legitimacy of the authority of mental health professionals, the correctness of the models of mental health they propound and are trained to point others towards.

The beneficence of treatment might profoundly alter the cost-benefit analysis of whether it makes rational sense to deny responsibility on mental health based grounds. The more respectful the treatment, the less risky it may be to wager like McMurphy did that treatment is preferable to punishment. Nevertheless, even if in denying responsibility on grounds of mental illness one does not invite the reactive attitude; such a denial still concedes that one is not qualified for full self-authorship and that one needs a professional authority to help manage one's existence.

V FORWARD-LOOKING RESPONSIBILITY

The therapeutic persuasion does not reject all conceptions of responsibility as the foundation of self-respect. The self-respecting person takes responsibility for improvement into the future in collaboration with the psy-industry. To turn again to Illouz, 'therapeutic culture has marked a major advance in the ethos of self-reliance; although it takes a stance of victimhood and moral disculpation for the past, it enjoins a voluntarist responsibility for the future'.[46] The therapeutic persuasion could never have emerged as the dominant cultural force it is, nor inspired such grand scale self-pathologization, had it not incorporated this future-directed, active, rational (though professionally supervised) conception of agency.[47] Future-oriented and confident of its prescriptions for health, the therapeutic persuasion is optimistic. Backward-looking conceptions of responsibility are, from the therapeutic perspective, characterized by unhealthy preoccupations with revenge and the impulse to inflict punitive suffering.

We can see the influence of the forward-looking notion of responsibility in various developments in the criminal law. This new forward-looking notion of responsibility is reflected, for example, in the theory and practice of mental health courts. In an article entitled 'Justice through therapy', Andrea Hartling explains that

> [e]ach individual who goes through the program is given a different set of guidelines to follow, which usually include living arrangements, medical appointments, involvement

[46] Illouz, *Saving the Modern Soul* (n 9) 186.
[47] ibid 158–59.

> with social programs and mandatory meetings with court workers who will track their progress . . . If they fulfil their contract, the Crown doesn't follow through with the initial charges.[48]

Likewise, in the field of restorative justice the distinction between causal and reactive fault tracks this shift in understandings of responsibility. As John Braithwaite explains, causal fault refers to the traditional criminal justice preoccupation with *actus reus* and *mens rea.* Reactive fault looks to how the offender orients herself toward the future, the responsibility she takes for making things better. The question of responsibility for the crime is bypassed in order to facilitate a focus on whether the alleged offender takes responsibility for improving the situation in the future. Past responsibility no longer holds our attention. It is future activity towards repair that is significant. Braithwaite writes:

> [I]f there is a level of apology . . . and undertakings that give tangible assurance of the prevention of recurrence (for example, participation in resocialization, anger control or drug treatment programs . . .) then the conference may judge criminal fault to have been acquitted reactively.[49]

The forward-looking notion of responsibility claims a moral superiority over ideas of responsibility that deny the offender the opportunity overcome the past.

Turning again to *The Sopranos*, moral scepticism about backward-looking ideas of responsibility is signalled by their predominance in mafia culture. Consider the following exchange between Dr Melfi and Tony Soprano after Tony discovers Coach Hauser has seduced one of his daughter Meadow's school friends and Tony is planning payback.[50]

> Dr Melfi: I'm interested in why you feel punishing this man falls upon you.
> Tony: Well it sure doesn't fall upon you.
> Dr Melfi: What do you mean?
> Tony: What would you do? You'd call the cops who would get some judge who would give him psychiatric counselling so maybe he could talk about his unhappy childhood and we could have sympathy for the fuck because he is the real victim here, right?

Tony seeks moral accountability for Hauser through punishment and rejects what he takes to be the legal system's therapeutic persuasion. We agree with Tony about the need for accountability but we recoil from the way he associates accountability with revenge, vigilantism, violence and the enforcement mentality of the Mafia. When Tony decides not to have Hauser kneecapped we see it as a huge positive breakthrough.

Although we do not accord the same benefit to Hauser, a forward-looking conception of responsibility characterizes our moral response to Tony himself. We are

[48] A Hartling, 'Justice through Therapy: The Mental Health Diversion Program Redirects London's Mentally Ill Criminals Away from the Courthouse and into Rehabilitative Programs' (6 December 2007) *New Media Journalism*, online: www.fims.uwo.ca/NewMedia2008/page122131722.aspx.

[49] J Braithwaite, 'Survey Article: Repentance Rituals and Restorative Justice' (2000) 8 *Journal of Political Philosophy* 115, 113. See also J Braithwaite, *Restorative Justice and Responsive Regulation* (Oxford, Oxford University Press, 2002) 119.

[50] Season 1, episode 9, 'Boca'.

at a moral distance from Tony's crimes; his brutal beating of Mahaffey the compulsive gambler, his blowing up of his friend Artie Bucco's restaurant, or his strangling FBI informant Fabian Petrulio with a piece of wire. Yet we are deeply morally engaged with his emotional work on himself. We don't care whether he takes responsibility for murder, arson or assault. We do care deeply about whether he is going to take responsibility for emotional self-transformation through therapy.

The forward-looking perspective is attractive. Why waste time on the past when we could be making a better future? Society, victims, offenders do not benefit from punishment. Thus the therapeutic notion of responsibility as future-directed is powerfully supported by critiques of revenge, the promotion of forgiveness, as well as arguments about the radical disutility of punishment.[51] This new form of responsibility, however, by no means puts the state out of the business of social control. Though punishment may become less of a concern for the state, the state, now in collaboration with the psy-industry, will still be very much involved in the process of remaking the offender through treatment. We should, I think, fear that this growing shift towards an aspirational conception of responsibility may authorize far greater intrusion in individual freedom in the name of social control than any punitive system could.

Returning to Kesey, we see the classic statement of this freedom based objection to denying responsibility and submitting to therapy as opposed to taking responsibility and incurring punishment. McMurphy wagers at the outset that treatment will be better than punishment. Later on he discovers the vastly greater threat to his liberty and autonomy that treatment entails. In conversation with one of the other inmates, McMurphy says that being in hospital is much better than being in jail. The other inmate disagrees. 'You're sentenced in a jail, and you got a date ahead of you when you *know* you're gonna be turned loose. . . . I was picked up for drunk and disorderly and I've been here for eight years and eight months'.[52] Suddenly McMurphy understands Nurse Ratched's mysterious confidence and her smug self-assurance despite McMurphy's many victories in their encounters on the ward:

> He'd been close to a month in this nuthouse and, it might be a lot better than a work farm, what with good beds and orange juice for breakfast, but it sure wasn't better to the point where he'd want to spend a couple of years here.[53]

Suddenly he realizes that to regain his freedom at all he must satisfy Nurse Ratched and the rest of the authorities on the ward. She does hold all the cards.

[51] Critiques of retributivism are often derived from the critiques of revenge. WI Miller states the anti-revenge case perfectly. 'Revenge is not a publicly admissible motive for individual action. Church, state, and reason all line up against it. Officially revenge is thus sinful to the theologian, illegal to the prince, and irrational to the economist (it defies the rule of sunk costs). Order and peace depend upon its extirpation; salvation and rational political and economic arrangements on its denial'. See WI Miller, 'Clint Eastwood and Equity: The Virtues of Revenge and the Shortcomings of Law in Popular Culture' in A Sarat and T Kearns (eds), *Law in the Domains of Culture* (Ann Arbor, University of Michigan Press, 1998) 161–202, 161.

[52] Kesey, *One Flew over the Cuckoo's Nest* (n 7) 159–60.

[53] ibid 160.

While McMurphy's treatment was invasive and brutal in the extreme – brutal in ways that treatment now claims to have transcended – the important point is that a forward-looking notion of responsibility for improvement through treatment in the future has no logical limit. Not bounded by the finite nature of backward-looking responsibility, the incursions on freedom imposed by treatment, be they ever so beneficent, are also potentially limitless. Being finite, a responsible wrongdoing eventually runs out as a justification for interference. An illness, by contrast, warrants the potentially limitless invasions of therapy. Insistence on a backward-looking notion of responsibility fixes the state's justification for depriving the individual of freedom in the past. In that sense, it also limits that justification.

Thus denying responsibility on grounds of mental illness not only marks acquiescence in one's deposition as the ultimate authority on and over oneself, it marks such acquiescence indefinitely. An aspirational understanding of responsibility provides potentially limitless justifications for paternalistic intrusion. Thus denying responsibility should be the least appetizing alternative for a self-respecting, and often even a merely self-interested, accused.

VI CONCLUSION

HLA Hart's resolutely consequentialist moral theory and his insistence (as Gardner so succinctly articulates it) that 'the suffering of the punished wrongdoer, be he ever so guilty, is always a cost and never a benefit of the criminal justice system'[54] lead him to look for a completely forward-looking justification of punishment. He saw, however, how this future focus might well lead to the rejection of the principle of responsibility all together.[55] If all we care about is the benefit of punishment in the future ,then why worry about responsibility in the past at all? As Hart put it in his essay 'Punishment and the Elimination of Responsibility' the upshot of a purely forward-looking social response to wrongdoing would be that the criminal's 'act, lying in the past, is important merely as a symptom – one symptom among others – of his character, mind and disposition; it helps us to diagnose what he is like and predict the effects of our action on him and on society'.[56] Still, Hart's concern was with punishment, and the risk he saw in a fully forward-looking understanding of the justification for punishment lay in the possibility that it would not rule out punishment of the innocent.

Here we have been concerned with an even more troubling possibility. If treatment, rather than punishment is the best way of preventing future wrongdoing, and if treatment unlike punishment does not either seek or inflict suffering and if

[54] J Gardner and HLA Hart, *Punishment and Responsibility: Essays in the Philosophy of Law* 2nd edn (Oxford, Oxford University Press, 2008) xiv.

[55] ibid ch 7: 'Punishment and the Elimination of Responsibility'.

[56] ibid 160.

many wrongdoers are mentally ill, why worry about the erosion of backward-looking notions of responsibility at all? Why not just celebrate a more effective and beneficent paradigm of social control?

That it is morally wrong to punish those who are not guilty (no matter how much future wrong may be prevented) is so intuitively obvious that one marvels at the amount of philosophical energy devoted to the question. A question that is far more pressing for our day is whether it is morally wrong to treat those who are not sick, however beneficial to society the projected effects of that treatment may be. The question is in many ways a trickier one, especially from a consequentialist point of view, if, as the therapeutic persuasion would have us believe, we need not attach any intrinsic disutility to treatment. Hart posited the value of freedom as the reason for holding onto a backward-looking notion of responsibility in the justification of punishment. We may have even better reason here to see the value of freedom as a reason for resisting purely forward-looking notions of responsibility in the justification of treatment.

We have every reason to distrust the psy-industry's bid to take over our understanding of the human personality. Growing as it is, the industry has obvious financial and power incentives to expand the category of mental illness indefinitely to bring more and more people, especially offenders, into its fold. All this is made easier by its ability to harness the basic impulse towards compassion for the suffering of injury and illness. We do not like to exclude people from benefits and assistance that inclusion in the ranks of mental illness now seems to entail. However, if it is wrong to treat those who are not sick – and I think it is – then we will always have reason to insist on backward-looking notions of responsibility as justifications for state intervention and we will always have reason to resist the artificial expansion of the category of mental illness. One way of doing that is to take a moral stand for rational responsibility as the foundation of self-respect.

8

Excuses and Excusing Conditions

DENNIS KLIMCHUK*

In this chapter I would like to challenge a view about excuses that is widely held, though for the most part only implicitly. It was recently articulated by Marcia Baron through a contrast between excusing and two conceptually adjacent ideas:

> If you forgive me, you bring it about that I am forgiven, and the same holds for pardoning; moreover, I can only be forgiven or pardoned by someone. Excusing is different, at least in this respect: I can have an excuse without anyone giving it to me; I have it because excusing conditions apply.[1]

The view I want to challenge draws a particular link between excuses and excusing conditions, expressed here, and expressed as well by Jeremy Horder when he says that '[i]f I excuse you, that says something about *you* or, in particular, about the circumstances in which you acted. By way of contrast, if I forgive you, that says something primarily about me'.[2]

Before articulating the view I need to say something about what an excusing condition is. This is a bit tricky. The problem is that it is difficult to explain the idea of an excusing condition in the abstract without begging one or more questions.[3] So let us start with the less abstract, with Baron's and Horder's accounts of what the excusing conditions are. Both are very rich and nuanced but I think for the purposes of isolating the idea of an excusing condition can be fairly expressed briefly.

According to Baron, A has an excuse if: (1) owing to some feature that distinguishes A from most adults it was very difficult for her to conform to the law's requirements, *or* (2) owing to the circumstances in which A found herself, it was extremely difficult for her, as it would have been for nearly anyone else, to

* I am very grateful to the participants in the conference from which this volume arises for their many insightful and helpful comments, as well as to my colleagues Samantha Brennan and Carolyn McLeod and to Marcia Baron and Jeremy Horder for the same.

[1] M Baron, 'Excuses, Excuses' (2007) 1 *Criminal Law and Philosophy* 21, 33.

[2] J Horder, 'Excuses in Law and in Morality: A Response to Marcia Baron' (2007) 1 *Criminal Law and Philosophy* 41, 43.

[3] Principally: what are the excusing conditions and what distinguishes excuses from other defences?

conform to the law's requirements.[4] According to Horder, A has an excuse if (a) her wrongful actions can be explained in such as way as to shed such favourable moral light on her conduct that it seems wrong to convict her, at least for the full offence *and* (b) there are no broad common goods that would be jeopardized by her partial or full acquittal, as there would be if, for example, her partial or full acquittal would encourage citizens to resort to self-help when they ought instead to seek legal redress. An explanation of the sort that grounds an excuse is cast in terms of either or both adopted reasons – the reasons on which basis the accused acted – or explanatory reasons, reasons that otherwise explain the accused's actions (that she stumbled, for example). Excuses can engage one or the other sort of reason differently in different circumstances. In duress, for example, sometimes what is exculpatorily persuasive is the accused's own reason for acting as she did and sometimes is it is rather the extent to which her will was 'overborne' by the threat to which she was subjected.[5]

For both Baron and Horder, then, an excusing condition is a property of the defendant's decision to commit the wrong in question: that, for example, owing to a condition from which she suffered, it was not really a decision at all, that it was a decision few of us could have resisted making or that it can be explained by reasons (either the agent's own reason or reasons independent of those) that cast it in a particular moral light. So it follows – to return to the passages from Baron and Horder quoted above – that an excusing condition is something that someone has without anyone giving it them, and in excusing A we say something about her rather than ourselves.[6]

The view I want to challenge holds that it is necessary and sufficient for having an excuse that one's decision to act as one did can be explained (or explained away) by an excusing condition.[7] This view is implicit in accounts of excuse that otherwise are in as fundamental disagreement as could be. For example, on JL Austin's account – the starting point for the contemporary debates about excuses and justifications – the principal characteristic of an excuse is that in raising an excuse one cedes the wrongfulness of one's action but denies responsibility for it.[8] John Gardner argues that Austin got it exactly wrong: if one was not responsible for one's action, then one doesn't need an excuse. An excused agent, on Gardner's

[4] Baron, 'Excuses, Excuses' (n 1) 23.

[5] J Horder, *Excusing Crime* (Oxford, Oxford University Press, 2004) chs 1.1–2, 2.5.

[6] Horder says, we saw above, that in excusing you we say 'something about *you* or, in particular, about the circumstances in which you acted' (underscore added). But the circumstances matter, as I understand it, only insofar as they provide an excusatory explanatory reason: they matter, that is, because of the light they cast on my decision to act as I did.

[7] Horder holds only the first half of this view, that is, he holds that A's being able to point to an excusing condition is a necessary but insufficient condition of A's having an excuse. Above I gave an example of one of the conditions that complete A's claim, namely that her partial or full acquittal would encourage citizens to resort to self-help when they ought instead to seek legal redress. Horder lists a number of others. See *Excusing Crime* (n 5) ch 1.2.

[8] JL Austin, 'A Plea for Excuses' in *Philosophical Papers* (Oxford, Clarendon Press, 1961) 124. Justifications, on Austin's account, are the mirror image of excuses: in raising a justification one accepts responsibility for one's action but denies that it was wrongful.

account, was responsible for what she did, but in acting as she did she made a mistake for which, owing to its character, she can be forgiven. One mistook a threat as real owing to having justifiably been in terror, for example.[9] Notwithstanding this basic difference (excuses deny responsibility; excuses presuppose it) Austin and Gardner share with Baron and Horder the view that if A is excused her wrongdoing can be explained (or explained away) by some feature of the defendant's decision to do as she did.

As opposed to what you might ask. The claim I aim to challenge seems analytically true, or nearly so. What I will argue is that at least some excuses at least sometimes exhibit one of the properties in terms of which Baron and Horder contrasted excusing with forgiving. Put very loosely, sometimes whether A merits an excuse rests importantly on something about the excuser. Put a bit more precisely, my claim is that sometimes a person may be entitled to an excuse owing to the fact that we lack standing to hold her to answer for her actions and conversely, sometimes a person may be denied an excuse owing to the fact that we cannot accept the exculpatory consequences of her excusing condition. In putting it this way, I have been deliberately imprecise about who 'we' are. The first part of my claim, that sometimes a person may be entitled to an excuse owing to the fact that we lack standing to hold her to answer for her actions, holds both in the context of ordinary morality and in the criminal law. Possibly there is an instantiation in ordinary morality of the claim that sometimes a person may be denied an excuse owing to the fact that we cannot acknowledge the exculpatory consequences of her excusing condition, but as I will defend this claim the relevant 'we' is the state.[10]

I will proceed as follows. In the first section, I will argue that it is sometimes not necessary, and in the second section, that it is sometimes not sufficient to be excused that one can point to an excusing condition. In each I will work with a particular criminal defence: necessity and provocation, respectively. In the first, I will defend the view that in some circumstances one is entitled to a defence of necessity because the state lacks standing to punish you. In the second, I will argue that sometimes one ought to be denied the defence of provocation notwithstanding that one has satisfied the requirements of the defence, on the grounds that the state cannot vindicate a claim implicit in one's defence. In the concluding section, I will consider the objection that my argument is not really about excuses: that,

[9] J Gardner, 'In Defence of Defences' in *Offences and Defences* (Oxford, Oxford University Press, 2007) 86. See also, 'The Gist of Excuses' in the same volume.

[10] One might suggest that my claim – that sometimes excuses rest on something about the excuser rather than the excused – is better cast as an expansion of the concept of an excusing condition rather than a denial of the biconditional relationship between excuses and excusing conditions. That is, one could say, if my arguments are sound, that some excusing conditions are properties of the defendant and her decision to do what she did and some are properties of the those who stand in judgement over her and their capacity or right to do so. I cast the point as I do – that is, I confine excusing conditions to conditions that explain or explain away the accused's wrongdoing – because I think it represents the way the idea of an excusing condition is generally understood. So, for example, Baron characterizes a view according to which whether someone merits an excuse is within another's discretion as a counter-example to the view that excuses rest on excusing conditions. See Baron, 'Excuses, Excuses' (n 1) 34.

even if the arguments of the first two sections are sound, all I have shown is that sometimes necessity is not an excuse and that sometimes we ought to reject the defence of provocation for extra-excusatory reasons. It is a central claim of this paper that this objection is false.

One final introductory point: I have so far said little about what counts as an excuse, about, that is, what distinguishes excuses from other defences. That is because I want to avoid some of the issues raised by the question, and postpone others. Controversies lurk around every corner, but I hope we can all accept that whatever excuses are, they are not justifications. A justification shows that one's actions were, in the end, permissible.[11] An excuse does not. If the distinction was exhaustive, then excuses would comprise those defences by which one was, we might say, 'let off the hook', notwithstanding having committed a wrong. While the justification/excuse distinction thus drawn captures, I think, the morally most significant distinction in the taxonomy of defences, this broad sense of excuse obscures some important distinctions, and in recognition of this everyone agrees that 'excuse' ought to be reserved for a subset of the category of non-justificatory defences.

There are two principal distinctions at issue here. It is helpful to think of these as marking points on an ascending scale, along which the accused concedes more of the conditions that collectively make her answerable for the crime with which she was accused. At the first step the accused denies that, in a sense, she committed a crime at all. Suppose A has taken from B something of B's without B's permission, and now exercises control over it as though it is hers. This looks like theft. But it may not be, if, for example, A was sleepwalking (and so would raise the defence of automatism) or thought that the disputed item was hers (and so would raise the defence of mistake of fact).[12] Whether and how to distinguish these defences from excuses proper is a question I will leave aside here, because the defences I will discuss – necessity and provocation – belong in the next step of the ascending scale, after the point at which the accused allows that she has committed a wrong. What I will postpone is the question whether and how to draw the step after that, at which point an accused allows that she has committed a wrong and concedes that she has no excuse, but proffers a non-justificatory defence nonetheless. Examples of these include diplomatic immunity and entrapment. Here an admitted fully guilty person is let free on the grounds that some good is thereby promoted (as in the case of diplomatic immunity) or on the

[11] By saying that justifications show that one's actions were, *in the end*, permissible, I am being deliberately ambiguous as between two views. According to the first, a successful justification shows that one's action was not, in fact, wrongful. According to the second, a successful justification shows that one's action was a kind of wrongdoing, namely a justified one. For what it is worth, I believe the second view is correct, but nothing turns on that here. The basic contrast between justifications and excuses comes out equally well on either.

[12] As I have drawn it, this category collects defences that some may want to sort further into those that deny that the accused had the capacity to perform a crime (infancy, perhaps insanity, in at least some cases) and those do not (such as, again, mistake of fact). There are other possible subdivisions as well.

grounds that a public body's misinterpretation of its mandate would otherwise be vindicated (as in the case of entrapment).[13] It is, we will see, an important objection to my argument that I have pushed necessity up into this final range on the ascending scale and have placed limitations on provocation that reflect considerations akin to those underlying defences like entrapment. This is the objection I will consider in the final section of this chapter.

I NEITHER NECESSARY

The claim I want to defend in this section is that sometimes a person may be entitled to an excuse owing to the fact that we lack standing to hold her to answer for her actions. I will argue, first, that this is a principle of ordinary morality. I will then consider an argument that aims to show that there is a principle that sets the limits of legal authority that bears the same structure.

The thought I have in mind is sometimes captured by the sentiment expressed in saying 'There but for the grace of God go I' in accounting for one's reticence at condemning another for his actions. The idea is that we recognize our shared vulnerability to circumstances and are not always confident that we could or would act as we believe we ought when faced with challenges that, owing to our good fortune, we have not faced. We sometimes withhold or mitigate blame, in other words, as an expression of a kind of moral humility.

I say *sometimes* because, as Anthony Duff points out, recognizing that I would have acted wrongfully as another did in the same circumstances does not quite by itself deprive me of standing to criticize him. What that recognition does is make my standing conditional on my willingness to criticize myself.[14] In some cases – suppose we share a blameworthy vulnerability to certain sorts of temptation – the right response is to let neither you nor myself off the hook. There are, however, some circumstances in which we would properly judge that (most) *anyone* would be vulnerable to wrongdoing in the circumstances in which the wrongdoer found himself,[15] and in at least some of these (the most dire) morality arguably requires humility. This judgement exhibits two features that distinguish excuses from cognate concepts such as forgiveness and pardon, and so, I suggest, entitles us to say that it is a judgement that the wrongdoer merits an excuse. First, while one can only be forgiven by the person one has wronged, in the sort of case I am considering, moral humility is required of all of us. Secondly, while forgiveness possibly and pardon almost certainly involve discretion, the judgement that moral

[13] I develop this understanding of entrapment below, in the final section of this chapter.

[14] A Duff, 'Blame, Moral Standing and the Legitimacy of the Criminal Trial' (2010) 23 *Ratio* 123, 124–30.

[15] Marcia Baron pointed out to me that whether the judgement that anyone might have acted as someone did in a particular case is true will depend on how fine or course-grained are the descriptions of the particular wrongdoing and the circumstances of its commission. This is very important and interesting. I believe that it complicates the claim I am making but does not undermine it.

humility in a particular case is required by all of us is no less objective than the claim that another has done no less than we could have expected of him – it is no less objective, that is, than the judgement that another has an excusing condition.

Now, not everyone will agree that this sort of objectivity is possible in morality.[16] I think it is. But my claim that it is here in a sense *obiter*. That is for two reasons. First, what really matters is that we recognize that some moral judgements exhibit the structure I have tried to describe. Secondly, and in any case, the analogous judgement in law, we will see, is objective or no less objective than many other legal claims.

I want to suggest that a familiar way of thinking of the defence of necessity exhibits a structure analogous to the morality humility judgement in ordinary morality, and defend what I believe to be the strongest version of this view. The basic structure of the moral humility argument is this: there is a condition that permits us to pass judgement on others – that we are reasonably confident that we would have acted otherwise in the circumstances in which they found themselves – that in some cases is not satisfied.[17] Let me emphasize that I do not mean to defend what we might think of as the *substantive* legal analogue of the moral humility judgement, the view that necessity ought to excuse in those circumstances in which we (judges or jurors) judge we would be vulnerable to the temptation to which the accused succumbed. On the contrary, nothing in what follows requires us to reject Lord Coleridge's claim in *Dudley and Stephens* that, in law, '[w]e are often compelled to set up standards we cannot reach ourselves, and to lay down rules which we could not ourselves satisfy'.[18]

The idea that there is a condition that permits the state to punish wrongdoers that is not satisfied in some cases of necessity has been variously expressed.[19] It is, for example, arguably invoked by the maxim *necessitas habet non legem* – necessity knows no law. But the view that necessity suspends the law *tout court* is blunter than the idea under consideration here.[20] Its clearest expression is in Kant's analysis of necessity:

> [T]here can be no *penal law* that would assign the death penalty to someone in a shipwreck who, in order to save his own life, shoves another whose life is equally in danger, off a plan on which he has saved himself. For the punishment threatened by the law could not be greater than the loss of his own life. A penal law of this sort could not have

[16] Baron argues that the judgement by which we ought to excuse another on grounds of moral humility is discretionary – which is not to call it subjective, but to deny that it is objective in the sense I have defended. See Baron, 'Excuses, Excuses' (n 1) 34.

[17] 'He that is without sin among you, let him first cast a stone' (John 8:7) exhibits the same structure, except that the condition it names is never satisfied (by us). See Duff, 'Blame' (n 14) 127 for a nice analysis of this passage and of Matthew 7:1, 'Judge not, that ye be not judged'.

[18] *R v Dudley and Stephens* (1884) 15 QBD 273, 288.

[19] Malcolm Thorburn suggested to me that there is an imprecision to the analogy that I aim to draw here. While the conclusion of a moral judgement is blame and perhaps criticism, the conclusion of a legal judgment is punishment, and the conditions of each are significantly different. That is true, and important. But I think even when cast abstractly enough to accommodate this difference, the analogy is illuminating, because the same basic structure of the standing analysis obtains in both cases.

[20] It is also false. Necessity only excuses those actions necessary to save oneself or another.

> the effect intended, since a threat of an ill that is still *uncertain* (death by judicial verdict) cannot outweigh the fear of an ill that is *certain* (drowning). Hence the deed of saving one's life by violence is not to be judged *inculpable* . . . but only *unpunishable.*[21]

At first glance, this argument sounds surprisingly un-Kantian, an impression deepened by noting how much it seems to parallel Bentham's analysis of the same category of case. Among the cases 'unmeet for punishment', Bentham tells us, are those in which punishment must be inefficacious. This category includes those cases

> [w]here, though the penal clause might exercise a full and prevailing influence, were it to act alone, yet by the *predominant* influence of some opposite cause upon the will, it must necessary be ineffectual; because the evil which he sees himself about to undergo, in the case of his *not* engaging in the act, is so great, that the evil denounced by the penal cause, in case of his engaging in it, cannot appear greater. This may happen . . . [i]n the case of *physical danger*; where the evil is such as appears to be brought about by the unassisted powers of *nature.*[22]

But the parallel is only superficial. Seeing the difference will help isolate Kant's view.

The difference comes out when we ask, what is the significance of the fact that the threat of punishment will prove ineffectual?[23] For Bentham, this matters because it follows that punishment of the imperilled wrongdoer will increase the amount of harm suffered by members of the community, and that matters because punishment is justified only when its imposition promises to diminish the amount of harm suffered by persons.[24] This is not Kant's point.[25] For Kant the inefficacy of the threat of punishment matters, not because punishment will be to no effect, but rather because it shows that compliance with the law cannot be expected of anyone moved only by those incentives it is possible for the legal system to provide. *This* matters, in turn, because it shows that there has been, in Kant's language, a failure of external lawgiving.[26] Let me explain.[27]

A lawgiving, in Kant's sense, is the placing of someone under an obligation to do or forbear from doing something. Lawgiving consists of two elements: a law and an incentive sufficient for the addressee's compliance. Lawgiving is external if it is possible to discharge the obligation imposed by the law for reasons provided

[21] I Kant, *The Metaphysics of Morals* (Cambridge, Cambridge University Press, 1996) 28.

[22] J Bentham, *An Introduction to the Principle of Morals and Legislation* (Oxford, Clarendon Press, 2005) 162.

[23] It is important to note how narrow this claim is. What matters is that the threat of punishment will be ineffectual, on an abstract decision theoretic measure. The claim is not that no other consideration would prevent, say, any particular person from taking another's life to save her own.

[24] Bentham, *An Introduction to the Principle of Morals and Legislation* (n 22) 158.

[25] And that is to his credit because, as Hart argued, Bentham misses an important point, namely that even if the accused could not have been deterred, it does not follow that others might be by the example of his punishment. HLA Hart, *Punishment and Responsibility* (Oxford, Clarendon Press, 1968) 18–20, 40–43.

[26] L Mulholland, *Kant's System of Rights* (New York, Columbia University Press, 1990) 194.

[27] I defend the interpretation of Kant summarized in this section D Klimchuk, 'Necessity, Deterrence and Standing' (2002) 8 *Legal Theory* 339.

by an external incentive. An incentive is external if it is not internal, and there is only one internal incentive: regard for the duty itself. The domain of right – of, we would say, the legitimate exercise of legal authority – is set by the limits of external lawgiving. The law's authority extends only to the enforcement of those duties that it is possible to discharge with the sort of incentive the state may provide: that is, in this context, the threat of punishment.

An example will help make all this clear. One acts beneficently, on Kant's account, only if one acts with a particular motive. For example, if I give to a charity just to impress someone, I have not discharged the duty of beneficence, even if in acting as I did I in fact contributed to others' wellbeing. That is because I act beneficently only if I give owing to the fact that morality requires it of me, and I do this, in Kant's language, by making the wellbeing of others my end. Thus, in Kant's scheme, beneficence is a duty of virtue. Beneficence cannot be a duty of right because the threat of punishment cannot compel me to adopt any end. It can only compel me to act (or forbear from acting) in certain ways. The duty to pay taxes – and so in part to act *as though* I have adopted others' wellbeing as my end – can be a duty of right, because I can discharge it merely as a means to avoid sanction. Thus, the duty to pay taxes is a duty for which external lawgiving is possible.

Benificence, however, is not. Neither is the duty to refrain from killing another to save oneself when circumstances force the choice – this, I suggest, is what Kant means when he says that there could be no penal law that would assign a death penalty to someone who killed another in such circumstances. The reasons are different in each case. The attempt to make beneficence a legal duty is essentially self-defeating: to the extent that I would obey the law owing to its incentives, I would fail to act beneficently. Subjecting to punishment the imperilled wrongdoer in the dire circumstances Kant considers is not self-defeating in the same way but it is, for related reasons, beyond the state's authority. It is beyond the state's authority because compliance with the law in the circumstances cannot be induced by the incentives that the law can provide. Kant's claim – it must be emphasized – is not that compliance with the law in the dire circumstances he considers is impossible, or even unlikely. Indeed, it is required (bear in mind that Kant's point is not that the killing is justified or otherwise permissible). But it is required by a duty that one cannot be induced by the threat of punishment itself to discharge.[28]

By concluding that the state may therefore not punish the wrongdoer, I would argue, Kant is saying something surprising but less controversial than it seems. His claim echoes, and expands in breadth and depth Locke's argument in the *Letter Concerning Toleration* that the state may not undertake to compel belief because it cannot succeed.[29] The state's authority, in short, runs out at the point

[28] At least not by punishment that the state is entitled to threaten. For an account and defence of this and other factual and conceptual constraints in Kant's example, see Klimchuk, 'Necessity, Deterrence and Standing', ibid 349–51.

[29] J Locke, 'A Letter Concerning Toleration' in R Vernon (ed), *Locke on Toleration* (Cambridge, Cambridge University Press, 2010) 8.

set by the means at its disposal. We, fellow members of the human community, may well be justified in condemning the imperilled wrongdoer's action (is there a plainer example of treating another as a means only?) but the state lacks standing to punish her.[30]

II NOR SUFFICIENT

The claim I want to defend in this section is that sometimes a person may be denied an excuse owing to the fact that we cannot acknowledge the exculpatory consequences of his excusing condition. I will defend this claim by defending an argument that invokes it, found in the dissenting opinion in *Thibert*, a Canadian provocation case.[31]

The following are the facts. Mr Thibert killed the man for whom his wife had left him. He went to their place of work with a loaded gun, seeking to speak to his wife in private. She refused. They all met in the parking lot, and at one point the victim held Mrs Thibert in front of him saying 'Come on big fellow, shoot me? You want to shoot me? Go ahead and shoot me'. He then let go of Mrs Thibert and advanced towards the defendant, ignoring his requests to stay back. The defendant shot him and drove away.

Thibert argued that he lacked the intention to kill or, alternatively, that he was provoked. The provocation provision of the Canadian Criminal Code[32] reads, in part:

> **232.** (1) Culpable homicide that otherwise would be murder may be reduced to manslaughter if the person who committed it did so in the heat of passion caused by sudden provocation.
>
> (2) A wrongful act or an insult that is of such a nature as to be sufficient to deprive an ordinary person of the power of self-control is provocation for the purposes of this section if the accused acted on it on the sudden and before there was time for his passion to cool.
>
> (3) For the purposes of this section, the questions
>
> (*a*) whether a particular wrongful act or insult amounted to provocation, and
>
> (b) whether the accused was deprived of the power of self-control by the provocation that he alleges he received,
>
> are questions of fact, but no one shall be deemed to have given provocation to another by doing anything that he had a legal right to do, or by doing anything that the accused

[30] This was arguably the judgment finally passed on the defendants in *Dudley and Stephens*. After several days adrift in the dingy of their sunken ship, Dudley and Stephens killed a third member of their crew and ate his body. Their conviction for murder was upheld by the House of Lords, but then commuted to six months, time served. They were, in short, found culpable but un-punishable (or, at least, unworthy of punishment).

[31] *R v Thibert* [1996] 1 SCR 37. My analysis here develops an argument I first made in a brief comment on Thibert: D Klimchuk, 'Circumstances and Objectivity' (1996) 45 *Criminal Reports* 24.

[32] Criminal Code RSC 1985 ch C-46.

> incited him to do in order to provide the accused with an excuse for causing death or bodily harm to any human being.

The defence thus imposes an objective and a subjective test. For the defence to be made out, the finder of fact must be satisfied, first, that the defendant was subject to 'a wrongful act or an insult that is of such a nature as to be sufficient to deprive an ordinary person of the power of self-control' (the objective test) and secondly, that he acted 'in the heat of passion caused by sudden provocation' (the subjective test). Subsection (3) says that these are questions of fact – that is to say, questions to be answered by the jury – but the Court has held that it is a question of law – a question to be determined by the judge – whether there is an 'air of reality' to the claim that either is satisfied on the facts. In asking whether there is an air of reality to a defendant's claim to a particular defence, a judge asks whether there is such evidence as might convince a properly instructed jury acting judiciously that the defence has been made out. At issue in *Thibert*, in part – the part on which I will focus – was whether the trial judge erred in thinking that there had been such evidence. The majority found that there had been. The dissent disagreed.

At issue in the disagreement is the question how to integrate into the question the significance of the background of the relationship among the three parties. Implicit in the majority's opinion is the view that it is only in light of that relationship that the victim's words and actions could be considered provocation. The main question to answer, on the majority's reckoning, is whether it is consistent with the objective standard to set it in this context – that is, to invest the ordinary person with those of the defendant's characteristics that explain why he might have found the victim's words and actions provocation. They hold, soundly, that it is, on the grounds that insults, for example, often depend on particular characteristics of their audience for their effect. The ordinary person standard serves to uphold the defendant to a standard of self-control we feel entitled to impose. Investing the ordinary person with, for example, the defendant's ethnic identity is, in some cases, not only permissible but necessary to see whether the standard was satisfied.[33] The Court held that the fact of the parties' relationship is like a defendant's age or ethnicity in this regard. So contextualized, there was sufficient evidence of provocation to justify putting the defence to the jury:

> Taking into account the past history between the deceased and the accused, a jury could find the actions of the deceased to be taunting and insulting. It might be found that, under the same circumstances, an ordinary person who was a married man, faced with the break-up of his marriage, would have been provoked by the acts of the deceased so as to cause him to lose self-control.[34]

Major J, writing for the dissent, disagreed. It is worth reproducing his analysis in full:

[33] On this point see too the earlier case of *R v Hill* [1986] 1 SCR 313, 331. It follows that the Court's habit elsewhere of calling a contextualized objective standard 'modified' is misleading. See, eg, *Arndt v Smith* [1997] 2 SCR 539 and *R v Beatty* [2008] 1 SCR 49.

[34] *R v Thibert* (n 31) 52.

> In my opinion, in this case there is no evidence of a wrongful act or insult sufficient to deprive an ordinary person of the power of self-control. That the deceased may have positioned Mrs Thibert between himself and the appellant cannot constitute a wrongful act or insult. Nor can the statements 'You want to shoot me? Go ahead and shoot me' and 'Come on big fellow, shoot me' be considered a wrongful act or insult. Those actions are not contemptuous or scornful; they are legitimate reactions to a dangerous situation. It would be improper to require victims to respond in a certain way when faced with armed, threatening individuals. The defence claim that the wrongful act or insult came from the appellant's evidence that the deceased used Joan Thibert as a shield while taunting him to shoot is ironic. The appellant had control of the only true weapon involved in this situation, the rifle.
>
> Further, that the deceased had a personal relationship with Mrs Thibert is not a wrongful act or insult sufficient to cause an ordinary person to lose the power of self-control. The breakup of a marriage due to an extramarital affair cannot constitute such a wrongful act or insult. I agree with the statement of Freeman JA in *R v Young* (1993) 78 CCC (3d) 538 (NSCA), at p 542, that:
>
> > It would set a dangerous precedent to characterize terminating a relationship as an insult or wrong act capable of constituting provocation to kill. The appellant may have been feeling anger, frustration and a sense of loss, particularly if he was in a position of emotional dependency on the victim as his counsel asserts, but that is not provocation of a kind to reduce murder to manslaughter.
>
> Similarly, it would be a dangerous precedent to characterize involvement in an extramarital affair as conduct capable of grounding provocation, even when coupled with the deceased's reactions to the dangerous situation he faced. At law, no one has either an emotional or proprietary right or interest in a spouse that would justify the loss of self-control that the appellant exhibited.[35]

The way Major J put his final point is revealing: *at law*, he held, no one has either an emotional or proprietary right or interest in a spouse that would justify the loss of self-control the appellant exhibited. Now the language of justification here is misleading, but I think not essential to the main point. That point is that, in accounting for why the actions or words with which one was faced constituted provocation, as a matter of law one cannot invoke what amounts to an emotional or proprietary right or interest in a spouse. One has no such right, and the court cannot vindicate one's claim to have such a right by permitting a defence of provocation that invokes it, even if only implicitly, to proceed.

Major J makes this claim in support of his finding that 'there is no evidence of a wrongful act or insult sufficient to deprive an ordinary person of the power of self-control'. If this were right, then the point would go to denying Thibert's claim to having an excusing condition.[36] But I think that while Major J's claim is exactly right, he miscasts its implication. Rather than forming part of the content of the

[35] *R v Thibert* (n 31) 64–65.

[36] I should clarify that I am not equating having an excusing condition in this case with satisfying the statutory requirements of the defence whatever they turn out to be. The equation works in this case because satisfaction of the subjective and objective elements of s 232 would qualify one for having an excusing condition in the way I have characterized it.

objective standard the limit imposed by Major J is better regarded as independent of it.[37] This is because I think that (regrettable as this is) a properly instructed jury acting judiciously may well conclude that an ordinary person would regard as provocative words or deeds that disrespected his emotional or proprietary right or interest in his spouse. One might respond that this would be possible only if we took 'ordinary person' to be a descriptive, statistical idea. It is, the objection continues, normative rather than descriptive. The question it asks is whether the accused exhibited such self-control as we are *entitled* to ask one another to exercise. I think this is right, but would add that the limits of what we are entitled to ask of one another are set, in part, by what we judge that as a matter of fact we can expect of one another. Consider the standard of care in tort. While that standard sets a norm against which each person is held – including in some cases persons incapable of reaching it – our natural capacities and other causal limits set the range in which that norm operates. The standard of care cannot require, for example, the physically impossible. Similarly, the boundaries of behaviour in fact accepted in a culture or society constrain (though neither strictly nor indefeasibly) the behaviour its members will judge that they are entitled to expect of one another.

Let me emphasize that my claim does *not* rest on its being a sound judgement that we are not entitled to expect someone in Mr Thibert's position to exercise self-control. Nor does my claim rests on its necessarily – or even, for that matter, likely – being true that a properly instructed jury acting judiciously would conclude that an ordinary person would regard as provocative words or deeds that disrespected his putative proprietary right in his spouse. It rests instead on the fact that a jury might, consistently with its mandate, so find *and* that that would not, on the principle Major J invokes, then entitle the defendant to the defence of provocation. He would be disentitled to the defence, I argue, because by allowing it the court would vindicate a view inconsistent with the equality of persons, something it cannot be heard to do.[38] The upshot, then, is that the accused would be denied an excuse because a court cannot cognize, we might say, the exculpatory consequences of his excusing condition.[39]

[37] As, I would argue, is the limit in ss 232(3) that 'no one shall be *deemed* to have given provocation to another by doing anything that he had a legal right to do, or by doing anything that the accused incited him to do in order to provide the accused with an excuse for causing death or bodily harm to any human being' (emphasis added). Kent Roach advances an interpretation of ss 232(3) that finds in it something akin to the principle I claim to be implicit in Major J's reasons: 'It could be argued that people have a legal right to leave relationships and even to make disparaging comments about ex-partners'. K Roach, *Criminal Law* 4th edn (Toronto, Irwin Law, 2009) 359. On this interpretation, the principle that one cannot, in making out one's claim to a defence of provocation, invoke a proprietary right or interest in a spouse would defeat the accused's claim independently of the question raised by the objective standard. The Supreme Court of Canada recently rejected this interpretation of ss 232(3) in *R v Tran* (2010) SCC 58 [29], and held that the objective standard ought to be interpreted in such a way as to exclude from ordinary person such views as that one's spouse is one's property (para 34).

[38] This is the point on which Doherty J's judgement of the Ontario Court of Appeal in *R v Humaid* (2006) 81 OR 465 ultimately turns.

[39] One might argue that a similar consideration bars or ought to bar necessity (and the closely related defence of duress) from being raised in defence to some crimes, at least murder. Notwithstanding that the defence is not a justification, and so its successful deployment does not announce that the

III AN OBJECTION AND THE CONCLUSION

In conclusion I would like to clarify my argument by considering the most important objection to it. That objection is that, if sound, my claims about necessity and provocation have only shown that they are not always or not in all respects excuses. They are or overlap with – the objection holds – what Paul Robinson calls non-exculpatory public policy defences.[40] These form a conceptually heterogeneous class. Within that class, the defence in terms of which the objection can most plausibly be made is entrapment. I will articulate the objection as strongly as I can, and then respond to it.

The objection can be particularly well made out in terms of the official Canadian judicial account of entrapment. In *Mack*, the Supreme Court of Canada held *per* Lamer J (as he was then) that

> there is . . . entrapment when: (a) the authorities provide an opportunity to persons to commit an offence without reasonable suspicion or acting *mala fides* . . . or, (b) having a reasonable suspicion or acting in the course of a *bona fide* inquiry, they go beyond providing an opportunity and induce the commission of an offence.[41]

(a) protects citizens against what the court calls 'random virtue testing' and (b) against not just wrongful compulsion, but the exploitation of characteristics that ought to be respected; in Lamer J's example:

> [I]f the law enforcement officer or agent appeals to a person's instincts of compassion, sympathy and friendship and uses these qualities of a person to effect the commission of a crime, we may say this is not permissible conduct because it violates individual privacy and the dignity of interpersonal relationships, and condemns behaviour that we want to encourage.[42]

The objection, then, is that the defence of entrapment can be accurately described as upholding the limits of legal authority, just as on Kant's account, the defence of necessity does. It is extended to the defendant rather than have the court vindicate a false view of the respect persons owe to one another. This is just the basis on which, I argued, the defence of provocation ought to be rejected in cases like *Thibert*. Entrapment is plainly non-exculpatory, and so not an excuse. So if the arguments in this chapter are sound, all that I have shown is that sometimes necessity is not an excuse, and that sometimes we ought to reject the defence of provocation for extra-excusatory reasons.

accused's actions were permissible, one might argue that in allowing the defence to go through a court would be vindicating the treatment of someone by another as a mere means in a way that is inconsistent with principles that lie at the heart of criminal (and other) law. This is a powerful argument. If sound, it doesn't affect the main point about necessity I hope to make – which is that we cannot understand its scope on the view that explains excuses just in terms of excusing conditions.

[40] P Robinson, 'Criminal Law Defenses: A Systematic Analysis' (1982) 82 *Columbia Law Review* 199.

[41] *R v Mack* [1988] 2 SCR 903, 959.

[42] ibid 963.

My response is that this argument ignores an important difference between entrapment, and necessity and provocation, even on the accounts I have given above. A successful defence of entrapment indicts another for his misconduct: it is, loosely speaking, about someone else and what he did. Though it is strange and perhaps a bit misleading to put it like this, there is a sense in which the defendant in an entrapment case is (permissibly) the beneficiary of another's wrongdoing. His culpability is, in a very important sense, not at issue at all.

Now one might say that *that* is just what I have argued in claiming that in some circumstances one is entitled to a defence of necessity because the state lacks standing to punish you, and that sometimes one ought to be denied the defence of provocation notwithstanding that one has satisfied the requirements of the defence, on the grounds that the state cannot vindicate a moral claim implicit in one's defence. But I think the point is better put differently. My claim is that the conditions of exculpation under law are set in part by principles that set the scope of legal authority and ensure that its exercise conforms with basic substantive principles that lie at its foundation. In other words, the scope of the excuses is set in part by principles of the rule of law, an insight that the view about excuses and excusing conditions I have sought to challenge here threatens to obscure.

PART II

Rethinking the Philosophical Foundations of the Domestic Criminal Process

9

The Law of Evidence and the Protection of Rights

HAMISH STEWART*

I INTRODUCTION

The protection of rights in the law of evidence is often associated with exclusionary rules that promote values external to the trial, that is, with Wigmore's 'rules of extrinsic policy', such as privilege and the exclusion of unconstitutionally obtained evidence. It is said that these rules interfere with the truth-finding function of the trial; a regrettable but necessary price to pay for the protection of values that the trial is not intrinsically concerned with. In contrast, Wigmore's 'rules of probative policy', the traditional common law rules of evidence, are usually understood as serving values internal to the trial process, notably, the search for the truth.[1] In this chapter, I suggest that the contrast between the rights-protecting and truth-finding functions of the criminal trial should not be drawn so starkly. If we understand the common law trial process as a method for resolving disputes about rights in a legal order that is in general committed to defining and enforcing the rights of free and juridically equal persons, then both the truth-finding and the rights-protecting function of the criminal trial, including its procedural and evidentiary rules, might be explained in relation to that goal. This approach might well affect our understanding of the rules of extrinsic policy in that the harm of, for example, excluding unconstitutionally obtained evidence is not just the failure to get at the truth, but the failure to vindicate a violation of right committed by the accused.[2] But in this chapter I focus not on constitutional exclusionary rules,

* For comments on a draft of this chapter, I am very grateful to Ekow Yankah, Arthur Ripstein, Marc Rosenberg, Thomas Cromwell, Dina Zalkind, the participants in the conference on 'Rethinking Criminal Law Theory' at Osgoode Hall Law School in September 2010 and the participants in a faculty workshop at the Faculty of Law, University of Toronto in November 2010.

[1] See JH Wigmore, *Evidence in Trials at Common Law* vol 1 (P Tillers rev, Boston, Little, Brown and Company, 1983) §11.

[2] Under the Canadian exclusionary rule, the 'societal interest in adjudication on the merits', which includes the interest in bringing wrongdoers to justice, is a relevant consideration in the decision to admit or to exclude unconstitutionally obtained evidence: *R v Grant* [2009] SCC 32 [79].

but on the common law. I sketch an understanding of the trial process as an institutional process for determining disputes about rights in a rightful condition. I then consider how two Canadian common law rules of evidence – issue estoppel and the balancing of probative value and prejudicial effect – serve a rights-protection as well as a truth-finding function in the criminal trial. The evidentiary aspect of the doctrine of issue estoppel helps to preserve the right to be judged guilty or innocent in proceedings concerned with specific allegations of wrongdoing, while the balancing of probative value and prejudicial effect helps to protect the right of the accused to be judged fairly.

II THE RIGHT TO A FAIR TRIAL

Suppose that the legal system is a set of institutions creating and applying rules and principles that are designed to provide a structure in which purposive and juridically equal individuals can interact as free persons, that is, as subject to restrictions on their conduct that each could accept as justified for the sake of the freedom of all. This picture of the legal system as constituting a 'rightful condition' is very abstract and, at this level of generality, is commonplace in the liberal tradition. It evidently requires considerable spelling out in all sorts of ways; but it is reasonably clear that one of the main tasks of such a legal system would be to define and protect the rights of the individual persons who constitute it, because rights are the institutional means for defining the freedom that each has in relation to each other and in relation to the state. But rights are not self-applying or self-enforcing. The legal system therefore requires institutions of adjudication for resolving disputes about rights. And the process of adjudication must itself be constrained by the rights of the participants; it would be normatively inconsistent for the system to deny that the participants were bearers of rights in the very process of determining a dispute about what those rights were. (If the participants were not rights-bearers, there could be no dispute about the existence or content of those rights.) The rules of procedure and evidence must therefore also be consistent with the rights of the persons who are disputing about their rights.[3]

Consider the following example. It is often said both that in the litigation process, the state has the right to every person's evidence, and that there are limits on that right.[4] This principle applies in both criminal prosecutions and civil actions:

[3] The authors of *The Trial on Trial* argue very persuasively that the criminal trial in a liberal state should be understood normatively not as a simple instrument for getting at the truth, but as part of a performative process of calling fellow-citizens to account for their (alleged) wrongdoing. While 'calling to account' may not be exactly the right description of the criminal trial process form the perspective of the Kantian version of the rightful condition that I invoke in this chapter, my project shares with theirs a non-instrumental conception of the trial and so there are naturally many points of contact between the two projects with respect to specific doctrinal issues. See A Duff, L Farmer, S Marshall and V Tadros (eds), *Towards a Normative Theory of the Criminal Law, The Trial on Trial* vol 3 (Oxford, Hart Publishing, 2007).

[4] *National Post v Canada* [2010] SCC 16 [1].

like the Crown and the defence in criminal cases, the parties to private disputes about rights can, subject to certain exceptions, invoke the coercive powers of the state to compel other individuals who have information relevant to the dispute to give evidence. Both the principle and its exceptions can be explained in a manner consistent with the functions of the trial process in resolving disputes about rights in a rightful condition. The state has the right to every person's evidence because the requirement to give evidence is a necessary element of a system of rights protection (how else would the tribunal determine the facts on which to base its decision?); every person can therefore accept the obligation to testify in proceedings to resolve disputes about others' rights as part of the system that itself protects her rights. But the right to every person's evidence cannot be exercised in a way that denies the rights of witnesses or potential witnesses. So the right to every person's evidence does not include the right to invade solicitor/client privilege, where that privilege is itself understood as necessary for an individual's participation in the process of determining her rights,[5] and it can be qualified by constitutionally protected privacy interests.[6] Nor does it include the right to use evidence obtained through severe rights-violations such as torture.[7]

But the most basic right of an individual in the adjudicative process is the right of a party to the proceedings not to be subjected to a penalty or civil sanction until it has been shown that he did in fact commit the rights-violation or other wrong or offence that is alleged. As Kant put it, every person has, just in virtue of being a person, the right to be 'a human being *beyond reproach* . . . since before he performs any act affecting rights he has done no wrong to anyone'.[8] In a rightful condition, a mere allegation of wrongdoing cannot be enough to deprive anyone of the right to be beyond reproach; there must be a fair and public process for deciding whether the allegation is, to the required degree, true. The presumption of innocence is an obvious legal manifestation of the right to be beyond reproach: everyone is presumed to be innocent of an allegation of criminal wrongdoing until guilt has been established, usually beyond a reasonable doubt, in a fair and public proceeding. And not just any procedure will do; rolling a pair of dice and finding the accused guilty if the sum is four or more would be fair in the way that a lottery is fair, but it would not be a test of the allegations against the accused. The procedure has to be a public process with procedural rules that could be accepted by all and that determines the truth of the allegation in a reasonable way, while respecting the rights of everyone involved, such that the verdict is not only likely to be true but also justified.[9]

[5] This theme has figured prominently in the Supreme Court of Canada's recent jurisprudence: see, eg, *Canada (Privacy Commissioner) v Blood Tribe Department of Health* [2008] SCC 45 [9]. It may help to explain why the Court has recently been so protective of the privilege.

[6] Criminal Code RSC 1985 ch C-46, s 278.1; *R v Mills* [1999] 3 SCR 668.

[7] Compare Criminal Code, s 269.1(4), which provides that any statement obtained through the commission of the offence of torture is inadmissible in proceedings governed by federal law.

[8] I Kant, *The Metaphysics of Morals* (Mary Gregor ed and trans, Cambridge, Cambridge University Press, 1996) 6:238 (in the Royal Prussian Academy pagination). Compare: *The Trial on Trial* (n 3) 113.

[9] Compare: *The Trial on Trial* (n 3) ch 3.

Thus, the rules of evidence and procedure for the criminal trial in a rightful condition cannot be designed solely to reach an outcome, or to satisfy the public's desire for a reassuring narrative of righting wrong or restoring order, or even to find out the truth – though they may indeed achieve all of these purposes – but they must also be consistent with the rights of the participants. The rules will, of course, also be conditioned by the purposes of punishment in a rightful condition, and writers in the tradition where I situate this chapter do not agree on what that purpose is.[10] But for the purposes of this chapter, it will be sufficient to stipulate a number of basic features of criminal punishment. First, persons are punished for their wrongful conduct, not for their bad characters.[11] Secondly, the universe of punishable conduct includes conduct that is privately wrongful (such as theft and assault), conduct that is damaging to the public order (such as treason), conduct that is damaging to the trial process itself (such as perjury and obstruction of justice) and conduct that is harmful to the state's legitimate regulatory objectives (such as traffic offences). The substantive doctrines of penal responsibility may apply differently to these different wrongs, but where a person is alleged to have committed any of them, she is entitled to a fair process to determine her liability. Thirdly, while it is not necessary to accept the extreme position that all offences must be punished,[12] I will assume the truth of the weaker claim that a rightful condition must at least sometimes punish conduct that violates private rights or the norms of public law because a state that never punished such conduct, limiting itself to civil remedies for the wrongs and harms that the conduct caused, would not live up to its own aspiration to define and to maintain a rightful condition.

I now explore how two common law rules of evidence can be understood through thinking of the trial process as a way of resolving allegations of wrongdoing in a rightful condition.

[10] Contrast the accounts offered by Kant, *The Metaphysics of Morals* (n 8) 6:331–337; S Byrd, 'Kant's Theory of Punishment: Deterrence in its Threat, Retribution in its Execution' (1989) 8 *Law and Philosophy* 151; A Ripstein, *Force and Freedom: Kant's Legal and Political Philosophy* (Cambridge MA, Harvard University Press, 2009) ch 10; A Brudner, *Punishment and Freedom* (Oxford, Oxford University Press, 2009) ch 1. See also, *The Trial on Trial* (n 3) 62.

[11] Character-based accounts of punishment do, of course, provide explanations of why there must be a criminal act before there can be criminal punishment, even though punishment is for character and not for conduct. But, for reasons that have been persuasively developed by Brudner, *Punishment and Freedom* (n 10) 64–70, the character-based account is incongruent with the features of the criminal trial process that I am trying to explain in this chapter.

[12] Kant's notorious claim that a society, about to dissolve, is under a duty of right first to execute any murderers (Kant, *The Metaphysics of Morals* (n 8) 6:333) has recently been echoed in Ripstein's strong claims about the necessity for criminal punishment in a rightful condition. Ripstein, *Force and Freedom* (n 10) 320.

III THE EVIDENTIARY EFFECT OF A VERDICT OF ACQUITTAL

It is often said that a verdict of acquittal is not a positive finding of innocence, and there is a way in which this statement is obviously true. Since the Crown has the burden to prove guilt beyond a reasonable doubt, strictly speaking, a verdict of not guilty as a matter of law always rests on failure of proof: the accused is legally innocent if the Crown fails to prove one or more of the elements of the offence (or fails to disprove at least one element of a defence). The fact finder may be completely convinced of the innocence of the accused; or the fact finder may think that the accused is probably guilty but not be satisfied to the required degree; or the fact finder may think the accused is certainly guilty but be prevented from giving effect to that conclusion because of a rule preventing it from taking into account the decisive evidence.[13] And in trials by judge alone, the public and the parties may be able to observe in the reasons for judgment the differences between fact finders who are convinced of innocence and those who are merely not satisfied of guilt. But from the point of view of the law of evidence, these are just different ways in which the Crown has failed to satisfy its burden of proof.

Since a verdict of not guilty never requires positive fact finding, it might be thought that the evidentiary effect of a verdict of not guilty, unlike the evidentiary effect of a verdict of guilty,[14] would be negligible. Yet that is not so, at least in Canadian law. It is true that a verdict of acquittal has little significance in subsequent civil proceedings involving the same alleged wrongdoing.[15] But an acquittal has a profound evidentiary effect in subsequent criminal proceedings. Canadian courts have consistently refused to recognize any legal difference between acquittals on different grounds or to make declarations of innocence.[16] And a verdict of acquittal is decisive in subsequent criminal proceedings not just in that it supports

[13] A possibility nicely captured by the Ontario Court of Appeal in a decision where evidence was excluded on constitutional grounds: 'The [accused] sought an order that his costs be paid . . . Having regard to his obvious guilt, I think the acquittal is a sufficient remedy': *R v Young* [1993] 79 CCC (3d) 559 [28] (Ont CA).

[14] Canadian courts have generally treated a conviction as prima facie proof that the accused committed the acts constituting the offence: see, eg, *Demeter v British Pacific Life Ins Co* [1983] 150 DLR (3d) 249 (Ont HCJ), aff'd 13 DLR (4th) 318 (Ont CA), and compare Evidence Act RSO 1990 ch E.23 s 22.1. Moreover, doctrines such as abuse of process have recently been applied to prevent a person from disputing a finding of guilt in subsequent proceedings, both civil and criminal: see, for instance, *Toronto (City) v Canadian Union of Public Employees, Local 79* [2003] 3 SCR 149; *F(K) v White* [2001] 198 DLR (4th) 541 (Ont CA); *R v Jesse* [2010] 252 CCC (3d) 442 (BCCA).

[15] *Fishman v R* [1970] Ex CR 784, 827.

[16] 'There are not different kinds of acquittals': *R v Grdic* [1985] 1 SCR 810 [35]. In a case where it was satisfied that the appellant was actually innocent, the Ontario Court of Appeal declined to make a formal declaration of innocence for two reasons: first, it lacked jurisdiction to do so under its enabling statute; secondly, it was unwilling for policy reasons to 'create two classes of people: those found to be factually innocent and those who have benefited from the presumption of innocence and the high standard of proof beyond a reasonable doubt': *R v Mullins-Johnson* [2007] ONCA 20, 228 CCC (3d) 505 [24]–[25]. A declaration of innocence does not appear to be a possible outcome of a trial: *Mullins-Johnson* [23].

the plea of *autrefois acquit* if the accused is subsequently charged with the same offence, but in that it sets up an estoppel against the opposing party. In proceedings against the accused for a different offence, the Crown cannot relitigate any factual issue that was, or must have been, decided in the accused's favour in a trial where he was acquitted.[17] This form of issue estoppel in criminal proceedings has several ramifications. If the accused is acquitted of offence A, and the Crown wants to use the facts relating to offence A as similar fact evidence in a prosecution for offence B, the Crown cannot do so in a manner that calls into question any issue that was decided in the accused's favour in his trial on offence A.[18] If in trial A, the Crown had to prove that the accused was at a certain place at a certain time and the accused was acquitted on the ground that he was not at that place and time (or if that finding is necessary to the acquittal), then in trial B, the Crown is estopped from asserting that the accused was in that place at that time.[19] In many cases, this will make it impossible for the Crown to use the evidence; for example, if the issue in the trial of offence A was identity or was whether the conduct occurred at all, the Crown cannot during the trial of offence B lead evidence supporting the proposition that the accused was the person who committed offence A and therefore cannot use the evidence from trial A as similar fact evidence in trial B because the acquittal breaks the link between the accused and the prior bad conduct,[20] or for any other purpose that depends on a finding that the accused engaged in the earlier conduct. This result follows even though the trier of fact may have thought that the accused probably committed offence A; it is not the burden of proof that matters, but the policy concern that underlies the law of double jeopardy in general: that the accused not be repeatedly vexed with the same allegation of misconduct.[21]

If determining the truth was the overriding purpose of the criminal trial process, then this form of issue estoppel would be puzzling.[22] But if determining the truth is understood as part of the process for deciding whether the accused has committed the offence charged and has therefore lost his right to be beyond reproach in respect of that allegation of wrongdoing, then the application of issue estoppel in criminal proceedings makes perfect sense. For criminal law purposes, the trial of offence A authoritatively and finally determines the question whether the accused committed offence A; if the trier of fact in that proceeding says 'no', the accused is conclusively deemed not to have committed the offence; his right to be beyond reproach survived that proceeding intact. Where another act of wrong-

[17] *R v Mahalingan* [2008] 3 SCR 316.

[18] *R v Cullen* [1989] 52 CCC (3d) 459 (Ont CA); *R v M(RA)* [1994] 94 CCC (3d) 459 (Man CA), leave to appeal refused 96 CCC (3d) v (SCC). The principle expressed in these cases may have to be narrowed somewhat in light of *Mahalingan*, but the result would be the same.

[19] *R v Grdic* (n 16) 825–26, and compare the discussion in *R v Mahalingan* (n 17) [18]–[24]. If the acquittal in trial A is consistent with the finding that the accused was in that place at that time, then the Crown is not prevented from proving that fact in trial B.

[20] On the necessity of linking the accused to similar fact evidence, see *R v Sweitzer* [1982] 1 SCR 949.

[21] *R v Mahalingan* (n 17) [39].

[22] Compare the arguments described and criticized in H Stewart, 'Issue Estoppel and Similar Facts' (2008) 53 *Criminal Law Quarterly* 382, 387ff.

doing is alleged, the court must continue to assume that the accused is beyond reproach in respect of the previous allegation, and so any fact which must have been decided in his favour at the first trial cannot now be contested. Otherwise the criminal trial court will be in the position of simultaneously affirming and denying his right to be beyond reproach, or as the court puts it, there is a danger of inconsistent verdicts.[23]

IV THE EVIDENTIARY BALANCING PRINCIPLE: PROBATIVE VALUE AND PREJUDICIAL EFFECT

Quite apart from any other exclusionary rule, Canadian trial judges have the power – indeed the obligation – to exclude evidence that is excessively prejudicial. Where evidence is led by a party to a civil action or by the Crown in criminal proceedings, the trial judge must exclude the evidence if its prejudicial effect outweighs its probative value. Where the evidence is led by the accused in criminal proceedings, the balancing formula is different: the trial judge must exclude the evidence if its prejudicial effect substantially outweighs its probative value. This common law evidentiary balancing principle[24] is explicitly built into some exclusionary rules, such as the similar fact rule;[25] it is presumed to be implicit in any statutory rule of evidence;[26] and it is always potentially applicable to any otherwise admissible piece of evidence.[27] The evidentiary balancing principle is central to the 'evidence revolution' in Canadian law: as the trial judge's task has shifted from the application of rules to the application of a set of principles, she is increasingly called on to judge probative value and prejudicial effect as a precondition to the admissibility of all kinds of evidence.[28] And the evidentiary balancing principle is, as an aspect of the constitutional right to a fair trial, a principle of fundamental

[23] *R v Mahalingan* (n 17) [2], [45].

[24] It is difficult to find a concise and accurate phrase to describe the trial judge's obligation to exclude excessively prejudicial evidence. I have previously referred to it as the 'discretionary exclusionary power' (see H Stewart, 'Section 7 of the Charter and the Common Law Rules of Evidence' (2008) 40 *Supreme Court Law Review* (2d) 415), but that phrase misleadingly suggests that the trial judge has a discretion to admit or to exclude excessively prejudicial evidence. While the trial judge's assessment of probative value and prejudicial effect is 'discretionary' in the sense of being resistant to appellate review, once the trial judge has made that assessment and has concluded that prejudicial effect outweighs probative value, he or she must exclude: *R v Handy* [2002] 2 SCR 908 [153].

[25] See *R v Handy* (n 24), and the discussion in M Rosenberg, 'Similar Fact Evidence' in *Law Society of Upper Canada Special Lectures: The Law of Evidence* (Toronto, Irwin Law, 2004).

[26] See the cases discussed in Stewart, 'Section 7' (n 24).

[27] See, for instance, *R v Starr* [2000] 2 SCR 144, applying the evidentiary balancing principle as the final step in the admissibility of hearsay evidence, though it is not clear how much work this step does on the facts of the case.

[28] For general descriptions of the 'evidence revolution', see S Lederman, AW Bryant and M Fuerst, *The Law of Evidence in Canada* 3rd edn (Toronto, LexisNexis Butterworths, 2009) ch 1; D Paciocco and L Stuesser, *The Law of Evidence* 5th edn (Toronto, Irwin Law, 2008) ch 1; H Stewart, 'Justice Frank Iacobucci and the Revolution in the Common Law of Evidence' (2007) 57 *University of Toronto Law Journal* 479.

justice under section 7 of the Canadian Charter of Rights and Freedoms;[29] any statute or common law rule applicable in criminal proceedings that does not comply with it – that permits the admission of excessively prejudicial evidence – is almost certainly unconstitutional.[30]

Colin Tapper has recently questioned the coherence of the evidentiary balancing principle, on two grounds: first, that concepts of probative value and prejudicial effect are of limited utility in making decisions about admissibility and secondly, that there is in any event no way to balance these two concepts:

> [T]he use of very high-level concepts . . . is prone to generate some form of compromise, frequently categorised as 'balancing', despite the patent absence of any common unit to which the concepts can be reduced. One of the most flagrant examples in the law of evidence is the balancing of prejudicial effect and probative value, despite one existing in the realm of emotion, and the other in that of logic, and despite the fact that in this context the prejudicial effect of a piece of evidence is understood to connote its being given a weight greater than its true value. So since there is no difference between the true value of a piece of evidence and its probative force, there is nothing left to balance since the probative force of the evidence has already been taken into account in determining whether there is any prejudicial effect at all.[31]

Exploring Tapper's description and critique of the principle will illuminate the ways in which the evidentiary balancing principle operates as an instance of proportionality reasoning, as a proportional limit on what might otherwise be excessively powerful common law rights of an accused person relating to prejudicial evidence.

Tapper defines probative value as the 'true value' of the evidence and prejudicial effect as giving evidence 'a weight greater than its true value'. But these definitions do not correspond to the best understanding of probative value and prejudicial effect, and certainly not to the way those terms are used in Canadian law. The balancing of probative value and prejudicial effect is part of the process of determining admissibility; thus, neither probative value nor prejudicial effect can be equated with the value or weight of the evidence at the end of the trial. Rather, both have to be understood as predictions about the effects of admitting the evidence on the trial and on the criminal process more generally, not as judgements about the ultimate value to be attached to it.

[29] *R v Seaboyer* [1991] 2 SCR 577, 610–11; see also Stewart, 'Section 7', (n 24) 423–25.

[30] There is a remote possibility that such a rule could, though inconsistent with s 7 of the Charter, be justified under s 1; however, the Supreme Court of Canada has never found a violation of s 7 to be justified.

[31] C Tapper, 'The Law of Evidence and the Rule of Law' (2009) 68 *Cambridge Law Journal* 67, 72; I have incorporated one of Tapper's footnotes into the quotation. Tapper thinks that the prominence of the evidentiary balancing principle is just one symptom of a larger and more serious problem in the law of evidence: he argues that recent developments in English law have compromised the rule of law by increasing the discretionary power of judges. But Tapper understands the rule of law almost exclusively in terms of certainty, that is, as the application or transmission of 'factually determined content' to disputes rather than as a process of reasoning from the legal materials towards a just resolution of disputes. Compare: D Dyzenhaus, *Hard Cases in Wicked Legal Systems* 2nd edn (Oxford, Oxford University Press, 2010) 229. Tapper therefore overlooks the possibility that developments in the law of evidence have made adjudication fairer.

Consider probative value first. The trial judge has to assess probative value at the point of admissibility, but the true value of the evidence will not be known until the end of the trial, when the trier of fact finds the facts in the light of all the evidence and in accordance with the trial judge's instructions. So probative value is not the true value of the evidence; it is rather the capacity of the evidence to justify a relevant inference, judged on the basis of the trial record and counsel's submissions at the point when admissibility is determined. Suppose, for example, that the accused person is charged with robbery and that identity is in issue. The Crown calls its first witness: an impartial eyewitness who is familiar with the accused's appearance, had a good opportunity to observe the offender at the time of the offence and was sober and alert. At this point in the proceedings – the start of the Crown's case – the evidence is highly capable of supporting the inference that the accused is the offender and therefore has very high probative value. Now, suppose that during the defence case, the accused offers a compelling alibi, and that the trier of fact accepts the alibi and acquits the accused. At some point in its reasoning, the trier of fact would have to conclude that the eyewitness was mistaken. So the eyewitness's testimony would have considerable probative value when originally offered, yet have no true value at the end of the trial.

Now consider prejudicial effect. As we have seen, Tapper defines prejudicial value as evidence 'being given a weight greater than its true value'. While this possibility is one kind of prejudicial effect,[32] the concept is much broader than that. There are several process-oriented forms of prejudicial effect: evidence may prejudice the trial process by distracting the trier of fact from the main issues, unfairly surprising the opponent, or usurping the function of the jury. Some factual issues may consume undue amounts of time, which not only complicates the trial at hand but delays the hearing of other matters.[33] And the most important form of prejudicial effect is not giving evidence excessive weight for a proper purpose, but using it for a prohibited purpose, that is, giving it any weight at all with respect to a particular factual issue when it should have none, for example, inferring guilt from evidence of bad character that is completely unconnected with the charge.[34] This form of prejudicial effect should be understood as the evil twin of probative value: the capacity of the evidence to found an improper, impermissible, or irrelevant inference, judged on the basis of the trial record and counsel's submissions at the point when admissibility is determined. When a trial judge assesses the prejudicial effect of an item of evidence, she is estimating how harmful the evidence is likely to be in the trial process, including the possibility that it will be used for an improper purpose.

If probative value and prejudicial effects are understood in this way, there is indeed something for the trial judge to consider at the stage of admissibility: the potential value of the evidence if properly used versus the potential dangers of the evidence if improperly used.

32 Compare: *R v Handy* (n 24) [31].
33 *R v Clarke* [1998] 129 CCC (3d) 1 (Ont CA) [34]–[35].
34 See, eg, *R v Handy* (n 24) [144].

But even if probative value and prejudicial effect are properly defined to reflect the trial judge's forecast of the benefit and the harm of the evidence to the trial process, the problem of balancing the two effects remains. Tapper is right to say that there is no common unit to which probative value and prejudicial effect can be reduced. But the coherence of the evidentiary balancing principle does not depend on the existence of such a common unit. 'Weighing' or 'balancing' probative value and prejudicial effect are metaphors for the trial judge's assessment of whether the trial will better serve its function of fairly deciding disputed factual matters with or without the evidence in question. This assessment, though difficult, is no different in principle from other 'balancing' exercises that courts are called on to make, such as deciding whether the 'balance of convenience' favours the granting of an injunction,[35] or whether a limit on a constitutionally protected right is justified.[36] If trial judges could not engage in this kind of assessment when balancing probative value and prejudicial effect, the law of evidence might have to choose between two extreme rules: outright exclusion of any evidence that had an impermissible purpose, regardless of the value it might have in the trial process; or outright admission of any evidence that had a permissible purpose, regardless of its detrimental effects on the trial process.

As the examples of the injunction and the limitation of constitutional rights suggest, a general problem facing any rights-based systems of law is how to reconcile or 'balance' competing claims of right – or, if you prefer, how to define the limits of competing rights without denying the reality of any of the rights involved. In private law, this problem is often addressed by resort to conceptions of reasonableness. For example, my right to carry out my activities is subject to the requirement that I take reasonable care to avoid injuring others who are foreseeably affected by them; the reasonableness requirement helps to define the scope of the competing rights to freedom of action and to security.[37] In constitutional law, this problem is typically resolved with resort to the concept of proportionality: the legislature may limit a constitutionally protected right where the limit is imposed in pursuit of the valid public objectives of a rightful condition in a manner that is rational, minimally impairing, and not excessively damaging to the right itself.[38] For example, the media's right to publish information concerning proceedings conducted in open court may be limited – if necessary and only to the extent necessary – by the right of an accused person to a fair trial or by the public interest in

[35] *American Cyanamid Co v Ethicon Ltd* [1975] AC 396 (HL).

[36] *R v Oakes* [1986] 1 SCR 103; *R v Secretary of State for the Home Department, ex parte Daly* [2001] 3 All ER 433 [25]–[28]; D Grimm, 'Proportionality in Canadian and German Constitutional Jurisprudence' (2007) 57 *University of Toronto Law Journal* 383, 393–97. The damage to a right and the effects of a rights infringement on a legislative objective cannot be measured in terms of a common substance, yet courts manage to make principled decisions concerning justification of infringements.

[37] Compare: A Ripstein, 'Philosophy of Tort Law' in J Coleman and S Shapiro (eds), *The Oxford Handbook of Jurisprudence and Philosophy of Law* (Oxford, Oxford University Press, 2002).

[38] *R v Oakes* (n 36). Academic proponents of proportionality include R Alexy, *A Theory of Constitutional Rights* (Oxford, Oxford University Press, 2001); D Beatty, *The Ultimate Rule of Law* (Oxford, Oxford University Press, 2004) ch 5.

law enforcement.[39] Both the private law and the public law version of this exercise involve comparing values that cannot be reduced to a common substance:[40] the benefits of liberty of action versus the harms of personal injury; the value of an objective such as the promotion of effective law enforcement versus freedom of expression.

The balancing of probative value and prejudicial effect is a similar exercise in proportionality. It is a way of reconciling the right of the accused person to a fair trial with the systemic need to determine the facts of the case for the purpose of rendering a judgement about the Crown's allegation that the accused committed an offence. Consider, first, the evidentiary balancing principle as it applies to evidence led by the Crown: the trial judge must exclude otherwise admissible evidence if its probative value is outweighed by its prejudicial effect. One begins with the thought that – consistent with the right to be beyond reproach and the right to a fair trial – the accused would have a right against the admission of any evidence that had any prejudicial effect because the introduction of prejudicial evidence always creates the possibility that the fact finder will decide the case on a legally improper basis, and therefore a risk that the right to be beyond reproach will be improperly taken away. But a rule of evidence requiring exclusion of any evidence creating a risk of improper fact finding would significantly restrict the admissibility of evidence that does have legitimate uses in fact finding and therefore would significantly interfere with the ability of the Crown to prove the commission of offences. The evidentiary balancing principle can therefore be understood as a proportional limit on the accused's right not to face prejudicial evidence. Prejudicial evidence is admissible for the purpose of facilitating the prosecution of offences, but only when it has sufficient probative value and when the trier of fact is properly instructed on its permissible and impermissible uses; that is, only when, in the trial judge's assessment of the issues in the trial and the ability of the trier of fact to follow instructions, the evidence is sufficiently capable of justifying a relevant inference to overcome the danger of improper use, consumption of time, confusion of issues, etc.

The principles governing the admissibility of similar fact evidence in Canada provide a good illustration of this way of thinking about the evidentiary balancing principle.[41] In *Handy*, the leading Canadian case on point, Binnie J, speaking for a unanimous court, linked the similar fact rule to the constitutional right to be presumed innocent:

> It is frequently mentioned that 'prejudice' in this context is not the risk of conviction. It is, more properly, the risk of an unfocussed trial and a *wrongful* conviction. The

[39] *Dagenais v Canadian Broadcasting Corp* [1994] 3 SCR 835; *R v Mentuck* [2001] 3 SCR 442.

[40] If rights are understood as instruments for promoting an outcome that is desirable independently of its effects on the particular individuals involved, as in utilitarianism and its cousins (eg, economic analysis of law), then the problem of balancing is solved by asserting that the effects of the rights in question can be reduced to a common substance – utility, wealth, happiness, or what have you – but at the price of denying the normative significance of the rights themselves.

[41] For a comparative discussion of the similar fact rule, assigning it the normative role of protecting the accused's moral autonomy rather than his legal rights as such, see HL Ho, *A Philosophy of Evidence Law* (Oxford, Oxford University Press, 2008) 285–316.

> forbidden chain of reasoning is to infer guilt from *general* disposition or propensity. The evidence, if believed, shows that an accused has discreditable tendencies. In the end, the verdict may be based on prejudice rather than proof, thereby undermining the presumption of innocence enshrined in ss 7 and 11(*d*) of the *Canadian Charter of Rights and Freedoms*.[42]

I interpret these remarks as holding that an accused person has a constitutional right to a verdict 'based on . . . proof' and a right against a verdict 'based on prejudice'. Evidence that shows only general bad propensity is inadmissible because it can have only a prejudicial effect. To protect the right to a verdict based on proof rather than prejudice, the accused has a right against the Crown's leading such evidence.[43] Evidence that shows a bad propensity is nonetheless admissible if it has sufficient probative value to overcome the associated prejudice. The principles governing the admission of the accused's prior discreditable conduct (or prior bad acts) may be stated as follows: evidence of prior bad acts is admissible to support a character-based inference to guilt if the prior bad acts demonstrate a specific propensity that is relevant to a clearly identified, live issue in the trial, and have sufficient probative value on that issue to overcome the moral prejudice and the reasoning prejudice that the evidence will occasion. Probative value derives from the improbability that independent witnesses would testify to conduct indicating the specific propensity in question. Whether the probative value is sufficient depends on the trial judge's assessment of a number of factors connecting the prior bad acts with the offence charged. The probative value of the evidence will be insufficient if the prior bad acts demonstrate a mere generic propensity (for example, dishonesty or violence), and will be non-existent if the prior bad acts cannot be sufficiently linked to the accused (if the conduct in question is not the accused's, it cannot show his propensity) or if the witnesses testifying about the prior bad acts and about the offence have colluded or tainted each other's testimony (if the witnesses are not independent, the coincidence between their accounts is not objectively improbable). Potential prejudicial effects include the danger that the jury will convict the accused simply because he is a bad person ('moral prejudice') and the potential confusion of issues and distraction caused by the need for the jury to make factual findings concerning the uncharged bad acts ('reasoning prejudice'). These principles are designed to ensure that any intrusion on the right of the accused against prejudicial evidence is a proportionate response to the general interest in prosecuting offences in a rightful condition.

Now, consider the evidentiary balancing principle as it applies to evidence led by the defence: the trial judge must exclude otherwise admissible defence evidence only if its probative value is *substantially* outweighed by its prejudicial effect. This principle is of relatively recent origin. Before 1991, while defence evidence was in general subject to the same rules of admissibility as Crown evidence, there was good authority for the proposition that the rules of admissibility might

[42] *R v Handy* (n 24) [139].

[43] ibid [72].

be relaxed in favour of the accused and for the proposition that prejudicial effect was never a reason for excluding defence evidence.[44] But in *Seaboyer*,[45] in the context of a constitutional challenge to a provision of the Criminal Code limiting the admissibility of evidence concerning a complainant's sexual conduct in trials of sexual offences, McLachlin J for the majority held that a trial judge did have a common law power to exclude defence evidence on the ground of prejudice to the trial process. But because of the need to avoid the conviction of the innocent, the formula for exclusion required 'that the prejudice must *substantially* outweigh the value of the evidence' (emphasis added).[46] McLachlin J then constitutionalized this version of the evidentiary balancing principle, identifying it as a principle of fundamental justice under section 7 of the Charter.[47] Thus, any statute or common law rule that prevents the defence from leading evidence whose probative value is not substantially outweighed by its prejudicial effect is unconstitutional.[48]

It might be thought that the common law background rule permitting the accused to lead any relevant and otherwise admissible evidence regardless of its prejudicial effect is required by the right to a fair trial. The Crown, after all, cannot be prejudiced in the way that an individual can, and the acquittal of the factually guilty, while unfortunate, cannot be regarded as a miscarriage of justice at the level of the conviction of the factually innocent. And the exclusion of probative defence evidence does raise the possibility of a wrongful conviction. On the other hand, the defence, like the Crown, can have no right to lead evidence that is merely prejudicial: the right to a fair trial does not include the right to acquittal on an improper basis.[49] So the version of the evidentiary balancing principle applicable to defence evidence can be understood as a proportionate limit on a right the defence would have under some idealised version of the common law rules of evidence. The purpose of limiting the accused's use of evidence that has both probative and prejudicial aspects is to avoid the possibility that the fact finder will follow an improper chain of reasoning. Exclusion of evidence is a rational means of achieving that purpose; so is admitting the evidence accompanied by a jury instruction concerning proper and improper uses. The requirement that the prejudicial effect of the evidence substantially outweighs its probative value ensures that exclusion – rather than admission plus jury instruction – is the means of achieving this objective only when there is no other means of doing so and when

[44] *R v Williams* [1985] 18 CCC (3d) 356 (Ont CA) 378 (rule against hearsay might be relaxed in accused's favour); *R v Valley* [1986] 26 CCC (3d) 207 (Ont CA) 239 (there is 'no discretion . . . to exclude relevant evidence offered by an accused on the ground that it is prejudicial to the Crown').

[45] *R v Seaboyer* (n 29).

[46] ibid 611.

[47] ibid 61.

[48] As the majority found to be the case for the statute that was at issue in *R v Seaboyer* itself; the successor statute, enacted in response, satisfied this test and was constitutionally valid: *R v Darrach* [2000] 2 SCR 443.

[49] Except, perhaps, the apparent right to jury nullification: *R v Krieger* [2006] SCC 47. But there is no right to lead inadmissible or prejudicial evidence in the hope of encouraging jury nullification; indeed, at the end of a properly conducted trial, the jury cannot be encouraged, or even told that it has the power, to nullify: *R v Morgentaler* [1988] 1 SCR 30 76–79.

the potential deleterious impact on the accused's right to a fair trial is clearly less than the beneficial effect on the trial process.

The proportionality of the evidentiary balancing principle as applied to defence evidence is best illustrated with reference to the problem that gave rise to it: admissibility of evidence of the sexual history of the complainant in a prosecution for a sexual offence. There is, of course, a long common law history of admissibility of this kind of evidence, a history notable not only for the unfairness it caused to victims of sexual offences, but for its questionable internal logic and inconsistency with other common law rules.[50] The Parliament of Canada attempted a number of times to draft a statutory rule limiting the use of evidence of the complainant's sexual history; the first was interpreted perversely by the courts,[51] the second was declared unconstitutional.[52] The third, currently in force, focuses on the permissible and impermissible inferences that may be founded on such evidence. Section 276 of the Criminal Code prohibits two inferences entirely: evidence of the complainant's sexual activity is not admissible 'to support an inference that, by reason of the sexual nature of that activity, the complainant . . . is more likely to have consented to the sexual activity that forms the subject-matter of the charge; or . . . is less worthy of belief'.[53] Evidence capable of supporting only those inferences is inadmissible. But evidence capable of supporting other, permissible inferences is admissible if it has 'significant probative value that is not substantially outweighed by the danger of prejudice to the proper administration of justice'.[54] Prejudice to the proper administration of justice can include many things, notably the danger that the trier of fact, despite being instructed not to do so, may reason that the complainant consented simply because she has consented in the past, or may decide that the complainant, as an 'unchaste' woman, may indeed have refused consent but is not entitled to the protection of the laws.[55] The evidence may nonetheless be probative of an issue in the trial; for example, if the accused's theory of the case is that the complainant's allegations have been fabricated and if that theory is connected to her prior sexual conduct[56] or where a material prior inconsistent statement by the complainant is inextricably linked to

[50] eg, unchaste female complainants in sexual cases were considered to be less credible because of their lack of chastity. The generalisation about truthfulness underlying this rule is dubious on its own merits, but the rule in any event did not apply to unchaste witnesses in general, or to unchaste male witnesses. For an overview of the Canadian law on point, see H Stewart, *Sexual Offences in Canadian Law*, ch 7 (release 7); for an absorbing account of individual trials illustrating some of the effects of these rules, see C Backhouse, *Carnal Crimes: Sexual Assault in Canada, 1900–1975* (Toronto, The Osgoode Society, 2008).

[51] As in *R v Forsythe* [1980] 2 SCR 268.

[52] *R v Seaboyer* (n 29).

[53] Criminal Code, s 276(1). Both inferences were permissible at common law.

[54] Criminal Code, s 276(2)(b). The Supreme Court of Canada has held that the insertion of the word 'significant' before the phrase 'probative value' should be read as indicating no real departure from the common law rule enunciated in *R v Seaboyer*, noting in particular that the equally authoritative French version of the statute contains no equivalent to the word 'significant' but refers simply to 'valeur probante': *R v Darrach* (n 48) [38]–[43].

[55] Compare: *R v Darrach* (n 48) [33].

[56] *R v Seaboyer* (n 29) 613–14.

her prior sexual conduct.[57] To be admissible in such a case, its probative value on that issue must not be substantially outweighed by its prejudicial effect, including especially the danger that even a properly instructed jury[58] may use it for an impermissible purpose. The objective of this limit on the common law right to lead any probative evidence is to promote the fair treatment of witnesses, rational fact finding, proper reporting of sexual offences and any other public interests that the old common law rules governing evidence of sexual history frustrated.[59] But the objective is not pursued by tightly defining the category of cases in which such evidence can be led; that was the fatal constitutional flaw in the predecessor to section 276.[60] Instead, the objective is pursued by giving the trial judge the responsibility to assess the pros and cons of admitting the evidence.[61]

In an ideal trial process, the admission of evidence that had both probative value and prejudicial effect would have no distorting effect on the outcome because fact finders would always follow the directions they are given about how to use evidence to reach factual conclusions; they would therefore always avoid improper reasoning (even if tempted by it). Evidence that had no probative value would be inadmissible because irrelevant, but evidence that had some probative value and some prejudicial effect would be admissible for what it was worth, and fact finders would simply disregard its prejudicial aspects. In that ideal process, the right to a fair trial would include the right of the defence to lead any otherwise admissible evidence, regardless of its prejudicial effect, and the right against the Crown's leading evidence that has only prejudicial effects would be merely one specific instance of the general rule against irrelevant evidence; there would be no need for a right against the Crown's leading evidence that has both probative

[57] *R v Crosby* [1995] 2 SCR 912.

[58] A limiting instruction is required by statute: Criminal Code, s 276.4, but would undoubtedly be required in any event by common law governing jury instructions.

[59] Compare: Criminal Code, s 276(3).

[60] *R v Seaboyer* (n 29). L'Heureux-Dubé J dissenting would have upheld the former s 276, but she interpreted it more expansively than the majority, reading it to permit some evidence that the majority thought it barred; though under her interpretation, it would still have been more restrictive than the current s 276.

[61] Constitutional lawyers may object to my use of s 1, *Oakes*-style reasoning in what appears to be a common law or s 7 analysis. They might say that the argument for the proportionality of the evidentiary balancing principle should arise only once a court has concluded that a statutory or common law rule of evidence violates s 7 of the Charter. But proportionality is not only a test for justification of the express limitation of rights under s 1; it is a style of reasoning about the scope of rights in general, for example, the right to self-defence (compare: *R v Walker* [2007] 217 CCC (3d) 254 (BCCA)), the right to claim an evidentiary privilege on a case-by-case basis (compare *National Post* (n 4) [58]–[68]), or the scope of constitutional rights (compare: S Breyer, 'On Handguns and the Law' (19 August 2010) *The New York Review of Books* 18. The extreme reluctance of the court to countenance a s 1 justification for a violation of s 7 flows largely from the fact that most – if not all – the work that would be done by proportionality analysis under s 1 is now done through the court's construction and application of the principles of fundamental justice under s 7. The constitutional right to a fair trial, for instance, has never been construed solely from the perspective of the accused person, but has always taken into account the public interests served by the trial process. Although the court does not put it quite this way, the right to liberty is proportionately limited because liberty can be taken away only in accordance with the principles of fundamental justice. A similar point could be made about the Supreme Court of Canada's understanding of the concept of 'discrimination' under s 15 of the Charter.

value and prejudicial effect. In the real world – where prejudicial effect does matter because of the real possibility of improper reasoning by the fact finder – these rights have to be qualified or limited to make effective prosecution of offences possible. The evidentiary balancing principle is a way of using the idea of proportionality, of assessing the impact of two competing considerations that cannot be reduced to a common substance and weighed in the process of determining rights, to define the scope of the accused's evidentiary rights in an inevitably imperfect trial process.

V CONCLUSION

The Supreme Court of Canada's revolution in the common law of evidence coincided with the advent of the Canadian Charter of Rights and Freedoms, and the corresponding development of a jurisprudence of constitutional rights and exclusion of evidence on constitutional grounds. These two developments proceeded more or less in parallel, and their influence on each other has been largely indirect;[62] it is possible that one could have occurred without the other. But with or without the constitutional guarantees in the Charter, the common law rules of evidence can and should be understood as protecting the basic right of everyone in a constitutional order to be treated as a person, a member of a community of free persons governed by institutions that operate by respecting their rights, including notably the right not to be punished or sanctioned without a proper procedure – itself rights-protecting – for determining the truth of the allegation of wrongdoing. The law of evidence can do this, not only by excluding evidence as a remedy for the violation of a right, but by constructing rules of admissibility that forward the goals of the trial process without denying the basic human dignity of the participants in it.

[62] Compare: D Paciocco, 'Charter Tracks: Twenty-Five Years of Constitutional Influence on the Criminal Trial Process and Rules of Evidence' (2008) 40 *Supreme Court Law Review* (2d) 309; Stewart, 'Section 7' (n 24). On the dangers of conflating Charter and common law protections, see H Stewart, 'The Confessions Rule and the *Charter*' (2009) 54 *McGill Law Journal* 517.

10

Packer's Blind Spot: Low Visibility Encounters and the Limits of Due Process versus Crime Control

JAMES STRIBOPOULOS*

I INTRODUCTION

Those who study the criminal process owe a tremendous debt to Herbert Packer. Nearly 50 years have passed since Packer provided what continues to be the dominant theoretical account of the criminal process. In a now famous law review article,[1] Packer theorized that the criminal process is most usefully described as being in a perpetual state of tension as between two competing models, which he defined as the 'Crime Control Model' and the 'Due Process Model'. In his groundbreaking work, Packer sketched out the contours of these competing models. His theory has supplied the framework for nearly five decades of debate regarding the criminal process. Today, little is written on the topic that doesn't acknowledge Packer's foundational contribution. The longevity of Packer's ideas is clearly testament to the perceptiveness of his insights.

Over the intervening years, however, much of what has been written in response to Packer has been fairly critical. Packer has come under attack not so much for what he includes in the two models he constructs, but mainly for what he leaves out. For example, the role of victims in the criminal process does not figure into Packer's account. Similarly, restorative justice practices go unmentioned in the binary model that Packer developed. In addition, drawing on empirical research that has revealed much about the actual workings of the criminal justice system,

* I would like to thank my research assistant, Richard Diniz, for his invaluable assistance in researching and editing this chapter. A debt of gratitude is also owed to François Tanguay-Renaud and Ekow N Yankah, both of whom provided invaluable feedback on an earlier draft. Of course, any errors remain mine alone.

[1] See generally HL Packer, 'Two Models of the Criminal Process' (1964) 113 *University of Pennsylvania Law Review* 1. Packer elaborated on his theory and tied his writing on process into a critique of substantive criminal law in a later book. See HL Packer, *The Limits of the Criminal Sanction* (Stanford, Stanford University Press, 1968).

many have challenged some of Packer's key assumptions. This includes critical legal studies scholars who question Packer's models as unhelpful caricatures that camouflage the influence of class and race on how the criminal process actually operates.

Criticism of Packer's theory often overlooks an important aspect of his account. As Andrew Ashworth reminds us, Packer's models are 'not designed to be prescriptive either generally or specifically'.[2] Packer quite deliberately distinguished between what he characterized as the 'Is' and the 'Ought' of the criminal process.[3] His models were intended neither to describe nor to prescribe. Rather, as Packer explained,

> [t]he kind of criminal process we have depends importantly on certain value choices that are reflected, explicitly or implicitly, in its habitual functioning. The kind of model we need is one that permits us to recognize explicitly the value choices that underlie the details of the criminal process. In a word, what we need is a normative model, or rather two models, to let us perceive the normative antinomy that runs deep in the life of the criminal law. These models may not be labeled Good and Bad, and I hope they will not be taken in that sense. Rather they represent an attempt to abstract two separate value systems that compete for attention in the operation of the criminal process. Neither is presented as either corresponding to reality or as representing what the criminal process ought to be. The two models merely afford a convenient way to talk about the operation of a process whose day-to-day functioning involves a constant series of minute adjustments between competing demands of two value systems and whose normative future likewise involves a series of resolutions, of greater or lesser magnitude, of the tensions between mutually exclusive claims.[4]

In short, Packer's aim was to provide us with a vocabulary for labelling and thereby better understanding the choices that are perpetually being made within the criminal process. These are choices that Packer plotted along a spectrum of values (or ideological commitments), with Crime Control at one end and Due Process at the opposite pole. Packer's models were therefore not intended as complete abstractions. They were meant to assist in better understanding the *actual* criminal process.

In addition, it is important to remember the context in which Packer was theorizing. As Packer explained, he was 'not postulating a criminal process that operates in any kind of society at all, but rather one that operates within the framework of contemporary American society'.[5] His starting point was therefore the American legal system, with its legal traditions, institutions and Constitution. Not surprisingly, however, Packer's theory has also proven useful in better understanding the criminal process in other common law countries. Perhaps the best example of this is Canada, where the entrenchment of the Canadian Charter of Rights and Freedoms[6] has resulted in strong parallels with the United States. In

[2] A Ashworth, 'Criminal Justice and the Criminal Process' (1988) 28 *British Journal of Criminology* 111, 117.

[3] Packer, 'Two Models' (n 1) 3.

[4] ibid 5–6.

[5] ibid 7.

[6] Part I of the Constitution Act, 1982, being Schedule B to the Canada Act 1982 (UK), 1982, ch 11.

both countries the judicial branches are formally vested with responsibility for checking executive and legislative action based on the terms of an open-ended and value-laden constitutional text.

It is also important to remember the period in American legal history when Packer developed his theory. Packer constructed his models at a time when the effect of the Bill of Rights on the criminal process was just beginning to be felt. For example, it was only three years before Packer published his groundbreaking article that the United States Supreme Court decided *Mapp v Ohio*,[7] in which the Court reconsidered its earlier decision in *Wolf v Colorado*[8] and concluded that the Due Process Clause required that the exclusionary rule also apply to state court proceedings. In short, Packer crafted his theory at a time in American legal history when the Warren Court was just beginning to remake the formal rules of the criminal process.[9] The conservative backlash against the activism of that Court was only just starting. Despite this, to his considerable credit, Packer's models proved invaluable in explaining both the criminal procedure revolution and the eventual retreat from it by both the Burger and Rehnquist Courts.[10]

Even more importantly, it should be remembered that Packer was writing at a time when empirical research into the criminal process was still in its relative infancy. For example, even though the American Bar Foundation Survey of the Administration of Criminal Justice in the United States was by then underway, the final results of that research had yet to be published.[11] Undoubtedly, Packer appreciated the potential significance of those efforts. In the introduction to his paper, in defining the 'criminal process', he explained that:

> It can be described, but only partially and inadequately, by referring to the rules of law that govern the apprehension, screening, and trial of persons suspected of crime. It consists at least as importantly of patterns of official activity that correspond only in the roughest kind of way to the prescriptions of procedural rules. As a result of recent emphasis on empirical research into the administration of criminal justice, we are just beginning to be aware how very rough the correspondence is.[12]

[7] *Mapp v Ohio* 367 US 643 (1961). Packer referenced this development in his article, see Packer, 'Two Models' (n 1) 8.

[8] *Wolf v Colorado* 338 US 25 (1949).

[9] eg, Packer published his article only just the year after the United States Supreme Court had decided *Brady v Maryland* 373 US 83 (1963) (holding that the Due Process Clause requires state prosecutors to disclose all material evidence to a defendant) and *Gideon v Wainwright* 372 US 335 (1963) (holding that state courts are required under the Sixth Amendment to provide counsel to criminal defendants who cannot afford their own lawyer). Important decisions, like *Miranda v Arizona* 384 US 436 (1966) and *Katz v United States* 389 US 347 (1967) had still not been decided.

[10] On the American criminal procedure revolution, see generally JH Israel and WR LaFave, *Criminal Procedure: Constitutional Limitations* 6th edn, (St Paul, West, 2001).

[11] eg, two of the major survey final reports on police detention and arrest powers were not published until later in the decade. See LP Tiffany, DM McIntyre and D Rotenberg, *Detection of Crime: Stopping and Questioning, Search and Seizure, Encouragement and Entrapment* (Boston, Little, Brown and Company, 1967); WR LaFave, *Arrest: The Decision to Take a Suspect into Custody* (Boston, Little Brown, 1965).

[12] Packer, 'Two Models' (n 1) 2. In this regard, Packer cited some of the preliminary research that had been published from the findings of the American Bar Foundation Survey of the Administration of Criminal Justice in the United States. See ibid, fn 3.

During the intervening years, the *considerable* rift between the law on the books and the reality of how the criminal justice system often operates has since been more fully revealed. An impressive body of empirical research has now served to expose the substantial divide between the law's formal demands and the actual workings of the criminal process. The goal of this chapter is to constructively revisit a key assumption underlying Packer's theory in light of that research and the lessons learned from the experience in both the United States and Canada during the intervening years.

Operating in the United States in the early 1960s, Packer suggested a key division in the respective roles of legislatures and courts under his two models. According to his theory, the legislature is the institution of crime control, while the courts are concerned with due process. Undoubtedly, the courts are often instrumental in vindicating the interests of due process. However, when the empirical research into the actual workings of the criminal process is considered, along with the experience in both the United States and Canada during the intervening years, a fair amount of doubt emerges with respect to Packer's assumption regarding the predominance of courts in facilitating due process.

Because of their institutional limitations, courts alone are incapable of meaningfully regulating police authority. That goal also requires a serious legislative commitment. The legislature has a critically important role to play if due process is to be realized. On their own, courts are simply not up to the task. Only legislation can clearly, comprehensively and prospectively delineate police powers and establish the sorts of procedural safeguards needed to check routine and low-level exercises of police discretion. Unfortunately, Packer's account of due process versus crime control depends on a fictionalized description of the courts, a view that actually serves to exacerbate the problem of low visibility abuses of police powers. It does so by reinforcing the rather misguided view that courts are capable of single-handedly vindicating the interests of due process. Experience has aptly demonstrated that they are not; that a collaborative effort between courts and legislatures is necessary for due process to be realized.

This chapter will proceed in three sections. In section II, Packer's seminal theory will be introduced and his two models briefly explained. In section III, the chapter will review the competing accounts of the criminal process that have emerged to challenge Packer's theory. Finally, in section IV, the chapter will offer a critique of Packer's theory by drawing on the empirical research (reviewed in section III.A), as well as the experience in both the United States and Canada since Packer penned his account.

II PACKER: CRIME CONTROL VERSUS DUE PROCESS

Packer's theory is of course well known. Nevertheless, a brief review of his account will be useful in understanding some of the criticisms that have since been levelled against his ideas. In addition, because the purpose of this chapter is to supplement Packer's theory with the benefit of learning during the intervening years, having a clear sense of his models will prove invaluable.

Packer of course theorized that the criminal process is most usefully described as being in a perpetual state of tension as between two competing models or poles, which he defined as the 'Crime Control Model' and the 'Due Process Model'. As noted above, Packer's models were not meant to describe the criminal justice system in any particular jurisdiction. Instead, the models are an attempt to 'abstract two separate value systems that compete for attention in the operation of the criminal process'.[13] In other words, for Packer, the criminal process is best understood as a series of compromises or choices as between the values that populate the two competing models he defines.

In describing these models Packer drew on two evocative metaphors, characterizing the Crime Control Model as an assembly line and the Due Process Model as an obstacle course.

A The Crime Control Model

The Crime Control Model is chiefly concerned with repressing criminal conduct. To achieve this goal, this model places a premium on efficiency at every stage of the process, from the screening of suspects, to determining guilt and the sentencing of offenders.

Efficiency is optimized through an administrative and managerial approach. Informal fact finding procedures that are controlled by police and prosecutors are favoured. As a result, police should be conferred broad and largely unfettered discretion to detain, search and interrogate suspects, so they can most efficiently separate the innocent from the guilty as early in the process as possible. Once they have done so, the system should move the undoubtedly guilty individuals who remain as quickly as possible towards conviction and punishment. Pre-trial release should be rare, as it only serves to discourage the timely resolution of charges by guilty defendants. It is this unceasing focus on efficiency in the processing of the guilty that makes the assembly line metaphor an apt descriptor of the Crime Control Model.

The emphasis on efficiency in convicting and punishing the guilty has a number of other consequences as well. One such effect is that illegally or unconstitutionally evidence obtained should always be admissible. The search for truth should take precedence over concerns about the manner in which evidence was acquired. Under the Crime Control Model, the criminal process is viewed as an inappropriate forum for identifying and remedying police and prosecutorial misconduct. Criminal trials should not get bogged down with such collateral matters and should instead focus on convicting and punishing the guilty.

[13] Packer, 'Two Models' (n 1) 5. It is worth noting, however, that Packer does concede that the legal backdrop he has in mind is the legal system in the United States, in other words an adversarial system operating against the backdrop of a constitutional Bill of Rights.

Another consequence is that whenever possible criminal cases should be resolved by way of guilty pleas thereby avoiding wasteful and needlessly time consuming trials. Remember, under the Crime Control Model, the innocent are supposed to have been screened out of the criminal process relatively early on by police or, failing that, by prosecutors.

On this view, although the potential for appellate review is necessary, it is only marginally so. In general, appeals should be discouraged. After conviction the emphasis should be on swift punishment, not review. Appeals should therefore be restricted to correcting those occasional slips where the trier of fact makes a plain error about factual guilt or makes some kind of procedural mistake so gross as to seriously undermine the reliability of the verdict. Justice Learned Hand, who penned the following warning nearly 90 years ago, effectively captures the sentiment that informs the Crime Control Model:

> Our dangers do not lie in too little tenderness to the accused. Our procedure has been always haunted by the ghost of the innocent man convicted. It is an unreal dream. What we need to fear is the archaic formalism and the watery sentiment that obstructs, delays, and defeats the prosecution of crime.[14]

B The Due Process Model

The Due Process Model is not simply the converse of the Crime Control Model. For example, the Due Process Model does not deny the social desirability of repressing crime. It approaches that goal, however, with an emphasis on a set of values that differs substantially from those that populate the Crime Control Model.

Unlike the Crime Control Model, which emphasizes efficiency and places great faith in police officers and prosecutors, the Due Process Model is informed by considerable scepticism. First, there is scepticism regarding the utility of the criminal sanction as an instrument for social control. Next, there is scepticism regarding the effectiveness of informal fact finding procedures and the supposed infallibility of official actors within the criminal justice system. The result is a strong preference for procedures that are both adversarial and judicial in their structure.

Under the Due Process Model, the individual who comes up against the apparatus of the criminal justice system is seen as vulnerable and in need of protection from the excesses of those responsible for investigating and prosecuting crime. On this view, the potential for abuse of official power is a pervasive part of the criminal process, beginning out on the street at the point of first contact between police and suspect, continuing back at the station house and persisting right into the courtroom where the criminal accusation is tried.

The scepticism of the Due Process Model is constant and informs a fear that the potential for wrongful convictions is ever present. The only perceived antidote for

[14] *United States v Garsson* 291 F 646 (NY Dist Ct 1923) 649 (Hand J).

this danger is scrupulously fair procedures. In contrast to the preoccupation with efficiency that animates the Crime Control Model, the Due Process Model is obsessed with quality control.

Quality control is achieved by strict adherence to legal rules and procedures that serve to control the exercise of discretion by official actors within the criminal process, including police officers, prosecutors and judges. Hence, the obstacle course metaphor.

Under the Due Process Model, 'the means' of the criminal process matter just as much as 'the ends'. 'Legal guilt' and 'factual guilt' are therefore equally important concerns. Consequently it is not enough to show that an accused person committed the crime charged; it is also necessary to establish that the process followed in acquiring the evidence and trying the allegation was procedurally sound.

The focus on fair process means that the criminal trial is seen as an appropriate forum to pursue claims of official malfeasance against police and prosecutors for their handling of an investigation or prosecution. A sensible remedy for such misconduct is the exclusion of any evidence that was illegally or unconstitutionally obtained or, in more extreme cases, the dismissal of charges. In addition, because police misconduct does not necessarily lead to criminal charges, other remedies are also required, including tort, internal discipline and robust civilian oversight.

Under the Due Process Model, trials are not perceived as an undesirable burden. Rather, they are seen as the logical and proper culmination of the criminal process. In contrast, the resolution of cases by means of guilty pleas is frowned on because of two concerns. First, this sort of informal resolution will mean that procedural irregularities will escape notice and remedy. In addition, an innocent individual might plead guilty to obtain some advantage, for example timely resolution and/or a reduced sentence. Given these dangers, guilty pleas should be rare and be subject to safeguards to ensure that the accused is acting in a voluntary and informed manner.

Scepticism also animates the appellate procedures contemplated by the Due Process Model. Convicted defendants should have easy access to appellate relief, including the assistance of counsel on appeal without regard to financial resources. Given the fallibility of everyone involved in the criminal process, including trial courts, appellate courts must possess broad remedial authority to not only correct factual errors, but to vindicate procedural protections.

If we were to choose an epigraph for the Due Process Model it would be the oft quoted claim by Justice Felix Frankfurter that: 'The history of liberty is the history of the observance of procedural safeguards'.[15]

C The Competing Institutions of Crime Control and Due Process

It will be remembered that Packer was not positing his models in the abstract. Rather, his construction of each was laid against the backdrop of the American

[15] *McNabb v United States* 318 US 332, 347 (1942) (Frankfurter J dissenting).

legal system, its particular legal customs, institutions and constitutional order. In sketching out the details of each model, Packer explained that, in the main, both look to different institutions for their enabling authority. That is, the legitimacy of each account depends on different institutional sources.

For example, Packer explained that because 'the Crime Control Model is basically an affirmative model, emphasizing at every turn the existence and exercise of official powers, its validating authority is ultimately legislative'.[16] This is no small point. On this view, since the agents of crime control (that is, police officers and prosecutors) derive their power primarily from the legislature, its outputs will invariably be aimed at enabling and legitimizing their crime control functions.

In contrast, the values that inform the due process account originate in the Constitution and are vindicated by the courts. As Packer explained, 'the Due Process Model is basically a negative model, asserting limits on the nature of official power and on the modes of its exercise, its validating authority is judicial and requires an appeal to supra-legislative law, to the law of the Constitution'.[17] It is ultimately the courts that are charged with the responsibility of interpreting the Constitution's guarantees and vindicating individual rights in specific cases.

Under Packer's theory, legislatures and the courts play importantly different, and even antagonistic roles. The former empower state actors with the authority they require to engage in the competitive endeavour of ferreting out crime, apprehending wrongdoers and efficiently bringing them to justice. In contrast, courts stand between the actors empowered by the state and the individuals ensnared by the investigative net that they cast. They do so by promulgating rules of fair process through their interpretation of the legal rights guarantees found in the Constitution, and vindicating those rights in instances where state actors have failed to respect the procedural rules. Under the Due Process Model, it is only after an accused person's case has successfully made its way through the obstacle course that a court is empowered to find the accused guilty and mete out punishment.

In section IV we will revisit the division of institutional labour described by Packer as between his competing models. Before doing so, it is necessary to lay the groundwork for better understanding of what I characterize as Packer's blind spot – a gap that has in part only been revealed because of the empirical research that has taken place since Packer first developed his two models. To bring that shortcoming into focus, we will need to gain a better understanding of the various critiques that have emerged in response to Packer's bipolar account. We move to that next.

[16] Packer, 'Two Models' (n 1) 22.
[17] ibid.

III PACKER UNDER ATTACK

Packer's account of the criminal process as involving a series of choices as between two bipolar models has been subject to ever increasing criticism over the last five decades. Although the perspective of critics has varied, the complaints reflect a growing consensus that Packer's models are inadequate. In this section, we will review the main challenges, with special emphasis on the Canadian context.

A The Empirical Challenge

Although writing in the early 1960s, Packer appreciated that empiricism was beginning to challenge the view – dominant until then – that the criminal process was fairly described in the formal legal rules that govern the apprehension, screening and trial of persons suspected of crime. As noted above, Packer acknowledged that the criminal process 'consists at least as importantly of patterns of official activity that correspond only in the roughest kind of way to the prescriptions of procedural rules'.[18] At the time, however, empirical research examining the criminal process was just getting underway. Packer's focus was therefore rather understandably on the formal rules, and how those rules would be differently constituted under the competing models he describes.

Since Packer developed his models, there has been a virtual explosion of research empirically examining how close the resemblance actually is between the formal legal rules and the realities of criminal justice practices. As noted above, these efforts began with the American Bar Foundation Survey of the Administration of Criminal Justice in the United States. That ambitious programme of qualitative and ethnographic research revealed that low-visibility discretionary decision-making pervaded every aspect of the criminal justice system, or in other words, that a great deal of official authority was exercised well beyond the reach of any formal rules.[19] Since these early beginnings, as Kent Roach notes,

> empirical studies have illustrated that police, prosecutors, judges, and defence counsel share common organizational interests that defy the contrasting ideologies of crime control and due process. These professionals are bureaucrats who habitually cooperate to maximize their own organizational interests, not warriors for crime control or due process.[20]

Exposing the extent to which there is deviation from the law's formal demands is no easy task. Unfortunately, many parts of the system are not at all transparent,

[18] Packer, 'Two Models' (n 1) 2.

[19] See generally LE Ohlin and FJ Remington (eds), *Discretion in Criminal Justice: The Tension Between Individualization and Uniformity* (Albany, State University of New York Press, 1993).

[20] K Roach, *Due Process and Victims' Rights: The New Law and Politics of Criminal Justice* (Toronto, University of Toronto Press, 1999) 20.

which means that 'short cuts, deviations and outright rule violations'[21] can too often escape detection and therefore meaningful remedy.[22]

From the very beginning, a major focus of empirical study in the criminal justice system was on the police, especially their detention, search and arrest practices.[23] Once the breadth of police discretion was revealed, scholars like Skolnick[24] and Davis[25] began studying how police behave in these legally grey areas. Through field study, they exposed the inherent potential for abuse in the myriad of low visibility discretionary decisions made by police.

Richard Ericson's groundbreaking study of police patrol behaviour revealed that (just like their American[26] and English[27] counterparts) Canadian police officers use legal rules quite pragmatically.[28] In the field, the formal limits on police authority are not usually foremost in an individual officer's mind. Much more important are the informal rules of police occupational culture. The law is often little more than a 'residual resource', deployed after other methods of resolving a situation have failed.[29] At other times, it is used as an after-the-fact justification where proactive policing, sometimes driven by oblique considerations like race or class, fortuitously leads to the discovery of evidence.[30] More recently, an extensive body of empirical research has emerged in the United States,[31] Great Britain[32] and Canada[33] to suggest that racial profiling is a widespread phenomenon in all three jurisdictions. For example, Canadian research strongly suggests that both

[21] MM Feeley, 'Two Models of the Criminal Justice System: An Organizational Perspective' (1972–73) 7 *Law and Sociology Review* 407, 417.

[22] ibid 422.

[23] Two of the survey reports focused on these powers. See Tiffany et al, *Detection of Crime* (n 11); WR LaFave, *Arrest* (n 11).

[24] See JH Skolnick, *Justice without Trial: Law Enforcement in Democratic Society* (New York, J Wiley, 1966).

[25] See KC Davis, *Police Discretion* (St Paul, West Publishing Co, 1975).

[26] Those who have studied American police also report that 'the law is used pragmatically by patrolmen to accomplish ends that are important to them'. See MK Brown, *Working the Street: Police Discretion and the Dilemmas of Reform* (New York, Russell Sage Foundation, 1981) 221. See also E Bittner, *Aspects of Police Work* (Boston, Northeastern University Press, 1990) 245; E Bittner, 'The Police on Skid Row: A Study of Peace Keeping' (1967) 32 *American Sociological Review* 699, 710; E Bittner, *The Functions of Police in Modern Society: A Review of Background Factors, Current Practices, and Possible Role Models* (Chevy Chase MD, National Institute of Mental Health, 1970) 109.

[27] Those who have studied the English police similarly report that: 'The police use the law as a control device. The aims of stops and arrests are often not to enforce the law *per se*, but to secure broader objectives: the imposition of order, the assertion of authority, the acquisition of information'. See M McConville, A Sanders and R Leng, *The Case for the Prosecution: Police Suspects and the Construction of Criminality* (London, Routledge, 1991).

[28] RV Ericson, *Reproducing Order: A Study of Police Patrol Work* (Toronto, University of Toronto Press, 1982).

[29] ibid 13–14.

[30] ibid 15, 200–01.

[31] See generally DE Harris, *Profiles in Injustice: Why Racial Profiling Cannot Work* (New York, New Press, 2002).

[32] See generally M FitzGerald and R Sibbitt, *Ethnic Monitoring in Police Forces: A Beginning* (London, Home Office, Research and Statistics Directorate, 1997); W MacPherson, *The Stephen Lawrence Inquiry* (London, The Stationery Office, 1999).

[33] See generally DM Tanovich, *The Colour of Justice: Policing Race in Canada* (Toronto, Irwin, 2006).

Aboriginals[34] and African Canadians[35] are detained by police at disproportionately higher rates than members of other racial groups.[36] In short, the empirical research suggests that legal rules alone will often have limited effect in controlling abuses of police powers.

B Critical Legal Studies: Due Process is for Crime Control

Seizing on the empirical research, some critical legal studies scholars have hypothesized that official deviation is no accident. They contend that both courts and legislatures create rules and procedures that are deliberately elastic, providing official actors with considerable discretion that is largely immune from meaningful scrutiny. On this view, the legal rules are little more than cover for what in practice is mostly unchecked power. In other words, they contend that 'due process is for crime control'.[37]

This thesis gained traction in Canada in the immediate aftermath of the Charter. Some scholars argue that, while seeming to limit state action, the Charter has in actuality served an enabling function. It has done so by giving more power to economic and political elites, while reinforcing, if not widening, existing social and economic divisions within Canadian society, all under the cloak of rights rhetoric.[38] On this account, the Charter is not 'a tool to control the discretion of

[34] See Public Inquiry into the Administration of Justice and Aboriginal People, *Report of the Aboriginal Justice Inquiry of Manitoba. Volume 1: The Justice System and Aboriginal People* (Winnipeg, Queen's Printer, 1991) 595; Task Force on the Criminal Justice System and Its Impact on the Indian and Metis People of Alberta, *Justice on Trial* (Edmonton, Task Force, 1991) 2–5, 2-46–2 51.

[35] See Ontario, *Commission On Systemic Racism In The Ontario Criminal Justice System* (Toronto, Queen's Printer for Ontario, 1995) 349–60; CE James, 'Up To No Good: Black on the Streets and Encountering Police' in V Satzewich (ed), *Racism and Social Inequality in Canada: Concepts, Controversies and Strategies of Resistance* (Toronto, Thompson, 1998) 157; R Neugebauer, 'Kids, Cops, and Colour: The Social Organization of Police-Minority Youth Relations' in R Neugebauer (ed), *Criminal Injustice: Racism in the Criminal Justice System* (Toronto, Canadian Scholars Press, 2000); J Rankin et al, 'Police Target Black Drivers' (20 October 2002) *Toronto Star*, online: www.thestar.com/specialsections/raceandcrime/article/761200--police-target-black-drivers. But see R Melchers, 'Do Toronto Police Engage in Racial Profiling?' (2003) 45 *Canadian Journal of Criminology* 347. But see also S Wortley, 'Data, Denials, and Confusion: The Racial Profiling Debate in Toronto' (2003) 45 Canadian Journal of Criminology 367. More recently, see J Rankin, 'Race Matters: Blacks documented by police at high rate' (6 February 2010) *Toronto Star*, online: www.thestar.com/specialsections/raceandcrime/article/761343--race-matters-blacks-documented-by-police-at-high-rate.

[36] See also WJ Closs, 'Bias Free Policing: The Kingston Police Data Collection Project – A Preliminary Report to the Kingston Police Services Board' (17 March 2005), online: www.turtleisland.org/news/profiling.pdf.

[37] DJ McBarnet, 'Arrest: The Legal Context of Policing' in S Holdaway and MR Chatteron (eds), *The British Police* (London, Arnold, 1979) 156. See also DJ McBarnet, 'Pre-trial Procedures and the Construction of Conviction' in P Carlen (ed), *The Sociology of Law: Sociological Rev Monograph* 23 (University of Keele, Department of Sociology, 1976) 172; DJ McBarnet, *Conviction: Law, the State and the Construction of Justice* (London, Macmillan Press, 1981) 26–69.

[38] See AC Hutchison and A Petter, 'Private Rights/Public Wrongs: The Liberal Lie of the Charter' (1988) 38 *University of Toronto Law Journal* 278; RV Ericson, *Making Crime: A Study of Detective Work* (Toronto, University of Toronto Press, 1993) 11–12, 219; RV Ericson and KD Haggerty, *Policing the Risk Society* (Toronto, University of Toronto Press, 1997) 64–66. See more generally M Mandel, *The Charter of Rights and the Legalization of Politics in Canada* rev edn (Toronto, Thompson Educational Publishing, 1994).

government and its agents, but a means to enable, justify and legitimate their discretionary power'.[39]

In a Canadian context, the 'due process is for crime control' thesis has been criticized for lacking balance. It ignores some undeniable due process developments that have operated to the considerable advantage of suspects and accused persons, and that are unlikely to have taken place without the Charter. For example, the generous right to disclosure which individuals charged with a crime now enjoy in Canada. This right clearly goes some distance towards reducing the risk of wrongful convictions and is hardly inconsistent with vindicating the interests of due process.[40]

C Victims' Rights

Packer's binary model has also been criticized for conceiving of the criminal process as involving a struggle between the state and the criminal suspect/accused. On Packer's account, victims barely merit mention.[41] This omission has not escaped notice.[42]

The historic alienation of victims by the criminal process is now widely acknowledged.[43] Over the past 30 years, a number of scholars have chronicled the profound unfairness occasioned by this historic injustice and have advocated in favour of a vision of the criminal process that places the interests of victims on equal footing with concerns about crime control and due process.[44] In practical terms, advocacy groups have successfully pushed for protection of victims' interests in the criminal process, including informational and participatory rights.[45]

For example, in Canada, every province and territory now has some form of victims' rights legislation.[46] Although these Acts vary in content, each requires that victims be kept abreast of developments regarding the investigation or prosecution of their case. Unfortunately for victims, in most provinces there is no enforcement mechanism for these 'rights'. As one judge noted about Ontario's legislation, it is nothing more than 'a statement of government policy wrapped up

[39] RV Ericson, T*he Constitution of Legal Inequality* (Ottawa, Carleton University, 1983) 28.

[40] See J Stribopoulos, 'Has the Charter Been for Crime Control? Reflecting on 25 Years of Constitutional Criminal Procedure in Canada' in M Beare (ed), *Honouring Social Justice: Honouring Dianne Martin* (Toronto, University of Toronto Press, 2009) 351.

[41] In his 68-page law review article, Packer mentions the 'victim' only twice! See Packer, 'Two Models' (n 1) 9, 12.

[42] For a review of the relevant scholarship, see Roach, *Due Process* (n 20) 26–27.

[43] In Canada, recognition of this historic shortcoming began in the early 1980s. See, eg, B Dickson, 'The Forgotten Party – The Victim of Crime' (1984) 18 *University of British Colombia Law Review* 319.

[44] See, eg, DE Beloof, 'The Third Model of Criminal Process: The Victim Participation Model' (1999) *Utah Law Review* 289.

[45] For a review of Canadian developments over the past 30 years, see J Barrett, 'Expanding Victims' Rights in the Charter Era and Beyond' in J Cameron and J Stribopoulos (eds), *The Charter and Criminal Justice: Twenty-Five Years Later* (Toronto, LexisNexis, 2008) 627.

[46] See, eg, Victims' Bill of Rights SO 1995 ch 6.

in the language of legislation'.[47] The empty symbolism of victims' rights legislation to one side, within the criminal process itself there have been some significant reforms.

Many of these reforms have been directed at child victims. In Canada, for example, child witnesses may now testify behind a protective screen or outside the courtroom via a video link;[48] they may also be permitted to have a support person present and close by while giving evidence[49] and in addition, a videotaped statement made by a child complainant within a reasonable time after the alleged offence is admissible into evidence if the witness adopts its contents while testifying.[50]

Other reforms are aimed at protecting victims of sexual violence. In Canada, for example, sexual assault complainants have now been granted standing to make representations to a court that is considering an application for production of their personal records (that is, psychiatric, medical or educational) to the accused.[51] In addition, there are now legislated restrictions in place to prevent unjustified questioning of a complainant regarding her prior sexual history[52] or sexual reputation.[53]

More generally, under contemporary Canadian legislation courts can preclude a self-represented accused person from personally conducting the cross-examination of any witness, including the victim.[54]

Finally, as part of the Canadian sentencing process, victims are now entitled to file and even read a Victim Impact Statement before a court decides on the appropriate sentence for an offender and the court is obligated to inquire as to whether

[47] *Vanscoy v Ontario* [1999] OJ No 1661 (Ont SCJ) [41]. In this case, two victims unsuccessfully sued for non-compliance with the Act alleging that they were not notified of pending court dates and not consulted with respect to plea bargaining agreements. The court rejected a Charter challenge to s 2(5) of the Act, which provides that: 'No new cause of action, right of appeal, claim or other remedy exists in law because' of the Act. But see The Victims' Bill of Rights SM 2000 ch 33, which entitles a victim who feels the Act has not been respected to lodge a complaint with the Director of Prosecutions in the province (s 28(1)) and obligates the Director of Prosecutions to conduct an investigation and report the results to the victim (s 28(2) through (5)). A victim who is dissatisfied with the results of that report may seek a review by the provincial Ombudsman (s 30).

[48] See Criminal Code RSC 1985 ch C 46 (as amended), s 486.2. This provision has been upheld as constitutional by the Supreme Court of Canada. See *R v Levogiannis* [1993] 4 SCR 475.

[49] See Criminal Code, ibid s 486.1.

[50] ibid s 715.1. The constitutionality of the predecessor provision was upheld by the Supreme Court of Canada. See *R v L(DO)* [1993] 4 SCR 419.

[51] See Criminal Code (n 48) ss 278.1–278.91, which legislates a protective scheme more robust than that set down by the Supreme Court of Canada at common law in *R v O'Connor* [1995] 4 SCR 411. The constitutionality of these provisions was then upheld by the Court, even though they appear to deviate from the criteria set down by the majority judgment in *O'Connor*. See *R v Mills* [1999] 3 SCR 668.

[52] See Criminal Code (n 48) ss 276–276.5, enacted in response to the Supreme Court of Canada's judgment in *R v Seaboyer* [1991] 2 SCR 577 declaring the predecessor provision unconstitutional. These provisions have now been upheld as constitutional by the Supreme Court of Canada. See *R v Darrach* [2000] 2 SCR 443.

[53] See Criminal Code (n 48) s 277.

[54] See Criminal Code (n 48) s 486.3. There is a presumption in favour of such an order where the witness is under 18 years of age (s 486.3(1)) or is the complainant in a criminal harassment prosecution (s 486(4)) and the authority to make it in all other cases where the court considers it necessary 'to obtain a full and candid account from the witnesses of the acts complained of' (s 486.3(2)).

the victim has been appraised of this right.[55] These are all welcome and important reforms.

Some commentators contend however that the reforms have not gone far enough. They argue that the time has arrived to go beyond what are mostly symbolic developments. In Canada, some contend that the solution is for the judiciary to interpret the Charter to offer more robust protection for victims' privacy and equality rights.[56] Alan Young goes even further. Echoing proposals that have been made in the United States[57] he argues that a constitutional amendment might be necessary.[58]

At the same time, there are those who contend that victims have already come to wield far too much influence over the criminal process in Canada.[59] They express serious reservations about amending the Charter to entrench victims' rights.[60] For this group, 'a criminal trial is about determining guilt and just punishment of accused, not about personal redress for victims'.[61] It is feared that constitutionally mandating a greater role for victims 'would hopelessly burden and confuse an already overtaxed and under-resourced criminal justice system'.[62]

Between these two extremes is Kent Roach. He observes that in recent years the interests of victims have often been co-opted by politicians anxious to score easy political points with an electorate clamouring for law and order. The result, he argues, is the 'criminalization of politics', a phenomenon that promotes 'the power of the traditional agents of crime control – legislatures, police, and prosecutors – while not necessarily empowering crime victims and potential victims'.[63] Exploited in this way, victims' rights are put to work for crime control. As a result, Roach advocates for a new 'non-punitive' model of victims' rights, which moves beyond past struggles between due process and crime control and looks towards a 'more holistic integration of criminal justice with social, political, cultural and economic justice'.[64] In other words, Roach favours a vision of victims' rights imbued with the conciliatory aims of restorative justice.

[55] See Criminal Code (n 48) ss 722 and 722.2.

[56] See, eg, Barrett, 'Expanding Victims' Rights' (n 45).

[57] See Senate Report (Judiciary Committee), 'Senate Committee Report on Crime Victims' Rights Amendment' (2006–07) 19 *Federal Sentencing Report* 58.

[58] See A Young, 'Crime Victims and Constitutional Rights' (2005) 49 *Criminal Law Quarterly* 432.

[59] See D Stuart, 'Charter Protection against Law and Order: Victims' Rights and Equality Rhetoric' in J Cameron, (ed), *The Charter's Impact on the Criminal Justice System* (Toronto, Carswell, 1996); DM Paciocco, 'Competing Constitutional Rights in an Age of Deference: A Bad Time to be Accused' (2001) 14 *Supreme Court Law Review Second Series* 111.

[60] See eg DM Paciocco, 'Why the Constitutionalization of Victim Rights Should Not Occur' (2005) 49 *Criminal Law Quarterly* 393.

[61] D Stuart, *Charter Justice in Canadian Criminal Law* 4th edn (Toronto, Carswell, 2005) 40.

[62] ibid 41.

[63] Roach, *Due Process* (n 20) 5.

[64] ibid 8.

D Restorative Justice

Arguably, the most ambitious challenge to Packer's bipolar account has come from proponents of restorative justice. They reject Packer's claim that the criminal process inevitably entails 'a struggle from start to finish'.[65] That idea is at the foundation of Packer's theory of a system in perpetual conflict between two irreconcilable poles, with crime control and due process locked in an intractable struggle.

Proponents of restorative justice seek a wholesale transformation of our existing criminal justice practices.[66] They favour a move away from the current emphasis on competing legal interests that are negotiated by professional justice system participants who are preoccupied with ideas of retribution, for example deciding guilt, attributing blame and doling out punishment.

As its name implies, the restorative justice approach instead envisions a system that focuses on restoring relationships damaged by crime including not only victims, but offenders and affected communities. Restorative justice practices aim to bring these constituencies together and make them whole through mutual understanding, accountability, forgiveness and compassion.[67]

Restorative justice practices may take a variety of forms. Over the last 20 years, some of these practices have made substantial inroads in Canada.[68] One of the best examples is a judicial initiative – the use of circle sentencing for Aboriginal offenders convicted of serious crimes.[69] Still others are the result of legislated changes, for example allowing for the diversion of accused persons out of the formal court process and into alternative measures programmes.[70]

Restorative justice is said to hold great benefits for everyone affected by crime. For victims, it offers a voice in the process, an opportunity to ask questions of the

[65] Packer, 'Two Models' (n 1) 2.

[66] See generally J Braithwaite, *Restorative Justice and Responsive Regulation* (Oxford, Oxford University Press, 2002); DW Van Ness and KH Strong, *Restoring Justice: An Introduction to Restorative Justice* 3rd edn (Ohio, Anderson Publishing Co, 2006). For a Canadian perspective, see Law Commission of Canada, *Transforming Relationships through Participatory Justice* (Ottawa, Minister of Public Works and Government Services, 2003).

[67] See H Zehr, *Changing Lenses: A New Focus for Crime and Justice* (Scottdale, Herald Press, 1990), who explains that retributive justice sees crime as 'a violation of the state, defined by lawbreaking and guilt' whereas restorative justice 'sees things differently . . . Crime is a violation of people and relationships . . . It creates obligations to make things right. Justice involves the victim, the offender and the community in a search for solutions which promote repair, reconciliation, and reassurance'. Ibid 181.

[68] See generally BP Archibald, 'Co-ordinating Canada's Restorative and Inclusionary Models of Criminal Justice: the Legal Profession and the Exercise of Discretion under a Reflexive Rule of Law' (2005) 9 *Canadian Criminal Law Review* 215.

[69] Beyond the ordinary courtroom participants (judge, prosecutor, defence lawyer, offender), circle sentencing normally also includes members of the offender's family, the victim and/or members of his family and members of the community which can include respected elders. See *R v Moses* [1992] 71 CCC (3d) 347 (Y Terr Ct), which is generally recognized as the first sentencing circle undertaken in Canada. The practice has grown since. See H Lilles, 'Circle Sentencing: Part of the Restorative Justice Continuum' in A Morris and G Maxwell, *Restorative Justice for Juveniles: Conferencing, Mediation and Circles* (Portland, Hart Publishing, 2001) 161.

[70] In the case of adults, see Criminal Code (n 48) s 717. With respect to youths, see Youth Criminal Justice Act SC 2002 ch 1, Pt 1, ss 4–12.

wrongdoer, to understand the cause(s) of the offence, to play a role in deciding the outcome and a real opportunity for reconciliation and healing. For offenders, restorative justice practices provide an opportunity to understand the harm caused to the victim, to express remorse, make amends, seek forgiveness and achieve reconciliation, all of which can serve as important steps on the road to rehabilitation and eventual reintegration into the community. For communities, restorative justice practices provide a forum for members of the community to express their concerns about crime, to address offenders directly, to reaffirm community values, to recognize and redress underlying causes of crime, to lay the groundwork for reintegrating the offender and take important steps towards building a safe and peaceful community.

Despite the optimism of its supporters, restorative justice also has its detractors. Perhaps the most searing criticism is that its goals are simply unrealistic. Especially for crimes that occasion serious harm, its Utopian vision seems to run up against the reality that for many victims and their families, retribution equals justice.[71]

E In Packer's Defence

Up until this point we have covered a fair amount of ground. We have surveyed not only Packer's theory, but the main critiques that have emerged in response to his account. Caution is necessary, however, when comparing these competing theories with Packer's models. Packer neither intended for his models to describe nor to prescribe the workings of the criminal process. Unlike competing theories, there is nothing aspirational in Packer's account; rather, his object was to develop a vocabulary by which to better label and thereby understand actual developments. As a result, to the extent that Packer did not anticipate nor account for the rise of the victims' rights movement or the ascent of restorative justice reforms, he cannot in fairness be faulted. After all, he did not have a crystal ball.

IV PACKER'S BLIND SPOT

Beyond developments that Packer simply could not anticipate, there were also variables that were undoubtedly operable when Packer wrote but that he simply *could not* see. These are the considerations that were, for our purposes, in Packer's 'blind spot'. In this section we will consider these variables, why Packer could not see them and how they require a tweaking of his models in order to properly reflect the significance of these unnoticed factors.

[71] See A Acorn, *Compulsory Compassion: A Critique of Restorative Justice* (Vancouver, UBC Press, 2004).

On Packer's account, it is the courts that vindicate the interests of due process. What Packer could not see – given the state of empirical knowledge at the time – was the extent to which law enforcement officials fail to respect the formal limits on their legal powers and employ the law in an instrumental rather than a principled way. He could not, therefore, appreciate the extent to which courts fail to account for rights violations which result from such practices. After all, it is usually only those cases in which official malfeasance yields evidence of criminal wrongdoing that come before the courts. Cases involving innocent individuals whose rights are violated largely remain hidden from view.[72]

Certainly, Packer was far from naïve. In constructing his Due Process Model, he recognized that not all police misconduct necessarily leads to criminal charges, a fact that he acknowledged as propelling proponents of due process to press for remedies beyond evidentiary exclusion, including tort, internal discipline and civilian oversight. Since then, however, experience has convinced most civil libertarians that vindicating rights through the use of civil suits and police complaint procedures is destined for failure. A combination of high costs and low damage awards deters most potential civil claimants.[73] In addition, those already marginalized individuals who are most likely to be affected by police abuses are also the least likely to have the wherewithal to pursue a civil action or a formal complaint.[74]

The other important variable that Packer failed to see was the institutional limitations that impede the effectiveness of courts in vindicating the interests of due process. These are impediments that, as will be explained below, actually serve to exasperate the problem of low-visibility abuses of police powers.

It will be remembered that on Packer's account of the Due Process Model, it is ultimately the courts that serve to validate the interests of due process by vindicating individual rights under the Constitution. In attributing this role to the courts under the Due Process Model, Packer was no doubt influenced by the activism of the Warren Court. At that time, that Court was busy championing individual rights in the criminal process under the US Bill of Rights. Subsequent developments, however, have revealed that characterization as overly simplistic. To understand this shortcoming we need a bit more insight into how events subsequently unfolded in the United States, and how they have similarly played out in Canada under the Charter.

The key provision in the US Bill of Rights that governs police detention, arrest, search and seizure powers is the Fourth Amendment to the federal Constitution. It is the provision that guarantees the 'right of the people to be secure in their

[72] The result is a form of acoustic separation, with the lived reality of law experienced one way on the street and its construction in court resembling only a small fraction of that reality. On 'acoustic separation' more generally, see M Dan-Cohen, 'Decision Rules and Conduct Rules: On Acoustic Separation in Criminal Law' (1984) 97 *Harvard Law Review* 625.

[73] See PC Weiler, 'The Control of Police Arrest Practices: Reflections of a Tort Lawyer' in AM Linden (ed), *Studies in Canadian Tort Law* (Toronto, Butterworths, 1968) 416, 448–49.

[74] Weiler, 'The Control of Police', ibid 462. See also A Goldsmith, 'Necessary But Not Sufficient: The Role of Public Complaints Procedures in Police Accountability' in PC Stenning (ed), *Accountability for Criminal Justice: Selected Essays* (Toronto, University of Toronto Press, 1995) 110, 124.

persons, houses, papers, and effects, against unreasonable searches and seizures'. In interpreting that guarantee the United States Supreme Court essentially sets minimum standards for the nation that both state and federal officials are required to meet.[75] Under the American federal system, criminal law and procedure is a federal and a state responsibility. The bulk of criminal law, however, is enacted and enforced by the states.[76] In enforcing these laws, state officials must respect the requirements of the Fourth Amendment, as interpreted by the federal courts. That said, provided that they meet these minimum standards, state legislatures and courts, operating within the parameters of state constitutions, are entitled to create additional protections for their citizens.[77]

The constitutional judgments of the U.S. Supreme Court, in the context of police powers, speak not only to Congress but also to 50 state legislatures, which, at any given time, may be employing rather varied approaches to the regulation of police practices.[78] By default, if state law is silent on the scope of a police officer's authority in a given situation, then the officer is entitled to act up to the limits imposed by the federal Constitution. In this indirect way, the decisions of the US Supreme Court actually serve to *create* police powers, at least in a negative sense, by not prohibiting police conduct in certain situations.[79]

[75] Although initially the Fourth Amendment only served as a restraint on the federal government, as explained above, like many of the provisions in the Bill of Rights, the US Supreme Court eventually concluded that it was so 'fundamental' that it was 'incorporated' into the due process guarantee found in the Fourteenth Amendment. This had the effect of extending the Fourth Amendment to the states. See *Wolf v Colorado* (n 8). See also *Mapp v Ohio* (n 7) (which, as noted above, also served to incorporate the exclusionary rule).

[76] The federal government has the power to create criminal laws that deal with matters falling within the heads of federal power. See US Const Arts I § 1 and I § 8. By default, everything else is left to the states. See Israel and LaFave, *Criminal Procedure* (n 10) 3–7.

[77] See *Ker v State of California* 374 US 23 (1963) (noting that '[t]he States are not. . .precluded from developing workable rules governing arrests, searches and seizures to meet the 'the practical demands of effective criminal investigation and law enforcement' in the States, provided that those rules do not violate the constitutional proscription of unreasonable searches and seizures [contained in the Fourth Amendment]'.) [34].

[78] eg, in *Terry v Ohio* 392 US 1 (1968), the case in which the United States Supreme Court recognized a police 'stop-and-frisk' power, Ohio did not have legislation in place conferring authority upon police officers to stop-and-frisk suspects. In contrast, in a companion case to *Terry*, the Court was dealing with a stop-and-frisk from New York State, where state legislation was in place that expressly conferred a stop-and-frisk power on the police. See *Sibron v New York* 392 US 40, 43–44 (1968) (setting out the relevant provisions from §180 of the NY Code of Criminal Procedure).

[79] For example, in *Sibron v New York*, ibid 60–62, the US Supreme Court refused to decide whether or not the New York stop-and-frisk statute conformed with the requirements of the Fourth Amendment. It explained that:

> New York is, of course, free to develop its own law of search and seizure to meet the needs of local law enforcement . . . and in the process it may call the standards it employs by any names it may choose. It may not, however, authorize police conduct which trenches upon Fourth Amendment rights, regardless of the labels which it attaches to such conduct. The question in this Court upon review of a state-approved search or seizure is not whether the search (or seizure) was authorized by state law. The question is rather whether the search was reasonable under the Fourth Amendment. *Just as a search authorized by state law may be an unreasonable one under that amendment, so may a search not expressly authorized by state law be justified as a constitutionally reasonable one* (emphasis added) (60–61).

In the aftermath of the Charter, something very similar but far less subtle has taken place in Canada. By holding out the prospect of excluding unconstitutionally obtained evidence,[80] the Charter rather unexpectedly served to expose the numerous gaps in the patchwork of statutory and common law rules that make up the law of police powers in Canada. In the Charter's early years, the Supreme Court of Canada vindicated the rule of law by applying the principle of legality and insisting that clear legislative authority license intrusions on constitutionally protected interests.[81] Over time, however, the Court succumbed to the pressure of filling the many gaps in formal police powers that Charter litigation was continually serving to expose.

Ignoring its own pronouncements about the need to avoid far reaching changes to the common law,[82] over the past 25 years, when confronted with gaps in police powers, the Supreme Court of Canada has often been willing to use its 'common law' law-making authority in order to fill them. The device developed by the Court for creating new 'common law' police powers is known as the 'ancillary powers doctrine'. It allows for the recognition of police powers by deploying what is essentially a cost-benefit analysis. This law-making device has two parts. First, it begins with a query as to whether the impugned actions of a police officer fall within the scope of her broad duties.[83] Assuming the answer is 'yes',[84] the second step involves a weighing of the apparent benefits, usually for law enforcement and public safety, as against any resulting interference with individual liberty interests. If the benefits are characterized as outweighing the costs, the action is said to be 'justifiable' and a new police power is born.[85] Over the last 25 years the Supreme

[80] See Charter (n 6) s 24(2).

[81] See *R v Wong* [1990] 3 SCR 36. The Court refused to read a statutory provision authorizing police to obtain a warrant to intercept private 'communications' so as to authorize its use for the issuance of warrants to engage in surreptitious videotaping. The Court explained, at 56: The common law powers of search were extremely narrow, and the courts have left it to Parliament to extend them where need be . . . it does not sit well for the courts, as the protectors of our fundamental rights, to widen the possibility of encroachments on these personal liberties. It falls to Parliament to make incursions on fundamental rights if it is of the view that they are needed for the protection of the public in a properly balanced system of criminal justice.

[82] See *Watkins v Olafson* [1989] 2 SCR 750, indicating 'that major revisions of the law are best left to the legislature. Where the matter is one of a small extension of existing rules to meet the exigencies of a new case and the consequences of the change are readily assessable, judges can and should vary existing principles. But where the revision is major and its ramifications complex, the courts must proceed with great caution' (760–61). See also *Winnipeg Child and Family Services (Northwest Area) v DFG* [1997] 3 SCR 925 [18]; *Bow Valley Husky (Bermuda) Ltd v Saint John Ship Building Ltd* [1997] 3 SCR 1210 [93] (McLachlin J); *R v Cuerrier* [1998] 127 CCC (3d) 1 (SCC) [43] (McLachlin J concurring).

[83] The source of police duties is derived from legislation, usually the legislation governing the police in the particular jurisdiction, and tends to define police duties in rather broad terms: 'preserving the peace', 'preventing crimes and other offences', 'apprehending criminals and other offenders' etc. See, eg, Police Services Act RSO 1990, ch P15, s 42.

[84] It invariably will be, unless the officer is involved in some entirely illegitimate activity completely unrelated to his official duties. See *Brown v Durham Regional Police Force* (1998), 131 CCC (3d) 1 (Ont CA) 116–17.

[85] See *R v Dedman* [1985] 2 SCR 2. See also *R v Mann* [2004] 3 SCR 59 [24].

Court of Canada has embraced the ancillary powers doctrine as bases for recognizing a host of entirely unprecedented police powers.[86]

Given the era in which he was writing, Packer's failure to anticipate the law-making role that would ultimately be played by courts operating under a constitutional Bill of Rights is understandable. That alone does little to cast doubt overall on the insightfulness of his models. For example, if courts are inclined to develop rules that are more due process orientated than those promulgated by the legislatures, then despite their unanticipated law-making role, their functions may still be considered more aligned with due process. By acting to fill gaps, they may very well be forestalling more regressive legislative responses by legislatures and thereby continuing to serve the interests of individual rights in a way that Packer could not have anticipated, but which is entirely in keeping with courts as the key institutions of due process. Such a view is not, however, a fair characterization of the impact of judicial law-making in this context. To the contrary, there is good reason to believe that the judicial elucidation of police powers can often cut hard against the interests of due process.

Take for example the experience in the United States under the Fourth Amendment, which, as noted, bears on police detention, arrest and search powers. There is rare consensus from critics on both the Right and Left that, as Amar has put it, this body of law 'is a vast jumble of judicial pronouncements that is not merely complex and contradictory, but often perverse'.[87] Maclin notes that while 'Fourth Amendment law is certainly complex' even more troubling is that 'over the last two decades the trend of the Court's cases has been to expand police power'.[88] As a result of these developments, some writers have gone so far as to label the whole American criminal procedure revolution a failure and to call for sweeping legislative reforms.[89] The ambiguous but ever expanding nature of police authority under such a system is the direct result of the institutional limita-

[86] See *R v Dedman*, ibid (recognizing a police power to briefly detain motorists at sobriety check-stops); *R v Godoy* [1999] 1 SCR 311 (recognizing a police power to enter premises in response to disconnected 911 calls); *R v Mann*, ibid (recognizing a police power to briefly detain individuals who are reasonably suspected of involvement in recently committed or unfolding criminal activity, and to conduct protective weapons searches of such individuals where an officer has well-founded safety concerns); *R v Orbanksi*; *R v Elias* [2005] 2 SCR 3 (recognizing a police power to ask drivers questions about alcohol consumption and request their participation in sobriety tests without first complying with s 10(b) of the Charter); *R v Clayton* [2007] 2 SCR 725 (recognizing a power to conduct criminal investigative roadblock stops where such a stop is tailored to the information possessed by police, the seriousness of the offence being investigated, and the temporal and geographic connection between the situation being investigated and the timing and location of the roadblock); *R v Kang-Brown* [2008] 1 SCR 456 (recognizing a power to use a drug detecting dog to sniff at an individual, as well as her belongings, where the police have reasonable grounds to suspect the individual is carrying narcotics, in order to confirm or refute that suspicion).

[87] AR Amar, 'Fourth Amendment First Principles' (1994) 107 *Harvard Law Review* 757, 758. For Amar, an originalist, the solution is a return to 'first principles'. See also AR Amar, *The Constitution and Criminal Procedure: First Principles* (New Haven, Yale University Press, 1997).

[88] T Maclin, 'What Can Fourth Amendment Doctrine Learn From Vagueness Doctrine' (2001) 3 *University of Pennsylvania Journal of Constitutional Law* 398, 422–23.

[89] See CM Bradley, *The Failure of the Criminal Procedure Revolution* (Philadelphia, University of Pennsylvania Press, 1993).

tions of courts more generally. Packer could not see this because experience had not yet served to reveal it. Those limitations however are now well recognized.[90]

First, unlike legislatures, courts cannot deal with the whole field of police investigative powers in a comprehensive and prospective way, but can address only those issues raised by the cases and the parties that happen to come before them. As the experience in the United States under the Fourth Amendment confirms, the result of developing police powers in this piecemeal fashion is a fair amount of uncertainty. Empirical research has since revealed that such uncertainty is no friend of due process. As Skolnick warns:

> Whenever rules of constraint are ambiguous, they strengthen the very conduct they are intended to restrain. Thus, the police officer already committed to a conception of law as an instrument of order rather than as an end in itself is likely to utilize the ambiguity of the rules of restraint as a justification for testing or even violating them.[91]

Secondly, judges are generalists and therefore lack the required expertise to choose between what are often rather specialized policy options. They are ill-equipped to distinguish between requests for new investigative powers that are actually required, and those that are motivated by little more than an effort to justify the idiosyncrasies of a particular investigation in a specific case in order to protect incriminating evidence from exclusion. The result can often be the judicial creation of a new police power that is entirely unnecessary. The needless expansion of police authority by judges is quite obviously not in keeping with a vision of the judiciary as redeemers of individual rights.

Thirdly, due to limitations inherent in the adjudicative process, the courts are ill-equipped to ascertain the sort of relevant social facts that are essential for the development of sound policy but often irrelevant to the disposition of individual cases. A good example of this is the Canadian case of *R v Ladouceur*.[92] In that decision, the Supreme Court of Canada upheld the constitutionality of a statutory provision that authorized police to stop motorists at will. Lacking any criteria to guide police discretion, the Court agreed that the provision violated the Charter right not to be arbitrarily detained guaranteed by section 9. Nevertheless, citing the perils of drunk driving, a slim majority of the Court upheld the violation as a 'reasonable limit' under section 1 of the Charter. In doing so, the majority dismissed as 'unfounded' concerns that the authority to arbitrarily stop motorists to make driving-related inquiries may be vulnerable to racial bias. Limited as it was to the record in that case, the Court could not empirically evaluate such concerns.

[90] I have elaborated on these limitations elsewhere, with special emphasis on Canadian developments. See generally J Stribopoulos, 'The Limits of Judicially Created Police Powers: Investigative Detention After *Mann*' (2007) 45 *Criminal Law Quarterly* 299. See more generally: DL Horowitz, *The Courts and Social Policy* (Washington, Brookings Institute, 1977); A Chayes, 'The Role of the Judge in Public Law Litigation' (1976) 89 *Harvard Law Review* 1281; M Capelleti, 'The Law Making Power of the Judge and its Limits: A Comparative Analysis' (1981) 8 *Monash University Law Review* 15.

[91] Skolnick, *Justice without Trial* (n 24) 12. See also T Maclin, '*Terry v Ohio's* Fourth Amendment Legacy: Black Men and Police Discretion' (1998) 72 *St John's Law Review* 1271, 1320.

[92] *R v Ladouceur* [1990] 1 SCR 1257.

Instead, the need for resolution took priority over the imperfect record, resulting in the Court upholding (and thereby constitutionally immunizing) a police power that is, as the empirical evidence has since revealed,[93] rather susceptible to abuse.

Fourthly, courts lack the ability to monitor the effects of their judgments and to modify the rules they create in a timely way in response to such effects. Again, *Ladouceur* illustrates this shortcoming. As noted, in upholding police authority to conduct roving and random stops, the majority gave short shrift to claims that racial considerations could influence who the police choose to stop. Within a decade, the majority was proven wrong,[94] but the open-ended power continues. It is unlikely to be revisited in a future case unless the Court takes the extraordinary step of signalling its receptiveness to a challenge.

Finally, it is important to remember that the courts usually grapple with the subject of police powers in cases involving individuals who are *in fact* guilty. Except for the very rare civil suit that makes it to trial, the courts almost never see cases involving innocent individuals who are unjustifiably detained, searched, or arrested by police. As Justice La Forest acknowledged, in explaining why courts should refrain from creating new police powers, they 'deal with specific cases that ordinarily involve people who have broken the law, a fact that does not encourage the broader perspective that should be brought to the issue'.[95] In such cases, hindsight exerts a subtle pressure on the court to uphold the conduct of the police and ensure that a wrongdoer is punished.[96]

The biggest problem with judicially created rules, however, is that no matter how clear the court might manage to make them, their enforcement ultimately depends on judicial censure, usually through the exclusionary remedy. If the police role is primarily that of crime fighters aggressively seeking out suspected criminals and acquiring evidence to make a case stick in court, then the prospect of courts excluding illegally obtained evidence could go some distance toward ensuring police compliance with the rules.[97] It is that assumption that seems to inform Packer's construction of his Due Process Model, with courts cast in the role of vindicating individual rights by excluding illegally or unconstitutionally obtained evidence.

[93] See nn 34–36 and accompanying text.

[94] ibid.

[95] *R v Evans* [1996] 1 SCR 8 [4] (La Forest J concurring).

[96] See WJ Stuntz, 'Warrants and Fourth Amendment Remedies' (1991) 77 *Virginia Law Review* 881, 912–13 making this point in the American context. See also C Steiker, 'Second Thoughts About First Principles' (1994) 107 *Harvard Law Review* 820, 852–53.

[97] Although the empirical research examining the deterrent benefits of evidentiary exclusion is far from conclusive. Some studies conclude that the exclusionary rule is an effective deterrent. See SR Schlesinger, *Exclusionary Injustice: The Problem of Illegally Obtained Evidence* (New York, Marcel Dekker, 1977) 50–56; Y Kamisar, 'Is The Exclusionary Rule an "Illogical" or "Unnatural" Interpretation of the Fourth Amendment?' (1978) 62 *Judicature* 67. While others find little evidence to suggest any deterrent benefits: see DH Oaks, 'Studying the Exclusionary Rule in Search and Seizure' (1970) 37 *University of Chicago Law Review* 665; B Canon, 'The Exclusionary Rule: Have Critics Proven that it Doesn't Deter Police?' (1979) 62 *Judicature* 398. Yet another study concludes that it has no deterrent benefits: see JE Spiotto, 'Search and Seizure: American Empirical Studies of the Exclusionary Rule and its Alternatives' (1973) 2 *Journal of Legal Studies* 243.

As empirical research has since revealed, however, maintaining order is a much larger part of what the police actually spend their time doing.[98] The trend towards community policing throughout North America,[99] with its emphasis on proactive police/citizen encounters,[100] has made that function even more important. When maintaining order is the objective, the threat of evidentiary exclusion has little purchase over police behaviour. The experience with Broken Windows[101] policing in New York City aptly demonstrates this point. If the police decide – as they did in New York City – that taking weapons off of the streets is more important than respecting civil liberties and securing convictions, the exclusionary rule stops having any protective effect.[102] And in extreme cases where a police officer harasses for the sole purpose of ordering 'disorderly people', the exclusionary rule again meets its limits, as the recent experience in Toronto at the G20 Summit aptly served to demonstrate.[103] These are the realities of policing that Packer simply could not see because of the state of empirical learning at the time that he penned his theory.

[98] See S Walker, *The Police in America: An Introduction* 2nd edn (New York, McGraw-Hill, 1992) 65–67, 112, who notes that less than one-third of police work is devoted to law enforcement or crime fighting, while the remainder is mostly spent performing peacekeeping or order maintenance functions.

[99] With respect to Canadian developments, see generally CT Griffiths, RB Parent and B Whitelaw, *Community Policing in Canada* (Scarborough, Nelson Thomson, 2001). With respect to developments in the United States, see generally JM Wilson, *Community Policing in America* (New York, Routledge, 2006). See also PF McKenna, *Foundations of Community Policing in Canada* (Toronto, Prentice Hall, 2000) 294–334.

[100] See R Trojanowicz, VE Kappeler, LK Gaines and B Bucqueroux, *Community Policing A Contemporary Perspective* 2nd edn (Cincinnati, Anderson, 1998) 3–24. But see DH Bayley, 'Community Policing: A Report from the Devil's Advocate' in JR Green and SD Mastrofksi (eds), *Community Policing: Rhetoric or Reality* (New York, Praeger, 1988) 225, 229.

[101] 'Broken Windows' policing concentrates enforcement efforts on disorder in public spaces – the metaphorical 'broken window' – in the belief that police/community relations will be strengthened, creating an atmosphere in which crime cannot flourish. The theory emphasizes the use of non-invasive methods first, and contemplates arrests as a last resort. See GL Kelling and CM Coles, *Fixing Broken Windows: Restoring Order and Reducing Crime in Our Communities* (New York, Free Press, 1996). See also JQ Wilson and GL Kelling, 'Broken Windows' (March 1982) *The Atlantic Monthly*. In practice, it has a demonstrated tendency to transform into something less benign. See BE Harcourt, 'Reflecting on the Subject: A Critique of the Social Influence Conception of Deterrence, The Broken Windows Theory, and Order-Maintenance Policing New York Style' (1998) 97 *Michigan Law Review* 291, 344. See generally BE Harcourt, *Illusion of Order: The False Promise of Broken Windows Policing* (Cambridge MA, Harvard University Press, 2001).

[102] See J Fagan and G Davies, 'Street Stops and Broken Windows: Terry, Race, and Disorder in New York City' (2000) 28 *Fordham Urban Law Journal* 457, 476–77, who explain that in practice Broken Windows policing in New York City 'drifted from street stops in quality of life crimes to widespread stops of citizens in search of guns'. While misdemeanour arrests rose almost 75% during the 1990s, the rate at which prosecutors were withdrawing misdemeanour charges also rose nearly 60% during this period, suggesting that many arrests were undertaken for ordering purposes only.

[103] See Canadian Civil Liberties Association, *A Breach of the Peace: A Preliminary Report of Observations During the 2010 G20 Summit*, online: ccla.org/wordpress/wp-content/uploads/2010/06/CCLA-Report-A-Breach-of-the-Peace-Preliminary-report-updated-July-8.pdf.

V CONCLUSION

With the benefit of empirical research and experience, it is now clear that Packer's vision of the courts vindicating the interests of due process by pushing back on police excesses through the exclusion of unconstitutionally obtained evidence is largely fiction. Subsequent learning has revealed that, due to their institutional limitations, courts alone are incapable of meaningfully regulating police authority. As it turns out, realizing that goal would also seem to require a serious commitment from the legislature.

The legislature has an integral role to play if the ends of due process are to be realized; the courts on their own are simply not up to the task. Only legislation can clearly, comprehensively and prospectively delineate police powers and establish the sorts of procedural safeguards that are needed to check routine and low-level exercises of police discretion. Courts simply cannot see the countless interactions between police and individuals that never culminate in formal charges. It is the legislature, not the courts, which possess the tools necessary to get at those encounters and vindicate the interests of due process. (How courts might go about prompting the legislature to take the necessary action is beyond the scope of this paper.)[104]

Despite his monumental scholarly contribution to our understanding of the criminal process, Packer's models are far from perfect. Contemporary critiques often focus on subsequent developments that Packer simply could not anticipate. What this chapter has served to expose are variables that were at work when Packer framed his theory but which he simply could not see; important matters that were unfortunately in Packer's blind spot.

On Packer's theory, the legislature is the institution of crime control, while it is the courts that are concerned with due process. The empirical research into the actual workings of the criminal process, along with the experience in both the United States and Canada over the intervening years, now serves to cast much doubt on that important assumption.

[104] In a Canadian context, I have previously sketched out a theory of how the Supreme Court could do just that. See J Stribopoulos, 'In Search of Dialogue: The Supreme Court, Police Powers, and the Charter' (2005) 31 *Queen's Law Journal* 1.

11

Social Deprivation and Criminal Justice

KIMBERLEY BROWNLEE*

This chapter concerns the use of social deprivation as a mode of lawful punishment. In this context, 'social deprivation' refers not to poverty and its associated social ills, but to a persisting inadequacy of access to minimally supportive social contact including interpersonal interaction, associative inclusion and interdependent care. In what follows, I elaborate a view that I articulate elsewhere – that there is a human right against social deprivation – and I argue here that modes of lawful punishment that involve social deprivation constitute human rights violations.[1] To the extent that interpersonal social needs have been considered in debates about either socio-economic human rights or lawful punishment, they have been largely subsumed under economic-welfare rights, in the first case, and under rights against torture in the second, which paints an incomplete and skewed picture both of the importance of the human need for social inclusion irrespective of economic needs and physical needs, and of the reasons not to employ socially privative punishment.[2]

Briefly, the position I defend is as follows. Human beings have a right to those conditions that are necessary for the realisation of a minimally decent human life. Having minimally adequate access to supportive social inclusion is a necessary

* I am grateful to Stuart Green for his very thoughtful response to this chapter at the 'Rethinking Criminal Law Theory' conference, Osgoode Hall Law School, Toronto (10–12 September 2010). I am equally grateful to Virginia Mantouvalou for her illuminating response to this chapter at the Royal Holloway conference on 'Margins of Citizenship' in London (12 November 2010). For very helpful discussions on these issues, I thank the participants at the 2010 University of Stirling 'Workshop on Human Rights' and the 2010 'Oxford Political Thought' conference as well as the research seminars participants at UCL and the Universities of Lancaster, Manchester, Rijeka, and York (UK). I thank François Tanguay-Renaud and James Stribopoulos for their excellent coordination of this project on Rethinking Criminal Law Theory. For their helpful comments on previous versions of this chapter, I thank Adam Cureton, Jules Holroyd, Jon Pike and Zofia Stemplowska.

[1] K Brownlee, 'Social Deprivation and Human Rights' (in progress).

[2] For defences of socio-economic rights as human rights, see H Shue, *Basic Rights: Subsistence, Affluence, and US Foreign Policy* 2nd edn (Princeton, Princeton University Press, 1996); J Nickel, 'Poverty and Human Rights' (2005) 55 *Philosophical Quarterly* 385, 391; J Nickel, *Making Sense of Human Rights* (Oxford: Blackwell, 2007) ch 9; TW Pogge, *World Poverty and Human Rights* (Cambridge, Polity Press, 2007). All of these philosophers give little attention to social needs independent of economic needs.

condition for a minimally decent human life (and indeed for a less than minimally decent human life) because, among other things, social deprivation threatens or undermines both the development and the maintenance of the cognitive, physical, emotional, linguistic and social abilities that both partly constitute a minimally decent human life and make other rights and domains of value meaningfully available.[3] I argue elsewhere that the human right against social deprivation is a secure right in the sense that it does not depend on either good community standing or good behaviour.[4] In what follows, I elaborate this view and consider its implications for the use of social deprivation in criminal justice.

I SOCIAL DEPRIVATION AND PUNISHMENT

To set the scene, let us begin in ancient Athens where the Assembly adopted an unusual formal practice to ease tensions among political rivals. The practice was that of voting annually on whether to banish one citizen from the city. If in a given year the majority of Assembly members held that it was necessary to banish a citizen, then a second vote would be taken and each Assembly member would write the name of the citizen he most wished to see banished on a broken piece of pottery called an 'ostrakon' (which is the etymological root of the word 'ostracism'). The citizen with the most votes would then be banished from Athens for an extended period of up to 10 years.[5]

Although banishment from Athens would undeniably have been a burdensome experience, it differs significantly from contemporary practices of forced social

[3] I do not mean to imply that persons who are unable to develop some of these abilities or who lose some of these abilities necessarily lead lives that are not minimally decent. Rather, I mean that a minimally decent life is one in which persons have the opportunities to develop and maintain these abilities according to their own capacity.

[4] I have borrowed the language of 'secure rights' and 'secure claims' from James Nickel, who uses it to articulate four areas in which, in his view, persons have secure, but abstract moral claims upon others: (a) secure claim to have a life; (b) a secure claim to lead one's life; (c) a secure claim against severely cruel or degrading treatment; and (d) a secure claim against severely unfair treatment. Nickel argues that these four abstract rights are 'secure' in the sense that they do not have to be earned through membership or good behaviour and their availability does not depend on that person's ability to generate utility or other good consequences. However, Nickel does qualify his view on their 'security'; he says that, although these claims do not depend on good behaviour 'claims to liberty can be justifiably suspended upon conviction of a crime'. See J Nickel, 'Poverty' (n 2); J Nickel, *Human Rights* (n 2) ch 9. This language is more attractive than that of 'inalienable rights' because, unlike the former, the latter implies that a person not only could not lose rights through poor conduct, but also could not voluntarily forfeit rights. Since the voluntary relinquishment of a right is a distinct issue from that of forfeiture through poor conduct, it is useful to have a distinct description that allows that rights can be immune to the latter, while remaining agnostic about the former.

[5] J Ober, 'How to Aggregate Knowledge in an Epistemic Democracy' (APSA paper 2008), online: convention2.allacademic.com/one/apsa/apsa08. Ober states that, typically, the majority response when asked if an ostracism was necessary in a given year was 'no'. Only about 15 ostracisms are known to have occurred during the 180 years of the Athenian democracy. During the period of his exile, an expelled citizen's property was not confiscated; his family could remain in Athens; and ostensibly he suffered no real loss of status.

exclusion, isolation and deprivation. In Athens, the practice of democratic banishment was not a formal part of the criminal justice system; there was no declaration of fault, no trial and no offering of a defence. And, when the period of banishment ended, the banished member could return to the city without stigma.[6] The procedure was essentially a pre-emptive measure designed to neutralize political conflicts that might pose risks to the community.[7] By contrast, in contemporary societies including Canada, much harsher ways of forcibly socially marginalizing or socially depriving persons are practised, and they do form formal parts of the criminal justice system. In contemporary Western societies, banishment is in fact a comparatively modest (and fairly rare) form of socially privative punishment. One example of its use is the 2010 case of Regina resident Gerald Klein, who was banished from his home city for one year for harassing a woman through three decades. In imposing this unusual peace bond, Dennis Fenwick J stated that 'The world's a large place. There's lots of places for Mr Klein to go'.[8] Such a view rests on the assumption that another community will be willing to accept, house and employ (or otherwise provide for) Mr Klein. That assumption may be reasonable in this case, but it nevertheless disregards the significance of this man's social ties, relationships and interdependences. Commenting on the judgment, Klein's lawyer Brian Pfefferle observed that:

> There's something about your home that can't be replaced . . . your friends, your family, the support network. And those are things that Mr Klein clearly does have in Regina that he does not have to the same extent in Saskatoon or any other city . . . Essentially being thrown out of Regina is akin to being sent to jail because you're removed from the people that you have contact with, removed from the people that you love, the freedoms that you enjoyed are taken away from you.[9]

The punishment imposed on Klein may have risked social deprivation, but it is far less severe than other kinds of socially privative punishments that are practised in Western democracies including Canada, and most particularly practised in the United States as in the examples outlined below.

The first is long-term solitary confinement, which, as the empirical evidence indicates, tends to cause persons to suffer acute psychological and physical deterioration.[10] Prisoners of war and long-term incarcerated offenders often report on their release that they initially experience solitary confinement with despondency and depression, but over time begin to feel themselves disintegrating. They sleep

[6] Plutarch Liues 135, 'This manner of banishment for a time, called Ostracismon, was no punishment for any faulte committed, but a . . . taking away of the enuie of the people' (T North tr, 1579) in *The Oxford English Dictionary*, online: oed.com/viewdictionaryentry/Entry/133172.

[7] Ober, 'Epistemic Democracy' (n 5).

[8] JG Pruden, 'Man banished from Regina after woman stalked for 35 years' *Regina Leader-Post* (9 August 2010).

[9] B Pacholik, 'No Christmas homecoming for banished stalker: Sask. judge reserves decision' *Montreal Gazette* (9 December 2010).

[10] For a general critique of the use of 'special, maximum-security' prisons in the United States, see R Lippke, 'Against Supermax' (2004) 21 *The Journal of Applied Philosophy* 109–24. See also, R Lippke, *Rethinking Imprisonment* (Oxford, Oxford University Press, 2007).

over 12 hours a day, forget facts and memories and lack the energy to read, eat or move. Some begin to hallucinate, have panic attacks and mutilate themselves.[11] Some go into a semi-catatonic state and become unable to respond to basic instructions. These individual accounts are corroborated by scientific studies which indicate that acute loneliness, understood as perceived social isolation, generates the same threat response as pain, thirst, hunger or fear; it sets off a chain of anxiety-inducing physiological reactions known as the 'fight or flight' response. Chronic loneliness is associated with obesity, the progression of Alzheimer's disease, increased vascular resistance, elevated blood pressure,[12] diminished immunity, a reduction in independent living, alcoholism, depression, suicidal ideation and behaviour, and mortality in older adults.[13] No doubt factors other than the solitude could account for some of a person's deterioration in solitary confinement, but there is a commonality among persons' recollections of long-term solitary confinement, namely, that they report it to be as agonising as torture.[14] And, for many, their psychological and emotional deterioration continues to affect them long after their release. One recent case of solitary confinement in Canada is that of James Bacon who was held in near total isolation for several months at the Surrey, BC, pre-trial detention centre. In this case, the isolation was not imposed as a punishment since it preceded Bacon's trial for gun offences. In June 2010, Bacon successfully argued that his pre-trial detention in solitary confinement breached his rights under the Canadian Charter of Rights and Freedoms.[15]

[11] In his memoir, journalist Terry Anderson reports on his solitary confinement in prison: 'The mind is a blank. Jesus, I always thought I was smart. Where are all the things I learned, the books I read, the poems I memorized? There's nothing there, just a formless, gray-black misery. My mind's gone dead. God, help me'. Cited from A Gawande, 'Hellhole: The United States holds tens of thousands of inmates in long-term solitary confinement. Is this torture?' *The New Yorker* (30 March 2009).

[12] Socio-neurological studies, such as those conducted by John Cacioppo, indicate that the blood pressure of lonely people can be as much as 30 points higher than that of people with healthy social connections. See, J Cacioppo, 'Research Summary' (Faculty of Psychology, University of Chicago) online: psychology.uchicago.edu/ people/faculty/cacioppo/index.shtml.

[13] Cacioppo states that human beings, whose abject dependency at birth is the longest of any species and who are dependent throughout life on conspecifics for survival and prosperity do not fare well when they either are living solitary lives or perceive themselves to be living in isolation. 'The average person spends about 80% of waking hours in the company of others, and the time with others is preferred to the time spent alone . . . Social isolation, in contrast, is associated not only with lower subjective well-being . . . but with broad based-morbidity and mortality'. Loneliness, Cacioppo notes, has also been associated with gene expression including the under-expression of genes that bear anti-inflammatory glucocorticoid response elements and the over-expression of genes bearing pro-inflammatory response elements. He concludes that social environment (and persons' perception of their social environment) is fundamentally involved in the sculpting, activation and inhibition of basic structures and processes in the human brain and body. For extensive references, see Cacioppo, 'Research Summary', ibid.

[14] According to Gawande, 'Hellhole' (n 11), a US military study of 140 naval aviators imprisoned in Vietnam reported that 'they found social isolation to be as torturous and agonizing as any physical abuse they suffered'.

[15] K Bolan, 'Judge rules Jamie Bacon's rights violated by treatment in jail' *Vancouver Sun* (10 June 2010). Mark McEwan J of the BC Supreme Court stated that BC Corrections had breached James Bacon's Charter rights on several fronts 'by creating circumstances and maintaining the petitioner in circumstances that manifestly threaten the security of his person (which includes both a physical and a psychological dimension) by the unlawful deprivation of his rights for an unlawful purpose'. For an

A second, severe mode of socially privative punishment commonly practised in prisons – though not formally sanctioned within Western democratic criminal justice systems – does not take the form of isolation, but rather that of brutality and degradation. Prison conditions that are marked by extreme brutality, hostility, degradation and cruelty are socially privative because the persons who endure them are deprived of minimally adequate access to the ordinary kinds of supportive social interaction that make for a minimally decent human life free from extreme degradation and cruelty. Data on the US and other Western countries indicate that tens of thousands of offenders are held in restrictive social conditions marked by brutality and hostility.[16] Recognizing that certain socially 'inclusive' conditions are nonetheless socially privative, enables us to assess the legitimacy of a person's accepting or even welcoming such conditions. Just as voluntary acceptance of social isolation should be looked at with some scepticism,[17] so too should acceptance of an extremely brutal or hostile social environment. It must be considered in relation to the range and value of the person's available options and her ability to assess those options. For instance, putting an offender in a prison cell with a deranged inmate can be likened – forgive the analogy – to giving a starving person contaminated water to drink. In neither case does the provision meet the relevant need. And yet, many persons who endure solitary confinement in prison report that, for them, any companion, no matter how horrific, is better than no companion.[18]

This last observation highlights a distinctive feature of the logic of the harm of forced social deprivation, namely, that the risk and reality of harm for any one person suffering this treatment is less when others are similarly treated. To make this point vivid, consider the proverbial desert island on which a bunch of shipwrecked hopefuls form a community. At some point, the community decides to punish one person, Robinson, for some offence, by socially isolating him. They do this either by banishing him to a neighbouring uninhabited island or by confining him alone within a large enclosure. In doing so, they force him to struggle for survival without the companionship, pooling of epistemic and physical resources and noble sense of purpose that come with interdependent social life. But, if they ostracize Crusoe along with Robinson, then Robinson and Crusoe each have the

examination of the use of segregation and isolation in Canadian federal penitentiaries, see M Jackson, *Justice Behind the Walls* (Vancouver, Douglas & McIntyre, 2002). For a comment on the ongoing use of solitary confinement in US prisons, see J Casella and J Ridgeway, 'No Evidence of National Reduction in Solitary Confinement' (15 June 2010) *Solitary Watch*, online: solitarywatch.com/2010/06/15/no-evidence-of-national-reduction-in-solitary-confinement/. Statistics on the number of convicted offenders held in long-term solitary confinement in the United States range from 20,000 to 120,000.

[16] For an examination of abuse in US prisons, see 'The Report of the Commission on Safety and Abuse in America's Prisons' (2006), online: prisoncommission.org/. See also Jackson, *Walls*, ibid.

[17] Brian Barry observes that voluntary self-exclusion is to be looked at with some scepticism. If the prevailing social context is one of discrimination and hostility, then a withdrawal from that environment may be voluntary, but the context makes it little different from non-voluntary exclusion. See B Barry, 'Social Exclusion, Social Isolation, and the Distribution of Income' in P Agulnik and J Hills (eds), *Understanding Social Exclusion* (Oxford, Oxford University Press, 2002).

[18] Gawande, 'Hellhole' (n 11).

prospect of being companion and helpmate to the other. And, if they ostracize Friday along with them too, then prospects improve even more for each of them and for the trio as a whole. Indeed, assuming that there is no scarcity of resources and no homicidal behaviour among those ostracized, their prospects for survival and good life become greater the more people thus ostracized by the original group (up to the point where no new additions to the rejected group will improve on their individual and collective conditions). It is because social interaction, inclusion and interdependency are so central to human life that a person's condition radically changes when she has the prospect of at least one companion.[19] The fact that *ceteris paribus* social isolation of two persons together risks or causes less harm overall and less harm for each than does the isolation of one alone shows how this kind of harming contrasts with many typical kinds of harming such as causing direct injury or death since doing the latter to more than one person does not lessen the harm done to any one person thus harmed.[20]

These observations about harm do not settle a consequentialist debate about the normativity of social deprivation as a mode of lawful punishment, since such a debate must attend to consequences other than those affecting the socially deprived person. The issue for consequentialists in the context of criminal justice is whether social deprivation can be expected to serve such aims as promoting general wellbeing, stability and general deterrence from wrongdoing no less well than otherwise. If the real or expected consequences of solitarily confining an offender were no less good than those expected from any alternative measure, then solitary confinement would be acceptable, and indeed obligatory, within simple consequentialist frameworks. The difficulty in affirming the antecedent of this conditional is that it is vulnerable to counter-evidence of the correlative variety, such as the fact that penal systems that impose very harsh punishments such as solitary confinement typically have higher recidivism rates and higher violent crime rates than do systems that eschew solitary confinement and, in general, impose milder punishments.[21] And, the data about solitary confinement in particular suggest that it not only does not deter offending, but creates new risks of greater and more deranged wrongdoing since it often leaves persons unable to lead socially integrated lives.[22]

Of course, irrespective of the empirical data, such crude consequentialist calculations are inadequate in being insensitive to salient normative factors such as intentions, the moral quality of acts in themselves, personal commitments, role-related duties, and rights. Taking a Kantian line, for example, we may argue that

[19] Of course, at T2, Crusoe and Friday may decide not to engage with Robinson, in which case he faces the same level of risk as when he excluded alone at T1.

[20] That said, in non-lethal cases, there may be both the derivative comfort for each victim of knowing she was not alone and the social benefits of having her experience be unexceptional. The point here is simply that social deprivation risks and causes less harm when there are other people willing to engage with you; these may be other ostracized people, or other people previously ostracized, or other people who simply are not part of the group that has isolated you.

[21] Gawande, 'Hellhole' (n 11).

[22] ibid.

there is a categorical prohibition against modes of lawful punishment that either threaten or undermine persons' abilities to lead autonomous lives. Since, in general, long-term socially privative punishment of the two forms described above can render a person unable to respond to instructions let alone appreciate the moral quality of her acts, such punishment fails to treat her as a reasoning agent; it fails to engage with her in a way that allows her to reflect on the reasons not to act as she did. Taking a different, non-consequentialist line that focuses not on our duties to persons as ends in themselves, but on persons' rights as persons, we may argue that there are human rights against modes of treatment that deny a person minimally adequate access to supportive social interaction and inclusion because such access is necessary for a minimally decent human life. It is to this position that I now turn.

II A HUMAN RIGHT AGAINST SOCIAL DEPRIVATION

As just noted, my case for the existence of a human right against social deprivation centres around the claim that human beings have a right to those conditions that are necessary for the realisation of a minimally decent human life, and that, irrespective of whatever else comprises a minimally decent human life, having minimally adequate access to supportive social inclusion is a necessary condition for such a life. More specifically, the right against social deprivation is not simply a negative right to be left free to endeavour to establish minimally adequate interpersonal ties; it is also a positive right to be provided, according to one's needs, with minimally adequate interpersonal contact and inclusion when one cannot secure it for oneself. For persons who have adequate means of securing their basic needs for social contact, little intervention by states or other parties is necessary or desirable. But for persons who lack the means to secure their basic needs or whose social ties have been forcibly severed, there is a duty to ensure the satisfaction of the basic minimum need for meaningful access to social contact. Consequently, in the context of criminal justice, the state's human rights obligations come into play unequivocally because offenders are under direct state control; the state is engaged in the practice of lawful punishment which, if not regulated appropriately, can result in the social deprivation of offenders.[23]

Even though the empirical and normative case for the human right against social deprivation is strong I believe, nevertheless this right is not a commonly recognized one. It is neither highlighted in contemporary theoretical debates about socio-economic human rights, nor identified as a distinctive right in most international treaties. No mention is made of interpersonal social rights in either the Universal Declaration of Human Rights or the International Covenant on Economic, Social, and Cultural Rights, which may be a reflection more of the

[23] I thank Virginia Mantouvalou for clarifying this point.

historical context in which these documents were written than of any general scepticism about interpersonal social needs as grounds for human rights. Only a few international documents refer to these social needs. For instance, Article 30 of the European Social Charter states that 'everyone has the right to protection against poverty and social exclusion'. However, the conjunction of 'poverty' and 'social exclusion' in this Article indicates that the Article may be taken to refer principally to the kinds of social marginalization that tends to accompany economic deprivation and not to persons' needs for interpersonal social inclusion irrespective of their economic situation. Social deprivation is neither unique to nor universal among the economically deprived.

Although the right against social deprivation cannot be subsumed under economic rights, it might be subsumable under, or derivative of, other presently recognized human rights (whose philosophical respectability I shall not question here). Could the right against social deprivation be subsumed under a right to basic education, or a right to basic health, or a right to physical security? Could it be subsumed under a right against torture, cruel and inhuman treatment, or some combination thereof? Constrained by space, I shall consider these various options only briefly. Human needs for interpersonal contact and care cannot be subsumed under a right to basic education for two reasons. First, this would require a highly non-standard notion of 'basic education' since our social developmental needs as children and young adults are akin to our subsistence needs. Just as adequate food is needed for us to grow taller and healthier, so too adequate social contact and care are needed for us to acquire language as well as the physical, social, emotional and cognitive abilities necessary for a minimally decent human life (which makes punishment through social deprivation particularly abhorrent when it is imposed on a young person). It is no more appropriate to say that socializing us during critical stages of development is part of 'basic education' than it is to say that feeding us is part of 'basic education'. Second, subsuming social needs under education needs or even, more broadly, under developmental needs would imply that, once we have developed into functioning adults, we no longer have social needs or, rather, we no longer have social needs that ground human rights. But, our social needs are not exclusively developmental. As the above empirical data indicate, the need of all persons for social contact and inclusion exists independently of any developmental or educative purpose it may serve, that is, the need for protection against social deprivation holds even for adequately developed and educated adults. The social nature of human life is not a contingent reality, but a necessary part of minimally decent human existence.

At first glance, it is more plausible to suppose that the right against social deprivation may derive from, or be subsumed under, the right to basic health since it seems that, in general, basic physical and mental health cannot be either achieved or fully maintained without minimally adequate access to social contact and inclusion. However, subsuming social needs under health needs could distract us from the distinctive interdependent nature and value of social interaction. Or, more optimistically, it could enable us better to recognize the distinctive interpersonal dimensions of our health needs. Thus, for example, if we appreciate the impact that our social needs tend to have on our health, then we might take a different view of the use of quarantine. Even though holding contagious patients in some form of quarantine may be necessary to contain the spread of a disease, we may be less likely to dismiss as a regrettable externality the likely negative impact on the persons who are thus isolated. That said, there is a more general concern about subsuming social needs under health needs, which is that social needs are not purely health related. Acknowledging the significance of persons' interpersonal social needs is part of respecting persons as persons, whose identities and autonomous choices draw much of their content, meaning and significance from meaningful opportunities for social inclusion.

Let me turn briefly to rights against torture and cruel, inhuman, or degrading treatment. In the context of criminal justice, the right against social deprivation does seem to be derivative of these rights taken together as a set. Subsuming the right against social deprivation under the right against torture alone would invite an overly narrow interpretation of the content of such rights as well as of the criminal justice contexts in which they are at issue and the kinds of suffering that social deprivation engenders. (As an aside, there is but weak international recognition of the inhumanity of solitary confinement as a mode of punishment. Principle Seven of the UN Basic Principles for the Treatment of Prisoners states insipidly that 'efforts addressed to the abolition of solitary confinement as a punishment, or to the restriction of its use, should be undertaken and encouraged'.) As noted above, social deprivation in prisons occurs not only through long-term solitary confinement – which may well be regarded as torturous – but through ongoing exposure to brutal and degrading social conditions that are not isolating, and which presumably are not torturous as such in most cases. To recognize that the latter conditions constitute rights violations, we must give sufficient attention to the content of the rights against cruel, inhuman and degrading treatment. Forced social deprivation of both the solitary and non-solitary variety is cruel, inhuman and degrading in itself and renders a person vulnerable to other forms of cruel, degrading and brutal treatment; protection from social deprivation is necessary to reduce persons' exposure to, and vulnerability to, treatment that persons credibly have a secure claim not to suffer.[24] That forced social deprivation is cruel, inhuman and degrading shows that, in the eyes of human rights law, the right against (forced) social deprivation would not be principally a social and economic (second generation) human right, since those rights are typically understood to centre around material conditions and economic resources. Rather, in the eyes of human rights law, the right against social deprivation would be a civil and political (first generation) human right and hence would receive more expansive and privileged protection under human rights law than do socio-economic rights.[25]

[24] Nickel, 'Poverty' (n 2); Nickel, *Human Rights* (n 2).

[25] I thank Virginia Mantouvalou for drawing my attention to this point. In her response to my paper at the Royal Holloway 'Margins of Citizenship' conference, she observed that the European

Although each of the human rights just discussed – basic education, health, torture, cruel and inhuman treatment – touches on an important dimension of persons' interpersonal social needs, none of them seems to capture fully the core content and distinctive value of the right against social deprivation. Thus, assuming that we have considered the most viable candidate 'cover-rights', there is reason to conclude, at a minimum, that the right against social deprivation is a distinct human right that protects persons' fundamental interests in having minimally adequate access to supportive interpersonal social interaction and inclusion. With this explication of the right against social deprivation in hand, let us turn to the issue of its security. In the next section, I elaborate my view that the right against social deprivation is secure in the sense that it does not depend on either good community standing or good behaviour.

III A SECURE RIGHT AGAINST SOCIAL DEPRIVATION

Secure rights are distinct from social and political privileges which flow from good standing and good behaviour, and which can be retracted or withheld when a person damages her standing in the community. Unlike political privileges, secure rights are not so vulnerable. They persist even when a person acts wrongly or lacks good standing; in other words, a person cannot forfeit these rights through poor conduct or loss of community standing. Several arguments can be marshalled in support of the view that the right against social deprivation is a secure right.

First, one argument for the security of this right is that it is a human right and that all human rights are secure in virtue of their special moral status. Human rights are claims that protect human beings' most fundamental needs and interests. Part of their purpose, as Peter Jones puts it, is to provide guaranteed safeguards for persons, particularly against the abuse of political power.[26] For such guarantees to provide the security they promise, it would seem that they must be secure and immune to changes in persons' conduct, community standing, or the declared needs of the community. Although attractive, this argument may claim too much for human rights, and may have some prima facie counterintuitive, though possibly legitimate, implications. For instance, if the right to life were secure, then a person would not forfeit that right were he to attempt to kill another person, which would mean that the victim who successfully defends herself and kills this attacker breaches the attacker's right not to be killed. For another

Court of Human Rights has considered one dimension of social deprivation in prison, namely, whether lengthy solitary confinement in prison violates Art 3 of the European Charter on Human Rights (ECHR), which prohibits inhuman and degrading treatment. She observed that, whereas the ECHR does not protect second-generation socio-economic human rights, it does protect first-generation human rights and thus the Court could afford legal protection to applicants through a civil and political rights procedure.

[26] P Jones, *Rights* (London, Palgrave, 1994). Jones does raise doubts about the security of all human rights.

instance, in the context of criminal justice, if all human rights including property rights and movement rights were secure, then any imposition of hard treatment as a form of punishment, be it a fine or (in serious cases) temporary incarceration, would be unjustified on the grounds that it is a human rights violation.

Despite these implications, we should not dismiss this argument too quickly. If indeed rights arise from those interests that are sufficiently strong to ground duties in others, and if, as I have argued, a person's interests in having minimally adequate access to supportive social contact are sufficiently strong to give rise to a basic right against social deprivation, then a person's right against social deprivation remains as long as she has sufficiently strong interest in social contact. It is only when she ceases to have the interests that give rise to such a right that she may be said not to have such a right. Her right may well be overridden by more pressing considerations, which may include, but are not limited to, others' rights. But that is a separate matter from whether her right still exists. The existence of her right depends on the presence of the relevant interests. And, there is reason to doubt that a person's interests in social interaction and inclusion lessen or disappear once she acts wrongly. Indeed, it is more plausible that a person's interests in social interaction and inclusion become stronger once she acts wrongly since such inclusion may serve to restore her sense of self-respect, may aid her to understand the wrongness of her act, may help her to overcome any proclivity for such behaviour, and may give her responsibilities and a sense of empowerment that reduce the likelihood of such behaviour.

Second, although it may be difficult to argue that all human rights are secure, it is plausible to hold that at least some human rights are secure. Indeed, the notion of a secure human right that cannot be forfeited through poor conduct is not controversial. Two uncontroversial and related examples of secure rights are the right to equal recognition before the law and the right to a fair trial. A third example that should be uncontroversial, despite recent debates, is the right against torture. These rights are not forfeited when a person acts wrongly. Indeed, the second of these rights – the right to a fair trial – only comes into play once a person is accused of acting wrongly. Thus, it is reasonable to think that other human rights, and certainly fundamentally important rights such as the right against social deprivation, may also not be conditional on good behaviour.

Third, the right against social deprivation is an important one on which the meaningful exercise of other human rights, such as personal security, subsistence, movement, employment, education, political participation and family life, depends. In consequence, interference with this right not only undermines it, but undermines the rights that are conditional on it, having a more expansive, damaging and morally problematic impact on the person than may be initially supposed. In brief, a society cannot deny a person adequate access to minimally supportive social contact and inclusion without threatening or undermining many, if not all, of her rights, most, if not all, of which society would have no intention or wish to impinge upon, and no grounds for impinging upon, by denying her adequate access to social contact.

Recognizing the security of the right against social deprivation has significant implications for criminal justice. Let me explore the implications by addressing some possible objections to the claims outlined above. These objections are the 'Problem of the Purposes of Punishment' and the 'Problem of the Intolerable Person'.

IV OBJECTIONS

The Problem of the Purposes of Punishment begins with the observation that a central insight of retributivism is said to be that the legitimate response to culpable wrongdoing is to suspend normal relations with an offending person until that person assumes the restorative responsibilities that flow from the wrongdoing.[27] On a typical interpretation, suspension of normal relations means withdrawing the respect and recognition that are otherwise appropriate to relations with that person. This is what it is to blame someone, and to be blameworthy is to lose the claim not to be subject to such a withdrawal of respect and recognition.[28] In serious cases, it is held to be acceptable, if not obligatory, retributively to ostracize, isolate or exile persons who engage in culpable wrongdoing so as to respond proportionally and to convey the appropriate degree of censure for the offence. If the use of social deprivation in punishment is, by nature, unjustifiable on the grounds that it constitutes a human rights violation, then it seems that we unduly restrict the community's capacity to respond proportionally to offending.

In reply, such retributive insights can be reconciled with a rejection of social deprivation as a justifiable mode of punishment when those retributive insights are given a sufficiently narrow interpretation, according to which the suspension of normal relations need not, and indeed should not, entail the suspension of minimally adequate access to supportive social relations with the culpable wrongdoer, which it does when it takes the form of long-term solitary confinement or extremely brutal and degrading incarceration. Rather, the suspension of normal relations entails that relations become focused, as much as possible, on the responsibilities that flow from the wrongdoing. Specifically, the relations should become oriented towards providing forums and opportunities for the wrongdoer meaningfully to make good on the restorative responsibilities that are hers in light of her past conduct without denying her minimally adequate access to supportive modes of social interaction and inclusion. This kind of approach to retribution also honours a person's right to be engaged with non-coercively as a reasoning agent who is responsive to moral reasons.[29] And, it retains a direct link between

27 See, eg, C Bennett, *The Apology Ritual* (Cambridge, Cambridge University Press, 2008).

28 See, eg, T Scanlon, *Moral Dimensions: Permissibility, Meaning, Blame* (Cambridge MA, Harvard University Press, 2008).

29 A practical model for this interpretation of the retributive insight can be found in some European penal systems which eschew the harsher methods of Anglo-American systems in favour of practices

the wrong done and the kind of punishment imposed in response, thereby giving the correct meaning to the communication of blame. This approach to punishment does not challenge the use of all socially limited forms of punishment; rather it focuses on the *minimum* level of adequate access to social inclusion, a level which falls far below what is typical or 'normal'. Thus, this approach rules out the use of socially limited punishments which undermine the base threshold for minimally adequate access to supportive social contact.[30]

The second problem is the Problem of the Intolerable Person, which is fairly self-explanatory. In brief, in prison settings and in communities in general, the question at issue is: How can either the state or its delegates honour the right against social deprivation in cases where an offender is a truly abominable human being whose presence is any social setting threatens or violates the human rights of others not to be socially deprived through extremely brutal, hostile, cruel or degrading treatment? There are at least four possible responses to the Problem of the Intolerable Person. First, there may be various ways to satisfy a minimum standard of adequacy in a person's access to supportive social interaction that do not risk others' human rights or general interests; possibilities include mediated or virtual interaction, regulated group interaction and other forms of non-standard social inclusion. Second, although it might be true of some 'intolerable' people that they could not but be as they are, this may not be true of all such persons. There is considerable evidence, some of which I note above, that the ways in which a person is treated in childhood and early adulthood have a significant impact on his or her ability to lead a socially integrated life. In consequence, focusing on prevention may be as important a solution to this kind of problem as looking to ways to manage persons who are presently socially intolerable. Third, a somewhat unattractive, but nonetheless plausible response is that, in extreme cases, there may be persons for whom the human right against social deprivation cannot be fully satisfied in view of the distinctive interpersonal nature of the social opportunities that satisfaction of this right requires. The possibility that not all persons' rights against social deprivation can be fully honoured does not mean that persons have no such right. Fourth, moreover, in the context of criminal justice, the matter at issue is the duties that the state itself has not to subject persons to those kinds of treatment and conditions that fall below a credible threshold for minimally adequate access to supportive social inclusion.

Despite the practical issues that attend this approach to lawful punishment, responsibility-focused retributive responses that eschew socially privative punishment are not only more in line with, and more directly communicative of, appropriate blame and censure than socially privative measures, but are more respectful

that respect offenders' sense of honour and dignity, give those in prison a voice about their conditions, assign to them transparently meaningful responsibilities related to reparation and enable them to retain many of their familial responsibilities (in some jurisdictions, families can live with prisoners). See, eg, JQ Whitman, *Harsh Justice: Criminal Punishment and the Widening Divide between America and Europe* (New York, Oxford University Press, 2005).

[30] I thank Leslie Green for helping to clarify this point.

of the wrongdoer as a person responsive to reasons. Resort to social deprivation in lawful punishment is not only coercive, intolerant, unimaginative and radical, but conveys the inaccurate message that the basic rights of socialization are privileges to be earned rather than secure claims that are essential for a minimally decent human life.

PART III

Rethinking International Criminal Law and its Specificities

12

Universal Jurisdiction and the Duty to Govern

MICHAEL GIUDICE AND MATTHEW SCHAEFFER*

Most defences of the moral legitimacy of international criminal law suppose that the key issue lies in the tension between respect for state sovereignty and protection of universal human rights, but maintain that once human rights abuses are sufficiently serious and widespread, state sovereignty is forfeited and third parties are justified in intervening.[1] Yet, on such views not only are third parties justified in intervening, they are, for the same reason, justified in enforcing standards of international criminal law. Once a state – or more accurately its government – has shown itself unable or unwilling to protect its citizens against egregious human rights violations, it forfeits its freedom from external intervention as well as its exclusive power to create, apply and enforce law, including criminal law. So long as principles of procedural and substantive justice are met, there is no special or additional argument required to justify trying and convicting wrongdoers guilty of international crimes.

Without doubt, the issue of the legitimacy of trying and convicting offenders under international criminal law is connected to the issue of the legitimacy of intervening in the affairs of sovereign states to end or prevent wide-scale human rights abuses. However, while connected, they are separable issues, and there is a danger in framing the question about the legitimacy of international criminal law entirely in terms of a balance between respect for state sovereignty and respect for universal human rights, whereby international criminal law is justifiably enforced

* The authors would like to thank François Tanguay-Renaud and James Stribopoulos for the invitation to present an earlier version of this chapter at the conference 'Rethinking Criminal Law: Canadian Perspectives in the Philosophy of Domestic, Transnational and Criminal Law' held in Toronto in September 2010. We also owe thanks to Antony Duff for helpful comments, and the Social Sciences and Humanities Research Council of Canada for funding support.

[1] See W Lee, 'International Crimes and Universal Jurisdiction' in L May and Z Hoskins (eds), *International Criminal Law and Philosophy* (Cambridge, Cambridge University Press, 2010); A Altman and CH Wellman, 'A Defense of International Criminal Law' (2004) 115 *Ethics* 35; and D Luban, 'Fairness to Rightness: Jurisdiction, Legality, and the Legitimacy of International Criminal Law' in S Besson and J Tasioulas (eds), *The Philosophy of International Law* (Oxford, Oxford University Press, 2010).

in contexts where state sovereignty is forfeited because of human rights abuses. There are plenty of good reasons to intervene on humanitarian grounds – mainly to end or prevent serious kinds of harms – but from these it does not necessarily follow that anyone has the right or authority to attempt to try and convict offenders who might be responsible for such harms, nor does it follow that standards of criminal justice or punishment are necessarily the proper or only responses.

In what follows, we shall investigate the grounds of moral legitimacy of claims to what is known as universal jurisdiction: claims of authority made by law-applying institutions to hold wrongdoers responsible for certain crimes regardless of the place where the crimes were committed or the nationality of the wrongdoer or victim. We shall focus on Antony Duff's recent work, as he offers the only account, to the best of our knowledge, which treats the legitimacy of the right or authority to try and convict offenders of international criminal law as a distinct issue, not collapsible into the issue of the legitimacy of humanitarian intervention or the fairness of criminal law procedures.[2] We should note, however, that it is beyond the scope of this chapter to address all the aspects of Duff's view which is developed on the back of his extensive and rich work on criminal responsibility, trials and punishment.[3] Instead, we propose to focus on two particular themes in his view, one substantive and one methodological. The substantive theme is the role of community deployed in justifying claims of universal jurisdiction. The methodological theme is the tendency to frame the issue of the moral and political justification in terms of an institution's right or authority to rule. We will suggest that Duff's appeal to a moral community is problematic, and that we also have good reason to resist framing the issue of the legitimacy of claims of universal jurisdiction in terms of a right to rule. Ultimately we aim to show that an account of a duty to govern might be a more apt way of assessing the justification of claims of universal jurisdiction.

The chapter is divided into five sections. In the first section, we identify some assumptions about international criminal law which we will not defend but which we believe are shared by others working on the issue of universal jurisdiction. In the second section, we will examine Duff's sophisticated account of the role of community in justifying trials and punishment. We will suggest that while he may be right to be sceptical of any sort of global or universal political community to which international criminals are legitimately called to answer, the core case for the legitimacy of universal jurisdiction cannot rest solely on defending the idea of a universal moral community of humanity. In the third section we will take up the second theme identified above, regarding the methodological issue of how to frame the moral and political issue of universal jurisdiction. Here we will argue that there are significant limitations to viewing the moral and political issue of the

[2] See RA Duff, 'Authority and Responsibility in International Criminal Law' in S Besson and J Tasioulas (eds), *The Philosophy of International Law* (Oxford, Oxford University Press, 2010).

[3] See, eg, RA Duff, *Trials and Punishments* (Cambridge, Cambridge University Press, 1986); RA Duff, *Punishment, Communication, and Community* (Oxford, Oxford University Press, 2001); RA Duff, *Answering for Crime: Responsibility and Liability in the Criminal Law* (Oxford, Hart Publishing, 2007).

legitimacy of universal jurisdiction in terms of an institution's right or authority to rule. In the fourth section we will propose an alternative account of the legitimacy of universal jurisdiction, what we will call the duty to govern approach, recently explored by Leslie Green. In the fifth and final section we will explore some of the implications of thinking about universal jurisdiction in terms of a duty to govern, with particular attention to the International Criminal Court (ICC).[4]

I SOME ASSUMPTIONS

A comprehensive account of the morality of claiming and exercising universal jurisdiction would require several elements, including an account of the nature of criminal wrongdoing, justification of the use of criminal law to respond to certain forms of serious moral wrongdoing, an account of the value and limits of state sovereignty and its relation to the morality of international law in general, identification and defence of rule of law limits to criminal law and its procedures, as well as rich empirical investigation of the successes and failures of law-applying institutions which act internationally. Clearly this is a large project, and one which we will not attempt here. Instead, we will identify some key assumptions, hopefully uncontroversial, but essential so that we can then focus on the two themes we have identified above. The assumptions are as follows:

1. **Assumption One:** In states torn apart by war or characterized by widespread human rights abuses, there are typically key actors whose wrongful acts or omissions ought to be addressed by means of criminal law. Notice that this assumption does not suppose that calling key actors to answer for their criminal conduct is the only response or step required to address the ills of war-torn states and widespread human rights abuses, nor does it suppose that all who participated ought to be held criminally responsible rather than called to answer in some other way (for example, through reconciliation, restoration, etc).[5]
2. **Assumption Two:** Some offences are universally and objectively morally wrong (for example, genocide and torture). With this assumption, we intend to put to the side any potential issues of ethical or cultural relativity relating to the moral wrongness of certain acts or omissions.

[4] We should note that the expression 'universal jurisdiction' is somewhat mis-used when applied to the ICC, as the term is typically associated with the jurisdiction claimed by particular state institutions, and the ICC's jurisdiction is typically characterized simply as 'international jurisdiction' by international criminal lawyers. However, since our primary concern is with the concept of universal jurisdiction and not particular uses of the expression, we shall refer throughout to 'universal jurisdiction'.

[5] See D Robinson, 'Serving the Interests of Justice: Amnesties, Truth Commissions, and the International Criminal Court' in J Harrington, M Milde and R Vernon (eds), *Bringing Power to Justice? The Prospects of the International Criminal Court* (Montreal and Kingston, McGill-Queen's University Press, 2006).

3. **Assumption Three:** International or domestic institutions, if their exercise of universal jurisdiction can be shown to be legitimate at all, should exercise universal jurisdiction only if a particular state is unable or unwilling itself to address effectively and justly criminal wrongdoing within its borders or involving its nationals. Thus we accept the force of the principle of complementarity which defines an essential part of the role and operation of the ICC.[6]
4. **Assumption Four:** Related to Assumption Three, we assume that while state sovereignty is valuable, it is not of absolute value. The exercise of sovereignty and its associated freedom from outside intervention is conditional on a state's ability and willingness to protect basic human rights.[7]
5. **Assumption Five:** Rule of law principles in the administration of criminal law ought to be respected to the greatest extent possible.[8] However, we leave it open whether the moral value of strict adherence to rule of law principles ought, under certain stringent conditions, to give way to competing moral demands of justice.[9]

At most, the foregoing assumptions set in place some necessary conditions for the morally legitimate exercise of universal jurisdiction (Assumptions One, Two and Three) as well as considerations to bear in mind in approaching the question of the moral justification of claims to universal jurisdiction (Assumptions Four and Five). What they do not establish, however, is an account of the sufficient conditions for the morally justified exercise of universal jurisdiction, for as Duff observes, they do not provide an answer to the question of *who has the right or standing* to try wrongdoers whose acts or omissions have taken place anywhere in the world, and particularly acts and omissions by and against persons with no connection to the institution claiming universal jurisdiction. In the next section we turn to Duff's account of the role of community in justifying the right or standing to try.

II THE ROLE OF COMMUNITY

Duff is sceptical of many of the prominent views of the legitimacy of universal jurisdiction, yet he nonetheless defends the view – which he has developed extensively in the context of states – that wrongdoers can be properly tried and pun-

[6] See the Rome Statute of the International Criminal Court 1998, A/CONF.183/9, art 1; B Schiff, *Building the International Criminal Court* (Cambridge, Cambridge University Press, 2009) 115–17; and A Cassese, *International Criminal Law* (Oxford, Oxford University Press, 2003) 351–53.

[7] See, eg Lee, 'International Crimes' (n 1). For a more general account of recognitional legitimacy of states in international law based on respect for basic human rights, see A Buchanan, *Justice, Legitimacy, and Self-Determination* (Oxford, Oxford University Press, 2004).

[8] See, eg, Luban, 'Fairness to Rightness' (n 1).

[9] See Altman and Wellman, 'A Defense' (n 1) 51–62.

ished through a communicative process which (i) treats them as rational and responsive agents and (ii) is conducted by members of their community or institutions acting on behalf of the community of which the wrongdoers are members.[10] We fully accept (i), so we will not examine it here. Regarding (ii), Duff identifies the relevance of the issue of standing with the following helpful analogy:

> Suppose that a group of my neighbours, worried about the decline in marital fidelity, take it upon themselves to bring local adulterers to book, and turn their attention to me, as an alleged adulterer. I might not deny that adultery is wrong, or that I am an adulterer who must answer for his adultery to those whose business it is – to my wife and family, to our mutual friends. But I might reasonably insist that it is not my neighbours' business: they have no right to call me to answer for my adultery; nor can the fairness of their procedures give them that right.[11]

The same is true, Duff argues, in the context of criminal law:

> Now a criminal trial . . . should be understood as a process which calls alleged wrongdoers to answer charges of wrongdoing, and to answer for such wrongdoing if it is proved against them. The legitimacy of that process depends both on its procedural fairness, and on the court's authority to call the defendant to answer; a deficiency in one of these dimensions cannot be compensated by adequacy, or even perfection, in the other.[12]

Part of Duff's message here is that accounts of the legitimacy of international criminal law, and its associated idea of universal jurisdiction, which attempt to 'bootstrap' from the fairness of its procedures are misguided, as they fail to answer the question of who has the right or authority to try and convict offenders. In Duff's view, the issue of who has the right to try and convict is essentially connected to the issue of what makes some particular wrong a crime:

> Crimes are 'public' wrongs, not in the sense that they harm 'the public' as distinct from any individual victims, but in the sense that they are wrongs that concern the 'public', ie, all members of the polity, in virtue of their shared membership; the criminal trial is the forum in which we formally call each other to account, as citizens, for such wrongs.[13]

In the context of a sovereign state – especially a liberal democratic state – the account of crimes as wrongs which concern the public explains well why jurisdiction rests primarily with the state: it 'is why the theft committed by a Polish citizen against a fellow Pole in Poland is not morally, as it is not legally, within the jurisdiction of English courts'.[14] At the international level, Duff follows others[15] in supposing that no political community – comparable to the sovereign state – exists, and so instead we must look not to a political community, but a moral community of humanity to justify the standing of law-applying institutions

[10] Duff, 'Authority and Responsibility in International Criminal Law' (n 2).
[11] ibid 591.
[12] ibid 591–92.
[13] ibid 595.
[14] ibid 595.
[15] See, eg, Luban, 'Fairness to Rightness' (n 1) 579.

claiming universal jurisdiction.[16] Where crimes of a particularly serious nature occur, such as crimes of genocide or torture, Duff supposes that others not connected by nationality are nonetheless properly concerned since such crimes are wrongs which concern all of humanity. It is simply in virtue of shared humanity that state borders can be crossed in the exercise of jurisdiction.

Duff is certainly not alone in appealing to the idea of a moral community or humanity to justify international criminal law and its use of universal jurisdiction.[17] While there is disagreement about how best to explain such an idea, and what its proper terms ought to be, virtually everyone defends the idea that there are some universal moral values which protect all persons regardless of their race, gender, nationality, ethnicity, etc. Yet, there is a particular danger which such appeals face. To avoid misunderstanding, we do not deny that some such moral community or idea of humanity is a necessary condition for the legitimacy of claims of universal jurisdiction.[18] The problem, however, is that since such appeals are meant to justify claims to universal jurisdiction in conditions where there is no political community, there is a danger of supposing that a political community is no longer needed because it has been replaced by a moral community. As we shall argue, appeal to a moral community on its own is insufficient to justify a claim to universal jurisdiction.

On Duff's account, for a wrong to count as a public, criminal wrong, 'we must be able to identify the relevant public to whom the wrongdoer is answerable: we cannot simply appeal to some impersonal demand of justice that the wrongdoer be punished'.[19] In the context of a sovereign state, the purpose of this observation is clear: it is meant to show that someone or some institutions, but not others, have the right to exercise jurisdiction. A general appeal to justice, unconstrained by boundaries of political community, is insufficient to show that wrongdoers can

[16] It is possible, however, to reject the claim that there is no global or universal political community. It is certainly true that there is no centralized global or political community, let alone a democratic one, and it is also certainly true, despite any pretensions some may hold for the United Nations, that there is no world government or world state. But neither is it true that all political communities, in which there are power-wielding institutions whose decisions affect the lives and well-beings of many persons, are systematic or self-contained in sovereign states and whose operations affect only those within its borders. The many dimensions of globalization, a vaguely defined collection of phenomena but not one without meaning, exhibit the various ways in which the decisions and actions of state institutions, institutions within states and groups of institutions of different states, including both governmental and non-governmental institutions, affect the lives and wellbeing of vast numbers of persons in different and often far away places. Such a globalized political community, while certainly nowhere near democratic nor, in many respects just, is nonetheless still a community in which the lives of persons in various distant places are connected by the actions and decisions of institutions capable of widespread influence. The trouble, we might say, is not that there is an absence of a global political community, but that the existing global community is one in which some of the most unjust inequalities and harms exist in part and parcel with existing institutions. There is, in other words, a global political community, but a highly objectionable one.

[17] See, eg, L May, *Crimes Against Humanity: A Normative Account* (Cambridge, Cambridge University Press, 2005) 81–95, especially 82.

[18] The idea of a moral community is also necessary, we believe, for claims of state jurisdiction to be justifiable.

[19] Duff, 'Authority and Responsibility in International Criminal Law' (n 2) 597.

be legitimately called to answer for their wrongdoing. If we replace the concept of 'public' with the concept of 'community', the idea remains the same: the idea of community is meant to convey the ideas of inclusion and membership, but just as importantly the ideas of borders, exclusion and non-membership.

There is something odd, then, in simply appealing to the idea of a moral community, or perhaps universal public, to justify the standing or right to try wrongdoers under the authority of universal jurisdiction. Who, or what institutions, are meant to be excluded from having that standing or right? Presumably no one, as we are all members of the moral community in virtue of our shared humanity. And this is part of the point. Appeals to the moral community or humanity are meant to show precisely that particular kinds of wrongdoing are not to be protected by appeal to the existence of particular political communities: the crime of genocide is so serious that it transcends respect for state sovereignty. This observation indeed shows the oddity of simply appealing to a community of humanity, as appeals to humanity are meant to show that particular community affiliations do not matter when it comes to certain types of crimes. The observation also reveals that there is no meaningful difference between an appeal to an impersonal demand of justice, which Duff maintains *is insufficient* to justify calling a wrongdoer to answer for their wrongdoing, and appeal to a moral community or public, which in Duff's view *is sufficient* to justify calling a wrongdoer to answer for their wrongdoing. The two collapse. Appeal to a moral community demonstrates a kind of universal concern for all persons in virtue of their humanity, but, given that an impersonal demand of justice is presumably fulfilled by and to persons, the two ideas are extensionally equivalent.

We should also spell out more clearly the coordination problem which moral communities face with the use of political power. Are all persons and all institutions, simply in virtue of being members or groups of members of the moral community, justified in claiming and exercising universal jurisdiction?[20] Assuming the answer is no, and the moral community needs agents, who, in particular, or which institutions, in particular, can justifiably act in the name of humanity? And under what conditions? In comparison, political communities tend to have solved the coordination problem of who can exercise political power: while we can always ask whether established political institutions (courts, legislatures, police, etc) can and do act legitimately in the name of the political communities they claim to represent, established institutions at least present themselves as the agents who are subject to such assessment in the first place. This makes established institutions, such as legislatures, courts and police at least necessary conditions for the legitimate exercise of political power. Without such institutions, political communities would be just as disorganized in addressing and handling certain issues, including criminal wrongdoing, as would moral communities which lack established institutions altogether.

[20] Can, for example, Richard Dawkins arrest the Pope (and perhaps even try him) on arrival in the UK for alleged crimes against humanity? See J Brean, 'Hitchens, Dawkins try for Pope's arrest during UK visit' *National Post* (12 April 2010), online: www.nationalpost.com/news/story.html?id=2789995.

There is another line of argument which reaches the same conclusion – that appeal to a moral community is insufficient to justify claims to universal jurisdiction. Duff says that crimes are wrongs that concern the public. The idea of concern, however, can be understood in one of two different ways: in either a descriptive or a normative sense. In the descriptive sense, anyone or any institution which actually is concerned would have jurisdiction to address criminal wrongdoing. However, there is no reason why such persons or institutions should fall within a single community; neither is it clear what would give any among them particular authority to address criminal wrongdoing. In the normative sense, persons or institutions have jurisdiction to address certain forms of wrongdoing if they ought to be concerned about them. In this sense, however, in the case of such serious crimes as genocide and torture, it seems clear that everyone, regardless of geography or political community, ought to be concerned. But again, what would justify any of them in particular to claim and exercise universal jurisdiction? If we add the conceptual problem about what it means to be concerned in the first place, there seems to be significant limits to its appeal.

These are, hopefully, uncontroversial observations, but their importance should not be overlooked. In particular, they point to an important conclusion: what is missing from the moral community such that it can act effectively and legitimately in responding to certain forms of wrongdoing is a set of established institutions capable of doing so. In other words, what is missing is a political community, since once the moral community acquires institutions, it acquires the sorts of things capable of exercising power in the name of the community, that is, political institutions capable of exercising political power.

To take stock at this point, we have argued that the morally legitimate exercise of universal jurisdiction requires not only an underlying moral community, but political institutions, and so a political community, which would solve the coordination problem bare moral communities face acting in the name of humanity. But of course we are not interested in just any solution to such a coordination problem: which political institutions can act legitimately – in the moral sense – in the name of the moral community? Here we arrive at the second theme to be explored: the methodological question about how best to frame the moral assessment of claims made by political institutions to exercise universal jurisdiction.

III THE RIGHT TO RULE AND DEMOCRACY

The question of the justification of claims of universal jurisdiction is typically framed in terms of a right to claim authority. As Duff says, 'by what right can English law claim authority over a Chilean torturer; by what right can English courts try and convict him?'[21] In this section, we will identify some limits to

[21] Duff, 'Authority and Responsibility in International Criminal Law' (n 2) 590–91 and 598. See also Luban, 'Fairness to Rightness' (n 1) 578; and Altman and Wellman, 'A Defense' (n 1) 45–46.

this way of putting the question, and in the next section we will offer an alternative.

To see the problem with the 'right to claim authority' approach we need to examine the concept of a right. There are two dominant, competing understandings of what a right is – the interest theory and the will or choice theory.[22] Neither view, however, is apt for explaining and evaluating claims to universal jurisdiction. According to the interest theory, most fully explained by Joseph Raz, a right exists when an individual has some interest which is sufficient to ground the duty on the part of someone else to respect, protect, or promote the individual's interest (or some aspect of it).[23] This explains why I have a right not to be tortured, as my right to bodily and psychological integrity is sufficient to ground a duty in others not to torture me, but also why I do not have a right to a sunny day, which, while a sunny day might be in my interests, it grounds no duties on anyone. Applied to claims of universal jurisdiction, it seems plain that courts, whether national or international, are not the sorts of beings which can have interests of their own, which in turn ground duties on others to obey them. Certainly courts, just like governments, are meant to act in the interests of others, and so can represent the interests of others. But, to speak of courts, or other kinds of institutions, as having rights of their own, in the sense of having sufficiently important interests, is to misuse the concept of a right.

What about the will or choice theory of rights? According to this theory, a person has a right if they possess a protected choice or liberty. For example, the practice of promising provides persons with the right to make promises, in that they have a choice of whether to make particular promises or not, or perhaps to make promises at all. Either way, it is up to them. Quite clearly this account of rights does not apply very well either to the question of the moral justification of claims to universal jurisdiction. Universal jurisdiction is a concept introduced to emphasize that crimes of the most serious nature – genocide, torture, etc – need to be addressed. These are crimes, as Duff and others say, which concern everyone in virtue of our shared humanity. To suggest that it is up to state or international institutions – which are capable of doing so – to choose whether or not to address such crimes would be nothing short of absurd.

It might be objected that those who use the concept of a right to frame the issue of the justification or legitimacy of claims to universal jurisdiction only mean to use the concept of a right in a legal, and not moral sense, as we have been discussing. In the legal sense, rights can of course be held by and given to just about anything, from persons to animals, plants and inanimate objects, and with the only condition that the right be authorized or validated by some system or source of law. If this is the case, then two responses are needed. First, it becomes unclear why appeal to a moral community is required to justify claims of universal jurisdiction, since what is needed instead is some defence of the existence of an

[22] For an overview of the debate, see M Kramer, N Simmonds and H Steiner, A *Debate over Rights: Philosophical Enquiries* (Oxford, Oxford University Press, 2000).

[23] See J Raz, *The Morality of Freedom* (Oxford, Clarendon Press, 1986) 165–92.

international legal system which authorizes claims of universal jurisdiction.[24] Secondly, for reasons we have given above, the moral justification of any such legal right to claim universal jurisdiction could not rest on identifying or appealing to any moral right which is held by a court or other institution, as courts or other institutions are not the proper bearers of moral rights.

There is one sense, however, in which it might be correct to speak of institutions having rights, understood in either an interest-based or will-based sense. If it is the case that individuals are the proper and ultimate bearers of moral rights – including the right or freedom of self-government – then the only way in which some but not others, acting through or within some institution, such as a legislature, could be justified in governing other persons is if they are chosen to govern as a result of some democratic procedure. In other words, the right to self-govern could be transferred, and so preserved, to institutions democratically created and operated. Such a right held by institutions would represent the collective interests of its subjects in self-government, and be authorized to make certain choices, or exercises certain liberties, if done in a way which represents the interests, choices or liberties of the demos.

Perhaps Duff's insistence that a wrongdoer can only be tried and convicted by members or some institution of his community indicates that it is democratic authorization which justifies the right of someone or some institution to try and convict, since as he says, 'the criminal trial is the forum in which we formally call each other to account, as citizens, for such wrongs'.[25] Democratic authorization would also seem to solve the coordination problem facing moral communities, in that it provides an answer to the question of who can justifiably act – and under what conditions – in the name of the moral community: those who are democratically chosen to do so under rules democratically created. Whether or not this is Duff's view, it is not an uncommon view to suppose that only democratic institutions are legitimate. As Allen Buchanan observes, democracy solves very neatly a central problem in political philosophy: among persons who are free and equal, how could some come to have legitimate normative power over the lives of others, if not chosen or authorized by those whose lives are affected?[26]

There are two implications to draw from the envisioned connection between democratic authorization and legitimacy. The first is that it would render suspect the legitimacy of all claims to universal jurisdiction made by states, as none of these have been democratically authorized by the international community over which they attempt to enforce standards of criminal justice, nor is it even minimally realistic to suppose that such widespread authorization would ever come about. As well as individual states, neither could the ICC be considered legitimate

[24] Here we are of course ruling out some immoderate – and likely implausible – version of natural law theory which supposes that the conditions of a moral community are identical to the conditions of an international legal system. No natural law theorist that we know of, Grotius included, has ever made such a claim, nor do we think it would be sensible to do so.

[25] Duff, 'Authority and Responsibility in International Criminal Law' (n 2) 595.

[26] Buchanan, *Justice* (n 7) 249–54.

as its democratic deficits are well known, both in its creation (while it was created by vote, not all states that voted are democratic) and operation (for example, cases can be chosen by the prosecutor alone[27] or referred by the UN Security Council, a notoriously undemocratic international institution). Notice, however, that this observation is not yet an objection to the view that democratic authorization is a necessary condition of legitimacy, as it simply might be the case that neither states' nor the ICC's claim to universal jurisdiction are legitimate to begin with. Surely this is a possibility which ought not to be ruled out. The objection comes, though, in a second observation. Is it true that only democratically authorized or operated institutions can be legitimate? An affirmative answer would seem to unduly restrict the concept, as well as the conditions of legitimacy, since there are surely other moral standards and principles which bear on an institution's legitimacy, including the protection of other basic rights besides a right to vote or participate in politics, the level of wellbeing or flourishing of persons subject to the rule of the institution, the absence of war and conflict, both within the community and with other communities, etc.[28] While democratic authorization is certainly desirable for any political institution, it seems doubtful that the legitimacy of all political institutions rests entirely or only on democratic authorization.[29]

Unfortunately, a full discussion of the relation between democracy and political legitimacy would take us beyond the scope of this chapter, but there is one final consideration worth bearing in mind. Suppose that, against the facts, state institutions and the ICC were fully democratically authorized to claim and exercise universal jurisdiction. What difference would this make to the moral legitimacy of their exercise of universal jurisdiction to try and convict persons guilty of serious international crimes such as genocide and war crimes? Likely none, and for a reason we have already introduced. Democratic authorization entitles political institutions to act in the name of their political community, but the political institutions are constrained to acting in ways which represent the will, interests and wishes of the political community. In other words, when representation is successful, it is really the political community itself whose choices and interests are governing. The problem, however, is that just as dependence on the interests and choices of particular political institutions is inappropriate as a condition of the moral legitimacy of institutional responses to serious international crimes, so is dependence on the interests and choices of particular political communities. International crimes such as genocide and war crimes, if taken seriously, would seem to demand response regardless of the particular interests and choices of particular political communities. Indeed, the grave nature of such crimes is what allows us to say, quite plausibly, that states which, by democratic means, choose

[27] Though the prosecutor's choices are subject to approval and review by the Pre-Trial Chamber. See the Rome Statute of the International Criminal Court (n 6) Arts 15 and 53.

[28] See John Simmons's account of the 'benefits of government' discussed throughout in AJ Simmons, *Moral Principles and Political Obligations* (Princeton, Princeton University Press, 1979).

[29] On the limits of democratic authorization as a requirement of political legitimacy, see Buchanan, Justice (n 7) 257–60.

not to respond are, morally speaking, failing. Democratic authorization is simply the wrong tool for the job.[30]

It is useful at this point to take stock again. In section two we showed how appeal to the idea of a moral community is insufficient to ground legitimate claims to universal jurisdiction; effective political institutions are also required. But which institutions can legitimately act in the name of the moral community? In this section we have suggested that framing the question in terms of who has the right to claim and exercise universal jurisdiction is either to misuse the concept of a right, or leads us down the unduly narrow path of justification in terms of democratic authorization. The upshot of this analysis is that on the right to rule view, there may be no institutions – state or international – which are capable of legitimately claiming universal jurisdiction. In the final two sections, however, we shall argue that the problem is not so much with existing state and international institutions, but rather with the way in which the moral issue has been typically framed.

IV THE DUTY TO GOVERN

In a recent article, Leslie Green notes that political and legal philosophers have, for too long, concentrated on only two questions a general theory of authority must answer: the question of what gives governments the right to rule and the related question of whether subjects have any general duty to obey.[31] Exploring some themes in the work of John Finnis, Green makes it clear that there is a third, and very important, question a general theory of authority must answer: under what conditions does someone or some institution have not the right, but the *duty* to govern?[32] To see how someone or some institution can come to have a fundamental duty to govern in a particular community, it may be useful to first imagine a community where no agent of the community yet exists or exercises political power. Persons in this bare, institution-less community will no doubt seek certain common goods in order to survive and flourish, which include natural resources properly distributed, public services, protected expectations and various substantive freedoms and group associations (for example, family, friendship, etc). These common goods, however, are not so easily acquired when disagreement and uncertainty about important matters permeate the community (for

[30] It might also be an outright obstacle in some cases. Consider the possibility of a democratic state which is able, without great cost to itself, to effectively and justly intervene in another state to end serious human rights violations, but whose government is unable or unwilling to do so because it lacks the political—ie, democratic—support of its citizens.

[31] L Green, 'The Duty to Govern' (2007) 13 *Legal Theory* 165.

[32] For Finnis's account of political authority, see J Finnis, *Natural Law and Natural Rights* (Oxford, Clarendon Press, 1980) 231–59. We leave for another time assessment of Finnis's view that a fundamental duty to govern entails (or grounds) a corresponding right to govern. For discussion, see Green, ibid, 179–80.

example, disagreement and uncertainty about basic institutions, how to respond to disputes and violations of social norms, etc). What is needed, if the common goods are to be enjoyed, is an institutional framework – itself a common good[33] – through which the disagreement and uncertainty about important matters can be settled.

Quite simply, there is a coordination problem in such a community that hinders access to the common goods, and the solution is a system of institutions to exercise political power. But there is another familiar dimension to the coordination problem: there might be a variety of reasonable ways to develop a system of political institutions, and the members of the community may very well disagree about this too. How, then, should some particular political institutions come to hold and exercise political power? It might be tempting to suppose that some sort of decision procedure should be adopted (for example, voting), but this misses the seriousness of the predicament. For there will be disagreement about what counts as a good decision-making procedure and when a decision-making procedure should be used, and there may even be circumstances where resorting to some sort of decision-making procedure is simply impossible (for example, if the community is in a state of civil unrest).[34] The key question then becomes: '*What* determines who should exercise political power in the community?' not 'How should the community *decide* who should exercise political power?'

It would seem, then, that political power ought to be exercised by those who can in fact effectively settle the coordination problem. As Green notes, the fundamental justification of the exercise of political power under the conditions of disagreement and uncertainty lies in a *task-efficacy* justification: if X can most effectively solve the coordination problem, X ought to exercise political power to do so. But what should we say about the normative status of those who can effectively settle the basic coordination problem? According to Green (and Finnis), they acquire a fundamental duty to govern.[35] The reason they acquire a duty ultimately rests on two facts: first, there is a serious coordination problem in the provision and enjoyment of certain common goods; and secondly, they are capable of effectively and justly providing those common goods.[36]

It is important to avoid possible misunderstanding here. On the account we are presenting, social power plays a key role in determining who should exercise political power. Now some may worry that this justification of political power may lead to varying degrees of tyranny, but this is not the case. Because political power is grounded in a duty to govern which is grounded in the need for coordinated provision and enjoyments of various important common goods, the scope of political power is clearly proscribed: an agent exercising political power (under

[33] Indeed, *the* common good, as Green notes. See, 'The Duty to Govern' (n 31) 171.

[34] ibid 178.

[35] See Green, 'The Duty to Govern' (n 31) 173; and Finnis, *Natural Law* (n 32) 246.

[36] We are here assuming that duties only exist (or typically exist) to protect, promote, provide, non-trivial goods or values, which if left unprotected, would amount to serious injustice. In this way, we identify duties from the other direction of a relation introduced earlier: duties exist when grounded in sufficiently important interests of individuals.

a duty to govern) should exercise political power only insofar as the exercise of political power is needed to provide the common goods. If an agent's exercise of political power does not or no longer satisfies this condition, their exercise of political power is not (or no longer) legitimate. Depending on the reasons for failure, the agent may simply have failed to meet their duty, for which they must now make amends, or they might have lost the duty altogether and so must relinquish political power.

No doubt there is much more to be said in fleshing out the details of the duty to govern approach to the morally legitimate exercise of political power. As Green notes, it is not so easy to judge whether any agent is capable of solving coordination problems in a community, nor is it clear what we should do when two agents are equally suited to govern.[37] Thankfully, we need not answer all of these questions here. Instead, in the next section we will return to our central question – what justifies or legitimates claims of universal jurisdiction in international criminal law – and use the opportunity to display the virtues of the duty to govern approach whose rudiments we have presented in this section.

V THE DUTY TO GOVERN AND THE ICC

The state of international criminal law is not unlike our imaginary bare, institution-less community. While international law in general has many institutions (United Nations, Organization for Security and Co-operation in Europe, World Trade Organization, etc), international criminal law is widely recognized to be in the early stages of development, with uncertain prospects. International criminal law is, then, best understood in terms of a project of political community building. Here our question arrives: who, if anyone, in international criminal law holds a duty to govern via claiming and exercising universal jurisdiction? If we recall that a duty to govern is grounded in a task-efficacy justification, we can begin to see the answer. What morally urgent task might call for the exercise of universal jurisdiction? The best answer seems to be this: because states occasionally do not or cannot hold wrongdoers responsible for egregious wrongs, there is a need to (i) create and promulgate international legal norms that prohibit egregious wrongs; (ii) monitor for unaddressed violations of these legal norms; and (iii) respond to unaddressed violations of these legal norms by calling alleged offenders to answer and holding wrongdoers criminally responsible. We can call this tripartite task the Task of International Criminal Law (TICL).

Is there anyone, or any institution, which is capable of completing TICL? There is good reason to think that an international institution is required for the job, given the fact that many states, more than occasionally, fail to prevent and subsequently address egregious moral wrongs. Even with those states which are power-

[37] Green, 'The Duty to Govern' (n 31) 175.

ful enough to enforce, even to a limited extent, international criminal law, their perceived legitimacy (that is, their sociological legitimacy) in the eyes of other states whose cooperation they need to be truly effective will not always be adequate.[38] Yet while we do not wish to rule out the possibility of states successfully claiming and exercising universal jurisdiction in sustained fashion, we would like to focus on the ICC, no doubt the most popular current contender.

The Preamble to the Rome Statute which created the ICC identifies several lofty goals, including the determination 'to put an end to impunity for the perpetrators of [serious crimes of concern to the international community]'.[39] Advocates of the Court are no less enthusiastic: Robert Johansen notes that the ICC 'could well be the most important institutional innovation since the founding of the United Nations'.[40] The problem, however, is that it seems clear that the ICC does not possess the ability to perform TICL. In terms of the components of TICL, the ICC does perform (i); and we can assume, for the sake of argument, that the ICC does a tolerable job of (ii). But real difficulty arises when it comes to (iii): trying and convicting wrongdoers. As David Wippman points out, the ICC is plagued by a variety of constraints that make it difficult to try and convict wrongdoers.[41] Two seem especially significant. First, the ICC is jurisdictionally constrained because it cannot, in most cases, try and convict citizens of non-signatory states unless it receives a referral from the UN Security Council, a referral unlikely to materialize because the United States, a permanent member of the Council and consistent critic of the ICC, possesses veto power over any possible referral. This effectively limits jurisdiction to violations within signatory states and violations outside signatory states by nationals of signatory states.[42] Secondly, the ICC is almost powerless to execute its arrest warrants and conduct investigations when signatory states or non-signatory states refuse to cooperate. Quite simply, it lacks the social power necessary to impose international criminal law.

Because the ICC cannot effectively complete TICL it may be tempting to declare that the ICC therefore has no duty to claim and exercise universal jurisdiction (since it has no duty to complete TICL). This would be a mistake. As is well known, the ICC cannot effectively complete TICL *on its own*; the support and cooperation of states, both signatory and non-signatory, is crucial for the success

[38] On this matter, then, we disagree with Win-chiat Lee who thinks it is no more difficult to justify a particular state's claim to universal jurisdiction than an international institution's. See his 'Terrorism and Universal Jurisdiction' in S Lee (ed), *Intervention, Terrorism, and Torture: Contemporary Challenges to Just War Theory* (Dordrecht, Springer, 2007) 214–15.

[39] Rome Statute of the International Criminal Court (n 6) Preamble.

[40] RC Johansen, 'A Turning Point in International Relations? Establishing a Permanent International Criminal Court' Rep No 1, 1 (Joan B Kroc Institute for International Peace Studies, 1997) quoted in WA Schabas, *An Introduction to the International Criminal Court* 3rd edn (Cambridge, Cambridge University Press, 2007) x.

[41] D Wippman, 'Exaggerating the ICC' in J Harrington, M Milde and R Vernon (eds), *Bringing Power to Justice? The Prospects of the International Criminal Court* (Montreal and Kingston, McGill-Queen's University Press, 2006) 101–08.

[42] And even then, the US has entered into several bilateral amnesty treaties with various signatory states. See Schiff, *Building the International Criminal Court* (n 6) 174–75.

of the ICC. Indeed, it would be unrealistic to suppose that the duty to address international crimes wherever they occur in the world could ever fall on any single institution. While individual states may not themselves have the sole duty to claim and exercise universal jurisdiction, the institutionalization of international criminal law – to the extent that it takes aim at a globally and morally urgent task – creates duties on the part of states (and, very likely, human rights NGOs) to assist and support the ICC.[43] Such states include both signatory and non-signatory states; the duty to support and assist could even be carried out, albeit incompletely, by states which refuse to allow their nationals to be tried by the ICC. This might strike some as further grounds for delegitimizing the ICC, but it must be remembered that international criminal law is still in its infancy, and achievement of full international criminal justice cannot be expected all at once. The most that can be done now is to identify who has a duty to do what to help bring about the goals of international criminal law. (Indeed, the ICC may even have an important role to play in identifying, and so coordinating, the particular duties of states.)

More of course remains to be said about how the duty to govern in international criminal law ought to be divided (for example, between arrest, trial and punishment) and distributed among state and international legal institutions (including but not limited to the ICC) to reach the goals of international criminal law. And while we have discussed in general terms the legitimacy of institutions themselves in their claims and exercises of universal jurisdiction, we have also left to the side the important issue of assessing the legitimacy of particular decisions made by international criminal law institutions (for example, with regard to their selectivity and impact on unsteady states in transition). These issues are certainly not to be overlooked. Our goal has been more modest, but important nonetheless: to show that given the moral urgency of international criminal law and the need to develop effective institutions and effective coordination among institutions, the terms in which we ought to assess the moral legitimacy of claims to universal jurisdiction are better cast as institutional duties, and not institutional rights.

[43] Jeremy Waldron argues that rights (which are grounded in morally important interests) often generate a multiplicity of duties. For example, the right to free speech grounds a duty on all of us to let others voice their opinions, but it also grounds a duty on all of us to praise free speech when appropriate, a duty on all of us to help those living under censorship, and so on. Indeed, the right to free speech even grounds further agent-relative duties: political authorities acquire a duty to protect and promote free speech via law, and journalists acquire a duty to expose censorship. In a similar way, we are suggesting that TICL – which is a morally urgent task because its completion will protect and promote morally important interests of people – generates a multiplicity of duties, too. In other words, TICL does not merely ground a duty on the ICC to undertake TICL; it also grounds countless duties on others to support the ICC in its morally important work. For Waldron's discussion of how rights can generate a multiplicity of duties see J Waldron, 'Rights in Conflict' (1989) 99 *Ethics* 503, 509–12.

13

International Criminal Law: Between Utopian Dreams and Political Realities

MARGARET MARTIN*

In the autumn of 2007 the current International Criminal Court (ICC) Prosecutor, Luis Moreno-Ocampo, delivered a talk at a conference in Montreal on the prevention of genocide.[1] During the question period, a journalist from Uganda urged him to withdraw the arrest warrants so peace talks could transpire between the members of the Lords Resistance Army (LRA) and her government.[2] She pleaded that her people wanted peace, not justice at this point in time. Moreno-Ocampo responded that once those responsible were arrested and prosecuted, the Ugandan people would have both peace and justice.

When the Prosecutor promises peace and justice he is assuming much. He assumes that a trial can deliver both simultaneously and that we can know this in advance. These assumptions are closely connected to another: for law to do its good work, it must not become enmeshed in the messy world of politics but, rather, international law must seek to transcend politics. Indeed, this apolitical vision of international law relies on the promise that justice and peace accompany the work of the ICC and this is an assumption that the Ugandan journalist was challenging. Can an international criminal trial deliver peace and justice? Can it solve serious political problems by holding a trial? And can it be staunchly apolitical in the process? Should it try?

While domestic criminal trials contribute to the causes of both peace and justice, the challenges facing international criminal law (ICL) are far greater and so

* I would like to thank all of the conference participants for their probing questions. I am especially grateful to Antony Duff for his insightful commentary. My sincere gratitude is also extended to Darryl Robinson, Thomas Telfer, Sean Coyle, Kristen Rundle and Mohamed Khimji for their helpful suggestions. Finally, many thanks to my research assistant Vera Dokter. My errors are my own.

[1] Global conference on the 'Prevention of Genocide', McGill University, Faculty of Law (13 October 2007).

[2] See generally KP Apuuli, 'The ICC Arrest Warrants for the Lord's Resistance Army Leaders and Peace Prospects for Northern Uganda' (2006) 4 *Journal of International Criminal Justice* 179; J Quinn 'Getting to Peace? Negotiating with the LRA in Northern Uganda' (2008) 10 *Human Rights Review* 55.

the aim of Moreno-Ocampo's promise is more idealistic than realistic. While many equate such idealism with a kind of optimism about what is possible, I will argue that this kind of hope and optimism is profoundly dangerous. Once it becomes clear that peace and justice may require different paths of action, Moreno-Ocampo's promise to the Ugandan journalist can be called into question alongside all the assumptions that inform the current self-understanding of ICL.

I begin my argument by defining the term 'apolitical'. I argue that both the realization and the pursuit of this ideal is a matter of degree. It is not simply an acontextual positivist approach that I am worried about, but the presumption in favour of prosecution endorsed by the Office of the Prosecutor. This presumption is problematic because it is supported by a directive to practitioners to narrow the scope of variables that are considered relevant in order to ensure that juridical justice is given priority over peace.

Section II is dedicated to an exploration of the dichotomy between peace and justice. I begin by arguing against the claim that the dichotomy is false and I do so by illustrating that a doctrinal version of this claim, forwarded by Linda Keller, breaks down on its own terms. The problem is that the coincidence of peace and justice via an international trial cannot be determined acontextually in advance. In certain circumstances, the requirements of justice demand a different set of actions than the requirements of peace. This, I will argue, is the case in Uganda.

By exploration of the practical effects and philosophical underpinnings of the ICC's operations in Uganda in section III, I seek to highlight the stakes of the debate. When the ICC pursues its legal mandate in this instance, the victim population is treated as a mere means to the ICC's ends. The end envisaged is a world order governed by international law. I challenge this Utopian vision of the future and the decision to subordinate victim populations to it. While peace talks may fail, they have the distinct advantage, at least in this instance, of aiming at the good of the victim community instead of the good of some future population.

In section IV, I will argue that this vision of the future world order is underpinned by the false dichotomy between bad politics and good law. Once this dichotomy is pierced, the decision regarding the best course of action becomes infinitely more complex and the possibility of law ushering in a better world becomes more susceptible to doubt. In fact, I will suggest that it is at the moment when international law comes closest to the apolitical ideal that it becomes the most dangerous. It is at this moment that it is most likely to work against the interests of vulnerable populations, such as the Ugandans.

The advantages of the victim-centered approach that I advocate are underscored when the dangers of pursing the legal ideal are brought into sharp focus. When law works against the interests of peace in a given instance, it can find itself on the side of war. Section V explores this possibility through an examination of Michael Scharf's legal analysis of the Iraq war. His support of law translates into a support for war signalling the dangers that accompany the apolitical ideal and the vision of the future that it contains. In my concluding remarks, which are offered in section VI, I defend the assumption that the interests of victims should be at the centre of the ICC's work at all times via a reflection on the potential purposes of criminal law in both the domestic and international contexts. In the international realm, we quickly find ourselves in the territory of consequentialist argumentation whereby the good of the victims is weighed against the goal to end impunity. My overarching argument is that the good of the victims should be given priority.

The starting point of my discussion may strike some readers as unconventional. Scholarship in the field of ICL tends to take two forms. Often arguments of both the critical and praiseworthy kind tend to be doctrinal in nature: they explore various problems, such as the tension between peace and justice, from the perspective of current doctrine.[3] This approach presupposes that the existing framework is adequate and needs only to be tinkered with. This is not a presupposition that I make.

The second approach is to seek the principles that legitimize international criminal law by considering whether or not a coherent normative account can be given.[4] While this method is not completely antagonistic to my own, the starting point I adopt, and the conclusions I draw may be competitive with the kinds of conclusions that this approach tends to yield. My discussion begins with a real world problem and moves backwards to see whether any potential boundaries of the ICL project can be articulated. The central claim of this chapter is that ICL is capable of doing good work in the world only when practitioners place the well-being of the most vulnerable populations at the center of their deliberations. In certain instances, this may mean that the ICC may have to cede to (and possibly support) other mechanisms that are better placed to protect the interests of the victims.

I THE APOLITICAL IDEAL

> The [Rome] Statute provides a clear framework to select situations and cases to investigate . . . I have to apply the law. Nothing more, nothing less. The decision that ending impunity will endure lasting peace and security was taken in Rome. I should not, and I will not take into account political considerations.[5]
>
> ICC Prosecutor Luis Moreno-Ocampo

This quotation is a more detailed expression of the Prosecutor's response to the Ugandan journalist. ICL, by seeking to end impunity, will bring with it both peace

[3] See, eg, J Wouters, B Demeyere and S Verhoeven, 'The International Criminal Court's Office of the Prosecutor: Navigating between Independence and Accountability?' (2008) 8 *International Criminal Law Review* 273; D Robinson, 'Serving the Interests of Justice: Amnesties, Truth Commissions and the International Criminal Court' (2003) 14 *European Journal of International Law* 481; Human Rights Watch, 'The Meaning of "the Interests of Justice" in Article 53 of the Rome Statute' (1 June 2005), online: www.hrw.org/en/news/2005/06/01/meaning-interests-justice-article-53-rome-statute.

[4] See, eg, WA Schabas, 'General Principles of Criminal Law in the International Criminal Court Statute (Part III)' (1998) 6 *European Journal of Crime, Criminal Law and Criminal Justice* 400; L May, *Crimes Against Humanity: A Normative Account* (New York, Cambridge University Press, 2005).

[5] L Moreno-Ocampo, 'Address to the Assembly of States Parties' (14 November 2008) 2–11, 6.

and justice. This is the promise that is codified in the Rome Statute and it is for this reason that Moreno-Ocampo refuses to take political considerations into account. The legal lens is a narrow lens that excludes extra-legal, or political, factors. Here the Prosecutor is offering us a rather robust vision of ICL's apolitical ideal.

One might interject at this early stage of the argument that the words of Moreno-Ocampo are best viewed as hyperbolic: he and his team are well aware of the complexity of the situations that they face. They are also keenly aware of the fact that the legal ideal is not realistic: no one actually believes that international criminal law can completely excise itself from the realm of the political.[6] While there is much truth to this response, an exploration of the position of the Office of the Prosecutor (OP) reveals a commitment to the apolitical ideal.

In 2007 the OP released a memo entitled 'The Interests of Justice' which directly addressed the issues that surround the relationship between peace and justice, and the interests of the victims.[7] The authors are particularly concerned with giving some determinate shape to the discretionary ambit accorded to the Prosecutor under Article 53 that maintains he can refrain from prosecuting individuals if it would be 'in the interests of justice' to do so. While this document is meant to clarify the official position, it does not in itself grant rights or duties, but seeks instead to carve out the contours of the Prosecutor's discretionary powers. A careful analysis of the content of this memo allows us to identify two different kinds of arguments, each of which expresses a commitment to the apolitical ideal, but to varying degrees.

The overarching goal of the authors is to defend what they refer to as a 'presumption in favour of prosecution'. A point confirmed by the OP, who explicitly state that the 'Prosecutor's discretion under Article 53(1)(c) and 53(2)(c) is exceptional in nature and that there is a presumption in favour of investigation or prosecution wherever the criteria established in Article 53(1) (a) and (b) or Article 53 (2) (a) and (b) have been met'.[8] This presumption is supported by a central assumption about the alignment of the victims' interests with the work of the ICC: 'the wording of Article 53(1) (c) implies that the interests of victims will generally weigh in favour of prosecution'.[9] Here there is an implicit acknowledgment on the part of the OP that the interests of the victims are central to their project but that, on occasion, legal action will not serve their interests. So the question arises, how precisely does the OP determine whether to proceed in a given case?

Tellingly, the OP protects the presumption in favour of prosecution by championing a division of labour which places the 'interests of peace' 'within the

[6] R Cryer, *Prosecuting International Crimes: Selectivity and the International Criminal Law Regime* (Cambridge, Cambridge University Press, 2005) 230.

[7] International Criminal Court, Office of the Prosecutor, 'Policy Paper on the Interests of Justice' (September 2007), online: www.icc-cpi.int/NR/rdonlyres/772C95C9-F54D-4321-BF0973422BB23528/143640/ICCOTPInterests OfJustice.pdf.

[8] ibid 1.

[9] ibid 5.

mandate of institutions other than the Office of the Prosecutor'.[10] Consequently, on their view, the phrase 'interests of justice' 'should not be conceived of so broadly as to embrace all issues related to peace and security'.[11] Such considerations do not fall within their *legal* mandate:

> In situations where the ICC is involved, comprehensive solutions addressing humanitarian, security, political, development and justice elements will be necessary. The Office will seek to work constructively with and respect the mandates of those engaged in other areas but will pursue judicial mandate independently.[12]

Insofar as the OP pursues its legal mandate with this level of independence, it cannot guarantee that it will also be contributing to, rather than working against, the process that seeks to address the wider set of social issues, including peace. This approach is worrying as it urges international lawyers to exclude certain considerations if they speak against and not in favour of prosecution. This method, I argue below, puts lives at risk.

The second strategy involves disregarding all issues relating to peace, justice and victims' interests: the law is the law and we are bound by it. When the OP retreats to this acontextual, apolitical vision of the ICC, a dangerous agenda shines through. This positivistic stance betrays an attitude of complete indifference to the consequences of their actions by ending the much needed discussion before it begins:

> With the entry into force of the Rome Statute, a new legal framework has emerged and this framework necessarily impacts on conflict management efforts. The issue is no longer about whether we agree or disagree with the pursuit of justice in moral or practical terms: it is the law.[13]

Now we no longer have a presumption in favour of prosecution, but a mandate to prosecute regardless of circumstance.[14] The apolitical, acontextual ideal is realized with this staunchly positivist approach to international law. Notice that it is at this point where a narrow technical approach to international law intersects with the idealism that underpins a lot of the work of international lawyers.[15] ICL's emancipatory potential is fulfilled (or so it is thought) via the strict adherence to the positive law. My claim is that all variables should be considered and continually reconsidered by international lawyers. The stakes are simply too high. They are high precisely because ICL may work for peace in certain instances, but it may also work against peace in other circumstances.

[10] ibid 1.
[11] ibid 8.
[12] ibid.
[13] ibid 4.
[14] International lawyers are often hostile towards the discretion the Prosecutor is granted by Art 53 and implicitly or explicitly endorse a purely legal lens. See, eg, H Olasolo, 'The Prosecutor of the ICC before the Initiation of Investigations: A Quasi-Judicial or a Political Body?' (2003) 3 *International Criminal Law Review* 87, 110–11. See also Human Rights Watch, *Uganda: No Amnesty for Atrocities* (New York, HRW, 2006).
[15] D Robinson 'The Identity Crisis of International Criminal Law' (2008) 21 *Leiden Journal of International Law* 925.

II IN THE NAME OF PEACE AND JUSTICE

It was during the drafting of the Rome Statute in 1998 that the idea of an international criminal court (ICC) gained traction, partly because a powerful case for its existence was made. International criminal trials could, it was argued, bring about justice *and* peace. As the OP argues, the 'ICC was created on the premise that justice is an essential component of a stable peace'.[16] It is not surprising that this argument was central to its coming into being. Juridical justice and its promise to end impunity is backward-looking – it arrives on the scene too late. Peace, on the other hand, is forward looking. It can provide the foundation for future flourishing. Insofar as international law can serve both masters, it will not simply seek to navigate the past, but it will lay a foundation for a better future. Thus not only does the ICC's existence partly hinge on this promise, so does our collective future insofar as one has faith that the international criminal trials can deliver both peace and justice.

Given these high stakes, it is not surprising that commentators have taken up the cause to demonstrate that the interests of peace and justice do coincide with the actions of the ICC. Consider, for instance, Linda Keller's argument, which seeks to dissolve what she sees as the false dichotomy between peace and justice.[17] She begins by admitting that she believes those drafting the Rome Statute chose not to deal with the issue of amnesties, thereby signalling a clear priority of justice over peace and reconciliation.[18] This point reaffirms the existence of a very real dichotomy, casting doubt on her ability to dissolve it. But it is nonetheless useful to explore her arguments, as they betray the futility of her aim.

Keller begins by attempting to absorb the requirements of peace into the definition of justice, arguing that the ICC should attempt to 'harmonize retributive and restorative justice principles'.[19] Here, processes like truth commissions and traditional forms of justice come into play. In this interpretation, justice is a broad concept that includes – but is not restricted to – the ICC's legal process. Despite her intentions, this argument simply reaffirms the potential tension between actions that promote peace and ICL's specific form of justice: the definition of 'justice' had to be broadened in order to incorporate peace.

Her second argument points to the fact that ICL makes room for peace. For instance, Article 53(2)(c) of the Rome Statute states that the Prosecutor can decline to prosecute when it is not in the 'interests of justice'. As Keller notes, this means that the law makes it possible to 'forego prosecution in deference to a state's conditional amnesty and truth commission'.[20] The problem with this argument is that Article 53's broad definition of justice, which

[16] International Criminal Court, 'Policy Paper' (n 7) 8.

[17] L Keller, 'The False Dichotomy of Peace versus Justice and the International Criminal Court' (2008) 3 *Hague Justice Journal* 12.

[18] ibid 16.

[19] ibid 14.

[20] ibid 1.

incorporates peace mechanisms, excludes the ICC's specific form of justice. Criminal proceedings, and the commitment to end impunity that such proceedings embody, are pitted against 'the interests of justice'. Article 53 does not dissolve the dichotomy, rather it absorbs it into the legal framework. The moral of the story is that ICL can but does not always serve peace and consequently difficult choices must be made. Keller implicitly acknowledges this point when she supports the work of the ICC over and above potential peace initiatives, despite the good they may bring.

Ultimately, Keller retreats to a legalistic definition of justice, admitting that the narrow brand of justice that the ICC offers can undermine the conditions required to bring about peace. When faced with the choice, she opts for justice over peace: 'There is arguably no justice where the criminals, particularly those most responsible, go free as a result of a peace deal'.[21] Moreover, Keller maintains that peace deals should not be offered for 'classes of cases involving genocide or grave breaches in light of the status of international law regarding the duty to prosecute'.[22] Her hostility towards peace deals is clear given that it would be the high-ranking individuals who would be positioned for such negotiations.

Not surprisingly, Keller prefers trials over peace negotiations in Uganda. On this issue, Keller is in good company: Moreno-Ocampo argues that the actions of the particular members of the Lord's Resistance Army amount to blackmail and extortion.[23] Keller is adamant that 'the ICC should not defer to a domestic non-prosecutorial alternative simply because it furthers peace, however desirable this outcome may be'.[24] Not only has the peace and justice dichotomy re-emerged in the course of her argument, but now Keller admits that peace negotiations may have desirable consequences, but that such potential outcomes should be ignored. By considering the case of Uganda in a little more detail, the cost of ignoring such 'desirable consequences' may prove to be extremely high. The cost may be a matter of life and death.

III THE STAKES: UGANDA

In order to see the challenge that faces the ICC, consider, once again, the Ugandan journalist's plea to Prosecutor Moreno-Ocampo. She wants the arrest warrants to be withdrawn so peace talks can proceed with the rebels. Now let us also assume that the Ugandan journalist is accurately capturing the opinion of the majority of

21 ibid 31.
22 ibid.
23 ibid 32.
24 ibid 33.

her fellow Ugandans when she states that her people want peace, not justice.[25] Why, we might ask, should the Prosecutor proceed against the wishes of the Ugandans?

International criminal lawyers tend to offer a tempered response: the trial will bring the Ugandans a kind of justice and hence some good. It is abominable to think that such individuals can get away with their horrific acts. In addition, there is no guarantee that the discussions proposed will bring peace (the Ugandan officials would be, after all, negotiating with those who carried out the atrocities).[26] So in light of this uncertainty, it is best to pursue the goals of ICL rather than allow normal power politics to play out.

The weaknesses in this response include its imperialistic bent coupled with the fact that there are also risks that accompany ICC's promise of justice. International lawyers cannot guarantee a guilty verdict insofar as the legal proceedings remain within the confines of the rule of law which offers protections to the accused; and if practitioners bend the rule of law to achieve a guilty verdict, then the version of justice the trial offers can be questioned – it becomes a show trial. Nor is the ICC able to guarantee that a trial can heal the fractures in any given society. This depends on numerous complex variables, many of which cannot be controlled by international lawyers.[27] There is, however, a more pressing problem with the Prosecutor's promise to deliver peace and justice: currently the ICC does not have any way of arresting the individuals it has indicted. It has no army. It has no police force. Because of this fact, there is no guarantee that the arrests will take place in the near future, if at all.

The moment it comes to light that the Prosecutor's promise to the Ugandan journalist is potentially empty the typical arguments that speak in favour of prosecution – peace, justice, reconciliation, retribution etc – no longer play a justificatory role. For any of these goals to be potentially realized, a trial is needed. Without a trial, the argument that speaks in favour of prosecution subtly shifts to very different, worrying grounds.

Uganda is an impoverished country. Because of the extremely poor quality of life many Ugandans endure, it is quite likely, if not guaranteed, that lives will be lost as they wait for the arrests to take place. Given that the arrests may never take place, the state of limbo that they find themselves in may persist indefinitely. When this fact is brought to the attention of international lawyers, the familiar response is as follows: 'yes this is the case, but some sacrifices must be

[25] It has been reported that 70% of the residents in Northern Uganda want Joseph Kony, the LRA leader, to be granted a conditional amnesty in order to allow peace talks to transpire. See Apuuli, 'The ICC' (n 2) 7. Note that my argument does not hinge on the issue of consent. It is possible for the population to believe that a trial will help their society, when in fact it may put the well-being of some of their citizens at risk.

[26] For an interesting discussion of both sides of this debate see R Cryer, 'Prosecuting the Leaders: Promises, Politics and Practicalities' (2009) *Goettingen Journal of International Law* 45, 66–72.

[27] LP Francis and JG Francis, 'International Criminal Courts, the Rule of Law, and the Prevention of Harm: Building Justice in times of Injustice' in L May and Z Hoskins (eds), *International Criminal Law and Philosophy* (Cambridge, Cambridge University Press, 2010) 69–71; M Koskenniemi, 'Between Impunity and Show Trials' (2002) 6 *Max Planck Yearbook of United Nations Law* 17, 5.

made in order for international criminal law to bring about a new world order'. In this instance, the sacrifice that must be made is the welfare of the Ugandan people.

The argument that is forwarded in favour of prosecution has quietly shifted to consequentialist grounds: the costs in terms of the welfare of the Ugandan people are outweighed by the perceived benefits for all of us of a world governed by the norms of international law. The victims' interests are no longer the focus. Recall that the initial set of arguments for prioritizing legal action over peace talks was victim centred: the Ugandans would benefit from the trials because they would enjoy both peace and justice. Trials can contribute to a lasting peace; criminals will be punished for their crimes. However, once the practical difficulty with realizing this goal is acknowledged, the decision to proceed legally is defended on the grounds of future gains of the world community. The interests of Ugandans (understood objectively or subjectively) are subsumed under the desire for law to create a better world order; they have unwittingly become the sacrificial lambs for a particular vision of a brave new world.

It is not simply the words of Moreno-Ocampo that are at issue, but his actions. The arrest warrants are still in place. Peace talks remain out of reach. We can now see that both the words and actions of Moreno-Ocampo go beyond the paternalism of imperialism, whereby what is done is done to 'help' the colonized; here there is a blatant recognition on the part of many practitioners that the actions of the ICC are not helping, but harming, the Ugandans. The moment practitioners in ICL are willing to sacrifice a victim population – the very population that ICL was introduced to help – questions must be asked about the nature of the ideal they are pursuing and of the enterprise more generally.

IV ICC: A NEW WORLD ORDER?

The vision of a new world order underpinning the ICC is one where law is able to tame the selfish actions of leaders. The hope is that the commendable values entrenched in international law can corral the transient and selfish interests of states. It is often assumed that international law will make the world a more peaceful and humane place. But in order for international law to perform this transformative role, practitioners must strive to be apolitical. Recall Moreno-Ocampo's pledge to 'apply the law', declaring that he neither 'should' nor 'would' 'take into account political considerations'.

Behind this promise lies a deep fear: if the ICC were to bow to political pressures – in this case the pressure for peace talks – it would be taking a step backwards. Too many backward steps, and the project of international criminal law, which is considered fragile and in its early stages, might cease to exist. One such argument is the idea that international law must be continually adhered to if future crimes are going to be deterred.[28] To fail to issue the arrest warrants, or worse to revoke or suspend them, would send the message that perpetrators can escape responsibility. The ICC's goal of ending impunity would be undermined.[29] Without a commitment on the part of practitioners to remain apolitical, law will become mere politics. Not only might this threaten the ability of the ICC to get funding, it also is akin to surrendering the promise that law brings to the international sphere. For these interconnected reasons, the need to refuse to bend to politics becomes urgent. Hans Peter Kaul, a judge at the ICC, urges practitioners to maintain this 'objective' stance in the face of the clear challenges that stand in the way:

> Obviously, there are also other limitations and obstacles. For example, it seems realistic to assume that 'Realpolitik' and states' interest will continue, in the future, to be important obstacles to the effectiveness of the ICC. In the apparently eternal struggle between brute force and the rule of law, further disappointments and setbacks seem possible. Steadfastness, stamina and the readiness to weather future difficulties and crises with determination will therefore be indispensable.[30]

Kaul assumes 'good' law has to do battle with 'bad' politics; that is, law has to do battle with self-interested 'brute force'. Given the nature of the enemy, determination is needed to usher in the better world; thus 'difficulties' linked with politics as usual must be overcome. Because of the nobility of ICL's goal – coupled with the need to be apolitical to achieve it – 'crises' must not deter international lawyers from their course. This is so even if the crisis comes in the form of harm to the most vulnerable individuals. This battle cry has been heard before. Human history is littered with examples that illustrate the cost of pursuing a better world order with a single-mindedness that will not bend to even the most worthy of pleas. The dream of a better world order is an earnest one, but it is nonetheless misguided in this instance.

The dichotomy between good law and bad politics is a false one: the interests of political actors, even selfish ones, may coincide with the best interests of the citizenry. Consider the controversial decision made by the Americans to not prosecute the Japanese Emperor, Hirohito. The decision was made based on the fact that the Emperor was a powerful symbol in Japan, the removal of which would threaten the stability of the nation. Historian Yuma Totani captures the issues clearly:

> For the Allied powers, Hirohito was as much a politico-military problem as a legal one because of the immense authority he continued to wield – based on his claim to divinity – over the Japanese people. Decisions regarding his treatment as a war criminal, there-

[28] Deirdre Golash questions the ability of international criminal trials to have a deterrent effect. See D Golash, 'The Justification of Punishment in the International Context' in May and Hoskins (eds), *International Criminal Law and Philosophy* (n 27) 215–17.

[29] M Ssenyonjo, 'The International Criminal Court and the Lord's Resistance Army Leaders: Prosecution or Amnesty?' (2007) 7 *International Criminal Law Review* 361, 384.

[30] HP Kaul, 'The International Criminal Court: Current Challenges and Perspectives' (2007) 6 *Washington University Global Studies Law Review*, 578–79.

> fore, had to be made not only in pursuit of justice but also for the maintenance of security in Japan, where the situation was still volatile and unpredictable.[31]

This is not an ideal scenario by any measure. It seems manifestly unfair to prosecute Japanese officials and leave the Emperor untouched. The American officials were faced with a difficult choice, but ultimately they chose not to risk the stability of Japan for the sake of justice. Given that the Americans had a stake in the future of Japan, it is not surprising that they chose peace and stability over justice: peace takes them forward, while juridical justice is primarily backward looking. Notably, the action that best served the interests of the citizens of Japan occurred because those making the decisions had a stake in the future of Japan.

Since the ICC does not have a stake in the future flourishing of Uganda in the same way that the United States had a stake in Japan, we can raise questions about whether international lawyers are best placed to make a decision about Uganda's future. More generally, questions can be asked about the ideal of detached justice. Detachment, in the case of the ICC, leads us more quickly towards Utopian impulses and away from a careful analysis of the particulars. Ironically, at the moment it looks like it might have succeeded in becoming apolitical; we should be most wary of adhering to its demands. This is so because the 'selfish' interests of states may also be the 'selfish' interests of the citizens of those states. It is certainly the case that the self-interest of politicians will not always coincide with the interests of the most vulnerable populations. However, if we make a pre-commitment to adhere to international law, or if we consider an artificially narrow set of variables, then the alignment of the interests of the victims with those of the ICC becomes a matter of mere coincidence and not of design.

In addition, it seems that lasting peace will only come if the causes of the current situation are dealt with. The roots of the problems in Uganda are manifold. The hope for a lasting peace would be more realistic and less Utopian if steps were taken to improve the living conditions of its citizenry. This is an issue of economics and development – of politics broadly construed – not of international criminal law. The ICC remains in a country for a limited time period and does not have an economy-based agenda.

In short, once the false dichotomy between good law and bad politics is undermined, the global moral landscape becomes infinitely more complex. It now becomes possible for law to work against peace. It is not simply the case that ICL may not bring with it both peace and justice, international law may find itself on the side of war rather than peace. This fact casts doubt on the Utopian vision that underpins the drive to pursue ICL at all costs. This drive is particularly noticeable in the push to create absolute duties to prosecute.[32] By exploring the idea of an absolute duty, it becomes more apparent that the future world order promised to us by international law looks very similar to the one we already have.

[31] Y Totani, *The Tokyo War Crimes Trial: The Pursuit of Justice in the Wake of World War II* (Cambridge MA, Harvard University Asia Centre and Harvard University Press, 2008) 43.

[32] DG Newman, 'The Rome Statute, Some Reservations Concerning Amnesties, and a Distributive Problem' (2005) 20 *American University International Law Review* 293.

V WAR, PEACE AND INTERNATIONAL LAW

By examining Michael Scharf's argument about the relationship between international law and the Iraq war, the danger of the apolitical ideal is punctuated. International law may advance the causes of war instead of serving as a foundation for lasting peace. Scharf argues that according to international law, it was legal to offer Charles Taylor exile in exchange for peace talks, but not so in reference to Saddam Hussein. He argues that the Bush Administration's actions were illegal:

> In the case of Saddam Hussein, the United States had accused the Iraqi leader of grave breaches of the Geneva Conventions and violations of the Genocide convention. Both the United States and Iraq were parties to these treaties, which contain an absolute obligation to prosecute offenders.[33]

Because it was illegal, it was wrong.[34] Notice that on this account, law is once again pitted against politics: politics is only allowed in when law lets it enter or when law is absent. Once law exists, it must be followed otherwise the rule of law will not be upheld. Consequently, the Bush Administration's offer to Hussein 'signaled that the provisions of these treaties are inconsequential, thereby undermining the rule of law in a critical area of global affairs'.[35] Scharf is relieved that 'the damage to the rule of law was negligible' because Saddam did not accept the offer.[36]

This leaves a key question dangling: 'Would greater damage to the rule of law have nevertheless been acceptable if it succeeded in averting a war that has resulted in tens of thousands of casualties on both sides since 2003?'.[37] Scharf's answer is 'no'. To defend his stance, he shifts his focus from the value of the rule of law to other, distinct considerations that appeal to the interests of Iraqi citizens.

This shift is informative as it signals that Scharf has made an important concession: an appeal to value of the rule of law in and of itself is not enough to justify his position. The key question is now: who will benefit from the adherence to the rule of law in this instance? The beneficiary seems to be international lawyers or the international community more broadly. International lawyers benefit insofar as they believe international law is being respected. But if this is the only interest being served, then the normative language of the 'rule of law' is being used to mask selfish interests. The international community benefits only if ICL can usher in a new world order – but if the world order is the one Scharf recommends, it does not appear to be markedly different from the old one. Once international law can find itself on the side of war, the future world order promises to be a world scarred by war, not simply one healed by peace.

[33] M Scharf, 'From the eXile Files: An Essay on Trading Justice for Peace' (2006) 63 *Washington and Lee Law Review* 339, 373. Note that I will not address the issue of the legality of the war.

[34] I will grant Scharf this point in order to explore the assumptions that inform his argument.

[35] Scharf, 'From the eXile Files' (n 33) 373.

[36] ibid 374.

[37] ibid.

By further exploring Scharf's argument, serious questions can be raised about the viability of the world order, and hence the desire to pursue it. He is aware that if he is going to convince us that the Iraq war was preferable to the illegal offer of exile, he must convince his reader that the Iraqi people are also being served.

His first argument is a familiar one in the international legal community: Hussein could have interfered with Iraq's transition to democracy.[38] Notice that this is a speculative argument which Scharf employs in the hopes of overcoming the brutal facts about the Iraq war. Indeed, even if this fear had materialized, it remains difficult to defend this position as it presupposes that Saddam would have created more problems for Iraq's transition to democracy than the war has to date.

Scharf quickly moves on to an additional argument. He claims that the trial of Hussein honoured the wishes of the Iraqi people. He wonders, '[m]orally, what right would American negotiators have to trade away the ability of thousands of Hussein's victims to see the dictator brought to justice?'.[39] Serious questions can be asked as to whether the Iraqi people, or any people, would choose war over amnesty for their former leader. And if they would choose war, the wisdom of making this choice can be questioned.[40] The wisdom of Scharf's argument can also be questioned.

Implicit in his argument are the claims that it is morally better to go to war, capture Hussein and prosecute him than to grant him exile in exchange for peace. My worry about the current allegiance to international law is that the apolitical ideal leads lawyers to treat law as a moral absolute. The desire to adhere to the law is stronger than the desire to avoid war, or to establish peace. In other words, those involved in the project see the rule of law as more important than lives – actual, tangible lives.

Not only does Scharf's argument confirm that peace and justice remain potential antagonists on the international stage (he opts for justice over peace), his argument also points to an additional reversal: law has traditionally been the enemy of war, now wars can (or should?) be fought in the name of law. Judith Shklar reminds us that in the domestic context law and war remain enemies:

> The ultimate spiritual and political struggle is always between war and law . . . The institutions of judicial citizen protection may create rights, but they exist in order to avoid what Montesquieu took to be the greatest of human evils, constant fear created by the threats of violence and the actual cruelties of the holders of military power in society.[41]

Once law becomes unmoored from its domestic underpinnings, it loses its natural enemies. This is dangerous, especially if one shares Montesquieu's (and Shklar's)

[38] ibid.

[39] ibid.

[40] MC Bassiouni worries that the rising death toll has actually vindicated Hussein in the eyes of the Iraqis (although he personally supports the trial). See MC Cherif Bassiouni and MW Hanna, 'Ceding the High Ground: The Iraqi High Criminal Court Statute and the Trial of Saddam Hussein' (2006–08) 39 *Case Western Reserve Journal of International Law* 21, 94.

[41] JN Shklar, 'Political Theory and the Rule of Law' in S Hoffmann (ed), *Political Thought and Political Thinkers* (Chicago, University of Chicago Press, 1998) 25.

judgement about the evils of fear and war and about the virtues of law. If law loses sight of these enemies it may unwittingly find it is fighting a battle on the side of war.

How did we end up with this extreme conclusion that adherence to international law is preferable to peace? The cornerstone of Scharf's argument is his claim that an absolute duty to prosecute exists in this instance. When we focus on the existence of this duty (which I will grant Scharf for the sake of argument), we become fixated on law's positive existence. Implicit in Scharf's argument is that the real (existing) law is the ideal. But at the very the moment we begin to focus on the positive law, we recall that states have chosen to commit themselves to this duty. But if the duty arose out of power politics, why is it so sacred so as not to be altered in the face of pressing political needs, like the avoidance of war?

Absolute duties are dangerous in a complicated world. So is the apolitical ideal that underpins them. The duty to prosecute in this instance seems to derive its normative force from the fact that it has revealed itself to be antagonistic to the self-interest of the states involved. Because the 'absolute duty to prosecute' operates against the best interests of both states, the positive law can be seen as more than power politics; conversely, when the demands of law coincide with the self-interests of states, it becomes difficult to determine if a leader's adherence to law is contingent on their political self-interests.[42] Law's 'objectivity' and its 'neutrality' stem from its indifference to what states want and the complexities of the political situation more generally. This means it is also indifferent to what is good for citizens.

This leads me to my paradoxical conclusion: at precisely the moment when international criminal law appears to be apolitical and neutral, it is most detached from the world and most in danger of causing great harm and sacrificing any hope of being legitimate. This conclusion is only uncomfortable if one adheres to the (false) dichotomy between good law and bad politics. Once peace can be on the side of politics then the interests of civilian populations may, in a given instance, coincide with the interest of the politicians. Peace, in the case of Iraq, was in everyone's interest (except certain international lawyers). Politics as usual is a force for good in this instance; law, on the grounds of Scharf's argument, is not. At the same moment it seeks to close the door on impunity, international law also closes the door on making context-sensitive judgements that are in the best interests of the citizens.

We can also ask what an absolute duty to prosecute looks like in international law. It certainly does not translate into the political world as such given that many, if not most, transgressions are not prosecuted (or even investigated). Given the undeniable element of discretion, why act in instances when it would place lives at risk? Why risk American and Iraqi lives? Why risk Ugandan lives? Once the idea of an absolute duty seems not to be absolute in an important sense – the realiza-

[42] M Koskenniemi, 'Politics of International Law' (1990) 1 *European Journal of International Law* 4, 7–8.

tion of the duty seems to depend on politics. The Americans did not, after all, wage war in order to uphold this duty. If ICL gets anything done it is because of past political agreements and present political will.

Once Scharf is forced to admit that the duty to prosecute materializes in a very circumscribed number of cases, his argument is weakened. Indeed, we begin to wonder if his argument is, at bottom, political. Is it an 'American pro-war' argument in the guise of a legal one? Does the normative language of justice and the rule of law function as a smokescreen for political self-interest? Why, after all, must this be one of the 'exemplary trials' when the cost is so very great?

This raises another quandary, built into the ICC: not only is it politically difficult to pursue hard targets because the ICC is reliant on their continued financial support and cooperation, the principle of complementarity poses additional (political) problems. This principle allows domestic legal systems to try accused individuals unless they are 'unwilling' or 'unable'.[43] Most powerful states would be willing and able. As Fred Mégret remarks:

> [I]nternational criminal justice is also the arena where some of the more utopian aspirations of international lawyers play out, and one where there is a significant clamor for resorting to international institutions as such, if only to give credibility to the idea that there is an 'actual' international community backing criminal sanctions.[44]

The need for the ICC to have its own institutions – its own trials – is echoed by Kaul J's concern that '[i]f the states generally discharge their primary duty to prosecute crimes, the Court will not be given anything to do and will have no cases'.[45] The ICC has selfish reasons for pursuing trials in Uganda.

The project is also driven by an idealistic vision – albeit a hazy one – of a future world order.[46] The second rationale is at least partly reliant on the first. The path to the realization of the apolitical ideal is deeply political in a certain sense. But, as I have argued, the ideal that motivates international lawyers becomes profoundly dangerous at the moment it loses sight of the interests of the civilian populations it is supposed to help. The problem is that the apolitical ideal encourages this kind of blindness – it even necessitates it. Instead of giving in to this blindness and heeding Kaul J's plea 'to weather future difficulties and crises with determination', his plea should be ignored. The voices that cry out at such moments should be listened to and acted on. Only then can the ICC play a role – albeit a limited one – in ensuring that tomorrow's world is a little better than today's.

Some argue that the potential for peace talks is directly related to the actions of the ICC: the accused wanted to negotiate peace only after the arrest warrants were

[43] For a discussion of this principle, see A Cassese, P Gaeta and J Jones (eds), *The Rome Statute of the International Criminal Court: A Commentary* (Oxford, Oxford University Press, 2002).

[44] F Mégret, 'In Defense of Hybridity: Towards a Representational Theory of International Criminal Justice' (2005) 38 *Cornell International Law Journal* (ssrn draft, 2–3).

[45] Kaul, 'The International Criminal Court' (n 30) 577.

[46] As mentioned, this vision intersects with a positivist approach to internal law.

issued.[47] This has embittered many international lawyers: not only do members of the Lord's Resistance Army escape trial, but they manipulate the situation to their advantage.[48] Letting the rebels get away with it would tarnish the standing of ICL. My reading of the situation is different. If the ICC plays a role, even if it is a supportive role in bringing about peace in a war torn part of the world, then it has done good work. If the threat of prosecution can be used to enforce the conditions of peace, then it can be useful in helping an impoverished community indefinitely into the future.

VI DOMESTIC VERSUS INTERNATIONAL CRIMINAL LAW: THE ROLE OF VICTIMS

In my concluding remarks, I wish to rearticulate my central claim by returning to the exchange between the Ugandan journalist and Prosecutor Moreno-Ocampo. At the same time, I will diffuse an objection about a foundational assumption of my argument. I am assuming that the victims matter – that their interests should not simply be a concern, but the central concern of international criminal lawyers. If legal action potentially harms vulnerable civilian populations, law should cede to other mechanisms that can work for the interests of these people. The claim that ICL is working for all humanity places an abstract ideal above the interests of an existing vulnerable population who are most in need of urgent help from international organizations.

One might interject at this juncture and ask why the victims' voices are relevant. Why, for instance, should we respond to the plea of the Ugandan journalist? In domestic systems such as Canada's, victims of crimes do not have a say: it is up to the state to determine whether an individual will be prosecuted. International law, one might argue, should seek to emulate this structure: the crime may take place against individuals, but the crimes in question are against all humanity. The criminal act triggers criminal proceedings, not the wishes of the victim.

Setting aside the difficulty the term 'humanity' has in bearing the weight of this argument,[49] a closer look at the analogy between domestic and international criminal law illuminates the nature of the obstacles that face the ICC that are not usually encountered at the domestic level.

Why, for instance, is it the case that a rape victim does not have a say about whether or not her attacker is prosecuted? One of the most obvious reasons is that if the rapist is not prosecuted, he will remain at large and might potentially reoffend. So for the safety and protection of the community, including the victim, the

[47] P Akhavan, 'The Lord's Resistance Army Case: Uganda's Submission of the First State Referral to the International Criminal Court' (2005) 99 *The American Journal of International Law* 403, 416.

[48] Ssenyonjo, 'The International Criminal Court' (n 29) 364.

[49] G Simpson, *Law, War and Crime: War Crimes, Trials and the Reinvention of International Law* (Cambridge, Polity Press, 2007) 33, 44–51.

rapist is prosecuted. It is in reference to this seemingly mundane point that the analogy between domestic and international law breaks down. In the domestic context the safety and wellbeing of the victim and the larger community is best served by proceeding with the legal process. Conversely in Uganda, it is by no means clear that the victim's interests are best served via the employment of the ICL. This is a case where good things that law can bring about in a domestic community (the safety and security of the victim and the community) cannot necessarily be brought about by the legal mechanism internationally. The Ugandan journalist is pleading with the Prosecutor to let other mechanisms help do the work that law is failing to do in this instance.

To sharpen my point about the dis-analogy between the two kinds of law, consider another purpose generally attributed to criminal law. Retributivists argue that criminal law is about punishing those who transgress society's norms.[50] The ICC's aim to end impunity echoes this message. In a functioning domestic system, however, this aim does not work at cross-purposes with the aim to keep the population safe and secure. In fact, the retributivist goals re-enforce the pursuit of a safe and secure community: by punishing dangerous wrongdoers, these other goals are served simultaneously. When the retributivist aim works to uphold the wider social goals of safety, security and wellbeing of the population, it brings with it both a backward and a forward looking aspect. By repeatedly punishing certain behaviours, it reinforces the normative structure of collective living.[51]

The retributivist ideal does not directly translate onto the international context: while international law can help to establish ideas about what is and what is not permitted, the establishment of these ideas does not necessarily coincide with the goal of protecting the victim community. Sometimes, one must choose between the two goals in a given instance. When such a divergence occurs, we are led into the world of consequentialist argumentation: we are left to weigh the relative value of the goals.

One might respond that we need not fall into consequentialist arguments in order to argue for the use of the ICC in cases such Uganda: Kant can help. Kant argues that consequences are irrelevant to the determination of whether or not an action is moral. This determination is made by focusing on intentions: the maxim underlying our action must be universalisable in order to be moral.[52] There are several problems with this approach, which seeks to support the strongest version of the apolitical ideal. First, given the discretionary ambit of the Prosecutor, all criminals are not prosecuted. The limited resources of the ICC combined with background considerations of power and politics renders Kant's categorical imperative unrealizable and thus unhelpful in the ICL context.[53] Moreover,

[50] See A Brudner, *The Unity of the Common Law: Studies in Hegelian Jurisprudence* (Berkeley, University of California Press, 1995).

[51] A similar argument can be made in reference to expressionist goals.

[52] I Kant, *Fundamental Principles of the Metaphysics of Morals* (TK Abbot trans, Amherst, Pometheus Books, 1988).

[53] I wish to thank Antony Duff for drawing my attention to this important point.

practitioners will end up treating victims as means in certain cases,[54] thereby violating Kant's claim that we are prohibited from treating individuals as mere means.[55]

At the moment when the victims become a mere means to the achievement of the goals of ICL, it should be that international law should cede to other mechanisms. In order to make this determination, the Prosecutor must carefully consider all of the variables that impact on the situation. In consequentialist terms, the wellbeing of the victim population should outweigh the idealistic goals of the ICC. Or in Kantian terms, the victims should be treated as ends in themselves. When international criminal lawyers place the victims' interests at the centre of their decision-making process, then ICC can find its place between Utopian dreams and political realities.

[54] See section III.

[55] Kant, *Fundamental Principles* (n 52) 65.

14

Joint Intentions

JENS DAVID OHLIN*

I INTRODUCTION

Collective criminal action has been – and remains – the most contentious area of substantive international criminal law. Three doctrines for imposing individual liability for collective endeavours have obsessively dominated the case law and literature, stretching from Nuremberg to the most current pronouncements of the International Criminal Court (ICC). These doctrines are: (i) conspiracy; (ii) Joint Criminal Enterprise (JCE);[1] and (iii) co-perpetration. Although the favoured doctrines keep changing, the central issue always remains how to hold a defendant responsible for the actions of another. This chapter attempts to cut across the spectrum in a new way and focus instead on the commonalities of these theories in an attempt to elucidate an underlying theory to explain and ground how individual liability can be generated from collective endeavours. In this regard, international criminal lawyers should be particularly concerned with finding a theory that adequately explains vicarious liability for group crimes, that is, the imposition of liability to all participants for the criminal actions of a colleague.

Section II explains that the doctrine of co-perpetration – in particular the 'control theory' version of the doctrine applied by the ICC – allegedly avoids the traditional problems associated with JCE. However, section II argues that control by itself does little to ground the imposition of vicarious liability and that a deeper theory regarding *mens rea* is required to do the job. Consequently, section III

* This chapter is excerpted from JD Ohlin, 'Joint Intentions to Commit International Crimes' (2011) 11 *Chicago Journal of International Law* 693–753.

[1] The three versions of JCE include co-perpetration by individuals who share the intent to commit the act ('JCE I'), concentration camp cases where the accused has 'knowledge of the nature of the system of ill-treatment and intent to further the common design of ill-treatment' ('JCE II') and vicarious liability for acts of others that fall outside the scope of the common criminal plan but are nonetheless reasonably foreseeable ('JCE III'). See *Prosecutor v Duško Tadić*, Case IT-94-1-A, Judgment (ICTY App Ch) (15 July 1999) [220]. In addition to its application at the ICTY and ICTR, joint enterprise liability is also used at the Special Court for Sierra Leone. See W Jordash and P Van Tuyl, 'Failure to Carry the Burden of Proof: How Joint Criminal Enterprise Lost its Way at the Special Court for Sierra Leone' (2010) 8 *Journal of International Criminal Justice* 591, 597–98 (discussing the 'doctrinal confusion and overreaching at the Special Court' regarding JCE application).

offers such a theory. *Regardless* of which doctrine a court applies – conspiracy, JCE, or co-perpetration – some theory must explain the mental state of participants who join together to pursue collective action. Strangely, although this question is absolutely central to the field, the international criminal law (ICL) literature has all but ignored the need to offer a philosophically sophisticated answer to this question.

Section III therefore explores the most plausible answer: individuals form a *joint* or *shared* intention that a group of individuals commits the crime.[2] By appealing to the philosophical literature on shared intentions (which has been generally ignored by ICL scholars),[3] this chapter offers a theory of collective criminal action that is both theoretically sound and yet also yields a legally workable doctrine for courts to apply. Defendants should only be held liable for each other's actions when each has the intention that they commit the crime together. Although the answer sounds simple at first glance, the theory offers a profound, and much needed, answer that both grounds ascriptions of vicarious liability, but also explains why courts should exclude liability for actions that fall outside the scope of the criminal plan.

II THE LIMITS OF THE CONTROL THEORY

While co-perpetration avoids many of the problems associated with JCE, the doctrine as applied by the ICC exaggerates the importance of 'control' as a defining characteristic of joint endeavours, while at the same time undervaluing the centrality of the distinctive mental states of the participants in joint criminal endeavours. By analyzing a series of hypothetical examples, section III will then conclude that intentionality – rather than control – must be the centre of any doctrine of group criminality.

A Co-perpetration at the ICC

The ICC Pre-Trial Chamber offered its analysis of the Rome Statute's Article 25 in *The Prosecutor v Thomas Lubanga Dyilo*[4] decision.[5] The Chief Prosecutor declined

[2] The terms 'joint intention' and 'shared intention' will be used interchangeably in this chapter.

[3] Bratman's work on joint intentions has been incorporated into the legal literature in several instances, though not in the ICL context. See, eg, D Markovitz, 'Contract and Collaboration' (2004) 113 *Yale Law Journal* 1417, 1451–56; SJ Shapiro, 'Laws, Plans, and Practical Reason' (2002) 8 *Legal Theory* 307; JL Coleman, *The Practice of Principle: In Defence of a Pragmatist Approach to Legal Theory* (Oxford, Oxford University Press, 2001) 95–100; C Bridgeman, 'Contracts as Plans' (2009) *University of Illinois Law Review* 341. See also C Finkelstein, 'Responsibility for Unintended Consequences' (2005) 2 *Ohio State Journal of Criminal Law* 579, 587–92 (Bratman on intentions generally).

[4] Decision on the Confirmation of Charges, *Prosecutor v Thomas Lubanga Dyilo*, Case ICC-01/04-01/06 (27 January 2007).

[5] See ibid [337].

to plead JCE and instead charged Lubanga under a theory of co-perpetration.[6] This in itself represented a substantial jurisprudential decision on the part of the Office of the Prosecutor. Although the ICTY Trial Chamber on a few occasions attempted to push a theory of co-perpetration in favour of JCE,[7] the Office of the Prosecutor at the ICTY never once pushed for co-perpetration as a mode of liability in place of joint criminal enterprise.[8] The ICC Pre-trial Chamber concluded that the notion of co-perpetration in Article 25(3)(a) best described the allegations against Lubanga because,

> the concept of co-perpetration is originally rooted in the idea that when the sum of the co-ordinated individual contributions of a plurality of persons results in the realisation of all the objective elements of a crime, any person making a contribution can be held vicariously responsible for the contributions of all the others and, as a result, can be considered as a principal to the whole crime.[9]

The Pre-Trial Chamber started its analysis by considering the various doctrines that can be used to distinguish between perpetrators and accomplices.[10] The traditional common law rule, which the Chamber termed the 'objective' approach, defined perpetrators as those who committed the *actus reus* of the crime, while supporters behind the scenes were branded as mere accomplices.[11] This is a counterintuitive result when the person behind the scenes orders the murder and the triggerman is a mere employee.[12] The alternative is a 'subjective' approach, which defines the perpetrator by virtue of his subjective mental state, that is, his intent to commit the crime.[13] In the case of a collective crime, what defines the perpetrators is their shared intent to commit the crime, regardless of their level of objective contribution (small or large). The Chamber identified the subjective approach with the JCE doctrine applied by the ICTY.[14]

The Pre-Trial Chamber swept both of these approaches to the side, preferring to chart a third way, co-perpetration, which combined subjective and objective

[6] However, the Legal Representative of Victims argued to the Court that Art 25(3)(a) codified joint criminal enterprise. See ibid [325].

[7] The most notable example was *Prosecutor v Milomir Tadić*, Case IT-97-24-T, Judgment (ICTY T Ch II) (31 July 2003) [440]. For a discussion of this case and its subsequent reversal by the Appeals Chamber, see JD Ohlin, '*Stakić* Commentary' in A Klip and G Sluiter (eds), *Annotated Leading Cases of International Criminal Tribunals* vol 14 (Mortsel, Intersentia Publishing, 2008) 739–41. See also H Olásolo, 'Reflections on the Treatment of the Notions of Control of the Crime and Joint Criminal Enterprise in the *Stakić* Appeal Judgement' (2007) 7 *International Criminal Law Review* 143, 143.

[8] The Office of the Prosecutor did allege on several occasions that defendants were responsible for co-perpetrating a joint criminal enterprise. See *Prosecutor v Milomir Stakić* (n 7) [504].

[9] See *Prosecutor v Thomas Lubanga Dyilo* (n 4) [326].

[10] See ibid [327]–[32].

[11] See ibid [328]. See also GP Fletcher, *Rethinking Criminal Law* 2nd reprint edn (Oxford, Oxford University Press, 2000) 654–55 (classifying theories to distinguish between principal perpetrators and accessories).

[12] For a discussion of the problems with the objective approach, see Ohlin, '*Stakić* Commentary' (n 7) 744. See also Fletcher, *Rethinking Criminal Law* (n 11) 655.

[13] See *Prosecutor v Thomas Lubanga Dyilo* (n 4) [329]; Fletcher, *Rethinking Criminal Law* (n 11) 657, citing *Stashchynsky* [1962] 18 BGHSt 87 (German court holding that KGB agent was not a principal because he was a mere instrument of his superiors).

[14] See *Prosecutor v Thomas Lubanga Dyilo* (n 4) [329].

elements in a different way. The Chamber based its understanding of co-perpetration in the Rome Statute on Roxin's control theory of perpetration.[15] This view is popular in German criminal law theory and has gained renewed currency in international circles as a result of the *Lubanga* decision.[16] The control theory of perpetration distinguishes between principals and accessories by asking who has control over the crime in question. If a defendant was in control of the criminal act, perhaps by virtue of ordering or soliciting a murder, then the defendant is an indirect perpetrator, even if he is not the *physical* perpetrator of the crime in question (that is, he did not pull the trigger).[17] The indirect perpetrator is indispensable because he controls the endeavour. If the individual with the gun is directed to conduct the crime by a military superior, then he has no direct control over the crime and is largely dispensable to the endeavour; he can be replaced by another soldier who can be ordered to commit the crime. If the indirect perpetrator works in tandem at the leadership level with others, then the leaders are classified as co-perpetrators because they share joint control over the crime. Control over the crime may be exercised through a hierarchical organizational structure (for example, *Organisationsherrschaft*), though there are other avenues for exercising control.

According to the ICC, the objective requirements for co-perpetration are the existence of a common plan among the participants and an essential contribution to the plan by the defendant.[18] The requirement that the contribution be essential means that the defendant could have frustrated the plan by withdrawing from it, thus establishing his joint control over the endeavour. The required mental state for an indirect perpetrator is *awareness* of his control over the crime.[19] For co-perpetrators, the required mental state is awareness of their *joint* control over a common plan and awareness of their essential contribution to it. Since both Lubanga and others had joint control over the crime, his participation was best viewed through the lens of co-perpetration, according to the Pre-Trial Chamber.[20] In addition to awareness of their control and essential contribution, co-perpetrators must also have the intent that the physical perpetrators should commit the crime.[21] However, the ICC completely watered down the intent requirement to the absolute minimum.[22] For purposes of this doctrine, co-perpetrators 'intend' the crime if they are aware of the risk that the physical perpetrators will commit

[15] Consider C Roxin, *Täterschaft und Tatherrschaft* 6th edn (Berlin, De Gruyter, 1994) 34; Fletcher, *Rethinking Criminal Law* (n 11) 655–56; *Prosecutor v Milomir Stakić* (n 7) [440], fn 945; *Prosecutor v Thomas Lubanga Dyilo* (n 4) [324], fn 414, [348], fn 425.

[16] For a complete discussion, see T Weigend, 'Intent, Mistake of Law, and Co-perpetration in the Lubanga Decision on Confirmation of Charges' (2008) 6 *Journal of International Criminal Justice* 471, 478–79. See also G Werle, *Principles of International Criminal Law* 1st edn (The Hague, TMC Asser, 2005) 123, [354].

[17] See Fletcher, *Rethinking Criminal Law* (n 11) 655–59.

[18] See *Prosecutor v Thomas Lubanga Dyilo* (n 4) [343].

[19] See ibid [331].

[20] See ibid [341].

[21] See Werle, *Principles of International Criminal Law* (n 16) 178.

[22] See Weigend, 'Intent, Mistake of Law, and Co-Perpetration' (n 16) 481.

the offence and the co-perpetrators reconcile themselves to this risk or consent to it.[23]

Criminal lawyers from common law jurisdictions would hardly describe this mental requirement as anything close to intentional or purposeful. At most, it is a form of advertent recklessness.[24] Criminal lawyers from civil law jurisdictions will often refer to this mental requirement as *dolus eventualis* and consider it uncontroversial, but the ICC's use of the concept here bears scrutiny. It is especially problematic because the ICC uses the same concept to conclude that the goal of the common plan need not be criminal at all: it is enough for the defendant to subjectively reconcile herself to the risk that her pursuit of the (lawful) common plan will entail the perpetration of various crimes by other actors.[25] The Rome Statute defines acting with 'intent' (in relation to a consequence) as meaning to 'cause [a] consequence' or to be aware that the consequence will happen 'in the ordinary course of events'.[26] The ICC put a gloss on this standard by concluding that a defendant's subjective awareness of a substantial risk of the consequence happening was sufficient to meet this standard.[27] Although this accords with the civil law doctrine of *dolus eventualis*, it is not at all clear that it accords with the meaning of the Rome Statute's requirement of 'in the ordinary course of events,' which suggests a higher standard than *dolus eventualis*. The result of the ICC's control theory approach is the combination of *awareness* of joint control over the crime with an intentionality requirement that is so watered down that the control requirement appears to be doing all of the heavy lifting in the doctrine. In the case of indirect co-perpetrators, what 'links' the defendants to each other is the common plan or agreement among them; but what links these defendants to the physical perpetrators is not the existence of a common plan but rather the defendants' joint control over the perpetrators, either as instruments or through an organizational hierarchy. However, the whole point of vicarious liability is the doctrinal need to provide a linking principle between the physical perpetrators of the crime and the defendants, and in the case of indirect co-perpetrators, the control criterion allegedly provides that link.

The second problem with the doctrine of co-perpetration is that it seems to imply a model of cooperation among a small number of individuals; the paradigmatic version of co-perpetration is cooperation between two individuals to complete a crime.[28] The Rome Statute's formulation of liability for crimes 'commit[ted] . . . jointly with another' suggests a crime committed by two persons;[29] the

[23] See ibid 481–82.

[24] See A Cassese, *International Criminal Law* 2nd edn (Oxford, Oxford University Press, 2008) 200–01 ('the test is . . . whether a man of reasonable prudence would have forecast that conduct, under the circumstances prevailing at the time').

[25] See Weigend, 'Intent, Mistake of Law, and Co-Perpetration' (n 16) 482.

[26] See Rome Statute, Art 30(2)(b).

[27] See *Prosecutor v Thomas Lubanga Dyilo* (n 4) [352]. See also Weigend, 'Intent, Mistake of Law, and Co-Perpetration' (n 16) 481.

[28] See Fletcher, *Rethinking Criminal Law* (n 11) 638.

[29] See Rome Statute, Art 25(3)(a).

provision does not say 'committed jointly with others'. International crimes, by contrast, are often committed by a great plurality of persons committed to a joint cause, and it is unclear whether describing such large-scale conspiracies as examples of co-perpetration is an accurate reflection of the facts on the ground. That being said, Roxin's theory of indirect perpetration through an organizational hierarchy nicely captures the relationship between a discrete number of leaders in a vast conspiracy, but it is unclear if the framers of the Rome Statute had this picture in mind when they crafted Article 25(3)(a) and its reference to 'jointly with another'. Such large-scale organizational criminality seems more suited to Article 25(3)(d) – contributions to a group endeavour – which the ICC has so far declined to utilize.

B A New Geography of Collective Action

Replacing JCE with the control theory of perpetration requires further scrutiny. We should conduct an independent and first order analysis of the criminality of group actors and decide what type of theory would best describe their culpability. A reactionary acceptance of the control theory would be just as unwise as blind acceptance of JCE. My own sense is that the control theory's attempt to move away from the subjective mental state of the perpetrators – and the idea of joint or shared intentions – is not ideal. Individuals often combine their efforts in order to achieve collective goals and, in so doing, demonstrate a particular intentional state that demonstrates their individual commitment to a joint activity.[30] Replacing this mental state with 'awareness' of the circumstances of joint control and a watered down intent requirement may have unintended consequences, which this section will now explore. Although it is clear that the doctrine of JCE is problematic, it is unclear whether the control theory, by sidestepping shared intentions, accurately responds to the particular problems in the doctrine. Ironically, it may be the case that the implicit idea of joint intentions was the one part of the JCE doctrine that ought to be retained.

In order to understand fully the mental states of individuals involved in group criminality, as well as their legal significance for criminal culpability, it would be best to consider a series of hypotheticals involving group action.

i The Love Parade

A large techno music festival is being held outdoors in an industrial city in Germany.[31] The crowd (hundreds of thousands of individuals) quickly exceeds the capacity of the outdoor location where the music festival is being held. The

[30] See this chapter, section III.B.

[31] The example is based on the stampede that recently occurred in Duisburg, Germany. See J Dempsey, 'Stampede at German Music Festival Kills 18' *New York Times* (24 July 2010).

main entrance to the festival is a small pedestrian tunnel that creates a bottleneck situation.[32] People continue to stream into the tunnel to get to the concert, but there is no room on the other side for them. At the same time, individuals inside the concert start to use the tunnel as an exit. People start to panic as they realize that there is not enough room in the tunnel to accommodate everyone. With people continuing to push from both sides of the narrow tunnel, those inside the tunnel become trapped with nowhere to move. More than 20 concertgoers are crushed to death by the surging crowd.[33]

ii The Essen Lynching

Three British pilots are captured in the German town of Essen during the Second World War.[34] A German officer orders a subordinate to transport the British POWs to a Luftwaffe post where they can be interrogated.[35] However, at the time of departure, the German officer issues the following additional order: the escort should not interfere with any civilians who might attack the prisoners.[36] The command was issued in public so that it could be heard not just by the escort but also by a crowd that had gathered in the vicinity.[37] As the POWs were marched down the streets of Essen, they were beaten by a growing crowd and eventually thrown over a bridge. One of the POWs died instantly after the fall from the bridge and the other two POWs were finished off by shots fired from the crowd and a final round of beatings.[38]

iii The Concentration Camp

Three military officers are all working as guards in a concentration camp in the former Yugoslavia.[39] The detention camp is specifically designed to serve as a system of mistreatment against the civilians who are detained there. Crimes, including murder, torture and rape, are being systematically committed against the civilians who live in the camp. The officers are all aware of the illegal nature of the camp and the officers all have the general intent to support the systemic

[32] See ibid.

[33] See J Dempsey, 'Deadly German Stampede Gets Its Villain' *New York Times* (30 July 2010).

[34] The example is based on the *Essen Lynching* case. See 'Trial of Erich Heyer and Six others (Essen Lynching)' (18th–19th and 21st–22nd December 1945) British Military Court for the Trial of War Criminals, Essen 1 *Law Reports of Trials of War Criminals* (UNWCC 1947) 88, 91. See also *Prosecutor v Duško Tadić* (n 1) [207]–[209] (citing *Essen Lynching*).

[35] See *Prosecutor v Duško Tadić* (n 1) [207].

[36] ibid.

[37] ibid.

[38] ibid.

[39] The classic concentration camp precedent is *Dachau Concentration Camp*, 11 *Law Reports of Trials of War Criminals* 5 (UNWCC 1947). The most significant concentration camp case to come out of the ICTY is the *Čelebići Camp Case*. See *Prosecutor v Delalić, Mucić, Delić, Landžo (Čelebići Camp Case)*, Case IT-96-21-T, Judgment (ICTY T Ch) (16 November 1998) [195]–[96].

mistreatment of the civilians in the camp by working as guards there.[40] One of the officers engages in the torture and rape of one of the civilian detainees. The other two officers do not directly help to commit this particular act, nor are they aware of this particular crime when it occurs.

iv The Deportation

A unit of soldiers is engaged in a campaign of ethnic cleansing in an attempt to remove all members of an ethnic minority from the region.[41] The soldiers forcibly remove 50 civilians from their homes simply because of their ethnicity and do not allow them to take any of their possessions with them. The soldiers agree among themselves that they will drive the civilians to a local train station, where a freight train is waiting to deport them, like cattle, to another region. The result will be an ethnically homogenous homeland (or at least progress towards that goal). However, when the detainees arrive at the train station, one of the soldiers decides that he prefers to kill the civilians instead of simply deporting them. He shoots all of them.

v The Attack against Civilians

A unit of 12 soldiers is ordered to seize a town that is located along a strategic roadway. By seizing the town, including its tall buildings, the soldiers will be able to locate and fire on any enemy soldiers who drive down the roadway. There are many civilians living in the town. Instead of evacuating and detaining the unarmed civilians, the soldiers decide to simply kill all of them. The soldiers agree that, in order to achieve this result, each of them will go into a building and kill any occupants that they find there.

C Analysis

What is the common factor among each of these hypotheticals? All of them involve collective action, although the degree of integration, the level of agree-

[40] See, eg, *Čelebići Camp Case*, ibid [325]–[26] (*mens rea* required for individual criminal responsibility for degrees of involvement in a crime is 'awareness of the act of participation coupled with a conscious decision to participate by planning, instigating, ordering, committing, or otherwise aiding and abetting the commission of a crime'); *Prosecutor v Duško Tadić* (n 1) [202]. See also *Trial of Josef Kramer and 44 Others (Belsen)* (17 September – 17 November 1945) British Military Court, Luneberg, Germany, 2 *Law Reports of Trials of War Criminals* 1 (UNWCC 1947) (45 staff of Belsen or Auschwitz concentration camps and others in positions of authority accused of committing murders individually and of having knowingly participated in a common plan to operate a system of ill-treatment and murder in these camps).

[41] See *Prosecutor v Stakić*, Case IT-97-24-A, Judgment (ICTY App Ch) (22 March 2006) [278] (Appeals Chamber's view of the *actus reus* and *mens rea* of the offence of deportation). For a full discussion of deportation as a crime against humanity, see R Cryer, H Friman, D Robinson and E Wilmshurst, *An Introduction to International Criminal Law and Procedure* 2nd edn (Cambridge, Cambridge University Press, 2010) 249–50 (specifically discussing ICTY case law regarding deportation in the context of ethnic cleansing).

ment and the mental state of the participants are different in each case. To start, consider the easiest case, the Attack against Civilians. In that case, the soldiers agree to commit the crime together. What is distinctive about the scenario is that the outcome would be impossible – or perhaps difficult – for each individual to achieve on his own. Consequently, the individuals agree on a collective course of action. So each individual not only has the intention to pursue his own particular course of action, but each individual understands and *intends* for the other individuals to fulfil their part of the programme as well. One can infer this intentional state – intending to commit one's own act and intending that others do similarly – on the basis of their shared commitment to the overall outcome, and the fact that the outcome is not achievable without this level of collective coordination. Arguably, this is the easiest case to justify vicarious liability for the actions of co-participants, because each individual has the mental state (intention) that grounds not only his own action but also the actions of his co-participants.

Contrast that situation with the most difficult hypothetical – the Love Parade example. In that case, the individuals at each end of the tunnel have a rather simple intention: to use the tunnel as a means of egress. When panic begins to set in and the individuals involved realize that there is a danger, each simply has an intention to escape the chaos in order to survive.[42] Taken together, the consequence of so many individuals acting on their individual intentions produces a deadly collective result: the crowd itself becomes a surging mass that ends up killing 20 individuals. However, the crucial distinguishing factor of the Love Parade crush, and others like it, is the attitude of each individual about the actions of the others. Although each individual intends to get through the tunnel, she does not intend for the others to do the same. This distinguishes the Love Parade crowd from the Attack against Civilians. In fact, each individual concertgoer would probably prefer that the others refrain from going through the tunnel in order to make it easier for her to pass through. Also, none of the concertgoers wants anyone to die. So what produces the deadly result is the confluence of so many concertgoers with individual intentions that result in a completely uncoordinated result. This notion of an *uncoordinated* result is significant, because a stampede is really just a collective action problem like the Prisoners' Dilemma.[43] If the concertgoers could have coordinated their behaviour properly, they could have exited the concert grounds in a safe and orderly fashion. But once the crowd started to panic, each individual was concerned that she might get trapped by the surging crowd, so each individual decided to push to get out in order to save herself. Of course, if each individual knew for certain that the other concertgoers would forgo pushing there would be no need for her to push as well in an attempt to

[42] See Dempsey, 'Stampede' (n 31) 1.

[43] But see J Wise, 'When Crowds Panic' *New York Times Blog* (3 August 2010), online: freakonomics.blogs.nyti mes.com/2010/08/03/when-crowds-panic/ ('[T]he most perplexing form of tragedy: one that unfolds entirely as a result of the normal psychology of healthy human beings. When crowds reach a critical density, they automatically become vulnerable to a contagion of blind fear that overwhelms any attempt at rational behavior[.]').

escape. But since there was no way of enforcing this norm, each individual had to engage in egoistic self-preservation and try to push her way out of the crowd, even if this helped create the very collective problem that caused the stampede. The problem of norm enforcement in such situations is particularly acute because even police officers screaming at people to stop will do nothing to change the people's self-interested behaviour if they risk death or injury when the rest of the crowd ignores the police officers' commands. And, given that the rest of the crowd is in the exact same situation, this guarantees that no one will listen to the police officers. The result is a Prisoners' Dilemma where everyone defects.[44]

This can be distinguished from the more *coordinated* result of the crowd behaviour in the Essen Lynching example. In that scenario, the members of the crowd hear the order of the German officer suggesting that it might be a good idea if the POWs were to meet a violent end.[45] The crowd then responds by beating the POWs. Each individual clearly has the intention to administer each individual blow.[46] But what is the attitude of each individual regarding the activities of the rest of the crowd? Although no advance coordination or deliberate planning sessions are conducted, it is possible to infer that each member of the mob intended for the rest of the mob to engage in the beating as well.[47] Unlike the Love Parade example where the collective violence is the unfortunate result of uncoordinated behaviour, the collective violence in Essen Lynching is the deliberate result of coordinated behaviour. Each member of the crowd intends to hit the POWs and similarly intends for the rest of the crowd to do the same, with full knowledge that together they might achieve a result that individually would be impossible to achieve: killing the captives.[48] It is important to realize that in such situations, the intention of each individual regarding the actions of the crowd arises somewhat spontaneously, without prior deliberation, but this does not mean that there is no

[44] See R Brown, *Social Psychology* (New York, The Free Press, 1965) 738–44 (stampede as *n*-person Prisoners' Dilemma); M Granovetter, 'Economic Action and Social Structure: The Problem of Embeddedness' (1985) 91 *American Journal of Sociology* 481, 490 (citing Roger Brown's *n*-person Prisoners' Dilemma).

[45] Compare with *Prosecutor v Duško Tadić* (n 1) [209] (concluding that 'not all of them intended to kill but all intended to participate in the unlawful ill-treatment of the prisoners of war'). It is not clear whether this is a legitimate inference from the Essen Lynching. The Court appeared to hold all the individuals vicariously liable regardless of whether they had fired a shot or delivered one of the fatal blows, though this does not entail the conclusion that defendants were convicted in the absence of an intention to kill. See especially *Prosecutor v Duško Tadić* (n 1) [209], fn 259 (discussing civilians, including Boddenberg, who were convicted in light of the fact that the motives of the crowd against the airmen 'were deadly').

[46] This issue is discussed in S Powles, 'Joint Criminal Enterprise: Criminal Liability by Prosecutorial Ingenuity and Judicial Creativity?' (2004) 2 *Journal of International Criminal Justice* 606, 616.

[47] See ibid ('The prosecution in *Essen Lynching*, as the Appeals Chamber noted [in *Prosecutor v Duško Tadić*], specifically stated that if the accused had the *intent* to kill, then they would be guilty of murder; if they had no such intent, then they could still be convicted of manslaughter. The accused were convicted of murder, implying that the court concluded that they all indeed intended the airmen to die').

[48] For another example of individual intent for the group to commit the act, see R Nordland, 'In Bold Display, Taliban Order Stoning Deaths' *New York Times* (16 August 2010) (execution where 200 villagers participated by throwing stones and were described as 'festive' and 'cheering').

intention or coordination at all. Spontaneous and intentional coordination should not be confused with no coordination. That is the difference between the Love Parade example and Essen Lynching.

Consider now the Concentration Camp example. This hypothetical sits in the middle – between the Love Parade example and the Attack against Civilians example. Each individual has the intention to work as a guard at the camp and in so doing has the intention to further the system of mistreatment that the camp represents. But each guard's attitude about the work of the others is a little more complicated. Each guard intends that the other guards also work to keep the system of mistreatment functioning, since each knows that it would be impossible to run such a system without the collective coordination of many guards who were similarly inclined. It would be literally impossible for a single individual to operate such a facility alone. However, it is probably not the case that the two guards intend for the third guard to commit that *particular* act of torture and rape.[49] This places the intentions of the guard in a liminal position between the two other hypotheticals. It is perhaps for this reason that the ICTY in *Tadić* designated an entirely separate doctrinal category, JCE II, for these cases.[50] Under the rule announced in *Tadić*, a concentration camp guard is vicariously liable for the actions of other guards if the defendant has the 'intent to further the common concerted design to ill-treat inmates'.[51] The defendant need not have the intent for the specific underlying criminal act charged in the indictment. So, in the case of the Concentration Camp example, the two prison guards would be convicted of war crimes for the torture and rape committed by the third guard. The *Tadić* court justified this rule by appeal to Second World War precedent, and in particular the *Dachau Concentration Camp* case, although the ruling is a bit thin on a doctrinal theory to explain the result.[52]

The most tenuous example is the Deportation hypothetical. In that case, the soldiers all have the individual intent to cooperate on the deportation. And each individual soldier intends that the other soldiers should complete their part in the plan as well. So we have a mutually reinforcing network of reciprocal intentions. However, the rogue soldier also has an intention that the others do not share: the intent to murder the civilians. The attitude of the other soldiers regarding this action might run the gamut from regret to a form of passive acquiescence.[53] In

[49] See, eg, *Prosecutor v Kvočka et al*, Case IT-98-30/1-A (ICTY App Ch) (28 February 2005) [184] ('The Trial Chamber found that Kvočka had actively contributed to the everyday functioning and maintenance of the camp and, through his participation, enabled the camp to continue unabated its insidious policies and practices, and is thus criminally responsible for the crimes committed as part of the joint criminal enterprise'); *Prosecutor v Momčilo Krajišnik*, Case IT-00-39/40, Judgment (ICTY T Ch I) (27 September 2006) [884] ('[P]ersons in a criminal enterprise must be shown to act together, or in concert with each other, in the implementation of a common objective, if they are to share responsibility for the crimes committed through the JCE[.]').

[50] See *Prosecutor v Duško Tadič* (n 1) [202].

[51] See ibid [203].

[52] See ibid [203], fn 250.

[53] At the most extreme end of the spectrum, one might describe the attitude of the soldiers as that of *dolus eventualis*. See Fletcher, *Rethinking Criminal Law* (n 11) 445–49. But see GP Fletcher and JD

any event, they clearly do not intend for the rogue soldier to take this action. The most that can be said is that they were negligent or reckless for participating in a joint criminal endeavour with a member whose capacity for rogue behaviour and straying from the criminal plan was arguably reasonably foreseeable. Under both common law conspiracy doctrine and JCE doctrine, this recklessness provides the justification for vicarious liability for actions that fall outside the scope of the original criminal plan.[54]

The co-perpetration theory applied by the ICC tends to analyze all of the following hypotheticals under the rubric of control.[55] According to the Pre-Trial Chamber's analysis:

> The notion underpinning this third approach is that principals to a crime are not limited to those who physically carry out the objective elements of the offence, but also include those who, in spite of being removed from the scene of the crime, control or mastermind its commission because they decide whether and how the offence will be committed.[56]

Fair enough. However, the required elements applied by the ICC to co-perpetrators provide confusing guidance. The objective elements include a common plan and an essential contribution to it.[57] The subjective elements include intent (*dolus eventualis*) that the crime be committed and awareness of their joint control over the crime.[58] So the control theory would provide the following answers to the hypotheticals. In the case of the Attack against Civilians, the soldiers are all guilty as co-perpetrators of the entire war crime because each one played an essential role in the crime and exercised joint control over the operation. In the case of the Love Parade stampede, it is difficult to determine whether there is a common plan and whether each individual's contribution is to be considered essential. First, the ICC's control theory does not require a common *criminal* goal; it allows prosecution for a non-criminal goal that creates a substantial risk of criminal consequences. As for judging the 'essentiality' of the contribution, the doctrine devolves into counterfactual analysis.[59] On the one hand, each individual's role was non-essential because 'but for' her conduct, the stampede would surely still have

Ohlin, 'Reclaiming Fundamental Principles of Law in the Darfur Case' (2005) 3 *Journal of International Criminal Justice* 554 ('If the purpose of an armed band is to rid an area of potential military opponents and they know that some people will die as a result, their attitude is not necessarily *dolus eventualis.* Their killing is *dolus* only if they realize that specific people will die, approve and desire this result in their hearts, and decide to continue with their action').

[54] See AM Danner and JS Martinez, 'Guilty Associations: Joint Criminal Enterprise, Command Responsibility, and the Development of International Criminal Law' (2005) 93 *California Law Review* 75, 164 (discussing mixed US circuit court reactions to charges under statute for providing material support or resources to an organization designated as a 'foreign terrorist organization' without a scienter requirement); M Osiel, 'The Banality of Good: Aligning Incentives Against Mass Atrocities' (2005) 105 *Columbia Law Review* 1751, 1785–86 (discussing the resemblance between JCE III and *Pinkerton* and felony murder).

[55] See, eg, *Prosecutor v Thomas Lubanga Dyilo* (n 4) [322].

[56] ibid [330].

[57] ibid [343], [346].

[58] See ibid [331], [366].

[59] See Weigend, 'Intent, Mistake of Law, and Co-Perpetration' (n 16) 480.

occurred in almost exactly the same way. On the other hand, this produces a paradoxical answer: the same thing could be answered about each defendant at which point the stampede would certainly *not* have happened. As for the criterion of joint control and awareness of control, the answer is complicated. In one sense, each concertgoer exercised joint control over the result by virtue of her actions that caused the result; had the concertgoers done otherwise, the stampede would not have occurred, thus implying a level of mutual control. On the other hand, the collective result was completely *uncoordinated*, thus suggesting a complete lack of meaningful control over the result and herein lies the difficulty: the lack of coordination stems from the lack of a common criminal plan. However, the ICC's control theory does not require that the common plan has a criminal goal, but only that the co-perpetrators realize the substantial risk of criminal consequences.

Consider now the Essen Lynching example. Although there is joint activity in this case (including a spontaneous plan to lynch the airmen), we again run into the same ambiguity over whether each individual punch from a member of the crowd is considered essential activity. In one sense, the actions of the crowd appear to be coordinated because each realizes that he is participating in a lynching, but the issue of control again appears elusive. One might resolve the anxiety here by declaring that the German officer who suggested to the crowd that they should lynch the airmen is the real perpetrator of the crime; he retained control over the crime because he could have refrained from issuing the order in the first place – and could have intervened and dispersed the crowd when it started. While *his* culpability is clear under the control theory, in situations where the top level actor is missing (the Love Parade example), the question of control is confusing.

The Concentration Camp and the Deportation examples are also difficult to resolve. Under the control theory, the camp guards might be considered as jointly in control because they exercise coordinated authority over the inmates. Moreover, they are clearly aware of the circumstances of their coordinated contributions and their joint control over the prison. On the other hand, they are in the middle of the organizational hierarchy, and perhaps ultimate control rests with the commandant of the prison, as in the Essen Lynching example.[60] The commandant presumably had the authority to relieve a camp guard of his duty and replace him with another soldier. Is this enough to conclude that the guard is not in joint control over the crime?[61] The Deportation case is the one example where a strict

[60] The commandant of the notorious Tuol Sleng prison was one of the first to be indicted and then stand trial at the ECCC. See *Kaing Guek Eav (Duch Case)* Case 001/18-07-2007/ECCC/TC, Judgment (ECCC T Ch) (26 July 2010) [679]–[81] (sentence of 35 years minus 10 years for time served and five years for illegal detention).

[61] Weigend helpfully suggests that control should be cashed out relative to the 'viewpoint of the concrete criminal plan', so that the relevant question is not whether the crime would have happened at all, but rather whether the crime would have still happened in the same way as agreed to by the participants. See Weigend, 'Intent, Mistake of Law, and Co-Perpetration' (n 16) 480. Of course, this requires an account of the level of specificity in the plan. The same plan might be described in different ways – a thick version that includes many specific details, a thin version that simply traces the broad outlines of the plan and excludes details and finally, versions of varying degrees of specificity along the spectrum between the thin and thick versions.

version of the control theory could offer a simple and elegant answer: none of the soldiers has control over the rogue soldier who strays from the pre-arranged criminal plan. Although each is guilty of co-perpetrating the war crime of deportation – and possibly a crime against humanity for persecution – the only soldier guilty of murder as a war crime is the rogue soldier. However, the ICC's expansive version of the control theory left the door open for vicarious liability provided that the other soldiers were aware 'of the substantial likelihood that his or her actions or omissions would result in the realization of the objective elements of the crime . . . [and decided] to carry out his or her actions or omissions despite such awareness'.[62] Applied to the current facts, this liability based on *dolus eventualis* would attach if the other soldiers understood that there was a substantial likelihood that the plan would result in the killing of the deportees by the rogue soldier and continued with the plan nevertheless.[63] This use of *dolus eventualis* simply rehashes the JCE III standard of 'reasonably foreseeable'.[64]

The control theory cobbles together a patchwork of requirements but never achieves a convincing account of group criminality. Although control is relevant for culpability, it is not the central element. By defining the mental element of the co-perpetrator as awareness of joint control combined with a watered down intent requirement, the doctrine effectively moves the mental element to the background in favour of the objective element.[65] Control becomes the *sine qua non* of the doctrine. True, this result is consistent with the PTC's motivation in adopting the control theory in the first place – avoiding the subjective approach embodied by JCE – but one wonders whether the result adequately captures the culpable mental state of the participants of collective crimes.

The ICC's control theory deemphasizes and undervalues the joint intention of the participants – no adequate theory of vicarious liability in international criminal law can be complete without a thorough understanding of the mental attitude of each participant to the participation of his colleagues. The basic structure of that answer must involve an appropriate mapping, at the philosophical level, of an individual's intentional commitment to the group endeavour. By drawing on the philosophical literature on shared intentions, the following section is devoted to briefly explaining that account and demonstrating its centrality in resolving these questions. Although a theory of shared intentions does not resolve every question of culpability raised by the hypotheticals in the previous section, the following section will demonstrate that a satisfactory ICL doctrine of collective participation cannot be constructed without one. It is a necessary but not a sufficient condition.

[62] *Prosecutor v Thomas Lubanga Dyilo* (n 4) [353].

[63] See ibid [352].

[64] See Fletcher and Ohlin, 'Reclaiming Fundamental Principles of Law' (n 53) 554 (arguing that *dolus eventualis* represents a higher degree of culpability than common law recklessness).

[65] See *Prosecutor v Thomas Lubanga Dyilo* (n 4) [329] (describing JCE as a 'subjective' approach which requires shared intent). Clearly, the Pre-Trial Chamber (PTC) was referring to JCE I, not JCE III. Also, it can be inferred from this paragraph that the PTC favoured the doctrine of co-perpetration over JCE because the latter was allegedly too organized around the mental states of the participants. For a further discussion of the subjective approach, see Fletcher, *Rethinking Criminal Law* (n 11) 655.

III A THEORY OF JOINT INTENTIONS

This section draws heavily on the work of Michael Bratman, who has offered the most philosophically convincing treatment of the matter of shared intentions.[66] John Searle and Raimo Tuomolo have also pursued similar accounts, which they called collective intentions and we-intentions.[67] For the most part, the philosophical differences between these theories will be of only partial concern to our analysis. True, it is important to get the theoretical details correct. But before we do that, we must demonstrate that the very idea of group intentionality is the relevant subject to discuss. Whether you call it a shared or joint intention, a collective intention, or a we-intention does not matter yet. We start with the definition offered by Bratman not because I am committed to its correctness, but rather because it offers the most concise and elegant formulation from which to start the analysis.[68]

A The Shared Intention Thesis

In numerous essays, Bratman defends what he calls the Shared Intention Thesis (SI thesis).[69] It consists of the following propositions:

> We intend to *J* [joint activity] if and only if:
>
> (1) (a) I intend that we *J* and (b) you intend that we *J*.
> (2) I intend that we *J* in accordance with and because of (1)(a), (1)(b), and meshing sub-plans of (1)(a) and (1)(b); you intend that we *J* in accordance with and because of (1)(a), (1)(b), and meshing sub-plans of (1)(a) and (1)(b).
> (3) (1) and (2) are common knowledge between us.[70]

Although the SI thesis sounds technical, it can be parsed rather simply. Step 1 codifies the requirement that a shared intention is simply a collection of two (or more) individual intentions that are related in the right way. The required relationship is then explained in Steps 2 and 3. The individual intentions referred to in Step 1 are a very specific kind of intention, which is the intention that you and I both engage in an activity *together*.[71]

The relationship between the intentions that is codified in Step 2 involves the reciprocal and coordinated nature of the intentions.[72] In other words, the

[66] See, eg, ME Bratman, *Faces of Intention: Selected Essays on Intention and Agency* (Cambridge, Cambridge University Press, 1999) 93–129.

[67] For a general discussion, see JR Searle, 'Collective Intentions and Actions' in PR Cohen, J Morgan and ME Pollack (eds), *Intentions in Communication* (Cambridge MA, MIT Press, 1990) 401; R Tuomela and K Miller, 'We-Intentions' (1988) 53 *Philosophical Studies* 367.

[68] Bratman's theory is arguably the most influential theory of joint intentions and has been widely cited in the legal field (although not in international criminal law). See, eg, Coleman, *The Practice of Principle* (n 3) 96–99.

[69] See Bratman, *Faces of Intention* (n 66) 131.

[70] ibid.

[71] See ibid 115.

[72] See ibid 124.

individuals do not simply intend for the cooperation to happen and then blindly hope that it comes to pass.[73] Rather, each individual desires that the group commits the action in full knowledge that the other individual so desires as well.[74] That is the first half of Step 2. The second half of Step 2 involves the meshing of sub-plans, or the coordination for how the activity will be conducted.[75] This does not necessarily mean that all possible sub-plans will be coordinated, but simply that each individual has an expectation that they will plan with the others how to carry out the activity, and it is within the context of this expectation that each individual has the intention that the group will conduct the activity.[76] Finally, Step 3 simply states that each member will be aware of the reciprocal nature of the intentions.[77]

Bratman's preferred example is the painting of a house by two individuals.[78] Suppose an individual wants to paint a house and starts in the front. As it happens, a second individual also wants to paint the house and starts from the back. Since neither is aware of the other, we could not conclude that they have a shared intention to paint the house.[79] Any coordination here is completely accidental. Suppose then that the individual in the front of the house is aware of the activity of the second individual, but not vice versa. This would also not constitute a joint intention to paint the house. Thirdly, consider a situation where both are aware of the existence of the other painter, but neither is doing the painting in accordance with – and because of – the other painter. (Such indifference might be strange, but not impossible.) This leaves us with the possibility that each one is aware of the other painter and in fact does the painting in full expectation that the other painter is doing the same from the opposite end. This, in fact, is quite easy to imagine where two individuals are committed to pursuing a project efficiently. However, what if the painter in the front starts painting in blue and the painter in the back starts painting in red, and each one is painting the house with the intention that it be *fully* painted in the colour that they were painting? In this situation, there would not be a joint intention either. A joint intention arises where there is some minimal planning activity such that each individual intends that the group commits the action because they have coordinated sub-plans that dictate how the action is going to be carried out.[80] Then and only then can we conclude that two individuals exhibit a shared intention to commit a particular action.

Several immediate observations can be drawn from this account. First, this account is highly individualistic. The basic building blocks of the account are individuals and their individual intentions, and the particular relationship between those intentions. There is nothing overly metaphysical or mystical about

[73] See ibid 118.
[74] See ibid 119.
[75] See ibid 125.
[76] See ibid 119–21.
[77] See ibid 119.
[78] See ibid 93–94, 98, 112, 120 and 153–56.
[79] See ibid 94.
[80] See ibid 95–98.

the concepts being deployed here.[81] There is no reference to corporate entities or group minds.[82] Indeed, if there is any fault here, it may be that the account is overly individualistic. Given that the account is so entirely individualistic, how does it manage to yield an account of a *collective* intention? The answer lies in the heavy use and deployment of the concept of planning.[83] Although many agents (including some animals) may have the capacity to form some kind of mental intention, only planning agents are capable of interacting with each other in a way that can yield a collective intention.[84] This is based on the full blown reciprocal nature of how planning agents interact with each other. Planning agents recognize each other as being uniquely capable of engaging in cooperative behaviour, through the process of deliberation regarding means, in a way that results in either the full or partial meshing of sub-plans.[85] Taken together, this yields a shared intention.

It does not matter (or it should not matter) what you call it. But one could offer a theory of shared intentions that is far less individualistic and far more collectivist. Searle, for example, argues that collective intentions of the type explained by Bratman are irreducible to their individual components.[86] By this he means that collective intentionality is not *wholly* reducible to individual intentions. His argument for the irreducibility of collective intentions stems from a simple intuition. A thorough individualistic account of collective intentions is only possible because it makes reference to cooperation.[87] This much is undeniable. The house painters only exhibit a collective intention to paint the house when there is some indication that they believe and intend that they will cooperate in the house painting project. Without this level of cooperation, one simply has two people individually painting a house with two separate individual intentions to paint the house. The reference to cooperation, though, may be problematic. How should one understand the concept of cooperation? Presumably it involves at least two individuals who work together to achieve a particular outcome. The 'working together' is a process that is not accidental, but rather is intentionally desired by the individuals who are cooperating. This is the very definition of cooperation. If this is the right understanding of cooperation, the appeal to cooperation is indeed problematic because it renders the entire account viciously circular.[88] The account of joint

[81] See also Searle, 'Collective Intentions' (n 67) 404 (discussion of group minds and collective unconscious 'at best mysterious and at worst incoherent').

[82] For a discussion of the history of corporate entities as it relates to legal discourse, see JD Ohlin, 'Group Think: The Law of Conspiracy and Collective Reason' (2007) 98 *Journal of Criminal Law & Criminology* 163–69.

[83] For a general discussion, see ME Bratman, *Intention, Plans, and Practical Reason* (Cambridge MA, Harvard University Press, 1987) 14–27.

[84] See C Rovane, *The Bounds of Agency: An Essay in Revisionary Metaphysics* (Princeton, Princeton University Press, 1998) 144–45. See also Bratman, *Faces of Intention* (n 66) 95–98.

[85] See Bratman, *Intention, Plans, and Practical Reason* (n 83) 36. Compare with Rovane, *Bounds of Agency*, ibid 144–45.

[86] Searle, 'Collective Intentions' (n 67) 404.

[87] See ibid 406.

[88] See ibid 405.

intentions is only rendered intelligible as an *individualistic* account because of its implicit appeal to the concept of cooperation.

But cooperation already has the notion of a collective intention imbedded within it.[89] So we are left with an uncomfortable dilemma. Either one includes cooperation in the formula and risks circularity, or one excludes cooperation from the formula and in the process leaves the account hopelessly under-broad. Neither alternative is particularly attractive. It suggests that collective intentions may not be easily reducible to individual intentions. As Searle puts it, they are a 'primitive phenomenon'.[90]

We need not resolve the problem here. Although I'm inclined to favour the irreducibility thesis, we are not absolutely required to resolve the philosophical debate in order to insist that some coherent theory of joint or shared intentions is necessary to ground an ICL doctrine for vicarious liability. I will rest content if I can demonstrate that a theory of joint intentions is required to ground the doctrine, without necessarily flushing out every last detail of the theory. Nor does this incompleteness render the theory suspect. It simply represents a promissory note that some less doctrinal aspects of the theory require future resolution. To confront them directly at this stage of the argument would risk entropy.

B Applying the Shared Intentions Theory to International Criminal Law

The appropriate course of action is to take the theory and apply it to the five hypotheticals presented at the beginning of the section and then compare the results it yields to the results that we achieved with the ICC's control theory of co-perpetration. If I am correct, a theory of joint intentions provides better answers to the hypotheticals than the control theory. This does not mean that control as a criterion is irrelevant, but simply that its centrality has been exaggerated. Just as the case law and scholarly literature in 1997 revealed an unreflective acceptance of JCE, we are rapidly and worrisomely coming to a current situation where blind and unreflective acceptance of JCE is being replaced with a hagiographic approach to the control theory of co-perpetration. Neither is particularly helpful; healthy scepticism should rule the day.

If we re-examine the Love Parade stampede, the notion of joint intentions explains why vicarious liability should be unthinkable in such a case. The concertgoers in the tunnel were not cooperating; nor did they reflexively make decisions in light of, and because of, the actions of the other concertgoers. Indeed, their interests were antagonistic. One might object that antagonism and joint intentions are not mutually exclusive. Consider two participants in a game competing against each other and with mutually incompatible interests; they still cooperate

[89] See ibid.
[90] ibid (defining these intentions as 'primitive phenomenon' in the sense that they are irreducible).

with each other *by playing the game*.[91] However, the Love Parade example can be distinguished from antagonistic game playing cooperation because game playing involves a joint intention to follow the rules of the game in order to mutually achieve the satisfaction of game playing. The Love Parade example is devoid of either actual rule following or a shared commitment to rule following in order to engage in game playing.

Compare this with Essen Lynching. Although the cooperation is rather spontaneous, it is clear that the members of the crowd share an intention to commit a collective act: the lynching of the airmen. Not only does each member of the crowd want to lynch the soldier, but each member of the crowd knows that the other members of the crowd are similarly inclined and that each will play his part in the gruesome deed by throwing a punch or kicking them. The aggregation of the individual acts does more than produce an accidental collective result like the Love Parade; it produces a planned action that each member desires. It should be noted that not all cases of mob behaviour will be exactly the same; they can cover the entire spectrum between Love Parade and Essen Lynching. Some brawls might be more haphazard and less coordinated than Essen Lynching, but still more organized than Love Parade, like a bar room brawl. The key to distinguishing them is the intentionality of the participants and their interrelation.

The Concentration Camp case and the Attack against Civilians example are also easy to resolve. The soldiers in the Attack against Civilians not only share a commitment to a particular goal, but they mesh sub-plans and each one is aware of his particular role in the overall endeavour. Indeed, the attack would not be possible (each soldier clearing a different building) without the coordination that results from their joint intention to commit the crime. This joint intention makes clear why vicarious liability is consistent with the principle of culpability. Although the physical actions are committed by several individuals, each one intends for the other to commit the action. By so doing, he makes it his own. To explain this argument, it might be helpful to consider other situations where actors might be legally responsible for the actions of another because they 'make it their own'.[92] In

[91] Situations involving cooperative activity at one level, and antagonism at another level, have long confounded judges in the case law. See, eg, *People v Russell* [1998] 693 NE2d 193 (NY) 194 (participants in gun battle were all convicted for intentionally aiding the shooter, even though they were shooting at each other). The court noted that 'unlike an unanticipated ambush or spontaneous attack that might have taken defendants by surprise, the gunfight in this case only began after defendants acknowledged and accepted each others' challenge to engage in a deadly battle on a public concourse'. *People v Russell*, 195. See also *People v Abbott* [1981] 445 NYS2d 344 (Ny App Div) 347 (applying similar rule in drag racing context). The rule has been frequently criticized. For a general discussion, see DB Yeager, 'Dangerous Games and the Criminal Law' (1997) 16 *Criminal Justice Ethics* 3. Bratman is more sympathetic to the general idea and acknowledges that competitive game playing involves cooperative activity. See Bratman, *Faces of Intention* (n 66) 107 (playing chess involves cooperation to play the game, though one's opponent does not, and cannot, be cooperative in his opponent's plan to checkmate him). Game playing therefore involves meshing of sub-plans among the players, although not all the way down.

[92] See, eg, *Nye & Nissen v United States* 336 US 613, 619 (1949), quoting *United States v Peoni* 100 F2d 401 (2d Cir) 402 (1938) (aider and abettor 'in some sort associate[s] himself with the venture, that he participate[s] in it as in something that he wishes to bring about, that he seek[s] by his action to

a case where a mob boss procures a subordinate to commit a murder, the mob boss makes the action his own because he wants the crime to be committed and uses his subordinate as an instrument to make it happen.[93] The Attack against Civilians exists on a spectrum with the mob boss, although this time each soldier makes the collective action his own, not because each uses the other soldiers as an instrument, but simply because each soldier intends for the group to commit the crime and intends to do his part to bring the collective plan into fruition. It is the mental state – not the *actus reus* – that provides the justification for the vicarious liability.

The Concentration Camp case is a little more difficult, but the existence of joint intentionality arguably captures the ambiguity of the situation. The two camp guards both share a joint intention to operate a system of ill treatment of civilians and each knows that the other is working with them on a coordinated plan to achieve that result. However, the two guards clearly do not share an intention with the third guard to commit that particular criminal act, that is, the torture and rape of the civilian. The torture and rape are at best a natural outgrowth of the system of mistreatment that the guards have the intention of promoting by working at the camp. Their culpability appears to remain in a liminal space between a hypothetical defendant who has a joint intention to commit a particular crime (most culpable) and a hypothetical defendant who merely recklessly participates in a criminal gang knowing that some crimes might happen (least culpable).[94] What is the moral and legal significance of their having a joint intention to operate a system of mistreatment, and what is the moral and legal significance of the *lack* of any joint intention with regard to that *particular* criminal act? My point here is not to defend a particular moral conclusion for how we should treat the two guards in the Concentration Camp example. Rather, my point is to emphasize that a theory of joint intentions gets to the heart of the nuanced culpability of the guards in this example.

One might object that the control theory was invoked by the ICC as a method of distinguishing between co-perpetrators and accomplices – that is, distinguishing between levels of participation in a criminal endeavour – and not grounding vicarious liability.[95] And certainly the ICC's use of the control theory suggests that they also implicitly considered some notion of a shared or joint intention as a relevant consideration, since the ICC requires a finding of an agreement or com-

make it succeed'); *State v Gladstone* 474 P2d 274 (Wash) 278 (1970) (defendant who directed an agent of the police to someone who might be willing to sell marijuana not guilty of aiding and abetting because no evidence that defendant did something in association or connection with the seller to accomplish the crime).

[93] This is best described as an example of indirect perpetration. The ICC case against al-Bashir is based on this doctrine. For a general discussion, see F Jessberger and J Geneuss, 'On the Application of a Theory of Indirect Perpetration in *Al Bashir*: German Doctrine at The Hague?' (2008) 6 *Journal of International Criminal Justice* 853.

[94] Compare *Prosecutor v Thomas Lubanga Dyilo* (n 4) [350] ('[aware] that a circumstance exists or a consequence will occur in the ordinary course of events') and [352] ('accepts such an outcome by reconciling himself or herself with it or consenting to it (also known as *dolus eventualis*)').

[95] See ibid [327].

mon plan among the co-perpetrators.[96] The question is whether control is the right barometer with which to distinguish between co-perpetrators and accomplices. According to the ICC, accomplices contribute to the endeavour but have no control over the outcome. They are not in a position to determine whether the crime actually happens or not. Although this is one plausible avenue for distinguishing between principals and their accomplices, one might also invoke the concept of joint intentions to do the job. Under this proposal, those who jointly intend to commit the crime with each other would be liable as co-perpetrators (or some other designation), whereas those who simply assist the group with *mere knowledge* that their assistance will help complete the crime are then labelled as accomplices. If the joint intentions theory is capable of making this distinction (and doing it better), it is unclear what is left for control – as a criterion – to do.

This is arguably what the ICTY Trial Chambers in *Kvočka* and *Stakić* were getting at.[97] The Trial Chambers in both cases insisted that JCE could be revised so that it distinguishes between those who co-perpetrated a JCE and those who aided and abetted the JCE.[98] And the distinction between the two categories was not based on control, but rather co-perpetrators were those who intended to commit the crime while the accomplices merely assisted with knowledge that they were helping the group to commit the crime.[99] Although both are concerned in the criminality, their modes of participation – and their mental states – are fundamentally different. The one problem with the doctrinal innovation of the Trial Chamber is that the Court failed to give the necessary theoretical analysis to explain why the distinction was both fruitful and necessary. Indeed, both decisions were rather skeletal on theory. I submit that if the Court had laid a proper foundation for its doctrinal distinction – by developing an explicit theory of joint intentions – the rationale for its decision would have been far clearer, and ultimately more influential.[100]

[96] See ibid [344]. The agreement can either be to commit a crime within the jurisdiction of the statute, or a common plan towards a non-criminal goal that will nonetheless result in a crime as a necessary outcome. See ibid [352] (describing this level of culpability as *dolus directus*).

[97] See *Prosecutor v Milomir Stakić* (n 7) [441]; *Prosecutor v Kvočka et al*, Case IT-98-30/1-T (ICTY T Ch) (2 November 2001) [249] ('The Trial Chamber also considers that it is possible to co-perpetrate and aid or abet a joint criminal enterprise, depending primarily on whether the level of participation rises to that of sharing the intent of the criminal enterprise. An aider or abettor of a joint criminal enterprise, whose acts originally assist or otherwise facilitate the criminal endeavor, may become so involved in its operations that he may graduate to the status of a co-perpetrator of that enterprise').

[98] See *Kvočka*, ibid [284].

[99] ibid.

[100] The Trial Chamber's attempt to split JCE into two separate categories – aiding and abetting a JCE and co-perpetrating a JCE – was immediately rejected by the Appeals Chamber. See *Kvočka et al* (n 49) [90]–[92]. The Appeals Chamber engaged in a similar rebuke of the Trial Chamber in *Stakić*. See *Prosecutor v Stakić* (n 41) [59]–[62].

C Restrictions on Vicarious Liability

It should now be clear why vicarious liability for actions falling outside the scope of the criminal plan is so controversial.[101] Insofar as the action falls outside the scope of the collective plan, there was no shared intention to commit the wayward crime. Since the joint action was based on an initial agreement to commit the crime, the defendant's intention is predicated on that initial agreement. Nor does it matter whether the wayward action was a reasonably foreseeable consequence of the criminal plan.[102] These individual wayward actions cannot be attributed back to the defendant; the shared intention was entirely different. The problem with the JCE doctrine was never its 'subjective' approach, but rather its insistence on vicarious liability for acts that fall outside the scope of the original criminal agreement (JCE III). Indeed, JCE III should never have been developed in the first place because, as demonstrated in this chapter, it is inconsistent with the very theory that animates the JCE doctrine.[103] Defendants in a JCE III case do not have a shared intention to commit the crime in question, and therefore they do not have the requisite mental state to place them in the same category as the principal perpetrator who committed the act. In addition to its deficiencies at the level of criminal law theory, JCE III is unsupported by either the current Rome Statute or the international case law; future international courts ought to reject it.[104] The ICC's control theory suffers from similar deficiencies: the use of *dolus eventualis* as a permissible mental state effectively guts the objective requirement of a common criminal plan.

A theory of joint intentions nicely explains why vicarious liability must be severely restricted, by eliminating vicarious liability for actions that fall outside

[101] See, eg, Danner and Martinez, 'Guilty Associations' (n 54) 137 (JCE as the nuclear bomb of the international prosecutor's arsenal); Powles, 'JCE: Criminal Liability by Prosecutorial Ingenuity' (n 46) 619 (broad nature of JCE could lead to 'unfortunate miscarriage of justice' if Trial Chambers are not vigilant in ensuring sufficient evidence in support of allegations and rigorous scrutiny of the evidence); Joint Criminal Enterprise Brief of Amicus Curaie Kai Ambos, *Kaing Guek Eav (Duch Case)*, Case 001/18-07-2007/ECCC/OCIJ (Pre-Trial Ch 2) (27 October 2008) 1, 13, 15–19 (rejecting JCE III as incompatible with fundamental principles of criminal law theory); JD Ohlin, 'Three Conceptual Problems with the Doctrine of Joint Criminal Enterprise' (2007) 5 *Journal of International Criminal Justice* 69, 81 ('The more subtle avenue would have distinguished between actions taken with mere knowledge of the conspiracy and those taken to intentionally advance the conspiracy. The former should yield the lightest liability while the latter should yield the heaviest. But the actions of a joint criminal enterprise cannot be attributed to both equally').

[102] Compare with *Prosecutor v Duško Tadić* (n 1) [224].

[103] For an example of this tension, see *D'Ottavio*, cited in A Cassese, 'The Proper Limits of Individual Responsibility under the Doctrine of Joint Criminal Enterprise' (2007) 5 *Journal of International Criminal Justice* 109, 119–20, fn12 ('There also exists a psychological causation in that all the participants shared the conscious will to engage in an attempt to unlawfully detain a person while foreseeing a possible different crime, as can be inferred from the use of weapons: it was to anticipate that one of them might have shot at the fugitives with a view to achieving the common purpose of capturing them'). The Italian Court of Cassation seems unbothered by the fact that the 'shared conscious will' of the participants did not include the crime for which they were convicted.

[104] A full defence of this assertion is offered in my 'Joint Intentions to Commit International Crimes' (2011) *Chicago Journal of International Law*, section III.A.

the scope of the original agreement, and by differentiating levels of participation in the group endeavour. The former restriction is required by the theory because, for those actions that fall outside the scope of the original plan, there is no joint intention with regard to that criminal action. And if the joint intention grounds vicarious liability in the first instance, the absence of a joint intention with regard to that one criminal act requires rejection of the application of vicarious liability to all other members of the group. The latter restriction is required because those who carry the joint intention for the group to commit the crime are categorically different from those who merely assist the endeavour with knowledge that their assistance will facilitate the group's efforts. What justifies this categorical distinction? Simply put, those who carry the joint intention are guilty of an *intentional* act, while those without the joint intention are, at most, guilty of a crime of knowing facilitation or complicity. If at some point an accomplice changes her attitude about the group's endeavour, and intends for the group to commit the crime, then the accomplice graduates to the status of co-perpetrator where greater liability is appropriate.[105]

IV CONCLUSION

In the end, the appropriate course of action is not to replace JCE with the control theory of perpetration, but rather reform JCE and eliminate JCE III because it fails to comply with the underlying theory supporting the doctrine. Despite the intense scrutiny regarding JCE and co-perpetration, international judges and lawyers have demonstrated insufficient interest in developing a deeper theory of criminal responsibility for group endeavours.[106] The case law of the tribunals is focused almost exclusively on choosing the appropriate doctrine that is consistent with statutory provisions and customary international law. Occasionally, judges consider compliance and fidelity to deeper principles of criminal law, although usually under the guise of discussing 'general principles of law' as the term is understood by public international lawyers. While some judges consider the issue

[105] One might object that this joint intentions theory could potentially label thousands of minor participants as co-perpetrators, simply based on their joint intention. Are factory workers making munitions guilty as co-perpetrators if they exhibit a joint intention to use the weapons as part of a criminal plan? The answer is simple: such cases should not be resolved by changing the required mental state for the doctrine, but rather by further examination of the level of contribution required to the plan as part of the objective element. If one adopts the differentiated version of JCE discussed in section III.B, the level of contribution could be used to distinguish between co-perpetrating a JCE and aiding and abetting a JCE. A full analysis of the required level of contribution (*de minimus*, substantial, or indispensable) for vicarious liability is outside the scope of the present chapter.

[106] The confusion surrounding Art 25 of the Rome Statute is just one example of this phenomenon. See, eg, A Eser, 'Individual Criminal Responsibility' in A Cassese, P Gaeta and J Jones (eds), *The Rome Statute of the International Criminal Court: A Commentary* vol 1 (Oxford, Oxford University Press, 2002) 767, 803 ('employment of obviously different mental concepts in this provision can hardly hide the lack of expertise in criminal theory when this provision was developed').

from the perspective of criminal law theory, others simply ignore it, and none hazards a foray into the philosophical landmines of collective action and the intentionality that generates it.

Perhaps this is not surprising. The autonomy of law in general – and international criminal law in particular – has supposedly liberated lawyers from engagement with the allegedly indeterminate and unanswerable pre-legal questions of philosophy, psychology and morality. But in nascent fields, such as international criminal law, there is more conceptual space (and need) for consideration of first-order moral and philosophical theories that ground the legal doctrines. Courts are often in the position of not just applying, but of announcing such theories. International tribunals have a greater responsibility to ensure that their rules and doctrines are defensible.

This is not to suggest that international courts ought to be ignoring the law when morality or philosophy counsels an alternative course. Nothing could be further from the truth. Rather, the point is simply that international lawyers are often in the position of applying modes of liability based on skeletal statutory language – namely, the word 'committed' in Article 7 of the ICTY Statute – that leaves great discretion to the court in terms of which criminal law doctrines ought to be applied. It is precisely in such situations that an international tribunal ought to be concerned with ascertaining the exact contours of individual criminal responsibility. And such an inquiry demands a broad examination of the foundation of that responsibility.

This process is especially difficult when the question is individual responsibility for collective criminal action. This chapter concludes that international courts ought to be developing their doctrine around the concept of joint or shared intentions – a philosophically nuanced theory that posits vicarious liability when groups of individuals each intend for their group to complete a crime and each individual acts according to the reciprocal nature of this joint intention. This phenomenon of joint intentions both justifies the application of vicarious liability imposed by international tribunals and also explains why it is so important to distinguish between criminal defendants who merely exhibit recklessness (under the current JCE III) from those who directly intend the consequences of their criminal participation. This is the doctrinal payoff of the joint intentions theory.

15

Theorizing Duress and Necessity in International Criminal Law

DWIGHT NEWMAN*

This chapter is among those specifically addressing issues of criminal law theory in the context of international criminal law. Canada, like other states, participates in an international criminal law order that arises at a complex set of intersections between national and international law, humanitarian law and criminal law and the domestic criminal law conceptions of a variety of legal traditions. To say that Canada participates in that order perhaps even understates the Canadian role, which has been one of significant leadership in the development of international criminal law and encompasses a substantial ongoing participation by Canadian lawyers. The international criminal law system has, of course, until recent years functioned through decisions of domestic courts (and, importantly, military courts martial), various ad hoc international courts and tribunals and various special hybrid institutions established to administer international criminal law, usually in the aftermath of particular conflicts in which violations have allegedly occurred. In recent years, a new international emphasis on seeking to end impunity for international criminal law offences has furthered the development of massive bodies of jurisprudence within some of the ad hoc bodies and contributed to the establishment of a permanent international criminal court. The development of much of international criminal law from various sorts of hybrid origins contains, of course, unique dangers for the theoretical coherence of this body of law, and even the permanent international criminal court emerged from a multi-textured negotiation process, all giving good reason to interrogate the theoretical underpinnings and texture of international criminal law.

In this chapter, I analyze the significance of what I will argue are actually normatively differing approaches to duress and necessity reflected in decisions of and debates concerning the decisions of two of the ad hoc institutions of international

* I am grateful to the editors for facilitating the discussion of my chapter in the intellectually rich setting of the conference that led to this collection, to Neha Jain for her thoughtful reply commentary and to the following for helpful comments in the discussion that ensued: Alan Brudner, Antony Duff, Dennis Klimchuk, Jens Ohlin, Dan Priel, Hamish Stewart and Victor Tadros.

criminal law, considering the widely discussed decision of the Appeals Chamber of the International Criminal Tribunal for the former Yugoslavia in the *Erdemović* case discussing duress[1] and the as yet less widely discussed decision of the Special Court for Sierra Leone in the *Fofana and Kondewa* case, also known as the *Civil Defence Forces (CDF)* case, particularly the parts of this latter case discussing necessity.[2] I will argue that the fractures around these concepts shown in these cases do not reflect simply theoretical problems with the defences themselves – albeit that both are already complex and contested in domestic contexts. Rather, they reflect also the very complex trans-systemic character of the international criminal law system.

In so doing, in section I, I will briefly introduce the relevant judgments, comment summarily on some problematic optics and then discuss a more concerning methodological point exposed by starting to think about these optics. In section II, I will turn to what I will argue is a problematic divergence of the normative underpinnings implicitly assumed for international criminal law in the two cases. I will argue that, contrary to first appearances that they fit neatly together, these two cases exemplify unresolved tensions between various hybrid sources of international criminal law. In section III, I will seek to show that the presence of a consequentialist-deontologist dilemma is a pervasive feature of international criminal law but may be more attenuated than is first apparent in some cases, including scenarios sharing a particular feature of the *Erdemović* case. In section IV, I will consider the possibility that the more unified approach of the Rome Statute has now made many of the prior problems mere accidents of history in terms of the modern shape of international criminal law. However, I will ultimately argue, rather, that the Statute's own trans-systemic character lurks under the surface in ways that risk bubbling over once again in future cases. These dangers make the application of criminal law theory distinctions both potentially intensely erroneous but also inherently necessary to future understandings of international criminal law.

I THE OPTICS OF *ERDEMOVIĆ* AND *FOFANA* AND *KONDEWA*

The defences of duress and necessity share, in many respects, a common moral currency,[3] making it natural to consider together the *Erdemović* and *Fofana and Kondewa* cases. In *Erdemović* , the ICTY Appeals Chamber considered the availability of duress as a complete defence against crimes against humanity or war crimes charges. These charges arose from Erdemović's participation as a member

[1] *Prosecutor v Dražen Erdemović*, Case IT-96-22-A (ICTY App Ch) (7 October 1997).

[2] *Prosecutor v Fofana and Kondewa* (CDF Trial), Case SCSL-04-14-J (SCSL T Ch I) (2 August 2007); *Prosecutor v Fofana and Kondewa* (CDF Sentencing), Case SCSL-04-14-T (SCSL T Ch I) (9 October 2007); *Prosecutor v Fofana and Kondewa* (CDF Appeal), Case SCSL-04-14-A (SCSL App Ch) (28 May 2008).

[3] *cf* M Gorr, 'Duress and Culpability' (2000) 19 *Criminal Justice Ethics* 3, 4.

of a Bosnian Serb firing squad that summarily executed approximately 1200 Bosnian Muslim civilians, with Erdemović having likely personally killed in the order of 70 victims, following a threat that he would join the victims if he did not participate. The majority, with the lead opinion on the point the joint opinion of Judges McDonald and Vorah, held that duress is not available as a complete defence (but only, possibly, in mitigation of sentence) in the context of an offender who has taken innocent life.[4] Judge Cassese issued an influential dissenting opinion that would have considered such a defence possible in principle, subject to the offender meeting a strict set of requirements concerned with imminence of the threat, lack of other means of averting the evil, proportionality and non-causation by the offender of the circumstances giving rise to duress.[5]

In *Fofana and Kondewa*, the Trial Chamber of the Special Court for Sierra Leone convicted the two accused for crimes committed in their capacity as leaders of the Civil Defence Forces in its efforts to restore the democratically elected government of President Kabbah. Because of their role and the specific actions they had urged, they were responsible for various crimes committed by the CDF (composed largely of Kamajors, a group of traditional hunters who acted as warriors for the CDF), leading to convictions on a number of charges. However, Justice Thompson wrote a Dissenting Opinion in which he would have acquitted on all charges, partly on the basis of a defence of necessity derived from Sierra Leonean law that was not put by defence counsel but that he considered arose based on the dire circumstances for Sierra Leonean democracy that the CDF combated.[6] The majority, somewhat peculiarly, responded on this point only in the later sentencing judgment, in which it wrote that the dissent on the trial judgment was inconsistent with common law precedent and with the norms of international humanitarian law;[7] however, it was ready to see the offenders' pursuit of civic duty as a major mitigating factor and gave sentences of only six and eight years.[8] In its 2008 decision, the Appeals Chamber, although not addressing it directly, implicitly alluded to the dispute below and referred to fighting for the restoration of democracy being 'no justification'[9] for serious humanitarian crimes; the majority of 3:2 also revised the sentences – in light of what it described as 'the revulsion of the international community' – to 15 and 20 years, with the two dissenting judges considering the contribution to civic duty as having warranted the more lenient sentences imposed at trial.[10]

What is perhaps initially striking in the commentaries on the two cases is a sheer difference in tone in relation to the two cases. Argument on *Erdemović* has

[4] *Prosecutor v Dražen Erdemović* (n 1) (Separate Joint Opinion of Judge McDonald and Judge Vohrah).

[5] *Prosecutor v Dražen Erdemović* (n 1) (Separate Dissenting Opinion of Judge Cassese) [16].

[6] CDF Trial (n 2) (Dissenting Opinion of Justice Thompson).

[7] CDF Sentencing (n 2) [73]–[76].

[8] ibid [94]–[95].

[9] CDF Appeal (n 2) (Majority Opinion) [565]–[66].

[10] CDF Appeal (n 2) (Dissenting Opinion of Justice King) [92]–[93] and [107]–[08] and partially Dissenting Opinion of Justice Kamanda, [15].

been divided, and criticisms of Judge Cassese's dissent direct but restrained by conventions of civility. The same is not necessarily true of comment on Justice Thompson's opinion in *Fofana and Kondewa*, where commentaries have chosen to express utter shock at Justice Thompson's raising of the defence of necessity, adopting a particularly abrasive tone unlike that directed toward Judge Cassese's Opinion.[11] Apart from the merits of either defence, this difference in the debates on the two cases has particularly troublesome optics in the context of recent concerns about an alleged anti-African bias by international criminal law institutions – with some talk of particular African states even considering withdrawing from the Rome Statute of the International Criminal Court.[12] The very tone of some of this debate has appeared to embody stereotyped assumptions that African judges were inferior to non-African judges, even when defending normatively analogous positions.[13] The differing tone may well actually not have stemmed from the sort of bias it appeared to embody but from differing vulnerability of the different judges to attack – it was, perhaps, easier for the international human rights movement, concerned with longer-term effects on international criminal law from the admission of additional exceptions to liability that would maintain impunity in further cases, to savage Justice Thompson than Judge Cassese. However, in so far as it has done so, I am critical of its actions that traded implicitly on stereotypes of the very sort against which the international human rights movement should be working. In any event, this is an issue more of optics than of substantive law or its relation to criminal law theory, on which the judgments bear further discussion.

When one turns beyond optics, both cases actually have their outright deficiencies. For example, the *Erdemović* case, although containing seemingly extensive doctrinal surveys and some normative discussion, could prompt relatively primordial worries about the methodology of modes of generation of norms of international law, a point perhaps rendered evident in a particularly tangible form through a Canadian lens. In surveying approaches and exceptions to a duress defence in various jurisdictions around the world with the aim of deriving general principles from domestic orders, the McDonald/Vohrah Opinion cited section 17 of the Canadian Criminal Code[14] as describing the Canadian position. This statement of the law ignored the likely unconstitutionality of parts of section 17, con-

[11] See, eg, V Oosterveld and A Marlowe, 'Prosecutor v Brima, Kamara and Kanu; Prosecutor v Fofana and Kondewa; Special Court for Sierra Leone' (2007) 101 *American Journal of International Law* 848, 853 (describing his reasoning, among other remarks, as 'regressive'). Commentary by human rights organisations outside scholarly journals has been even more unrestrained.

[12] This discussion has most recently arisen in the context of Kenya, although at one stage there was talk in Uganda as such as well. The more difficult aspect now is that the African Union is taking a greater interest in the matter.

[13] Justice Thompson also calls the majority judges on their potentially strategic and certainly prejudicial references to acts of cannibalism committed during the conflict: CDF Trial (n 2) Annex C (Dissenting Opinion of Justice Thompson) [3]. Although there may have been isolated acts of this sort, there is research suggesting the widespread exaggeration of such claims, with the claims thus functioning largely to generate fear and, when directed from outside, to perpetuate stereotyping of particular communities. See, eg, MC Ferme and D Hoffman, 'Hunter Militias and the International Human Rights Discourse in Sierra Leone and Beyond' (2004) 50(4) *Africa Today* 73.

[14] Criminal Code RSC 1985 ch C-46 (Canada).

firmed in respect of some dimensions of section 17 shortly thereafter by the Supreme Court of Canada's decision in *Ruzic*.[15] My claim here may appear to depend on a particular account of the nature of law in which a decision of unconstitutionality merely recognizes pre-existing norms rather than changing the law. However, the unconstitutionality of elements of section 17 was widely predicted during the period prior to the *Erdemović* decision. Adding that circumstance, I do not think it wrong to say that its unconstitutionality was part of a correct description of the law even prior to the *Ruzic* judgment and that merely copying the Criminal Code provision did not correctly describe Canadian law. While it is of course the case that the *Ruzic* decision pertained to overly stringent immediacy and presence requirements in the statutory duress defence, and it did not explicitly concern the exclusion of offences that was the principal matter at issue in *Erdemović* ,[16] the underlying logic of *Ruzic* might well tell against the exclusion of offences as well, and a full description of Canadian law on duress requires going beyond the statutory provision to case law and its underlying theoretical conceptions.

To suppose that the statutory section alone defined Canadian law was methodologically suspect, as then was the Tribunal's specific derivation of general principles of international law from domestic norms – if Canadian law was too inaccessible for the Tribunal, then how are we to trust its description of yet more different legal systems? The point is perhaps accentuated even further by the presence as one of the counsel of record in the *Erdemović* case of a Canadian-educated lawyer,[17] although the counsel of course would not have had the opportunity to review the judgment in advance for errors in its treatment of Canadian law. That said, the Tribunal itself limited, in the usual manner of international courts, the systems of law to which it referred in analyzing the general principles of law and referred only to common law and civil law traditions and not, for instance, Islamic legal principles that some of the Bosnian Muslim victims might have considered as possible references when one is considering the various legal systems of the world.

In the other case at issue, similar outright deficiencies are present. The Sierra Leonean Special Court simply did not engage in any particularly precise analysis of the possible argument for necessity. Some of the more moderate critics of Justice Thompson's invocation of necessity rightly noted that his attempt to apply a necessity defence was imprecise in not relating the defence to the particular offenders' circumstances so much as an overall military conflict.[18] The majority response was little better in so far as it merely made a quick claim about the normative demands of international humanitarian law and invoked old English common law without direct attention to Sierra Leonean law itself,[19] which Justice

[15] *R v Ruzic* [2001] SCC 24, 1 SCR 687.

[16] See ibid [19].

[17] Payam Akhavan was one of the counsel of record for the Office of the Prosecutor.

[18] Human Rights Watch, 'Political Considerations in Sentence Mitigation' (March 2008) 9–10.

[19] CDF Sentencing (n 2) [73]–[78], citing to *R v Dudley and Stephens* [1884] 14 QBD 273.

Thompson had actually used and in which he had genuine supporting expertise.[20]

The majority citation was to the old English precedent of *Dudley and Stephens*.[21] This unproblematized citation masks the more complicated position of English common law itself. Although the *Dudley and Stephens* principle that there is no defence of necessity to murder has received later support,[22] there are nonetheless later cases that also complicate this position. There are, for example, those permitting necessity as a defence to a medical operation inevitably causing the death of one of a pair of conjoined twins[23] or well-accepted views within English law that it would be lawful to shoot down a plane full of passengers if necessary to prevent a greater disaster.[24] This last example is in tragically ironic contrast to a German position that has now seemingly rejected the shooting down of such a plane,[25] in a case to which I will return in section III of the chapter, in the context of German law traditionally allowing duress and necessity a wider scope and English law imposing the *Dudley and Stephens* limit.

The fact that both the *Erdemović* and *Fofana and Kondewa* judgments have these kinds of surface difficulties in connection with their use of domestic legal norms, instantiates a larger methodological point. The interaction of the international criminal law system with domestic orders in the context of deriving general principles from these domestic orders is fraught with the usual challenges in such an exercise. However, it is subject to additional problems in so far as the choice to derive a particular norm from domestic orders may well import a norm that sits uneasily with other norms within the international criminal law system. Norms within a criminal law system do not exist as solitary norms but as norms within that system – and, indeed, not just a substantive system, but with substantive norms interrelated with procedural and evidentiary norms. One might easily derive specific norms from domestic orders on an individual basis but find that they do not fit together well within a system that does not have other norms making them work effectively together.

The Rome Statute provision on applicable law before the International Criminal Court recognizes some of the challenges that may be present in a last resort derivation from domestic law. The International Criminal Court is empowered to use

> general principles of law derived by the Court from national laws of legal systems of the world including, as appropriate, the national laws of States that would normally exercise jurisdiction over the crime, provided that those principles are not inconsistent with

[20] CDF Trial (n 2) Annex C (Dissenting Opinion of Justice Thompson) [69] (citing to portions of his textbook on Sierra Leonean criminal law).

[21] CDF Sentencing (n 2) [73]–[78], citing to *R v Dudley and Stephens* (n 19).

[22] *R v Howe* [1987] AC 417.

[23] *Re A (Children)* [2000] 4 All ER 961 (CA).

[24] D Ormerod, *Smith and Hogan Criminal Law* 11th edn (Oxford, Oxford University Press, 2005) 322.

[25] *Bundesverfassungsgericht Entscheidung* 115, 118 (2006) (German Federal Constitutional Court) [*German Plane Case*]. For a detailed discussion of the case, see T Hörnle, 'Shooting down a Hijacked Plane – The German Discussion and Beyond' (2009) 3 *Criminal Law and Philosophy* 111.

this Statute and with international law and internationally recognized norms and standards.[26]

The decision to require that general principles be imported in a manner promoting consistency recognizes some of the problems that otherwise arise.

At the same time, on one reading of the text, as a sort of two-stage text, it introduces yet another layer of argument, which now must be concerned, in the first instance, with analyzing whether particular norms are general principles and, in the second, with whether they must nonetheless be excluded. In the latter case, no further last resort source is set out, with a literal reading of the Article then implicitly leading to a lacuna within international criminal law in some instances. I might respectfully venture a different, one-stage approach to the analysis of general principles in the particular context of international criminal law. Such an approach would prioritize approaches having a close theoretical fit with international criminal law and then import them as general principles so long as they are not fundamentally contradicted by the experience of domestic orders. This reading is, perhaps, more at odds with the text of the Article. But we must seek possibilities that pursue coherence in international criminal law. In any event, as a general statement, a strong methodology of international criminal law surely requires greater attention to criminal law theory. That said, these methodological discussions warrant further treatment on another occasion, since they have been a mere side path from the main question of the availability of duress and necessity defences as discussed in the two judgments at issue.

II IMPLICITLY DIVERGING THEORETICAL VISIONS

The *Erdemović* approach to duress, although thought by some not to be the last word given the closeness of the decision and the persuasiveness of the Cassese dissent on this issue,[27] has recently been cited by the Cambodia tribunal as essentially setting out the determined position on duress and closing further debate on duress in customary international law.[28] Commentators on the *Civil Defence Forces* case have tended to write of wanting the majority position determined definitive and, in their more declamatory moments, to regret Justice Thompson's dissent even having been published.[29]

[26] Rome Statute of the International Criminal Court 2187 UNTS 90 (entered into force 1 July 2002) Art 21(1)(c).

[27] See JD Ohlin, 'The Bounds of Necessity' (2008) 6 *Journal of International Criminal Justice* 289, 291.

[28] *Prosecutor v Kaing Guek Eav alias Duch*, Case 001/18-07-2007/ECCC/TC (ECCC T Ch) (26 July 2010) [553]–[54]. *Cf* R Cryer, 'One Appeal, Two Philosophies, Four Opinions and a Remittal: The Erdemovic Case at the ICTY Appeals Chamber' (1997) 2 *Journal of Conflict and Security Law* 193 (arguing that the application of the majority approach has the potential to embarrass international criminal courts in potential future circumstances).

[29] See, eg, Oosterveld and Marlowe, 'Prosecutor v Brima, Kamara and Kanu' (n 11) (referring to the publication of the judgment as 'unfortunate').

If the underlying reasons of these two cases become entrenched in the corpus of customary international criminal law in their two specific forms – and further analysis might well question the extent to which they will – then my claim is that there will be the entrenchment of substantially divergent approaches to two defences that are closely related in normative terms.

On one reading, the theoretical approaches of the *Erdemović* majority and the *Civil Defence Forces* majority might appear to share an important commonality. Both arguably prioritize a policy preference for successful prosecution and the ending of impunity over possible normative arguments for exculpation from criminal responsibility. In *Erdemović*, the McDonald/Vorah Opinion saw as a central element justifying its position the policy goal of 'facilitat[ing] the development and effectiveness of international humanitarian law and . . . promot[ing] its aims and application by recognising the normative effect which criminal law should have upon those subject to them'.[30] In the *Civil Defence Forces* case, the majority in the sentencing decision expressed concern that the approach of Justice Thompson to necessity would effectively negate norms of international humanitarian law,[31] again prioritizing policy objectives of the effective enforcement of international humanitarian law.

This alignment might speak to a consistent theoretical position held to by both majorities, one enforcing a form of human rights fundamentalism. Judge Li's Concurring Judgment in *Erdemović* is ready to be explicit about his prioritization of the life of innocent human beings, which he terms the '*sine qua non* of international humanitarian law', in any situations where different views on the law have different results for the protection of innocent life.[32] But international criminal law, while advancing human rights objectives, does so through a criminal law system subject to various constraints rather than a system oriented unequivocally to innocent human life, making it appropriate to analyze the positions not only in terms of their relation to human rights norms, but their underlying approaches to criminal law concepts.

Finer distinctions between the cases in criminal law theory can begin to separate their normative underpinnings. The majority determination in *Erdemović* is not that there is no possible defence of duress in international criminal law but that it is subject to severe limits in not being available as a complete defence 'to a soldier charged with crimes against humanity or war crimes in international law involving the taking of innocent lives'.[33] The same judgment actually explicitly acknowledges a 'general principle of law recognised by civilised nations that an accused person is less blameworthy and less deserving of the full punishment when he performs a certain prohibited act under duress'.[34] By contrast, the major-

[30] *Prosecutor v Dražen Erdemović* (n 1) (Separate Joint Opinion of Judge McDonald and Judge Vorah) [75].

[31] CDF Sentencing (n 2) [78].

[32] *Prosecutor v Dražen Erdemović* (n 1) (Separate Concurring Opinion of Judge Li) [8].

[33] ibid (Separate Joint Opinion of Judge McDonald and Judge Vorah) [88].

[34] ibid [66].

ity position in *Fofana and Kondewa* is seemingly that there is simply no possible defence of necessity ever available in international criminal law, with the majority in the Appeals Chamber not even considering necessity arguments to be in mitigation of sentence.[35]

If, as is a common view, duress and necessity are both criminal law defences because of traditional voluntarist guilty mind requirements, then the cases arguably begin to diverge in so far as *Erdemović* acknowledges those normative underpinnings but places some policy constraints on the duress defence while *Fofana and Kondewa* implicitly rejects those normative underpinnings in the necessity context. However, several further distinctions may fruitfully be layered onto the cases.

We can usefully make explicit, first, a distinction between the varying roles of *mens rea*[36] within the criminal law context, which these cases help make clearer. Alan Brudner has recently noted the common tendency to elide two distinctive roles of subjective fault or *mens rea*, one pertaining to the threshold question of whether criminal responsibility attaches to a particular accused at all and the second to the further question of degrees of criminal responsibility in the context of certain offences where different sorts of *mens rea* alter the offence or the gradation of the offence.[37] However, even this distinction arguably understates the multiple roles of *mens rea* within a criminal law system based on subjective fault, as we might further distinguish in the second wing as between actual definitions or gradations of offences and questions related to sentencing for particular offences, the latter often not within the purview of criminal law theory discussions that rightfully have enough to grapple with simply dealing with foundational questions of criminal responsibility. Nonetheless, the cases at hand point to the possible role of defences that challenge *mens rea* in affecting criminal responsibility outright, the definitional classification of the charge applying to criminal responsibility and the aggravating and mitigating factors in sentencing if criminal responsibility attaches.

Secondly, we can invoke a normative distinction between excuses and justifications.[38] An excuse admits that the accused committed a wrongful act but nonetheless challenges the attribution of criminal responsibility. A justification admits that the defendant's acts meet the definition of the criminal offence but claims

[35] CDF Appeal (n 2) [247].

[36] Note that some Canadian jurisprudence would actually even come close to regarding duress as an *actus reus* issue in so far as it establishes a moral involuntariness: see, eg, *Perka v The Queen* [1984] 2 SCR 232 *contra R v Ruzic* (n 15) [42]–[47]. However, what is needed in each case even within the Canadian approach is an evaluation of whether the individual's choices were constrained, considering the morality of possibilities on each side of the choice, so even this description is arguably better regarded as a different description of a *mens rea* problem.

[37] A Brudner, 'Subjective Fault for Crime: A Reinterpretation' (2008) 14 *Legal Theory* 1.

[38] Some challenge the possibility of neat normative distinctions between concepts that they consider more muddied in actual law: see, eg, K Greenawalt, 'The Perplexing Borders of Justification and Excuse' (1984) 84 *Columbia Law Review* 1897; RA Duff, *Answering for Crime: Responsibility and Liability in the Criminal Law* (Oxford, Hart Publishing, 2007) 266.

that the act was nevertheless not wrong.[39] Many scholars have taken the view that a duress defence is an excuse and a necessity defence a justification.[40] On such an account, one could conceivably go on to develop strong arguments for permitting a duress defence in international criminal law but rejecting a necessity defence, or at least approaching the latter significantly more suspiciously, which we might read as the net position of the cases at issue. Two particularly plausible arguments would present themselves. First, one might put the argument that there is simply no possible way to present a justification for the horrific acts falling within the category of crimes against humanity or war crimes, given both the effects on the individual victims but also their nature as international crimes against the very essence of the human legal order.[41] Secondly, one might put the argument that there are problematic implications of admitting a justification defence in an international criminal law context because, dependent as it is on an overall account of the rightness of the actions, it implicitly affects the legal position of other actors complicit in the actions, acting in resistance to them, or relying on the precedent that the determination of necessity now establishes.[42]

These conclusions have, to some degree, a distinguished lineage. The explicit analysis of the possibility of particular kinds of acts that can be neither justified nor excused dates at least to Aristotle.[43] He writes of the act that can never be praised on the basis of its contribution to a greater good and can never be excused on the basis of any threats, with the example that he offers being that of matricide.[44] Part of Aristotle's discussion seems to presume that sufficiently heinous crimes are such that they simply cannot be subject to exculpation because there can be no explanation of the psychology of carrying out such acts. Part seems to pertain to the sheer heinousness of the acts. Though the psychological account may not be in keeping with modern psychology and a full gradation of the heinousness of crimes is a problem laden requirement for the application of the account, it is nonetheless not a difficult stretch, if without full theorization, to analogize Aristotle's matricide to the killing of innocents in the context of a war crime or crime against humanity. The majority positions in *Erdemović* and in *Fofana and Kondewa*, in one sense, simply affirm that certain heinous acts, as with matricide for Aristotle, by their nature fall outside the categories of the potentially excusable and the potentially justifiable.

But Aristotle's presumed factual scenario, as is the case with most of the past case law on duress and necessity, is framed at least implicitly against a set of factual assumptions from which at least the *Erdemović* scenario diverges. The

[39] See, eg, G Fletcher, *Rethinking Criminal Law* (Boston, Little, Brown, 1978) 759. *Cf* Duff, *Answering for Crime*, ibid 263.

[40] See, eg, J Dressler, 'Exegesis of the Law of Duress: Justifying the Excuse and Searching for Its Proper Limits' (1988–89) 62 *Southern California Law Review* 1331, 1348–49.

[41] See, eg, Ohlin, 'The Bounds of Necessity' (n 27) 295.

[42] See, eg, Fletcher, *Rethinking Criminal Law* (n 39) 760–62.

[43] Aristotle, *Nicomachean Ethics* 1110a–1110b. I thank Antony Duff for drawing my attention to Aristotle's consideration of these matters.

[44] ibid 1110a.

matricide example is de-contextualized, and it does not speak directly to, for instance, the horrible dilemmas of an actor who commits matricide to save the rest of the family when the mother was doomed anyway. Specific sorts of factual scenarios shift the ground of debate in a manner to which I will return in section III.

The horrific acts concern is ultimately subject to argument about the horrible dilemmas of an actor who violates international criminal law to prevent some greater violation of international criminal law, which would in many instances be legally permitted under the different doctrinal rubric of self-defence/other-defence but would surely normatively sometimes be an implicit instance of justificatory necessity. The argument against necessity justifications out of concern for pre-authorizing horrible acts by other actors is subject to arguments that implications for other actors do not automatically follow uniquely from necessity in the ways conceptualized by some scholars. Consider, for example, the fact that the availability of an excuse may also affect the obligations of other actors.[45] These points are obviously appropriately subject to ongoing debate beyond the scope of the present discussion.

More importantly for present purposes, what can illuminate these cases and what these cases can in turn illuminate is the possibility that duress and necessity do not fall within the strict respective pigeonholes of excuse and justification. The defence of duress, as nicely illustrated by Judge Cassese's approach, for instance, has strong justification-oriented components.[46] Conversely, although the first ring of necessity might sound justificatory, one could reasonably read Justice Thompson's account of why a necessity defence applied to the actions of Fofana and Kondewa as having excuse-oriented components. He actually began his judgment with reference to the possibility that an offender could 'be *excused* from criminal liability by reason of the proof of certain defences recognised by the law' (emphasis added).[47] His ultimate conclusion was that the acts of Fofana and Kondewa were '*excusable* in the eyes of the law on the grounds of the defence of necessity' (emphasis added).[48] Although there is the possibility that Justice Thompson did not choose to use the word 'excuse' with technical precision and actually meant 'justification', both his career and other parts of the judgment make clear that he was very much alive to the distinction.[49] In any case, one need not automatically read Justice Thompson as having claimed that the criminal acts at issue were justified but can easily read his judgment as instead claiming a defence of excusatory necessity. There would be more to be said about such a

[45] See, eg, Greenawalt, 'Perplexing Borders' (n 38) 1925 (considering the instance of rights to defend oneself against an aggressor who is not responsible for his actions).

[46] *cf* Dressler, 'Exegesis' (n 40) 1356–67 (describing duress as an atypical excuse given that the person is morally responsible for the action and the defence takes account of a balancing process concerned with whether the person could expect to resist the threat).

[47] CDF Trial (n 2) Annex C (Dissenting Opinion of Justice Thompson) [7].

[48] ibid [92]. See also [88] (also using the term excuse).

[49] ibid [75].

defence, and indeed there would be important conceptual criticisms of it.[50] But such a defence exists in a very much different normative relationship to duress than might have first been presumed.

If the majority in *Fofana and Kondewa* is then actually rejecting the possibility of a defence of excusatory necessity, its normative position is actually potentially further in tension with the normative underpinnings of the duress discussion in *Erdemović*. An excusatory necessity defence does not say that violations of international criminal law are justified and thus does not raise some of the criticisms cited against the possibility of a defence of necessity.[51] The introduction of the excuse-justification distinction and its complex tracking onto duress and necessity further illuminates the tensions present in these debates.

Thirdly, attempts to apply the concepts of justification and duress may call for yet further distinctions. As Duff has recently argued, a simple division between excuse and justification seems to leave certain conceptual gaps. Perhaps the most problematic for present purposes arises in what Duff terms the 'problem of putative justification'.[52] If an accused acts on a reasonable but mistaken belief as to facts that would have grounded a justification if true, a subjectivist approach to criminal law would surely identify a ground for exculpation even though it will fit neatly neither the excuse nor justification category. Duff argues for the further category of a 'warrant' partly in response to this specific problem (as well as for the further category of an 'exemption' in response to other problems in simple excuse/justification classification).[53] This problem might also reasonably arise in the context of what we might term a putative excuse situation. In particular, if there were reasonably believed to be facts that would have given rise to excusatory necessity as a defence to a violation of some norms of international criminal law if true, this situation might reasonably offer a warrant that would at least partly exculpate from liability. Some theories of excuse and necessity, of course, may avoid the need for this additional ground of exculpation as a separate category. For instance, Victor Tadros's powerful account of justification defences as based on reasons – and thus potentially based on reasonable but mistaken beliefs – effectively avoids the need for another category but instead frames situations based on putative justifications as simple cases of justification.[54] Such an approach differs in categorical lines at issue, which is important to address in general terms but does not alter the present issue.

Some will say that any such moves push matters too far. An approach based on subjectivist criminal law theory potentially offers a result that will be in tension with a forceful human rights orientation embodied in international criminal law.

[50] Dressler, 'Exegesis' (n 40) 1336–43 emphasizes the significance of duress involving – along with an imminent threat from a human being of sufficiently serious consequence – a threat as distinct from an offer, which some might see as differentiating it from any excusatory necessity analysis.

[51] See Ohlin, 'The Bounds of Necessity' (n 27).

[52] Duff, *Answering for Crime* (n 38) 271–72.

[53] ibid 275–76.

[54] See generally V Tadros, *Criminal Responsibility* (Oxford, Oxford University Press, 2005) 267–73, 280–90 (arguing against John Gardner and George Fletcher).

Some might even go so far as to derisively challenge the possibility of a defence founded on what would be, after all, an imagined excuse. To this point I shall return in section IV within the context of the Rome Statute. Different legal traditions at the foundations of international criminal law render complex all the discussion here, whether of normative underpinnings or even of positivist international law norms. One approach to the resolution of pulls in various directions from different legal traditions (whether traditions of different bodies of law or criminal law traditions of different systems), of course, has been the development of a treaty norm. I turn in section IV to the Rome Statute provisions, which interestingly are often described as adopting something more along the lines of the Cassese dissenting position on duress, with possible room to read in something akin to necessity. However, first, I turn in section III to the particular scenario giving rise to a more specific deontologist–consequentialist dilemma and argue that it is particularly apt to surface in the international criminal law context.

III A DEONTOLOGIST – CONSEQUENTIALIST DILEMMA IN DURESS AND NECESSITY SCENARIOS

The *Erdemović* situation has a particular structure that I suggested earlier made it different from many past cases and, for that matter, from Aristotle's example of an act that is subject to neither excuse nor justification. Judge Cassese's dissent alludes to the point as one affecting the proportionality analysis,[55] but the other dissent, by Judge Stephen, puts directly that the situation is distinct from that in, for instance, much of the past English case law in that a refusal by Erdemović to participate in the crime would have resulted only in the same group of people being killed plus Erdemović being killed and thus contributed nothing other than a heroic example that the criminal law cannot demand.[56] The lead majority Opinion of Judge McDonald and Judge Vohrah challenges and rejects what it terms the 'utilitarianism' present in such reasoning and reasserts the importance of absolute moral imperatives,[57] thus opening a deontologist-consequentialist front within the discussion.

Interestingly, Judge Li's Opinion, which concurs with the lead McDonald/ Vohrah Opinion, offers what could be read as a consequentialist-oriented response to Judge Cassese and Judge Stephen, noting as his main non-doctrinal concern with their argument the consequence that it would open the possibility of a defence that would 'justify every one of the criminal group who participated

[55] *Prosecutor v Dražen Erdemović* (n 1) (Separate Dissenting Opinion of Judge Cassesse) [12].

[56] *Prosecutor v Dražen Erdemović* (n 1) (Separate Dissenting Opinion of Judge Stephen) [54]–[58].

[57] *Prosecutor v Dražen Erdemović* (n 1) (Separate Joint Opinion of Judge McDonald and Judge Vohrah) [80]–[83].

in the joint massacre of individual persons'.[58] Judge Li's concern, though consequentialist, might appear to have a rule-utilitarian, as opposed to act-utilitarian emphasis. But the interesting result is nonetheless that only two of the five judges adhere to a deontological position, and three to variations of a consequentialist position – yet Erdemović is convicted for committing a criminal act that could arguably be excused or justified on a version of a consequentialist position, with the two judges writing most strongly for his conviction lambasting the place given to consequentialism were any excuse to be accepted when consequentialist positions actually attracted the support of the majority of the judges on the panel. There but for their circumstances went they.

The *Erdemović* situation is a more specialized case of a broader problem where the question is whether a decision to deliberately kill the set of persons A {A1, A2, . . . An} to prevent an action can be excused or justified when the alternative criminal loss of lives is to set of persons A plus set of persons B {B1, B2, . . . Bn}. The German Constitutional Court famously considered the related but slightly different issue of whether a legal provision could constitutionally stand that permitted the lethal use of force against an airplane where the plane was going to be used against the lives of others and the use of force was the only means of preventing this.[59] The Court rejected such a provision on the basis that an authorization of this sort did not respect the human dignity of the passengers and crew members in so far as it allegedly treated them as means rather than ends. At the same time, the Court explicitly differentiated its constitutional conclusion on the legislative pre-authorization from any conclusion on the availability of a criminal law defence to anyone who shot down the plane in such a scenario.

This problem is notably distinct from a more general consequentialist 'save-the-greater number' argument.[60] Although there will in reality always be some slight loss of duration of life to the set of persons A – and some have argued the possibility of the importance of those last five minutes from those persons' perspective to, for instance, make last phone calls or prayers[61] – there is nonetheless a situation very close to the possibility of the interventionist action saving other lives at the cost only of already 'doomed lives'. To the extent that there is no wilful destruction of these lives – but only the loss of doomed lives as part of the strike against a weapon threatening other lives – arguably, one could conceivably find the intervention permissible even under a natural law doctrine of double effect,[62] let alone the easier consequentialist case. An insistence on the McDonald/Vohrah deontological principle would, in these circumstances, appear harsh indeed, condemning (in epistemically definite scenarios of some sort) multiple thousands to death on the pretext of the five remaining minutes of two hundred passengers.

[58] *Prosecutor v Dražen Erdemović* (n 1) (Separate Opinion of Judge Li) [11].
[59] *German Plane Case* (n 25).
[60] I thank Victor Tadros for discussion on this point.
[61] Hörnle, 'Shooting Down' (n 25) 124.
[62] See, eg, T Aquinas, *Summa Theologica*, IIa-IIae Q 64 art 7.

In parallel, to the extent that Erdemović acted based on a reality of the lives at issue being doomed, and thereby saved his own life, there is a possible argument that his particular situation fell within the special scenario of saving some (one) among the lives that would otherwise be lost anyway. The scenario, though, is potentially complicated by the self-saving character of the act, not in any objective sense but in such possibilities as that the individual saving himself is more susceptible to misjudge the situation at issue and, for instance, to minimize the possibility of flight for the easier possibility of participation in the criminal act. The reasoning that would exculpate Erdemović may also seem to leave unaddressed Judge Li's concern about the possibility of every member of a group being excused or justified. Such a response effectively presumes that there must be individual culpability by someone in the context of a heinous wrong. The matter of whether the introduction of possibilities of collective responsibility, such as I have discussed elsewhere,[63] modulates this charge would take us too far afield from present issues. The Erdemović scenario nonetheless unfolds in a special factual context that may draw consequentialist and deontologist positions closer together.

The distinct problem of a situation where one kills a set of persons A to save a distinct set of persons B does not benefit, as it were, from the special feature of doomed lives. That said, the thoroughgoing act consequentialist will potentially argue that it does not differ from the prior scenario. After all, on this line of argument, to say that it did would effectively value different persons differently, if only out of adherence to a different moral account. There is no easy reconciliation with the deontologist in this scenario, which involves a clear trading off of some lives for others.

The natural thought that *Fofana and Kondewa* follows this scenario is not as automatic as it might first appear. If acts to try to save the state from disintegration and an associated massive loss of life do save massive numbers of lives, it is at least possible that those killed in the task of doing so correspond to some among that number. There is, obviously, no epistemic near-certainty on the point, as there arguably is with the plane. But there is also not an obvious dismissal of the point out of hand. Nonetheless, the consequentialist and deontologist will also part ways in this scenario. Justice Thompson's generalized necessity defence partakes of a different sort of consequentialist underpinning from Judge Stephen's defence for Erdemović, if not as compared with Judge Cassese's.

The international criminal law system will pervasively face a different type of case than do domestic orders. The international criminal law system is specifically focused on action that is part of large-scale action, with the elements of various offences requiring widespread and systematic attacks or intentions to destroy a community or with a jurisdictional focus being put on the most serious crimes by the most serious offenders. The mode of commission will typically involve actions by a number of individuals connected together in some manner in pursuit of a

[63] See, eg, D Newman, *Community and Collective Rights: A Theoretical Framework for Rights Held by Groups* (Oxford, Hart Publishing, 2011).

cause in the context of often complex political settings. The collective/individual interactions, the complexity of motives and the complex political landscape are all likely to lead to various consequentialist-deontologist dilemmas on a reasonably pervasive basis.[64]

IV THE ROME STATUTE UNIFICATION AND CONTINUING HYBRIDITIES

The Rome Statute provides, among its grounds for excluding criminal responsibility, a defence of duress arising from threats made by other persons or from circumstances.[65] It thereby follows some recent discussions of duress that have sought to include duress by circumstances, which some have seen as an excusatory necessity defence.[66] The relevant piece of Article 31 provides for a defence where

> [t]he conduct which is alleged to constitute a crime within the jurisdiction of the Court has been caused by duress resulting from a threat of imminent death or of continuing or imminent serious bodily harm against that person or another person, and the person acts necessarily and reasonably to avoid this threat, provided that the person does not intend to cause a greater harm than the one sought to be avoided.[67]

This wording contains special constraints related to causation, to imminence, to level of threat and to proportionality, many of these corresponding quite closely to the requirements within Judge Cassese's test in *Erdemović*.[68] On one component where the wording diverges – that in relation to causation – Eser's chapter in the widely used Triffterer commentary on the Rome Statute argues that the language of the Statute imposes a particularly high threshold in demanding in Article 31(2)(d) that the impugned conduct 'has been caused by duress'.[69] Counter to Eser's argument, however, we might note that this threshold does not exist in all linguistic versions of the Statute, with the French being one example which requires only that '[l]e comportement dont il est allégué qu'il constitue un crime relevant de la compétence de la Cour a été adopté sous la contrainte résultant d'une menace'. Acting 'sous la contrainte' does not require the action to have been 'caused by' the duress, and the offender will surely be entitled to the more

[64] For another issue giving rise to such dilemmas, consider the issue of amnesties in international criminal law, on which I make some theoretical arguments in D Newman, 'The Rome Statute, Some Reservations Concerning Amnesties, and a Distributive Problem' (2005) 20 *American University International Law Review* 293.

[65] Rome Statute (n 26) Art 31.

[66] See, eg, Ireland Law Reform Commission, *Defences* (2009) LRC 95-2009.

[67] Rome Statute (n 26) Art 31.

[68] See *Prosecutor v Dražen Erdemović* (n 1) (Separate Dissenting Opinion of Judge Cassese) [16].

[69] A Eser, 'Grounds for Excluding Criminal Responsibility' in O Triffterer (ed), *Commentary on the Rome Statute of the International Criminal Court: Observers' Notes, Article by Article* 2nd edn (Oxford, Hart Publishing, 2008) 863, 885–86.

favourable interpretation under typical principles of criminal statutory interpretation where two authentic texts are inconsistent. A different explanation for the Statute's wording here is precisely that it sought to capture that the causation of the duress could not have been by the offender.

What remains the case, though, is that the Rome Statute provision does not offer a definitively resolved or even sharpened theoretical position. Like past discussions of duress, the Rome Statute provisions shade the analysis of duress as between elements associated with justification and with excuse, with one theoretical effect being a conceptual blurring and another practical effect that it may become impossible to claim duress in clear cases of otherwise appropriate excusatory duress because the justificatory element (proportionality of evils) cannot be met.[70] Unification has actually been accomplished by negotiation between representatives from many different legal traditions, so it should perhaps be no surprise that the ultimate shape is a blend of different concepts.

This reality evokes the possibility that criminal law theory has little to contribute to understanding the now statutory terms. There may be no single clear theoretical view embodied in the Statute. To apply theoretical distinctions developed within particular legal systems too readily may make a mess of understanding a system at the conflux of different systems. At the same time, this circumstance may also make it immensely important to attempt to develop and apply theoretical distinctions that work within the international criminal law system.

Piecing together different concepts developed separately within the drafting further accentuates the challenges at hand. Article 32(1) provides that '[a] mistake of fact shall be a ground for excluding criminal responsibility only if it negates the mental element required by the crime'.[71] This phrasing both empowers and restricts the role of mistake of fact. In the end, building on the earlier discussion, does a mistake of fact combined with the mistaken facts' otherwise potential contribution to a situation of excusatory duress give rise to a defence (along the lines of Duff's warrants)? More generally, is there scope within Article 31 to distinguish the scenarios discussed in the last section? These as yet unresolved questions show the ongoing importance of criminal law theory simply to trying to grapple with some quandaries. At the same time, criminal law theory may help contribute to the development of a normatively coherent body of international criminal law.

Apart from its inherent objectives, the international criminal law system can be simultaneously a reflection of and lens for our understandings of our own domestic criminal law systems. The recent case law on the customary international law of duress and necessity can make us think again in new ways about the description of these defences and their underlying normative orientation. I have argued that some of that case law has emerged in sometimes problematic ways, but also that

[70] See also LE Chiesa, 'Duress, Demanding Heroism, and Proportionality' (2008) 41 *Vanderbilt Journal of Transnational Law*, 751–53.

[71] Rome Statute (n 26) Art 32(1).

even the now more unified instrument of international criminal law has not necessarily overcome some of the conceptual challenges at hand. Criminal law theorists might be inclined to wave the white flag, but they should instead be watching for the green flag being waved at them.

INDEX